ASP.NET:
A Beginner's Guide

ASP.NET:
A Beginner's Guide

Dave Mercer

McGraw-Hill/Osborne

New York Chicago San Francisco
Lisbon London Madrid Mexico City Milan
New Delhi San Juan Seoul Singapore Sydney Toronto

McGraw-Hill/Osborne
2600 Tenth Street
Berkeley, California 94710
U.S.A.

To arrange bulk purchase discounts for sales promotions, premiums, or fund-raisers, please contact McGraw-Hill/Osborne at the above address. For information on translations or book distributors outside the U.S.A., please see the International Contact Information page immediately following the index of this book.

ASP.NET: A Beginner's Guide

1234567890 FGR FGR 0198765432

ISBN 0-07-219512-6

Publisher Brandon A. Nordin
Vice President & Associate Publisher Scott Rogers
Acquisitions Editor Ann Sellers
Associate Editor Ben Walker
Project Editor Katie Conley
Acquisitions Coordinator Tim Madrid
Technical Editor Mark Goedert
Copy Editor Sally Engelfried
Proofreader Marian Selig
Indexer Irv Hershman
Computer Designers Carie Abrew, George Toma Charbak
Illustrators Michael Mueller, Lyssa Wald
Series Design Gary Corrigan
Cover Illustrator Kevin Curry
Cover Series Design Greg Scott

This book was composed with Corel VENTURA™ Publisher.

To the American heroes who lost their lives on 9-11-01.
Freedom forever.

"...I think perhaps of all the things a police state can do, distorting history is the most pernicious ... secrecy is the keystone of all tyranny. Not force, but secrecy ... censorship. When any government, or any church, for that matter, undertakes to say to its subjects, 'This you may not read, this you must not see, this you are forbidden to know,' the end result is tyranny and oppression, no matter how holy the motives. Mighty little force is needed to control a man whose mind has been hoodwinked; contrariwise, no amount of force can control a free man, a man whose mind is free. No, not the rack, not fission bombs, not anything—you can't conquer a free man; the most you can do is kill him."

—*Robert A. Heinlein,* Revolt in 2100

About the Author

Dave Mercer has been building databases professionally since 1993, and built his first website in 1995. He has a diverse background, including 15 years in industrial engineering and a degree in Business Administration from San Diego State University. He has worked on websites for businesses ranging from flower shops to car dealerships to real estate appraisers. He's been teaching website design and development classes since 1996, and has been writing books for the computer market since 1998.

Dave is currently CTO of a website design and database development company, and is building an Application Service Provider named Servata. He lives in Spring Valley, CA with his wife JoAnn, and practices his sailing in San Diego Bay whenever he gets the chance.

Contents at a Glance

Contents

Acknowledgments

Thanks to Jeffrey Davis for writing much of Module 12 and contributing to the Appendixes. Thanks to Ann Sellers, Tim Madrid, and Katie Conley at Osborne for providing all the support to keep me on track. And thanks to the folks at Microsoft for making an incredible platform and the high-tech tools that go with it.

Introduction

When I first began to encounter references to Microsoft's .NET ("Dot Net") technology, I wondered what it was: a software application, a programming language, a new web technology, or what? As it turns out, .NET contains elements of all these. And appropriately for me (since my last book in this series is all about XML), .NET relies heavily on XML for many things it does, especially Web Services. Although we don't spend lots of time on XML in this book (please see Osborne's *XML Beginner's Guide* for complete coverage of XML), we do cover the basics of this exciting new language-building specification.

So what's the big deal about .NET? Well, to beat another cliché to death, the holy grail of information systems is to provide access to just the right information at just the right time to just the right *person or computer*, and that's what .NET is supposed to accomplish. Microsoft is not alone in this endeavor; Sun, IBM, and several other big names in the computing world are building similar systems with similar foundations for similar reasons. You and your computer will be using information systems built with these technologies soon, if you're not already, and you may not even realize it when it happens.

If you've searched for and *found just the right piece of information* on the Web recently, you might be wondering if the goal mentioned in the last paragraph hasn't already been achieved. Let's define the goal succinctly, in parts, and then we'll review how ASP.NET can get us there.

The Right Information

Perhaps the best way to define information is as data that means something. Data by itself, such as 2, 22, 44, 45, 46, 47, 8, is meaningless. Although you could imagine a meaning for this set of numbers (such as ages of people, or the combination of a lock), without being informed of the meaning you have no idea what it represents. If this string of numbers represents the winning lottery numbers, it is potentially very valuable information. And if you bought a ticket and want to know what those numbers are, then this piece of information is the right information. Information such as today's winning lottery numbers is generated in a rather crude but supposedly random and secure process, often using bouncing balls sucked by air pressure into a tube one by one. In this book we show you how you can create a Web Services application that makes lotto random numbers for anyone with a browser (although they will not necessarily be the winning ones, unfortunately).

The Right Time

Information often has a shelf life, and sometimes it's a very short one. While some information retains a big part of its value for a long time, some information is only valuable for a short time. It would be great to know the winning numbers *before* the lottery is played, and it would be awful to find out the winning numbers (assuming you held the winning ticket) *after* the deadline for claiming the prize had passed. Rather than generating information, this part of the goal has to do with information delivery, and information of this kind is currently delivered in just about every conceivable format, from hard copies (such as newspapers) to analog (TV and radio) to digital (on the Internet).

The Right Person or Computer

Not everyone needs to know the winning numbers for the lottery, and quite a few probably prefer not to see them displayed on the evening news. But if you bought a ticket and were not the winner, you might want to find out the numbers to confirm what the odds already say (looooooser). And if you beat the worst odds in the world and really did hold the winning ticket, you definitely need to find out this information before it goes out of date. Being human, however, you might forget about the ticket (hey, it really happened not too long ago to a guy in New York, and he almost didn't get paid). That's where computers come in. Assuming your computer didn't take a dump (or better yet, that the server you use didn't crash) if the information had been relayed to your computer and your computer knew what to do with it (such as wake you up, or perhaps cash the ticket in for you) then life could get pretty easy, no doubt.

Now let's move from the outrageously improbable to the mundane. Everybody likes convenience, and automating all the routine, tedious little chores in life would be a blessing. Just for the record, what we're talking about here is not forcing everyone to lead a slothful life, turning into fat, useless morons while machines take over the world and eventually execute us all (good sci-fi, though, eh?). We're talking about *choice*. Of course you can do tedious, routine, boring things if you want, but you *wouldn't have to*. And in those instances in which tedious translates into life-threatening (like piloting a 747), then the case for computers is pretty easy to show.

Now, the heart of the matter. If we could completely automate the generation and delivery of the right information at the right time to the right person or machine, we could automate many of the things we now are forced to do the hard way. With technologies such as the Internet, XML, and .NET, we finally have all the tools in place. We can literally program just about any application that can be conceived. The only things remaining to go the whole distance are ubiquitous data acquisition devices and artificial intelligence (AI).

The point of this story is that we now have a tool whose capabilities really are almost limitless. Everyone and everything is or soon will be connected—not just people and their desktop computers, but literally everything. Any kind of sensor or input device can communicate with any programming logic contained in any device with communications and computation capability, many of which will soon become too small to even see. We're very close to living in a smart, connected world. And the basic technology many of the new applications will depend on is Active Server Pages and the .NET Framework (ASP.NET).

ASP.NET is not a programming language or database or markup language or application. Microsoft refers to it as a platform, extending the definition of platform to mean distributed applications on the Internet, whether or not they have a user interface. After all, why include a user interface if the communications are intended for machine consumption?

One of the major advances of ASP over ASP.NET is the use of XML as a messaging and data exchange format. As we mentioned earlier, XML is not a language either but a common and widely accepted specification for writing human-readable text-based languages. Like the Internet itself, so many people and organizations are using XML that it has taken on a life of its own, and that ensures broad compatibility (for the most part) for years to come. More than any competing platform of this type so far, ASP.NET is a means of harnessing the awesome power of logical instructions (programming), connectivity (the Internet), data sources (much more than just databases), and communications between devices (the user interface or IO functions). In one fell swoop it creates an environment in which you can put all these things to work for whatever purpose you desire. And it's only getting better. This is definitely a technology you need to know and understand.

Who Should Read This Book

So welcome to Osborne's *ASP.NET: A Beginner's Guide*. As the name suggests, this book is for everyone from raw programming trainees to programming professionals breaking into ASP for the first time. If you intend to program interactive websites, this book is for you. If you intend to manage those who program interactive websites, this book is for you. If you own a business and wish to understand one of the primary technologies by which developers will program interactive websites for you, this book is for you.

We hope you'll find the material interesting, well rounded, clear and concise, and just plain fun. For my money, Active Server Pages is one of the easiest, most immediately accessible, and most fun technologies for working with the Web, and at the same time it is incredibly powerful.

What This Book Covers

This book is broken into 11 modules and several appendixes. The modules contain pretty much all you need to know to immediately begin programming interactive websites and distributed applications with ASP.NET, from simple responses to server components all the way to complete database manipulation to e-mail applications. Because modern website applications are built from many different languages, technologies, and components, this book touches on HTML/XHTML, website design, business process modeling, XML, JScript, VBScript, VB.NET, SQL, ADO.NET, ASP objects and components, and database construction with SQL Server. You'll be exposed to working code fashioned in a plain, easy-to-understand format, demonstrating clearly all the basic functions you'll need to grasp and work with daily. In addition, we make extensive use of Visual Studio.NET and show you easy ways to quickly build working web applications from the templates provided.

At the back of the book there are several appendixes (the first being an answers guide) containing valuable reference material for quick review when you need a specific command, function, value or constant. All the code is available for easy download and insertion into your own site from the Osborne website (and also from **www.e4free.com/ASPNET**). If you follow along with the examples written in the book and produce code and databases to match, you can use the samples to immediately add powerful functionality to any website you already have.

Note

You *must* have a properly configured server running your examples and code before they will work (we talk about this extensively in Module 1).

Module 1, ASP.NET: Getting Set Up: In this module we discuss ASP, ASP.NET, and the .NET Framework. How they are related to websites, operating systems, and their effect on website design is reviewed. The installation of IIS 5.0 is covered, as well as hosting issues. Manual and automated development environments are reviewed, and an overview of the built-in objects and components of ASP and ASP.NET is included. In addition, some of the features of the programming languages for the CLR are discussed.

Module 2, ASP.NET Programming Basics: The ins and outs of traditional and object-oriented programming languages are reviewed, as well as how dynamic applications function as related to HTML, the DOM, VBScript and JScript, and content stored in databases. We discuss how HTML, XHTML, and scripting languages fit into the scheme of things, and we discuss the role of SQL. Differences in the way ASP and ASP.NET applications function and their file naming conventions are also reviewed.

Module 3, Programming ASP.NET with Visual Basic.NET: In this module there is a thorough review of VB.NET and JScript, including data types, operators, keywords, and so forth. Interactive objects such as the Request, Response, and Server objects are also examined. The Request and Response objects are the workhorses of ASP and can easily be useful in ASP.NET, and we discuss using them for basic interactions with your users in detail. Reading and writing data, cookies, buffering and flushing, and other methods and properties are explored in the module's project. In addition, we look at typical web server operations and cover basic server-side includes as well. The correct syntax and implications of creating object instances are explained, and the methods and properties of the Server object are used in the module's project.

Module 4, Web Forms and ASP.NET: This module begins our coverage of Visual Studio.NET and the creation of solutions and projects using Web Forms. We detail installing and setting up VS.NET and show how to create a Web Forms-based project. A simple application is built, including capturing data from the user and validating it.

Module 5, ASP.NET Configuration, Scope, and State: ASP.NET and the .NET Framework include some new methods for configuring applications, and we cover this subject in this module. In addition, we describe how to use the Global.asa file with ASP and the Global.asax file with ASP.NET to manage state and scope in many instances. This module reviews state and scope and how they can be managed using the Application and Session objects. The correct syntax is shown, and the properties and methods of each are outlined in examples and in the module's project.

Module 6, ASP.NET Objects and Components: Any application programming technology eventually needs access to the file system, and the SOM provides this functionality for ASP and ASP.NET on the server. The Dictionary object is covered in this module, as well as objects that allow access to drives, folders, files, and individual text streams. ASP Components include the Ad Rotator, the Browser Capabilities, and several others, all of which are reviewed in this module. Their relation to well-designed websites is discussed, and typical usage of each component is demonstrated in the module's project. Finally, third-party component issues are covered.

Module 7, Web Services and ASP.NET: Web Services are individual units of application logic that are hosted on a server and are available for other services or applications to connect with them. In this module, we cover using VS.NET to create Web Services, as well as how they are related to XML, SOAP, and WSDL.

Module 8, ASP.NET and SQL Server: ActiveX Data Objects (ADO) is a set of components used with ASP to access databases, and ADO.NET is the next upgrade to this technology. Both are discussed in detail, and the design and construction of a typical database is covered in this module. The SQL database query language is presented in basic format, so the syntax becomes clear, and common SQL queries are shown. Finally, ADO objects (Connection, Command, and Recordset) and ADO.NET objects (DataSet, DataAdapter, and DataReader) are discussed.

Module 9, The ADO.NET Connection-Related Objects: Using a SQL Server database, we demonstrate how to connect via DSNs and connection strings. Correct usage of the Connection object is shown, and several types of connections are made. Stored procedures are discussed, and a stored procedure is created and run in the module's project.

Module 10, The ADO/ADO.NET Recordset and DataSet-Related Objects: Manipulating data in a database gets going nicely using recordsets with ADO and datasets with ADO.NET. Applications allowing basic record navigation and edits, updates, and deletes are constructed using both technologies in the module's project.

Module 11, ASP Transactions and Mail: Part of working with data sources is forming changes into transactions, and the fundamentals of transactions are covered in this module. An SQL Server database is used with a transaction-based ASP.NET application to demonstrate performing transactions, sending mail, and securing the application.

Appendix A, Answers to Mastery Checks: At the end of each module is a section called "Mastery Check" that contains questions that check to make sure you've absorbed the basics; Appendix A provides the answers to these questions.

Appendix B, Visual Basic/JScript Reference: This reference includes Visual Basic and JScript keywords, functions, operators, and data types.

Appendix C, ASP.NET Server and HTML Controls: This reference is a guide to built-in controls that may be used on Web Forms.

Appendix D, XHTML 1.0 Reference: This reference summarizes the differences between HTML and XHTML and outlines the elements common to both HTML and XHTML.

How To Read This Book

This book can be read from beginning to end, starting with the first module, but you can also open any module for an easy-to-follow introduction to the specific ASP.NET objects or capabilities you are interested in. Each module explains in detail the objects it covers and includes many working examples demonstrating the capabilities of the object or components in question. In addition, at the end of most of the modules is a step-by-step project that gives you the opportunity to use the most important parts of the material discussed in the module.

Special Features

Throughout each module are ***Hints, Tips,*** and ***Notes***, as well as ***detailed code listings.*** The code all works fine and the source code can be downloaded in .zip files from the website in full, at **www.e4free.com/ASPNET**. There are ***1-Minute Drills*** that check to make sure you're retaining what you've read (and help focus your attention on the more important points). There are ***Ask the Expert*** question-and-answer sections that give in-depth explanations about the current subject. Included in the book and on the website are ***Projects*** that take what you've learned and put it into working applications. At the end of each module is a ***Mastery Check*** to give you another opportunity for review, and the answers are contained in ***Appendix A***. The properties and methods of each ASP or ASP.NET object are listed and explained, and coding techniques are discussed and illustrated. Overall, our objective is to get you up to speed quickly, without a lot of obtuse, abstract, and dry reference to formal coding practices.

There is quite a bit of additional information at the websites mentioned in the modules, from the Microsoft website to the W3C website to third-party ASP and ASP.NET developer's websites. I've also built some web pages containing links to Zip files that have all the code and examples found in the book, so you can visit and download what you need rather than copying from the book. You can find the URL to each module project listed next to the module's project heading.

So let's get started. You won't believe how easy and fun it is to use ASP.NET to program distributed applications and even basic website functions and pages. Good luck!

Module 1

Getting Set Up

The Goals of This Module

- Understand the range and relationships of ASP.NET technologies
- Explore operating systems (OSs) and their relationship to ASP.NET
- Install and configure Internet Information Server (IIS) 5.0
- Review manual and automated (Visual Studio.NET) development environments
- Examine ASP.NET objects, components, and ADO.NET
- Cover issues and concerns of website and application hosting
- Review programming with Visual Basic
- Create a simple ASP.NET page

Welcome to *ASP.NET: A Beginner's Guide*! In this and the next two modules, we'll cover all the basics of getting set up for .NET, as well as fundamentals of programming you'll need to survive here. Let me just say right now, it's not that hard to learn how to program, but you've got to think logically and never give up. All programming languages were made by people, and once you grasp how the programmers who cooked up this stuff think, you'll find each new problem a little easier and each new challenge less stressful. All the programming concepts, reserved words, methods, properties, and so on have a purpose, and they become your tools just as drills, saws, levels, and hammers are to carpenters.

So why all the fuss about ASP and ASP.NET? If you are familiar with the way websites work, you may have heard about HTML (Hypertext Markup Language, the language from which the bulk of web pages is constructed) and you may even have seen HTML code (click View | Source in your Internet Explorer browser and you'll see HTML code). HTML is a markup language written in plain text whose main function is to display text and graphics in a pleasant way. There is no real programmatic functionality in HTML, no calculations, no database access, nothing. HTML is used to create a simple user interface on what is called the *front end*. The front end is the part you see in your browser (or client). However, when you access a web page, your browser is making a connection and requesting the HTML for a web page from the web server (thus the term *client-server*) on what is called the *back end*. HTML doesn't do anything on the back end other than store static text and graphics in a format the browser can understand.

Although JavaScript and a few other scripting languages can make some neat stuff happen on the front end, including calculations, verifying form input, and so forth, the back end is ideally suited to accessing databases, talking to other applications across the Internet, and performing complex programmatic functionality (especially when you don't want to give away the code or ask the user to download and install applications). This power on the back end can take an ordinary website and transform it into a dynamic application immeasurably more valuable to users than plain-text, hard-coded web pages written in HTML.

Traditional ASP provided a means of coordinating these back-end capabilities and functions but was limited in terms of the programmatic features and performance available. ASP.NET not only provides a performance boost, it integrates and coordinates many other features as well, including XML Web Services, a standard method for accessing other applications and exchanging data, and the ability to run just about any programming language. ASP.NET is almost completely *backward compatible* with ASP, and ASP files run just fine in an ASP.NET environment. Because you will most likely run into many examples of ASP while programming ASP.NET professionally, this book often uses ASP examples to start the ball rolling and then immediately goes into a comparable ASP.NET example so you can easily see the difference. Many concepts that are easy to grasp in ASP are expanded on and extended in ASP.NET, providing another reason for the many ASP examples you'll see in each module.

In this module, we outline the technologies from which .NET is composed, and we provide a bit of background on ASP in particular. We also discuss system requirements for the various operating systems, servers, and development environments that are included in or required by .NET, and we conclude with some coverage of appropriate programming languages for .NET.

What Is ASP.NET?

The .NET portion of the acronym refers to Microsoft's .NET Framework, and we'll get into a complete discussion on that shortly. Obviously, ASP stands for Active Server Pages, so let's talk about that a bit. ASP is a technology rather than a language in itself, and it is very popular for writing website applications. Traditional ASP runs on networked operating systems such as Windows NT or Windows 2000 and requires a web server such as Internet Information Server (IIS). The most recent version of ASP was 3.0, and ASP.NET is the next step forward, although ASP.NET is really a whole new programming methodology rather than just an evolutionary advance in ASP.

As we cover in the section "Setting Up For ASP.NET," you'll probably be running ASP.NET on some version of Windows 2000 Server, and you'll also most likely be running both ASP and ASP.NET. They are separate installations (ASP is automatically installed with IIS), have separate processing engines, use different configuration models (ASP uses the registry, while ASP.NET uses XML configuration files), and work with different file types (ASP filenames end with .asp, .asa, and so forth, while ASP.NET filenames end with .aspx and so on). Therefore, you can run an ASP application on the same server and at the same time as an ASP.NET application. The disadvantage of doing so is that ASP will probably run more slowly and does not offer quite the same capabilities as ASP.NET.

How Does ASP.NET Fit In?

ASP.NET is a part of the .NET Framework, a new computing platform from Microsoft optimized for creating applications that are highly distributed across the Internet. Highly distributed means that the components of the application, as well as the data, may reside anywhere on the Internet rather than all being contained inside one software program somewhere. Each part of an application can be referenced and accessed using a standard procedure, whether it is a database, web page, application, component, and so forth.

ASP.NET is the part that provides the features necessary to easily tie all this capability together for coherent web-based applications. It is a programming framework, and one of the primary differences between it and traditional ASP is that it uses a *common language runtime* (CLR) capable of running compiled code on a web server to deploy powerful web-based applications. In Module 2, we cover the particulars of compiled versus interpreted programming languages; for now, let's just say that compiled programs (such as those used with ASP.NET) run much faster than interpreted programs.

What Is the .NET Framework?

The short answer to this question is that .NET is Microsoft's name for a platform for XML Web Services. XML is covered in greater detail in Module 7; for now, all you need to know is XML is a standard way for developing markup languages that can describe any kind of data or functionality (as a matter of fact, it's called a *self-describing* standard). Essentially, what this means is there is enough information in XML documents and their associated Document Type Definitions (DTDs) to allow them to be used as a universal data and functionality exchange system, and that's precisely what is being done. Across industries, organizations, and government entities, XML languages and documents are being created, and companies find it quite easy (compared to previous systems) to hook their data and applications together when a common XML language is used.

The "web services" part of XML web services refers to the data and application functionality that is available across the Internet, without regard to what operating system a particular computer or server is running or what programming language the application (or its logic) was written in. Microsoft's intention is to build XML Web Services capability into all its operating system, application, and server products.

What Are Active Server Pages (ASP)?

Active Server Pages (ASP) is the name Microsoft uses for a technology that is convenient for building dynamic web pages. Dynamic web pages contain content that may change from second to second, based on data or conditions that may change as time progresses. ASP, together with the scripting languages it supports and the data sources connected to an ASP website application, provides the functionality that allows the pages' content to change. In fact, unlike ordinary web pages, ASP pages may exist only as code until a user actually clicks them.

Unlike traditional programming languages, however, ASP is interpreted rather than compiled, meaning it runs much more slowly. For small programs this may not be noticeable, but for larger programs the difference can be quite significant. In ASP.NET, VBScript is not supported and, as we've mentioned, ordinary ASP applications can run side-by-side with ASP.NET applications on the same server (although the two do not communicate with each other). In this book, the majority of the examples will be in Visual Basic.NET (VB.NET) or VBScript, although a few will be JScript or C# (pronounced C sharp), Microsoft's new version of the C programming language.

1-Minute Drill

- What are traditional web pages made with, and how are they changing with advances such as ASP.NET?
- How is ASP.NET primarily different from ASP?

- Web pages are usually made with HTML, with perhaps some JavaScript included to add some limited programmatic functionality. ASP.NET and other such technologies offer the capability to go beyond static, hard-coded web pages to dynamic web pages, in which what the user receives may depend on how the user is interacting with the website.
- Traditional ASP is one way to make dynamic web pages and website applications, but the chief limitation is that ASP are interpreted when accessed, meaning they exist as source code until they are used, at which time the source code is turned into actual processor instructions. This method is rather slow but works well enough for fairly simple applications. ASP.NET applications may be much more complex because they are compiled (but they are only compiled at runtime, and you can still always review the source code when you need to make any changes) and offer an enormous performance increase over interpreted applications.

Ask the Expert

Question: I've seen lots of websites, but haven't built one of my own yet. How are websites created?

Answer: Traditional websites are made up of web page files (made from plain-text HTML commands) plus perhaps some graphics files and maybe some multimedia files as well. You can make a simple web page file by writing the HTML code by hand in Notepad, and you can even view it directly off the hard drive in your browser. Your browser contains the functionality necessary to turn the HTML into a beautifully rendered page, as well as the functionality to process any JavaScript instructions you might include in the HTML.

Although you can view simple web pages directly from the hard drive in a good browser, some functions on better websites require back-end processing and must be viewed by being served up by a web server. The standard way of releasing web pages across the Internet to the world is to load them onto some web space. Web space is space on the hard drive of a web hosting company's computer, typically connected to your domain name. The web server software processes requests web pages and user input, manages processing of back-end applications and database access (usually there are dedicated engines or drivers on the back end that perform these functions, with the web server controlling everything), and delivers the finished pages to the user.

Website creation may involve many software tools for writing the pages, creating the graphics, writing the scripting or programming, and working with various types of multimedia effects. This is normally done on a development machine and then loaded onto the server to test functionality. During construction, the server the pages are loaded onto is called the *development* or *construction* server; once development and testing are complete, the pages are loaded onto the *production* server.

Question: How are web pages published to the server?

Answer: The easiest way is to create your pages and then copy them to the default website folder on the server. If you are publishing remotely, you can use a File Transfer Protocol (FTP) program to copy your pages over. Most good HTML-editing tools these days also contain the ability to copy your files to the web server. If you use an FTP program to copy your files to the server, FTP must be running on IIS and you must know your hostname (the IP address of the FTP server), your username, and your password.

Question: What is the difference between a traditional website and an application-driven website?

Answer Traditional (or static) websites deliver their content by request without having any idea whether the requester has just been there or is visiting for the first time. There is no continuity between requests, nor any continuing information between requests. In technical terms, normal web requests and responses are *stateless*. In addition, normal web pages are built and then displayed as is. Little or no information in them is updated automatically, and they certainly aren't constructed on-the-fly or in direct response to user input or conditions.

Application-driven (or dynamic) websites, on the other hand, can keep track of each user and store information across page requests (or even across the entire website for all users about the state of interactions with each individual user). Dynamic websites can also build pages automatically, on-the-fly, and in response to conditions on the server, at the client, or unique to the user.

Question: How are communications conducted between the web server and the browser? It sounds like there are a lot of things happening that are not apparent to the user.

Answer: Hypertext Transport Protocol (HTTP) is the standard protocol for communications between a web server and a browser. We cover HTTP extensively in Module 2; for now, let's just say that each time you type an address in your browser and hit Enter (or click a link), lots of information about your request (including your location on the Internet and the type of browser you are using) is transmitted to the server in HTTP format. When the server responds with a web page, it also sends lots of information back to your browser as HTTP-formatted headers.

Setting Up for ASP.NET

One of the first things to do when getting ready to use ASP.NET is to make sure the development and operating environments are suitable for the tools and applications intended to be used. For example, basic operating systems such as Windows 98 can be used for development, but specialized operating systems such as Windows 2000 Server must be used to run the applications once developed. And if you're going to take advantage of specialized tools such as Visual Studio.NET, you'll need a high-powered computer and operating system to run them. In the next several sections, we discuss system requirements and setup procedures for IIS 5.0 and other required components.

As we discuss later in the section "The Development Environment," ASP.NET applications can be coded using a plain-text editor such as Notepad, although this is not the most efficient method to use. Developing all the other resources that might be required for a particular ASP.NET application, especially for the user interface, may involve a range of specialized tools, including image-editing programs, database programs, HTML-editors, and so forth. Obviously, for the development of ASP.NET applications, it doesn't really matter what image-editing tool you use, so for this book we'll stick to those tools you *must* have in order to develop ASP.NET applications and leave your choice of other tools to you. From time to time we may discuss other useful tools that work well for us, but please feel free to experiment and use whatever suits you best.

Operating Systems

An operating system (OS) works only on the central processing unit (CPU) or range of CPUs it has been especially made for. It is the translator of application and file system functions (among other things) for applications running on those CPUs. The components of an ASP.NET application can be *developed* using just about any operating system and software tools, but ASP.NET will only *run* on specific operating systems and servers: Windows 2000, Windows NT 4.0, and, as a web server, Internet Information Server (IIS). As a practical matter, if you are doing ASP.NET development, you'll want to be running the appropriate operating system and server so you can easily test and debug your applications.

Traditional ASP was developed up to version 3.0. The next version was originally called ASP+, but development of the platform has now proceeded to ASP.NET. There are several OS and hardware combinations ASP.NET will run on. The minimum recommended OS for ASP.NET is Windows 2000 or Windows NT 4 with Service Pack 6a. The minimum recommended OS for the Microsoft .NET Framework SDK is Windows 2000, Windows NT 4 with Service Pack 6a, Windows Me, Windows 98, Windows SE, or Windows 95.

The minimum hardware (this is pretty slow, mind you) required is a Pentium 133MHz with 128MB RAM.

The OS used as the web server for the examples in this book is Windows 2000 Advanced Server running on a Pentium 166MHz with 128MB RAM, and when used with Visual Studio.NET a 500MHz Pentium III with 256MB of RAM. These machines have Internet Information Server (IIS) 5.0 installed and, according to Microsoft, this web server is fully integrated at the operating system level, meaning it is capable of functions (such as security) and performance that take advantage of operating system capabilities, rather than requiring all this functionality to be built-in separately.

In addition, it is really best to run your examples from a separate machine running Internet Explorer 5.5 to 6.0. While you can run your examples directly on the server or from another browser, there will be examples that take advantage of IE 5.5's special features (but we'll point them out, of course). Running examples from a separate client machine also means you'll detect problems with permissions that may not be evident when you're logged directly into the server as an administrator.

Windows 2000 Advanced Server Edition

Windows 2000 has been on the market since February 2000, and as of this writing there are a number of patches, service packs, or other fixes available (although I'm sure we'll see more by the time you read this). You can find them listed at **www.microsoft.com/windows2000/downloads**. Download and install at least the latest security patches and upgrades. The installation of Windows 2000 Advanced Server Edition and IIS mentioned in the next few sections refers to a version that is most likely earlier than the one you will install (or you may not have to install anything if your system administrator has done these steps for you), so some of the screens and explanations may be a bit different on your machine if you are installing the very latest version when you read this book.

During installation of Windows 2000, you'll be asked quite a few questions about how you want Windows 2000 configured. The most important questions affecting your use of ASP.NET concern the installation of Internet Information Server (discussed in the next section) and how your hard disk (HD) drive partitions are formatted.

Microsoft recommends installing Windows 2000 as an application server if you intend to run the machine primarily as a web server. Doing this will make it use memory more efficiently. Since it installs as a file server by default, you need to follow this procedure to switch to an application server:

1. On the desktop, open My Computer and click Network and Dial-up Connections.
2. Double-click Local Area Connection and select Properties.
3. Select File and Printer Sharing for Microsoft Networks in the scroll box and click the Properties button.
4. On the Server Optimization tab, select Maximize Data Throughput for Network Applications.

For nonproduction servers, I recommend installing Windows 2000 to a FAT partition and setting aside another partition entirely for the installation of IIS. The IIS partition should be formatted as NTFS (the NT File System). This will make your Windows 2000 installation viewable by other FAT operating systems while allowing IIS to maintain the highest levels of security with NTFS.

Servers

The most important server you can install is Internet Information Server (IIS) because you'll need it to run your ASP.NET applications. There are a number of other servers specifically designed to work with the .NET Framework (Application Center, Biz Talk, Commerce Server, Exchange Server, and so forth), and we'll discuss them in Module 8. Once you get the operating system and IIS installed, you'll still need to install ASP.NET Premium, unless you are installing Visual Studio.NET. During the installation of Visual Studio.NET, you will need to install a series of Windows components, one of which is ASP.NET, and all these components should be on a separate disk that comes with Visual Studio.NET. VS.NET also requests installation of Microsoft Data Access Components (MDAC) 2.7. You can find MDAC 2.7 at the Microsoft website as a free download; it should also be on the VS.NET disks.

Installing Internet Information Server (IIS) 5.0

IIS 5.0 is installed by default during installation of Windows 2000 Advanced Server, unless you have another web server already installed. While you are installing the operating system, you will have the opportunity to specify configuration options for IIS. However, after the OS installation you'll immediately get a Configure Your Server screen (shown in Figure 1-1) that lets you start a variety of service installation and configuration wizards. We'll use this screen to walk through and discuss the options available for IIS 5.0.

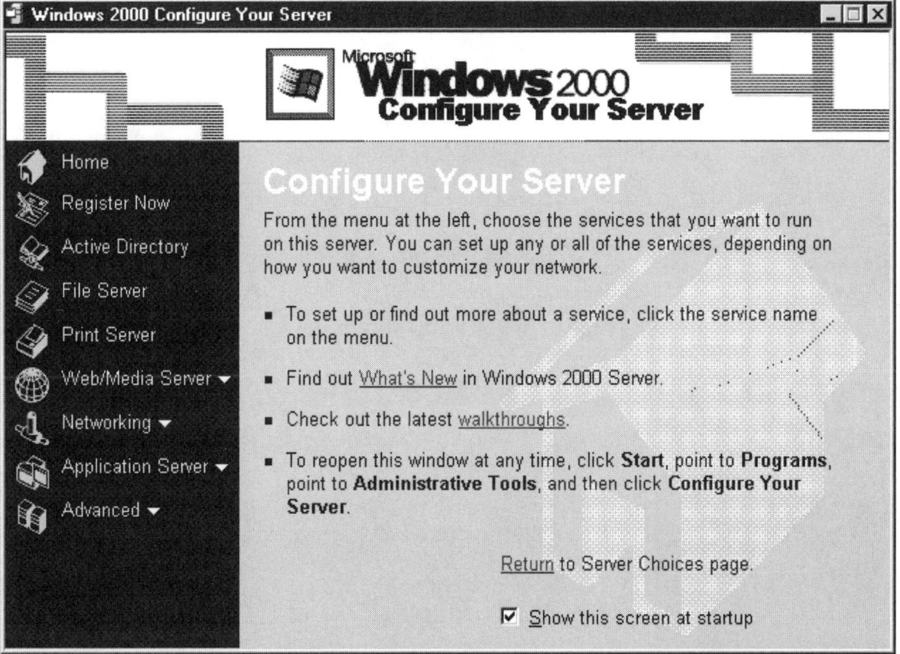

Figure 1-1 The Configure Your Server screen

When you click Web/Media Server on the toolbar along the left-hand side of the screen, a drop-down menu will appear (shown in Figure 1-2), and you'll be able to choose between web services and streaming media services. Choose Web Server, and you'll see the screen shown in Figure 1-3.

On the Web Server screen you get three choices:

- Create a new virtual directory
- Manage web services
- Learn more about web services

If you click the choice for learning more about IIS 5.0, a Help window will appear offering six options:

- Installing IIS
- Software Checklist

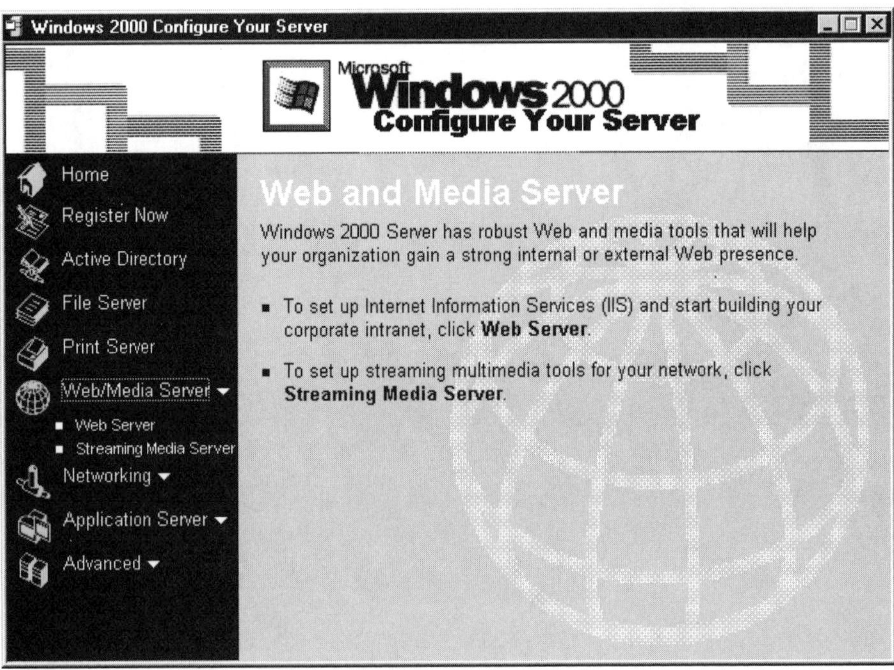

Figure 1-2 The Web and Media Server choices

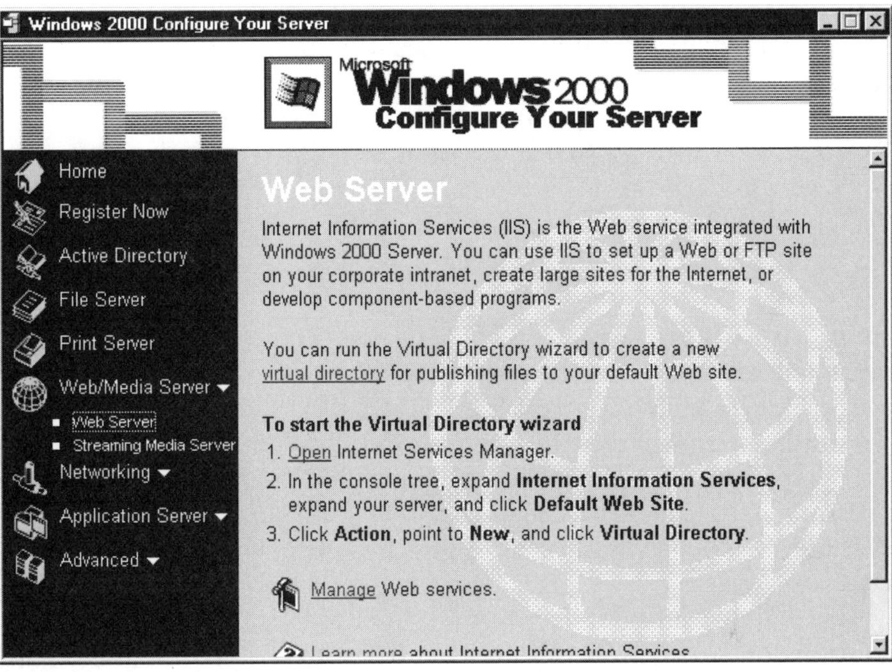

Figure 1-3 The Web Server screen

- Troubleshooting
- Electronic Mail
- Newsgroups
- FrontPage Server Extensions

Installing IIS The Installing IIS option simply tells you the procedure for installation in the most basic terms rather than explaining any of the configuration options or, more importantly, why you would want to configure IIS a particular way and the consequences of your decisions. We'll provide some of this information here, but you might want to consult your system administrator for tips about how to optimize the installation (and security issues) based on the way your own network and web publishing services are set up.

Software Checklist Prior to beginning installation, you must have TCP/IP installed. The Windows TCP/IP Protocol and Connectivity Utilities is the name Microsoft uses to denote this set of utilities. It should be installed by default. Microsoft also recommends installing Domain Name Service on one of the computers on the network so that users can enter "friendly" names, rather than IP addresses, to access other computers. That choice is up to you. As I mentioned earlier, IIS should be installed on an NTFS partition (there's more information about partitions and formatting schemes in the next "Ask the Expert" section).

Troubleshooting The Troubleshooting option gives you a method for determining whether or not your web server is working. Essentially, you must ensure that there are browser-readable (HTML) files in your wwwroot folder, open your browser, and enter the proper URL to find one of the HTML files. The URL should be the name of your computer preceded by http:// and followed by a slash and the name of the file to display; for example, **http://yourcomputer/myfile.htm**. You can find the name of your computer in the Control Panel under Network Settings.

E-mail and Newsgroups If you want to send e-mail or read newsgroups, you should install SMTP and NNTP during installation of the OS, or later from the Configure Your Server screen. The next two choices under Learning More about IIS (Electronic Mail and Newsgroups) each give you a URL you can use to review documentation for these services. The URLs are **file:\\%systemroot%\help\mail.chm** for e-mail and **file:\\%systemroot%\help\news.chm** for newsgroups.

FrontPage Server Extensions If you want to host Websites created with Microsoft FrontPage, you will want to install FrontPage Server Extensions. Microsoft FrontPage is an HTML-editor/Web-authoring program. Web pages created with it consist mainly of ordinary HTML compatible with any Web server, but Microsoft has also built-in features that can take advantage of special server extensions for added functionality, such as full-site searches. These special server extensions are the FrontPage server extensions, and they must be installed for these features to work.

Installing ASP.NET Premium

Installing ASP.NET Premium is pretty straightforward. It is currently about 18MB to download and took us about 20 minutes to install on a Pentium 166MHz machine. It will immediately request that you load Internet Explorer 5.5, so you might as well upgrade if you haven't already. It also recommends you load Microsoft Data Access Components (MDAC) 2.7, which you can find on the Microsoft and ASP.NET websites. Both of these can be installed from the Windows components disk that comes with Visual Studio.NET as well, so you may not have to download them at all. Once these two packages were loaded, the installation proceeded smoothly. A simple ASP.NET page (the example developed in Project 1.2) loaded into its own folder on the web server and ran fine the first time around.

Ask the Expert

Question: What is FAT and NTFS?

Answer: Information about the files on your hard drive, such as location, size, and so forth, is stored in a File Allocation Table, or FAT. A single physical hard drive can be logically divided up into multiple hard drive partitions, each with its own drive letter. Partitions can be formatted differently from one another, although, depending upon the formatting structure, they may or may not be able to "see" each other.

There are several file storage formats in common use, such as FAT16, FAT32, NTFS (Windows NT File System), and others for Unix and proprietary operating systems. Networked operating systems, unlike desktop operating systems, usually have a means to store permission information for each file or folder, along with the data mentioned previously. Windows 2000 can be installed on a FAT16 partition, but IIS should be installed on NTFS, because NTFS, in addition to providing a File Allocation Table, stores permissions information for each file and folder.

Question: What permissions information can be stored?

Answer: Permissions information dictates what a particular user or group can see, read, write, move, execute, author, delete, and edit. There are various levels of permissions that can be assigned, and the operating system reviews stored permissions information to decide if the user making the request has sufficient permission to perform the request. Permissions can be assigned to an individual user or to a group as a whole. Assigning permissions to a group as a whole (and then simply adding users to the group as necessary) makes managing permissions easier when large numbers of users are involved.

Question: **How can I tell if my drive is FAT or NTFS?**

Answer: Open Windows Explorer and select the drive (partition) on which the operating system or IIS is installed. Right-click it to display the shortcut menu, and select Properties. Under the General tab, the file system type is shown.

Question: **How can I change the format of a partition on my hard drive to NTFS?**

Answer: Partitions can be formatted to NTFS from Windows Explorer. Just find the partition you wish to change in Windows Explorer, right-click it, and choose Format from the shortcut menu. Note that once you change a partition to NTFS it cannot be changed back to FAT (at least, not according to Microsoft's documentation).

Question: **What are load balancing and performance throttling, and when should I use them?**

Answer: Load balancing is part of a general set of topics referring to your ability as a designer to scale up the hardware and software components of your website for increased numbers of visitors and more activity per visitor. Performance throttling or tuning is related as a means of controlling CPU performance, bandwidth consumption, and application performance.

The discussion really starts with clustering. Clustering lets you connect multiple servers via clustering software; to clients such as Internet Explorer they provide services as though they were one computer/server. In addition, clustering allows multiple servers to offer robust features not available with stand-alone server nodes, like failover and load balancing. Clustered servers can share clustered hard disk drives, further improving performance and reliability of critical database-contained information.

Often you'll hear of web farms or CPU farms, and this term is sometimes used interchangeably with clustering. Increased performance and reliability are the chief reasons for adding multiple servers in a cluster arrangement. For example, if a server dies within a cluster, other servers can immediately pick up the slack. This is called failover. When the dead server is reanimated and it resumes carrying its load, the term is failback.

Performance throttling is also part of a larger discussion about controlling and tuning resource usage among the various services at work on your server so that you can offer maximum performance for each service while not unnecessarily restricting or limiting usage of any service. The problem is rather complex and involves several issues.

First, any online services compete to use the CPU, the applications you've created, and the bandwidth available. Bandwidth available is determined by the data transfer speed of your Internet connection, so that a 28.8K modem is capable of transmitting 28,800 bits each second, while a T-3 line can transmit 45,000,000 bits each second. File size and protocol overhead (a percentage of the file size dedicated to nonfile data, such as packet source and destination addresses) added together equal the amount of data that must be transmitted to accomplish a given purpose, such as sending an e-mail or fulfilling an HTTP request for a web page. Data transfer speed (bandwidth) determines the maximum amount of data that can be transmitted, and therefore, the total number of files or communications requests that can be transmitted. Each online application will compete for bandwidth, and if some applications are transmitting larger files or more communications requests, other applications may slow down or stop altogether for a while, disrupting those services.

You can throttle bandwidth usage at the website level, and these settings will override settings made at the level of the entire computer. If you are running multiple websites on IIS, you can throttle each individually, an important consideration for web hosting companies and ISPs. System monitoring tools can tell you how well your settings are performing, and a good rule of thumb is that if you are exceeding 50 percent of your available bandwidth during peak usage times, you should consider getting a better (higher data transfer speed) connection.

The Development Environment

The term *development environment* refers to the software (and the tools associated with it) used to write or build all the components of an application. For example, in the user-interface, there may be graphics, video, audio, multimedia, and text components, and to perform functions within the user interface there may be many types of specialized controls, such as hypertext links, forms, and form controls (text boxes, lists, buttons, and so forth). Behind the scenes, there may be a number of data resources and programmatic functions. The tools used to build and integrate all these components, as well as test their functionality, are collectively referred to as the development environment. As a general rule, development environments are either manual or automated, although depending on the functionality of the tool or tools use, the overall development environment may fall somewhere in between completely manual or completely automated.

ASP.NET applications can be created using Visual Studio.NET (discussed soon in the section "Automated Development"), but there is no requirement to use a tool such as this for your development. According to Microsoft's ASP.NET documentation "ASP.NET follows the same 'just hit save' design principle of ASP: any text-based editing application may be used to create ASP.NET applications. When an ASP.NET page is first accessed, it is compiled automatically, and future requests will access the compiled resource." In Project 1.2, for example, the first time the page was accessed it took a few seconds to appear. After that, the server was accessing the compiled version, and the page appeared in the browser much more quickly.

General Working Environment

Set aside a folder named ASPNET on the hard drive of your working and testing computer to store all your working files, related resources, and examples. You can download all the examples and code mentioned in this book at **www.osborne.com**. The material on this website can be placed in subfolders of the ASP.NET folder, named for each module in the book, so you can keep the examples separated. Use the ASP.NET folder and its subfolders whenever you are working in this book.

For serving up ASP.NET pages and applications, make a similar folder within the published folder of your web server (typically Inetpub\wwwroot). Use these folders to keep all your pages and applications for proper rendering, processing, and display within the browser of your working and testing computer (of course, you can use one machine for both functions, but it's more realistic to access your pages across the Internet like any normal user).

Note

Simply browsing directly to files with IE or other browsers will not properly render your ASP.NET web pages! For example, if you click File | Open | Browse in IE and select a file with an .aspx suffix, you might be asked to save or edit the file, but it will not be rendered or displayed properly. In order to properly render the page you must access it by typing in **http://*computername/foldername/filename***, where *computername* is the name of your computer and *foldername* is the name of the folder under wwwroot in which the file is stored. If you have placed the file directly in the wwwroot folder, no *foldername* is required.

Manual Development

Manual development means you are writing the source code as plain text. Some programmers prefer to write all their code as plain text, and very complex applications can be developed manually with tools as simple as Notepad or WordPad. Typically, however, Notepad and WordPad are used for quick editing of existing files rather than construction from scratch, and even programmers who like to code by hand reuse prewritten code extensively. And although Notepad is convenient, some text editing programs have capabilities that provide for more efficiency than others, as we discuss next.

The Notepad Text-Editing Accessory Notepad is a very simple and lightweight text-editing tool that is supplied with all normal installations of Windows, as part of the Accessories group (from the desktop, click Start | Programs | Accessories to see it on the menu). It is capable of creating and saving text files, searching for text strings, and it produces ASCII text, plus carriage-return and line-feed characters at the end of each line. It is useful for creating very small HTML files or for editing HTML files, including scripting such as ASP, VBScript, JScript, and so forth. It is a popular tool because it is free with the operating system, small, and leaves no formatting characters in the file. However, there are almost no automated functions, so it pales in comparison to the more sophisticated page and scripting creation and debugging tools.

WordPad WordPad also comes with standard installations of Windows under the Accessories group, and it is a somewhat more advanced text or word processing tool. It allows you to save files in formats other than plain ASCII text, but this is actually a drawback for most code-writing and editing. It is primarily useful for working with files too large for Notepad, as long as you make sure to save your files in plain text format. Use WordPad with caution.

Programmer's File Editor Programmer's File Editor (PFE) is a very useful utility program for programmers, as its name implies. It is a plain text editor but has a number of features that make programming easier, such as the line number display function. It also has the standard features of text editors, such as Find and Replace for matching text strings. You can find shareware versions of PFE at **www.download.com**. Just search for text editors (or simply "Programmer's File Editor") in the Search box.

Automated Development Environments

Automated development environments, often called Integrated Development Environments (IDE), contain facilities that let you use visual- and text-based tools to program and construct elaborate applications, usually with several languages to choose from and with many visual tools to make development easier and more efficient. They are usually expensive and require a fair amount of knowledge for productive use. Although they may write a great deal of code for you, that doesn't mean you can use them without knowing the code because chances are good that you'll have to get right into the code on numerous occasions. The tool of choice for ASP.NET development is Visual Studio.NET [VS.NET].

Visual Studio.NET For developing ASP.NET applications, Microsoft's Visual Studio.NET has a wealth of features available to make the development process as painless as possible. It contains many of the features that made its predecessor, Visual Studio, so popular and supports all the new capabilities of the .NET Framework. We offer an introduction to using VS.NET in Module 4.

To run Visual Studio.NET you will need at least a Pentium II with a 450MHz CPU, plus anywhere from 92 to 192MB of RAM, depending upon the operating system you are running (Windows 2000, Windows XP, or Windows NT 4.0).

A variety of programming languages, tools, and capabilities are built into Visual Studio.NET, including Visual Basic and C#, plus easy-to-use visual development interfaces for Web Forms and Web Services. In addition, many of the features of Visual InterDev, Microsoft's high-end website development tool, are included in Visual Studio.NET. Visual InterDev contains a site designer for overall site construction, an integrated page editor for page construction, database tools such as the Data View and the Query Designer for working with databases and data sources, and debugging and collaborative development tools.

Project 1-1: Checking Deployment and Development Environments

Before you start using the example code and projects in this book, you should determine which operating system is running and what tools are installed. The following steps take you through that process. Installed on your system (or the development server you have access to) must be:

- The appropriate operating system. We're using Windows 2000 Advanced Server.
- The appropriate Web Server software. We're using IIS 5.0.
- ASP.NET. We're using Premium Edition.
- If you will be following the examples that make use of Visual Studio, you must have Visual Studio installed. We're using Visual Studio Enterprise Architect Edition. When we installed it, it also installed ASP.NET and other Windows Components.

Note

If you find that your machine does not have the appropriate software installed you will need to get things properly set up (or have the system administrator do it) before you can expect the examples and projects to function correctly.

Step-by-Step

1. Decide how you are going to proceed with development, testing, and serving. It's common to use a single machine for development and testing and another for serving, meaning that you write code on the client machine, load it onto the server, and then test it in the browser of the client machine. This is not a hard and fast requirement, so you may find yourself in the position of doing development, testing, and serving all on the same computer. Either way, the proper operating systems and application tools must be installed and running properly. We'll proceed as though you are running separate machines for development, testing, and serving.
2. On the development machine, click Start | Settings | Control Panel. The window with all the Control Panel icons should appear. Double-click the System icon. A small dialog box will open, and you should see the name and version of the

operating system running on the machine. You should also see the amount of RAM installed and the CPU version (although perhaps not the megahertz rating).

3. If the operating system is any version of Windows, it is likely that Notepad and WordPad are installed, as well as Internet Explorer. To check, close the dialog, minimize the Control Panel window, and click Start | Program | Accessories. You should see Notepad and WordPad in the list of Accessories. Internet Explorer can be found as an icon featuring a blue *e* either on the desktop or on the status bar (at the bottom of the screen when the desktop is displayed).

4. Double-click the Internet Explorer icon to start Internet Explorer, and once it is open click Help | About InternetExplorer to find the version of Internet Explorer installed. By the way, if IE says no Internet connection is available, you will need to make a connection to the Internet and to your web server if the server is running on another machine (unless you can simply make a connection through your local area network).

5. You can do your development and testing from just about any machine running Windows that has a text editing program installed and Internet Explorer 5.5, but if you want to use Visual Studio.NET, you will have to be running the minimum system requirements (mentioned earlier in the section "Visual Studio.NET").

6. If you have direct access to the web server or are running the web server and your development environment on the same computer, you can use a similar process to discover the version of the operating system and installed tools and services. One important point: Visual Studio.NET requires FrontPage Server Extensions to be installed and correctly configured on your web server. The documentation for installing Visual Studio.NET contains complete instructions on how to accomplish this; if Visual Studio.NET is already installed, FrontPage Server Extensions will also be installed and properly configured.

ASP and ASP.NET: An Overview

Active Server Pages 3.0 is the predecessor to ASP.NET, and the functionality to make it run is built into IIS and Windows 2000. When you install Windows 2000 Server, for example, ASP is automatically installed when the operating system and web server are installed. ASP is, quite simply, a technology for interacting with the user by intercepting incoming requests and processing outgoing responses. Ordinary HTTP requests and responses follow a very inflexible pattern during normal use and are not suitable for dynamic interactions. Please note that ASP and ASP.NET still use HTTP to communicate to the browser and back, but ASP and ASP.NET bring added functionality that makes the communication process much richer.

Web hosting with a version of the Unix operating system was, until recently, the default method of publishing your web content. Common Gateway Interface (CGI) is the name of the method used to interact with the web server on the Unix side.

When you have a website hosted on IIS and you run ASP scripts or ASP.NET applications, the server checks each file to see whether or not they have ASP or ASP.NET extensions. A file extension is the last three, four, or more characters following the dot at the end of the filename. ASP files end with .asp, while ASP.NET files end with .aspx. Also, files ending with an HTML extension (such as .htm or .html) are reviewed to see if they contain ASP coding (and server-side includes, discussed later in this book).

If any files have the appropriate extension or contain code, the server routes those files to ASP or ASP.NET for processing prior to sending them out to the client. The script or code is then processed and the appropriate content is generated for transmission back to the browser/client. Because processing takes place before the results are delivered to the user, all manner of functionality can be built-in, such as database access, component usage, and the ordinary programmatic functionality available with VBScript, JScript, or any other scripting language you'd care to use (for ASP). VBScript is the default language ASP uses, but both VBScript and JScript scripting engines are included with Windows 2000. Visual Basic.NET, JScript, and C# are the default programming languages supported by ASP.NET, and VBScript is not supported at all in ASP.NET.

ASP Objects

ASP is not a programming language; it is an engine for processing scripting language commands that has added functionality in the ability to instantiate components and use built-in objects. Think of it as the glue that holds together scripting, objects, components, and interactions with the web server (altogether these pieces make up your application). ASP objects are an important part of the overall technology. ASP objects are referenced in scripting language code (such as VBScript or JScript) to perform certain highly useful functions, such as capturing data submitted by users, responding to user inputs, managing applications and sessions, and manipulating the server. ASP.NET also supports the intrinsic ASP objects and adds numerous new objects and components to the mix.

Included ASP Objects

Objects in ASP have names (Request, Response, and so forth) and in code they can be referenced by their names. In addition, objects have things called methods, properties, and collections associated with them, and these items can also be referenced in your code.

Note

Objects are very useful for determining what is going on in your application and for making other things happen based on what you find at any given point. For example, the Request object has a collection called ServerVariables associated with it. Inside this collection you will find data about the server variables currently in the Request.ServerVariables collection. (Notice the dot notation separating the name of the object and its collection.) The number of variables in the ServerVariables collection is finite, and each variable also has a unique name. The data in the collection reflects the values produced during the most recent communication between the client and server.

Objects included with ASP are as follows:

- **The Request and Response objects** These objects capture incoming data from the user and respond with processed text, HTML, and other data.
- **The Application and Session objects** These objects allow the designer to set up the application both as an application, whose variables have scope over the entire set of scripts in use, and as a session, whose variables have scope over the scripts in use by an individual user.
- **The Server object** This object allows the developer to manipulate the server, encode HTML and URLs, set timeouts for scripts, and create instances of other objects and components within the application.

ADO and ADO.NET Objects

ActiveX Data Objects (ADO) is the term used for one of the most valuable components ASP can call. ADO objects allow direct and convenient access to databases and other data sources, and this functionality serves many common purposes on application-driven websites.

Included ADO Objects

ADO includes the following objects:

- **The Connection object** This object creates a connection between your ASP scripts and a database or data source.
- **The Command object** This object allows you to run specific commands against a data source.
- **The Recordset object** This object gives you control over a set of records and fields from a data source, such that you can perform all the common record functions available when working with a database table, such as finding, editing, adding, deleting, and so forth.

ADO.NET Objects

ADO.NET uses a somewhat different approach to retrieve data from databases, but although the names have changed, many of the functions performed are the same. After all, you still want to retrieve, modify, and return records to a database. Depending on what you feel most comfortable with, you can always import the old ADO type library (we'll discuss this further in Module 9) and then use ADO rather than ADO.NET. The names of the new ADO.NET objects are as follows:

- **DataSet and DataReader objects** The DataSet object is a set of records that you find, navigate, and modify, while the DataReader object is a read-only set of records.
- **DataTable object** The DataTable object is similar to a table in a database; one or more of them may be contained in a single DataSet object.
- **DataTableMapping, DataView, and DataRelation objects** These objects are used to manipulate or work with other objects in the DataSet object and will be discussed in greater detail in Modules 9 and 10.

ASP Components

As we mentioned, ADO is an ASP component, and the objects and components included with ASP and ADO work just fine in ASP.NET. There are other components included with ASP, and you can also buy third-party components online. Components are valuable because they offer preprogrammed functionality that would take many hours of effort for you to duplicate, even assuming you had excellent programming skills. Built-in components are essentially free, and the cost for most third-party components is relatively low; they are usually tested and debugged for reliability, and they expose methods and properties you can easily call and use, just like built-in objects.

The scripting engines provide access to their own set of objects, most notably the Dictionary object, FileSystemObject object, Drive object, Folder object, and File object. Collectively, these are called the Scripting Runtime Library objects. There is another class of objects that comes with ASP called installable components, discussed in the next section.

Included (Installable) ASP Components

Installable components included with ASP 3.0 are as follows:

- The Ad Rotator component
- The Browser Capabilities component
- The Content Linking component
- The Content Rotator component
- The Counters component
- The Logging Utility component
- The MyInfo component
- The Page Counter component
- The Permission Checker component
- The Tools component

We'll discuss these components in much more detail later on in this book, but keep in mind that ASP.NET makes extensive use of Web Forms and Web Services (discussed in Modules 4 and 7, respectively), and these can be thought of as functioning in a manner similar to components in their own right.

Relational DBMSs and Other Data Sources

Relational databases, such as Microsoft Access, SQL Server, and many others, contain data structured as tables, records, and fields. You can connect to these databases with the Connection object, as mentioned above, but you can also connect to and manipulate many other data sources with the tools developed for ASP and ASP.NET. For example, you can connect to spreadsheets and word-processing documents as well.

Just the same, you'll be primarily using databases with ASP.NET and ADO.NET for the immediate future, and while Microsoft Access isn't very scalable for production websites, it is a good tool for rapidly prototyping databases and the functionality required for a particular project. There are conversion and migration tools available that make it easy to go from prototype in Access to full-fledged industrial strength DBMS (database management system) when you've stabilized the functionality required.

- What are the general components of Active Server Pages?
- Are these components supported in ASP.NET? How does ASP.NET differ in its approach to object and components?

Developing Distributed Online Applications

Online applications are websites that offer an order of magnitude more functionality than static web pages or normal websites. On a normal website you can fill out a form and when you press the Submit button the contents of the form are sent to a CGI script and processed into an e-mail, or perhaps turned into

---

- The main components of ASP are the Request and Response objects, the Application and Session objects, the Server object, and built-in components such as the Ad Rotator component and the Browser Capabilities component.
- These components are supported in ASP.NET, but ASP.NET also allows the use of more sophisticated behind-the-scenes object and component processing in order to provide better management of objects and components; it also provides a framework for creating user-defined components based on Web Services and Web Forms.

a text file on the server. Everything else is simply the display of text and graphics in your browser, with a little hypertext linking around the web for fun.

A good example of an online application is a website that does your taxes. It gets its name from the familiar application programs we use like TurboTax, except that it doesn't run on your desktop, it runs online. To build one, you'll need to do some software development much like the programmers of TurboTax did.

The default website created for you when IIS is installed is the place applications start. Assuming you know what functions you want to build in, you can code them with ASP and VBScript (or another scripting language that appeals to you). For speed and scalability, you may wish to program particular functions of your program as executable components (ActiveX) using C++ or Visual Basic, or perhaps you'll buy some components off the shelf.

Most likely you'll also create some databases to store subscriber or customer data behind the scenes, as well as tables of information that may not change much, such as tax tables and forms.

Finally, you'll tie the functions, components, databases, and user sessions together using Active Server Pages objects and the scripting language you've chosen. ASP functions will manage user interactions and call the other components of your application within the scope of the application and session parameters you set.

Client/Server or Tiered Applications

A server or software service is called that because it serves up files or performs services for other computers, such as delivering web content. A client requests services from a server. Typical clients are web browsers and e-mail programs. To make it more fun, the distinction between servers and clients is beginning to blur, and servers and clients can also be clients and servers.

The term *client/server* fits the interaction between a web browser and a web server pretty well. The client makes a request for a web page or other website resource, and the server provides copies of the web page (and associated files) to the client. Obviously, the server (like most servers) is built to handle multiple client requests at once.

Related to client/server is another type of client/server interaction called multitiered applications. Multitiered applications involve several levels of interactions. For example, suppose you use your client to request data from a server, and the server must in turn request processing functions and data from a data source or an intermediate data interpreter or conversion program. These intermediaries are often referred to as the middle-tier in a multitiered application, and there may be a number of layers of processing going on between you the data or functionality you are using. Ideally, these layers should be transparent, so the functions of the application perform in a uniform way, using the (browser) interface you understand.

Multitiered applications can consist of components spread out anywhere online or on a network, so that applications can be more easily scaled, more reliable, and more powerful and data-rich. After all, think what you could do if you could combine multitudes of the resources available on the Internet into a monolithic application, even in just one industry or area of interest.

Hosting Issues

Website applications must be hosted on a web server somewhere, so picking a good hosting service is key to getting good response from your applications. It's very important to establish a rapport with the technical support folks at your hosting company early on. If they are not competent, you should complain or switch. In addition, get full details on what hardware/software combinations they are running and in what configuration. Depending upon the configuration, what works for one client on a platform may not work for another client on the same platform.

Choosing Connection Types The primary considerations when choosing a connection type or evaluating the connections of a web hosting company are how many ways are they connected and at what speed.

Each web hosting company or Internet Service Provider (ISP) purchases their Internet connections from larger companies upstream on the Internet (their upstream provider) until you get to the largest Internet connection providers. If your web hosting company claims to be *multihomed*, they are saying they have connections to several upstream Internet connection providers. This is important because even the biggest Internet connection providers have been known to fall out of service for days and weeks at a time, although this is relatively unusual. Having connections to three to seven upstream providers is not uncommon at the better hosting companies.

The amount of bandwidth available depends on the type of connection they have to the Internet. The amount of bandwidth available to you depends on how many other sites are vying for the same bandwidth (either on your machine, or on all the machines in your cluster). To estimate the amount of bandwidth required to support a given number of users, you can use a procedure similar to the following:

1. Find the size of the files to be transmitted. For HTML pages, multiply the number of characters per line (approximately 80) by the number of bits per character (8), times the number of lines per page (around 66), times the number of pages in the document, times an overhead factor of 1.5. For example, for a 10-page HTML document filled with code, there would be 10 pages times 66 lines per page (660), times 80 characters per line (52,800), times 8 bits per character (422,400), times 1.5 for overhead. The total bits to be transmitted would be 633,600, or about two-thirds of a million bits.
2. Divide the number of bits to be transmitted by the bandwidth available to find out how long it will take to transmit the page. If our page is really two-thirds of a million bits, it would take around four-tenths of a second to transmit if you're running a T-1 line (1.54 million bits per second). Conversely, dividing transmission speed by file size gives the number of pages that can be transmitted per second (about 2.36 for this example).

Note

This calculation is not representative of typical HTML pages because most do not contain characters in every column of every line. However, pages do usually contain graphics files that must be transmitted separately. All the files making up a page should be included in your calculations of bandwidth requirements. In addition, it's important to note that most people can't receive at T-1 speeds. If they are using a 56Kbps modem, you'd better make sure your pages are about one-tenth the size we just discussed, including graphics and related files.

3. Figure out how many users your available bandwidth can support. The amount of bandwidth used is commonly measured as the number of times your web pages (meaning all the files associated with a page) are downloaded per day times the typical file size downloaded, in kilobytes or megabytes. If you have 1.54 million bits per second available (a T-1 line dedicated to your web server only) then you can transmit (after the overhead factor) 11,088,000,000 bytes per day, or a little over 10GB. If each page hit averages 30KB, you can support approximately 333,000 page hits per day.

If each page hit is spread apart from the others, no user will suffer performance degradation. However, it is much more common to see users congregate at your site during peak times. You should also calculate the number of simultaneous users your site can support and still maintain acceptable download times. This is done by calculating the number of page hits that can be processed and transmitted within an arbitrarily chosen time frame. For example, if you want all your users to receive their page requests within three seconds of clicking, you would calculate the maximum transmission speed of your connection for the average page hit. If each page hit is 3.75KB and you're running a T-1 line, you can fit approximately 100 users into a three-second time frame (1.54 million bits per second divided by 30,000 bits per page*1.5 overhead divided by 3 seconds).

Ask the Expert

Question: I've heard that I can host multiple online applications from one installation of IIS via virtual directories. What is a virtual directory?

Answer: A virtual directory is a folder that is not in your home or root website folder but appears to browsers to be so. It is actually an *alias* to another directory elsewhere on the server. Among the advantages of using virtual directories are that users don't know the real location of critical files on your server, and it's easier to change directories later if you decide to move content (just change the alias mapping, not every URL reference in the website).

Question: It sounds like virtual directories are pretty useful. Is there an easy way to create them?

Answer: Yes. You can use the Virtual Directory Creation Wizard. Just follow these steps (these steps and the screens associated with them are from the Pentium 166MHz with an earlier version of Windows 2000 installed and may be somewhat different from your choices if you are running a very recent version of Windows 2000):

1. Open the Internet Services Manager from the desktop using Start | Programs | Administrative Applications | Internet Services Manager.
2. Find the Default website and right-click it to obtain the shortcut menu. Choose New | Virtual Directory. The Virtual Directory Creation Wizard, shown in Figure 1-4, will open.
3. On the first screen requiring an entry (Figure 1-5), enter the alias or name for your virtual directory. On the next screen (Figure 1-6), enter (or browse to) the physical folder represented by the name you entered on the previous screen.
4. On the next screen, you can choose what actions to allow the directory, such as Read, Run Scripts, and so forth (as shown in Figure 1-7). Make your choices, go to the final screen and click Finish. Your virtual directory will appear in the Default website with the alias you chose.

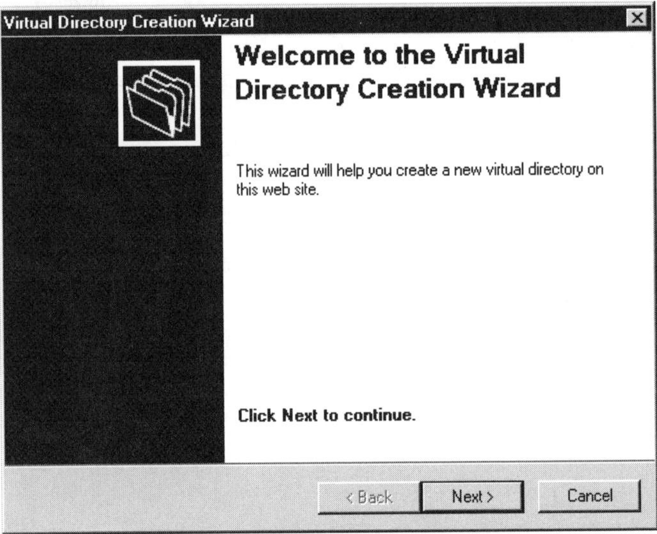

Figure 1-4 The Virtual Directory Creation Wizard

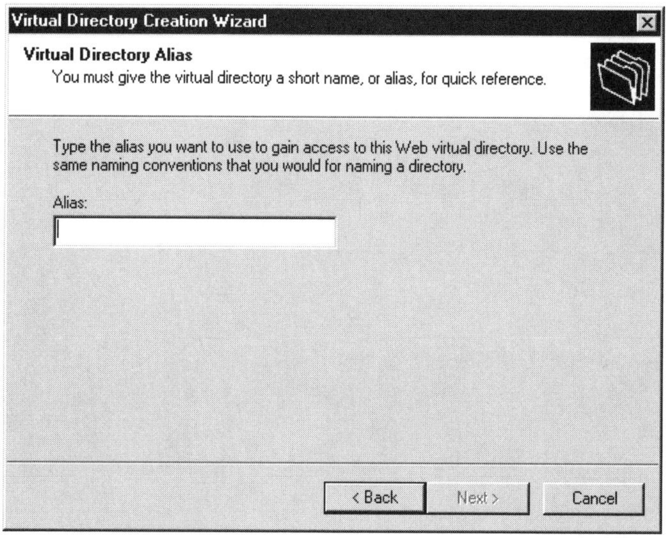

Virtual Directory Creation Wizard

Virtual Directory Alias

You must give the virtual directory a short name, or alias, for quick reference.

Type the alias you want to use to gain access to this Web virtual directory. Use the same naming conventions that you would for naming a directory.

Alias:

< Back Next > Cancel

Figure 1-5 The Virtual Directory Alias screen

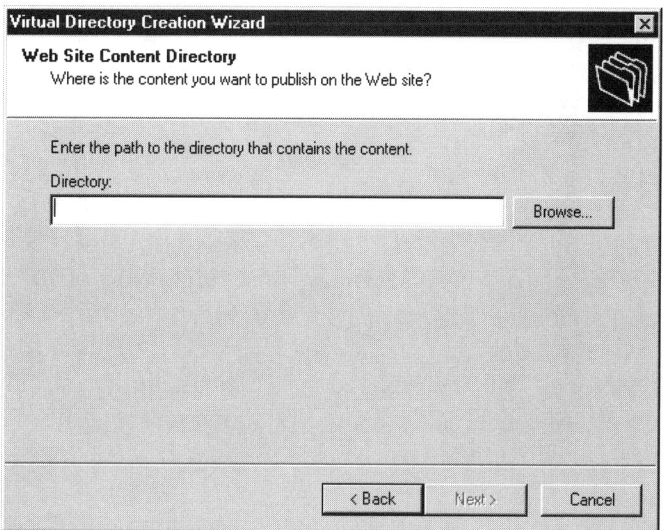

Figure 1-6 The path to the physical directory

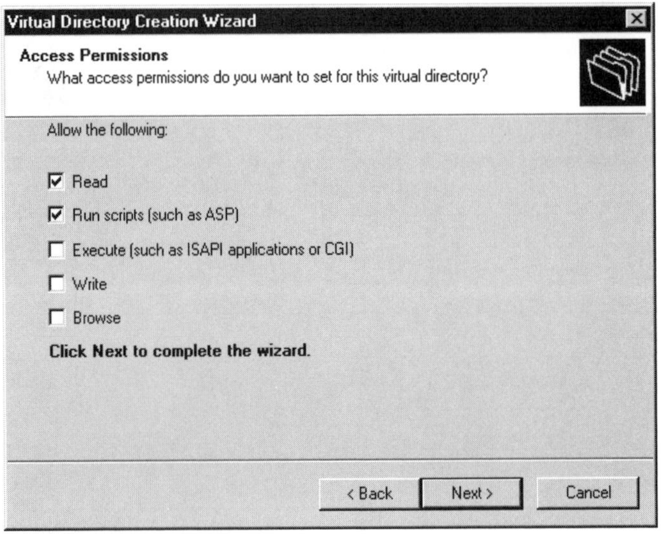

Figure 1-7 The virtual directory Access Permissions screen

ASP.NET Programming Languages

One way of categorizing programming languages is by general function, and the following types are offered: markup languages, interpreted scripting languages, traditional compiled programming languages, and database access languages. With ASP.NET, the supported languages are Visual Basic (VB), JScript, and C#, but you'll use a number of other languages (or language development standards) during application development as well, such as HTML, XHTML, CSS2, XML, XSL, and SQL. Each has its own particular best use, but there is some overlap.

In ASP you could use several languages on a single page of code, but in ASP.NET this is no longer allowed. As you will see in the project at the end of this module, you must declare the language you intend to use at the beginning of your page, although you can mix and match languages (each in its own page) across your application as much as you like. In the next sections we discuss these languages and where they work best.

Languages Available

Visual Basic.NET, JScript, and C# are supported in ASP.NET and the .NET Framework. They are compiled and run in the common language runtime

(CLR). The source code (plain-text commands written in the language) for each language that is supported is compiled into something called language-independent *intermediate language code* (IL). Any language can be used so long as a compiler is available that will produce IL code; Microsoft has made compilers available for the three languages supported. The CLR also provides memory management, security, garbage collection, and so forth.

Visual Basic.NET

In ASP the default language is VBScript, a scripting version of Visual Basic. In ASP.NET, Visual Basic.NET (VB.NET) is one of the supported languages. Since there are many areas in which VB.NET, Visual Basic 6.0, VBScript, and Visual Basic for Applications overlap, VB.NET is a good choice if you are already familiar with one of these other languages.

C#

C# is a derivative of the very popular C and C++ languages. It contains features similar to those found in C and C++, while at the same time automating or eliminating some tasks and functions that have been a source of errors in the previous versions.

JScript

JScript is a version of JavaScript developed by Microsoft and is also supported in ASP.NET. Although labeled a scripting language, it is also compiled in the CLR and is useful to developers familiar with JScript or JavaScript.

Project 1-2: Looping Program Structures

Programs perform actions based on input and feed out the results as output. The actions can be classed as one time or repetitive, and repetitive actions are called looping structures. One of the most common looping structures in a program is the For...Next loop. Each time through the loop, a series of program instructions (or even a single instruction) is performed. To keep track of the number of times through the loop, a counter is usually used and incremented each time. Eventually, the terminal value is reached, and the loop quits executing, after which the next instructions come into play. In this project, you'll build a simple web page that incorporates Visual Basic.NET programming.

Step-by-Step

1. Build a simple HTML web page to serve as the container/template for what you want the server to deliver to the user. Start by opening up Notepad and entering the following code:

```
<html>
<head><title> My first ASP.NET Page</title></head>
<body>
<center>
</center>
</body>
</html>
```

2. This provides a very simple web page. Save this file with the filename first.aspx in your ASP.NET folder, in the Module01 subfolder, in the working subfolder. Next, add the following code to the very top of the file:

```
<%@ Page Language="VB"%>
```

3. This code tells the server that this file uses Visual Basic (VB) as the programming language for this page. The server already sees and understands the HTML code by default but needs to be informed of the other languages present.

4. Now you can add programmatic functions to the body of the page. You're going to do some programming in Visual Basic, but you'll need to mix in some plain HTML as well wherever HTML is required ordinarily (we'll cover HTML in greater detail in Module 2). Start by putting in some delimiters, right after the beginning <center> tag in the HTML, to show where the ASP.NET begins, and make a variable act as a counter, like this:

```
<%
Dim i As Integer
```

5. The <% tells the server that this is the beginning of some programming language code (VB in this particular example), and the Dim statement in Visual Basic says you are going to "dimension" the variable. Dimensioning means making space in memory for the variable and whatever data it might contain, in this case an integer.

6. Now that you've got a variable to serve as the counter, you can set it to the value 1 for starters, and then you can enter the HTML <font> tag and some text to be displayed each time through the For…Next loop, like this:

```
i = 1
For i = 1 to 7
%>
     <font color="#FF0000" size="<% Response.write(i) %>">
Programmatically increasing font size</font><br>
<%
Next
%>
```

7. Setting the variable named *i* to the number 1 starts the sequence off, but what really makes it work is the combination of the For statement, the processing and text to output, and the Next statement. Each time through the loop, the variable *i* is automatically incremented by one, but if you want to choose a different increment you can easily do so. When the Next statement is reached, the loop begins again, but when *i* is equal to 7, the loop quits and the remainder of the page is processed. The final output is plain HTML to the browser, generated courtesy of the Response object's write method. Note that in ASP it was OK to put the text in quotes after the Response.write portion (like this: Response.write "text goes here"), but in ASP.NET the output text must be within parentheses after the object and method in the code.

8. Notice in the <font> there are some attributes: color and size. You've set the color to the HTML color code for red (#FF0000), so all the lines of text will be red, but you've set the size to change depending upon what iteration through the loop you happen to be on using the counter *i* to serve *not only* as a counter, but *also* as the value of the size attribute each time you go through the loop. Pretty slick, eh?

9. The entire document should look like this code example:

```
<%@ Page Language="VB"%>
<html>
<head><title> My first ASP.NET Page</title></head>
<body>
<center>
<%
```

```
Dim i As Integer

i = 1
For i = 1 to 7
%>
<font color="#FF0000" size="<% Response.write(i) %>">
Programmatically increasing font size</font><br>
<%
Next
%>
</center>
</body>
</html>
```

10. Don't forget to resave your file; then you can browse to it. It will be compiled, so it takes a while to load the first time; after that, it's very quick. The output on your screen should look like Figure 1-8.

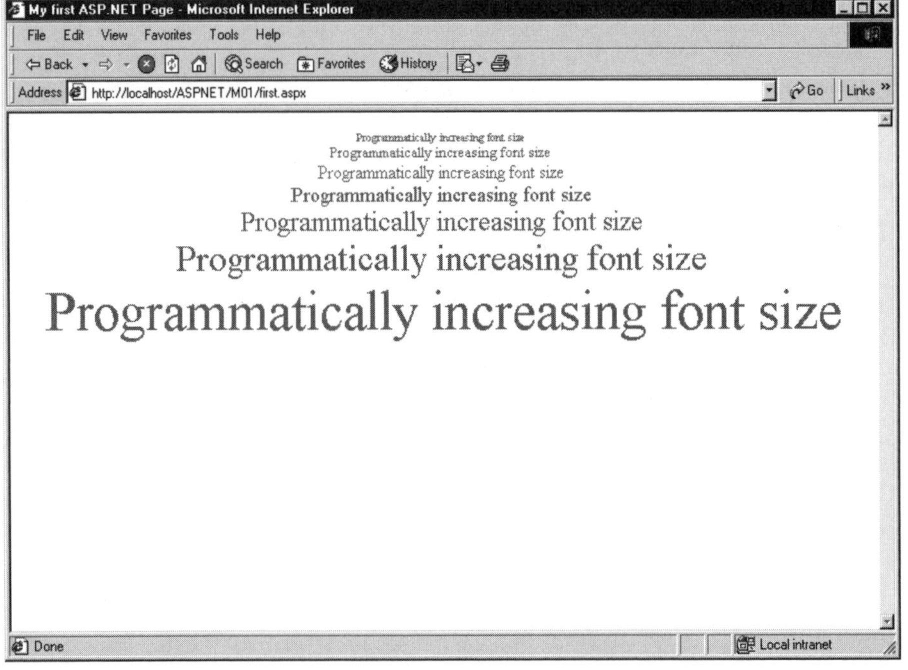

Figure 1-8 The output of the sample program

Mastery Check

1. On what platform does ASP.NET run, and how much does ASP.NET cost?

   A. Unix, and it costs around $1,000

   B. Windows NT, and it is free

   C. Windows 2000, and it is free

   D. B and C

   E. None of the above

2. What is the primary functionality ASP.NET brings to a website, and why is it so important?

   ____

   ____

3. What is a partition, and why does it matter how it is formatted when installing IIS?

   ____

   ____

4. What process is advisable to use when designing a web-based application?

   A. Start developing pages and functions first, and ask questions later.

   B. Do exactly as the client says.

   C. Ask plenty of questions up front, and then evaluate the client's needs and make recommendations based on those needs.

   D. None of the above.

5. What is bandwidth and why is it an important consideration in the design of a modern website?

   ____

   ____

Mastery Check

6. What is the difference between interpreted and compiled languages?

   A. Interpreted language refers to programs written in a foreign language, which must be interpreted to be modified.

   B. Compiled languages are for developing programs that are turned into processor instructions specific to the CPUs they run on, while interpreted languages remain in the form of source code until they are accessed. Compiled languages produce executable files that run much faster than code made with interpreted languages.

   C. Both end up being compiled at some point, so there is really no difference.

   D. All of the above.

7. What is XML?

   A. XML is Web Services.

   B. XML is a specification for creating markup languages.

   C. XML is eXtensible Markup Language.

   D. All of the above.

   E. B and C.

8. What programming languages are supported in ASP.NET?

   A. All programming languages

   B. Only Visual Basic.NET, C#, and JScript

   C. Any programming language for which a compiler capable of producing IL code is available

   D. None of the above

Mastery Check

9. What ADO objects are used for accessing databases?

    A. The Table object and the Recordset object

    B. The Connection, Command, and Recordset objects

    C. The Database object and its collections

    D. None of the above

10. What ADO.NET objects are used for accessing databases?

    A. The DataSet and DataReader objects

    B. The Data object and its collections

    C. ADO.NET uses only the ADO objects

    D. None of the above

11. What kinds of bandwidth are there, and how is usage calculated?

    A. There is available bandwidth and used bandwidth. Both are calculated the same way, by multiplying the sizes of files transmitted over a period of time.

    B. There is available bandwidth and used bandwidth. Available bandwidth is calculated as the total amount of data that could be transmitted in a given time frame, while used bandwidth is the amount of data actually transmitted in a given time frame.

    C. There is only available bandwidth, calculated as the amount of data that could be transmitted in a given time frame.

    D. None of the above.

12. What is a distributed application, and how is it different from normal applications?

    ____

    ____

Mastery Check

13. How can you find out what version of the operating system is running on your computer?

A. Look on the box the operating system came in.

B. Click Start | Setting | Control Panel and then the System icon.

C. Ask the system administrator.

D. Any of the above.

14. What is the advantage of using a set of tools such as Visual Studio to develop ASP.NET applications?

A. Visual Studio.NET contains the programming languages and integrated development environments that make development much more efficient, all in one package.

B. Visual Studio.NET has tools that write some of the code for you and includes tools with visual development interfaces, making programming much more intuitive.

C. Visual Studio.NET is optimized for creating applications for the .NET Framework.

D. All of the above.

15. What kinds of features are found in a web page made with ASP.NET?

____

____

Module 2

Programming Basics

The Goals of This Module

- Learn the basics of programming
- Learn how program logic is constructed and how programs flow
- Review the basics of website layout and design
- Review the basics of HTML and XHTML
- Explore fundamental interactivity methods in ASP.NET
- Learn basic Visual Basic.NET programming structure and syntax
- Practice error-handling techniques
- Examine good and bad debugging procedures

More and more, websites are becoming complete online applications. Whereas early websites used static pages to display text and graphics, today's websites perform very complex functions, much like traditional applications programs. Therefore, the development effort that goes into modern websites is similar to traditional software development efforts. Programming is a fundamental part of those efforts, and the same kinds of tools and procedures used to develop software are being transformed and used in website development.

This module covers programming basics, such as using HTML/XHTML, VBScript, Visual Basic, JScript, ASP, and SQL, and also touches on error handling and debugging. In addition, we'll offer some advice about site layout, as well as construction and process flow.

Basics of Programming

In a sense, computers are devices like any other designed to work for us. For example, a hammer is a simple device that increases the leverage in your arm to apply a driving force to nails, and it also provides a hard surface against which to do the driving. A hammer has no capability to turn into a screwdriver (but could be misused as one, no doubt). The ability to respond to varying circumstances with the appropriate capability is the mark of a device containing logic.

Not all devices that include logic are digital computers. A carburetor is an example of an analog computer. Devices employing analog computation often use mechanical linkages to receive inputs and generate outputs, as in the throttle linkage and system of fuel jets in a carburetor. Digitization offers the advantage of flexibility, and flexibility is the significant feature of modern digital computers. They can be used as the basis for just about any type of device, so long as analog inputs can be digitized and digital outputs can be reconstituted into analog form.

A further advantage of digital computers comes about when they are endowed with flexible program and data storage such as hard drives. Multiple programs can be present and may work individually or together to accomplish the objectives in any given situation. Finally, connecting digital computers to the Internet makes it possible to gather real-time data far beyond the capabilities of a typical desktop computer, and with flexible and standard communications using platforms like .NET, digital computers and the applications on them can finally collaborate effectively.

Data Types

Data is simply a value or values that may or may not mean anything in the real world. We apply types to data and so begin to apply meaning to data. For example, the string 2/2/01 by itself means nothing, but if we say it is a date, it immediately means something to a person. However, for a computer, the string is just a string until a date data type is applied, and then the computer understands that this string is really a date and that certain calculation methods apply to it. There are data types for many types of data, including numbers (quite a variety there, including several kinds of integers, currency, floating point numbers, decimal numbers, and so forth), plain text, dates, logical value (Yes/No, True/False, and so forth), and other more specialized types often constructed from combinations of the basic or primitive data types.

Programmed Instructions

Programming languages comprise the logical statements that manipulate or process data. As has been repeated so often, computers work with zeros and ones. These zeros and ones are represented as tiny switches (either on or off) within the central processing unit (CPU) of the computer, as well as other places where data resides (such as the random access memory [RAM] and the hard drive). Often called bits, the zeros and ones can be accumulated into bytes (a sequence of 8 bits, typically), with a byte often representing a letter or number. Some schemes for representing letters and numbers use more than one byte, but the purpose is to make it so that computers can communicate in terms we are familiar with. There is no inherent mandate that bits become bytes in the form of letters and numbers; bits can represent anything we want them to. Programming languages are the means by which we process bits and bytes from input data to output result.

Computer Programming Languages

At the lowest level, computers process instructions with their CPUs as strings of bits. One step above that, program instructions are formed in some type of assembly language. However, even at this level, the commands are far too basic for the average person. Higher-level languages such as C++ and Visual Basic are commonly used to create program instructions (a complete set of program instructions is called a *program*, and if the program has a user interface and fulfills the basic requirements to solve or work with a particular problem, it is often called an *application*). These languages are *compiled*, meaning they are processed by compiler software that converts the higher-level statements into lower-level assembly statements and then into processor instructions that are optimized to run only in a particular operating system on a given range of CPUs. That is why there are versions of programs that run on DOS, Windows, Unix, and the Mac; even within a particular operating system, there are limitations on what class of CPU is required or what version of an operating system a program will run on.

Compiled vs. Interpreted

Programs that have been compiled generally run faster than programs that are interpreted. A compiled program simply starts running as low-level instructions via the operating system, while programs made in interpreted languages (such as VBScript, JavaScript, and so forth) must be compiled by an interpreter when they run, the intervening step slowing things down considerably. If the difference in execution is the difference between a millisecond and a microsecond, a person won't notice, so interpreted languages are quite useful for quickly adding a bit of programmatic functionality to a web page, for example. Larger, more complex programs are required where speed is essential, as in complex functions happening back on the server.

Not too many years ago, compiling a program proceeded in the way we've described, but more recently compiling a program has taken on a variety of new meanings. For example, Java programs are compiled into what is called bytecode. This is a state in which the program is semicompiled and will run in the Java virtual machine (JVM) of any computer, regardless of the operating system of that computer. The JVM provides an environment in which the program can be processed for the operating system on which it is running; although the JVM adds overhead and slows processing a bit, it is much faster than strictly interpreted languages.

With the .NET Framework, as we mentioned in Module 1, programs run in the common language runtime (CLR) environment. Program instructions are compiled to the language-independent intermediate language code (IL) state, and after the first time they are accessed (and compiled) the CLR refers to the compiled resource rather than the initial source code, even though that file is still there.

Program Flow

Typically, programs have a flow of operations associated with them, meaning that the program will initiate processing following predefined steps, according to the inputs it receives. The way that processing progresses is called program flow. One mark of a program is that it bases the processing steps used on current conditions. For example, if a user is attempting to login, the program will check to ensure that the user has registered. If so, the program performs a set of instructions that log the user in. If the user is unregistered, the program will not log them in but instead may offer the opportunity to register. The flow from processing to checking conditions and on to further processing may be represented by a flow chart. A flow chart is a diagram of the processing steps and conditions that determine what processing steps to perform next.

Note

Often other useful diagrams are employed during the construction of an application in order to assist in the conceptualization of the design of the application and how it should properly function. See the section "Unified Modeling Language" later in this module.

Writing a program starts with defining the high-level requirements of the program. The actual development of a finished application may proceed from the bottom up or the top down, but in either case it is best to try to get the overall requirements defined first, so you at least have some idea where you are going.

Application Program Requirements

High-level application program requirements have much to do with the actual data processing that will occur and not so much with other considerations such as scalability, security, and so forth (even though these are very important considerations as well). The point is to try to define what the end results must be and then figure out what data is required to arrive at those results and what processing must be done to get there.

Programming languages often focused on a step-by-step approach, in which data inputs were processed and outputs returned in a very linear way. In fact, early programming languages relied on line numbers to mark areas of a program that might only be processed under certain conditions or might be repeatedly processed (as in looping structures). Modern programming languages use an object-oriented structure that tends to model real-world conditions better.

Object-Oriented Programming

Part of the latest upgrade to Visual Basic is to make the language completely object-oriented. This means that everything in the program is treated as an object. Objects have program instructions and data contained in them, and they typically have properties associated with them (data values representing something specific to the object) and methods that can be used to perform operations on their data.

Processing Data

Some languages are better than others for certain operations, and some languages are more familiar to developers than others. Almost any language can be used to write a given function, but it's best to use the language most suited to the processing requirement or most familiar to your developers if there is little difference in language capability.

Data processing is a matter of arranging the data into suitable structures and then processing the data by means of passing it through conditional and looping program structures. There are many ways to accomplish any processing requirement; programs are considered "good" or "elegant" when they perform processing in a compact, efficient way and yet are still easy to read and diagnose. Another important factor is good abstraction, meaning that important functions are separated so they can be changed without altering some other key function.

Writing Pseudocode

Any processing requirement can be written out in plain English sentences, and a helpful programming practice is to write out what you want the program to do first, before you code it. This is helpful to programmers because the code doesn't have to actually work at this stage, it just has to make sense. The process of writing out the code as *pseudocode* will help identify logical errors before they happen and serve as a guide to the correct program structures before a lot of coding and debugging time is spent.

Exception Handling

It's great when programs work properly and when all inputs and outputs match the expectations of the programmer and the user. However, in the real world, users often enter erroneous data, and programs often fail. How a program copes with bad data or failures is called *exception handling*. A program that copes well with problems is said to be "graceful"; one that simply crashes your computer or gives a technical error message to the user always creates a bad impression.

Any good programming language will provide a means by which exceptions may be detected and handled gracefully, and both VBScript and Visual Basic.NET have many ways to capture failures or unexpected data. We discuss exception handling for VBScript in the section "Error Handling," and we'll discuss VB.NET exception handling in Module 3.

Effective Coding Techniques

There are many ways to code an application, but some of them are more practical, readable, and easier to troubleshoot than others. This section reviews common coding practices that can enhance the value of your code and typical problems you might encounter that require debugging. Some of the examples refer to objects and components that have not been covered yet, but they will be in later modules, so be patient and focus on the techniques presented.

Common Coding Problems

Writing program code is partly a matter of personal style, but there are a few basic practices that will simplify things and help avoid common problems. Problems with your code cause exceptions, and exceptions can be classified as syntax errors (which VB.NET will check for as you enter code in an IDE), runtime errors (which may not be found until the application is running), and logic errors (unexpected results not caused by syntax or runtime errors).

This section demonstrates examples of problem code, explains why the code has problems, and shows how to correct the problems. Most of these techniques have to do with performance and maintainability issues.

Mixing Code with Your HTML

VBScript, Php, Python, and a variety of other languages make it easy to add code to your HTML. This makes it easy to add programmatic functionally to your web pages, but it mixes the code into the pages instead of maintaining a nice abstraction between code and display. This ASP code example (and Project 1-1, in fact) shows a mixing of code with HTML:

```
<html><head><title>My Web Site</title></head>
<body>
<h1>Welcome to my web site</h1>
<h3>Today is <% = FormatDateTime(Date, vbLongDate) %> </h3>
</body>
</html>
```

Mixing a little code into HTML is a quick and easy way to get a small application up and running, but in larger applications it makes the application rather hard to understand and debug. In some cases, a mixing approach is valid. A simple page that needs just a little ASP code to perform some function not available in HTML is one case. If you decide that the page is temporary and will be replaced with an improved version later, that's another case.

The major problem with this approach is how the server handles HTML versus ASP or ASP.NET. In order for ASP code to be processed, the file extension must be .asp. IIS reads the extension and loads the ASP engine to process it. As it's reading the ASP code, however, it encounters plain HTML. IIS then has to load the HTML processing engine to handle it. This continues through the whole page. Even with the new versions of ASP and IIS used for the examples in this book, processing can be slowed down.

The preferred approach is to use ASP to generate all output using the Response object's Write method. This method allows the ASP engine to handle all processing and finish processing faster.

Tip

Double-quote characters in your HTML must be converted to two double-quote characters, or ASP/VBScript gets confused. This is a minor annoyance when you consider the performance gains.

Declaring Variables

One of the holdovers from the original versions of Basic was the ability to start using a variable without first declaring it. In VB and VBScript, variables can be declared using the Dim statement, as shown here:

```
Dim intVariable
```

Visual Basic adds a data type designation to this declaration; VBScript does not. Declaring variables explicitly (rather than having them just appear the first time you write them into your code) offers several advantages. For one thing, explicit declarations make it impossible to create a new variable by typo (and these kinds of mistakes can be very hard to debug). For another, it's easier to track and maintain variables in one location in your code. The following ASP and VBScript example shows a variable that was accidentally created by typo:

```
<html><head><title>My Web Site</title></head>
<body>
<h1>Welcome to my web site</h1>
<h3>Today is <% = FormatDateTime(Date, vbLongDate) %> </h3>
<% strInput = Request.ServerVariables("SCRIPT_NAME") %>
<% If Day(Date) = 5 Then %>
<h3>Today is Thursday!</h3>
<% ElseIf Day(Date) = 1 Then %>
<h3>Today is Sunday!</h3>
<% End If %>
<% Response.Write stInput %>
</body>
</html>
```

Because the variable stInput was created accidentally (as opposed to the real variable strInput), the name of the script (stored in the SCRIPT_NAME variable) isn't being printed out. Is the Request.ServerVariables collection working?

Are you losing memory somewhere? No, you've got a typo in the name when you are printing it out at the bottom of the script. VBScript sees that you have a new variable, allocates space for it, and goes on its way. The variable, of course, starts out with no content, so strInput never gets printed.

The solution to this is twofold. First, always use the Option Explicit statement as the first line in every ASP page. This statement forces you to declare your variables by disabling VBScript's auto-declaration feature. It works best as the first line in a code block (<% Option Explicit %>). Then, declare all your variables for that page.

Note

VB.NET uses Option Explicit=False as the default, meaning you are not required to declare all variables. Since False is the default, you should include the statement and set it to True in your modules to make it easier to debug your applications. There is also an Option Strict statement, which, if set to True, disallows implicit data type conversions where precision is lost. Although it may seem like more work, doing these things will save you a great deal of time and frustration later, when you are trying to debug your applications. In Module 3 we also discuss the @Page directive, which accepts the Explicit and Strict attributes for the same purpose.

Another good VBScript coding habit is to list the data type in a comment following the variable. Both these techniques are shown in the following example:

```
<% Option Explicit
Dim dcnDB   ' As ADODB.Connection
%>
```

The type comment doesn't do anything in the program, but it does provide documentation for what the variable does. With VB.NET, you'll typically list the type following a variable declaration anyway, and if you use the Option Strict statement you'll have to.

Note

Comments in VBScript and VB.NET are started with an apostrophe (') and continue until end-of-line characters are encountered (end-of-line characters can't typically be seen, but are created when you press Enter at the end of a line of script or program code).

Putting a prefix on the variable name can also be helpful, although we don't always use this practice. While VBScript will let you put any type of data into a variable (all VBScript variables have a data type of Variant, meaning they can hold any type of data and most data conversions will occur automatically as necessary), using the prefixes on your variables provides a visual indication of the type of data that is supposed to be in the variable.

Hard-Coded Values

One of the annoyances with code is fixing hard-coded values. This means that everywhere a value is needed, such as a database connection string, the exact value is copied over and over. As an example, say every page in a company's intranet had an entire connection string copied everywhere it was necessary. If the connection string data ever changes, each page in which the hard-coded connection string appears has to be changed individually.

This happens in both numerical and textual data, as in one site that had a form with drop-down list boxes where one of the items was "Not Selected" and had a –1 for its value. This is a good idea, since you can trap the –1 in your error handling and validation code. However, the –1 was hard-coded everywhere it was needed.

Another less obvious example comes when pages are generating links to other pages. How many times have you had code that looked something like this?

```
Response.Write "<a href=test.asp?action=validate&id=" & intID &
">click here</a>"
```

This code is using the variable to supply the ID parameter to the URL, but what about all the hard-coded values in the URL? What hard-coded values, you might ask. Here's a list of all the hard-coded values in this particular link:

- Page name
- Action parameter
- Action parameter value
- ID parameter in URL

If you have to move your site to a different location, or if you rename your files, you'll have to find all the references to test.asp in your ASP code to make the application work again. If you are building your URLs and misspell the word "action" in either the generating code or in the code that checks the parameter value, you'll get errors that are tough to trace. The same thing goes for the value for the action parameter, as well as the name of the ID parameter. The solution is to use constants for everything: the page names, the parameter names, and so on. Constants can be defined using the Const statement, as shown here:

```
Const myConstant As String
```

Access and Security Control

How many times have you gone to a store and attempted to open the door, only to discover the store was closed? The owners of the store forgot to put out a sign saying they were closed, so you had to try the door first. Many computer programs use this method for security. They let you modify a record and when you're ready to save the record, the program displays an error message saying you don't have the security rights to do it. All that work down the drain without more than a rude warning.

The point is, don't let your users think they can do something when they can't. If they can't add a record, don't give them the opportunity to try to add a record. Hide the link or issue a warning on the page that tells users what's going on before they attempt a procedure and fail.

Poor Documentation

Early computer science classes emphasized that documentation was important. If you write the program, you are the only one using it, and you know what you're doing in the code, why is documentation necessary? Well, years pass and the old memory isn't quite what it used to be. In addition, you've got at least ten different applications' codes running around in your head, and it's confusing. If you write an application that works well, you might not revisit it until you need to add some enhancements. Depending on how busy you are, it may be several months before you put in those changes. Inevitably, you will open up a piece of code and stare at it for hours, trying to figure out what you were thinking at the time you wrote it.

The solution to this problem is simple: document everything in your code. If there is a complex bit of logic, add a line of comment to explain what's going on. If you made an assumption about input or output data, add a comment to remind yourself about it. File header documentation blocks are useful for tracking changes and additions to the file in a central location.

The point is not whether the code works, but whether the code is going to be useful in a different application or as part of an expanded application. If the code breaks these rules, the end result is code that will have to be reworked or entirely rebuilt.

Designing Applications

Although applications can be designed with just about any purpose in mind, the bulk of applications are designed to accomplish objectives of a business, work, entertainment, or educational nature. Extremely simple applications (a few pieces of code on a single page, perhaps) usually require no elaborate specifications, diagrams, or documentation, but even relatively unsophisticated applications (large blocks of code or multiple pages of code) benefit from good design practices.

More complex applications can be further categorized into those that have a user interface (that is, they are designed to be used by and interact with people) and those that function independently or work with other applications. An application may, of course, work with people *and* work with other applications, but when a user interface is required, the design process is a bit more complex.

Finally, there are issues that every application faces in daily use, such as availability, reliability, scalability, and securability. The application must be available where needed (on a wireless platform, for example), reliable enough to properly support users (no application is going to be 100 percent reliable), scalable to cope with user demand (usage often varies tremendously and is also often unpredictable), and securable (insecure applications can break, be broken into, and leave a company in very bad position).

Naturally, there are techniques available that assist in designing applications. In this section, we'll describe common methods for approaching the application design problem.

Process Modeling

Many objectives can be accomplished using a process. The broad outlines of a process include gathering data, interacting with users on the basis of that data, performing data processing, and providing outputs (including the final answer or resolution). Processes often contain subprocesses and conditional or branching processing that can be accumulated into larger and larger processes. The first step in building an application may be to model the real-world processes that are used to accomplish a particular objective and then to translate that model into processing steps that happen in your application.

Unified Modeling Language

Modeling business processes, and the programming constructs they relate to, is common in modern software and application development. Therefore, it's not surprising that standardization of modeling languages and concepts is occurring.

Unified Modeling Language (UML) is one standard that seems to be catching on across the board. Figure 2-1 shows part of an application design diagram in UML.

The developers of UML (Grady Booch, James Rumbaugh, and Ivar Jacobson) built UML with an object-oriented bias, so diagrams made with UML tend to contain information useful to programmers developing complex applications with many objects. We'll discuss object-oriented programming concepts in more detail in the section "Visual Basic.NET."

Designing a User Interface for the Web

Like the application itself, the process of designing a user interface for the Web benefits from a little forethought. It's a good idea to determine what the objectives of the owners of the site are. For example, do they want to increase sales, improve customer services, enable real-time interaction, or provide secure transactions? Perhaps there are several objectives or a mixture of objectives. In any case, finding out what the objectives are, and determining in advance how achievement of the objectives will be measured, makes it much easier to actually *meet* the objectives.

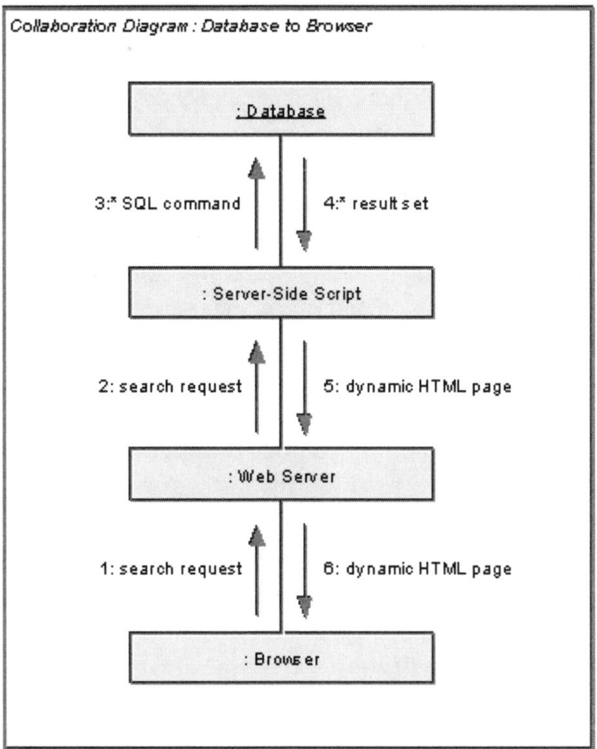

Figure 2-1 A UML diagram

There are a few parameters that most any website will have to conform to, such as ease of download and ease of navigation. After a while, you will find yourself working in a way that takes these parameters into account. In the next few sections we'll give each of these parameters a brief overview.

Convenience

People use website applications because they are convenient, or at least, more convenient than other solutions. To determine whether your idea is convenient, look at existing processes people use to accomplish the same thing and see if doing it online is truly more convenient. For example, if you're already connected to the Web with high-speed access and a clear understanding of what you're doing, going online to shop may seem like the most convenient thing in the world. For someone with low-speed access or with limited experience online, web shopping may be a pain, and cruising down to the local store could seem a lot more convenient. Making your website application as convenient to use as possible can bring in even reluctant visitors.

Navigation

Site navigation is crucial to any website. If folks can't find what they're looking for, they can simply click to one of the myriad other sites available. That doesn't mean you're forced to use the same layout as everyone else on the Web, just that you should spend some time making sure it is intuitive and perhaps test it on a few friends first. If a person unfamiliar with the site cannot find their way around, it is obviously not laid out in an intuitive manner.

Remember, traffic planners, department stores, and many other businesses spend big money on consultants to determine the best traffic pattern or store layout to accomplish their purposes. Consider using similar usability techniques for your website. If you're not sure how, consider hiring a consultant who specializes in testing websites for usability and making them more user friendly.

From an ASP standpoint, setting cookies can give you a glimpse into users' traffic patterns (click-stream) as they traverse your site. Combined with hit statistics, the data can be a valuable tool for determining flaws in your site's design, as well as for discovering or inventing ways to encourage sales and make life easier for users. And take user feedback seriously. For every user who provides feedback to you, there are probably many others with a similar complaint but less inclination to tell you about it.

Project 2-1: Design the Structure for a Website Application

This project will take you through the process of designing the layout for a new website from scratch. For graphics and layout, a graphic artist or professional layout designer may be needed, particularly if you don't possess those skills yourself. It's up to you to apply the information supplied here as you and your colleagues make design and layout decisions along the way.

Step-by-Step

1. Build a basic flowchart of the user and management pages on the site. Typical pages for a commercial site include About, Contact, Order, Terms, Privacy, and Catalog. On the flowchart, draw a box representing each page (or the response to each page), and draw lines between the pages showing how they link together.

2. Be sure to include spaces or controls for all the data captured or information displayed. Make sure your clients agree that the pages outlined give them enough data to perform their business processes and that the data is sufficient to support the calculations and processing required by your scripting or components.

3. If the project warrants it, conduct usability testing of several graphical formats as well as layouts. Make sure users can find what they are looking for and are able to navigate the site intuitively. For this project, usability testing can be simple; you might just present the format ideas to a person unfamiliar with the project and with the website creation process. Ask him or her to tell you if there are things he doesn't understand while trying to navigate the site.

4. List the number of web pages that will be created and for each page list the languages involved. For behind-the-scenes processing, list the scripts that will be required, giving each one a descriptive name. This list will grow as you gain a greater understanding of how ASP works, but for now building a conceptual list is fine.

5. Copy the flowchart, page formats, displayed and captured information, number and language requirements for each page, and scripting requirements for the application into a folder and review each design with the client. For this project, simply collecting the materials you've generated into a folder is enough. These materials become the basis for decision making and construction of the website.

How Dynamic Website Applications Work

Dynamic websites employ applications above and beyond the familiar capabilities of ordinary websites. We're not talking about Flash or animated graphics; we're talking about dynamically generated (and sometimes interactive) content, whether text, graphics, or flashy multimedia. In the next few sections we'll discuss the languages, protocols, and technologies that make dynamic websites possible.

HTTP and XHTML

Communications on the Web (just another part of the communications services provided by the Internet as a whole) take place mainly via Hypertext Transfer Protocol (HTTP). As the name indicates, HTTP is a *protocol*, a standardized format for exchanging web communications between client and server. The portion of these messages that make up web pages are written mainly with HTML, although some minor programmatic functionality is often added using JavaScript. Ordinary web pages made with HTML are called static web pages.

Static Web Pages

Static web pages are so called because they exist as plain-text HTML and JavaScript files rather than being generated on-the-fly from back-end scripting and content stored in a database. The content in them doesn't change except when the webmaster uploads revisions. Web pages usually contain the following:

- A header that, except for the title, contains information invisible to the viewer
- The body, into which the bulk of the content goes
- JavaScript or VBScript for limited programmatic functionality
- Graphics or multimedia to lend a pleasing appearance

XHTML 1.0 is the most recently updated version of the HTML specification (you can find more information about the spec, or recommendation, at **http://www.w3.org/**). The last "normal" version of HTML was HTML 4.01. HTML is a subset of Standard Generalized Markup Language (SGML), a complex but powerful markup language creator specification that has been around for many years. SGML can be used to create many different markup languages, and HTML is only one of them.

Basic HTML elements usually (but not always) have a beginning and ending tag, differentiated by the slash, as in the beginning and ending bold tags (<B> to begin bold text and </B> to end bold text). Tags are always delimited by (start and end with) the less-than and greater-than signs. Think of tags as bookends, alerting the browser to begin boldfaced font with the beginning tag, and end boldfaced font with the ending tag. Like most rules, there are exceptions. The image tag (<IMG SRC="image.gif">) is an example of an HTML tag that has no ending tag. Some HTML tags have ending tags that are required, some have ending tags that are not required, and some have no ending tags at all (and it is forbidden to use them). XHTML 1.0 is based on HTML, but is compliant with the XML standard, also a subset of SGML, but a markup language creator in its own right. Appendix E lists all XHTML tags as well as details about proper usage.

Some HTML tags, in normal use, offer users the opportunity to communicate with the server. For example, if you build a link into your page, the viewer will be able to click that link and request another page from your server (or any web server in the world, for that matter). Graphics files are accessed using a similar mechanism in the image tag. Form tags have the ability to specify the path and filename of a program or script to run when the submit button is clicked. ASP takes advantage of these mechanisms as a means to run scripts. For ASP.NET, there is an entire class of objects called Web Forms to use for similar functions (see Module 4).

Coding XHTML/HTML

There are many fine HTML primers and tutorials, both in print and on the Web, so we won't spend an inordinate amount of time on the HTML tags here (although we will cover essential tags as we encounter them in our scripting exercises). However, because you will be mixing HTML with your code frequently, there are some things you should know about HTML and XHTML conventions in general:

- HTML *is not* case sensitive, but URLs, paths, and filenames may be. XHTML *is* case sensitive, and all XHTML elements and attributes are written lowercase.
- HTML elements consist of the starting tag and any attributes or properties they may possess, plus content such as text (if content is allowed) plus the ending tag. If there is no ending tag, XHTML demands that the starting tag have a terminator inside it, as in the line break element (<br />). Notice the slash inside the less-than and greater-than signs, after the br. In XHTML, all elements must be properly closed.

- HTML tags can be separated (delimited) from ASP scripting within an HTML document by means of the ASP separation characters (<% and %>) and can also be generated in server output using the HTMLEncode function in ASP.
- JavaScript and VBScript can also be generated by or embedded in ASP scripts.
- XHTML elements must always be properly nested. This means that if you place one element inside another, the inside element must also end before the outside element, as in the bold and italics tags shown here:

```
<b><i>bold and italics correct</i></b>
<b><i>incorrect</b></i>
```

Browser Wars

No discussion of the Web would be complete without mention of the differences in web browsers. Not only do browsers run the gamut from text-only to fully 3D-capable, they also vary widely in their ability to handle conforming HTML tags, HTML extensions (the most popular of which are created by Microsoft and Netscape), and various file types. HTML extensions, by the way, are nonconforming HTML tags that can be properly interpreted (out of the box) only by the maker's browser, unless another browser maker builds acceptance of these tags into their product. In the war for market dominance, the big players seldom adopt each other's extensions.

To add to the confusion, various browser versions also differ in their ability to interpret tags, and sometimes tags fall out of favor or are replaced by more effective tags (they may become *deprecated*, meaning they are scheduled to be phased out). Moreover, some browsers (the mini-browser for WAP phones, for instance) don't even use HTML or XHTML.

The common solution is to detect the browser or media type on which a page is to be displayed (or within which an application is supposed to run) and supply content and rendering specifications appropriate for that platform. For example, you could output a page for a browser with XHTML elements while outputting the same page for a WAP phone in Wireless Markup Language (WML).

Hypertext Transfer Protocol (HTTP)

The World Wide Web Consortium (the same organization that develops XHTML specifications) also builds the Hypertext Transfer Protocol, currently in version 1.1. Like most Internet-related specifications, it is tracked as a Request for Comment (RFC), and the most recent RFC for HTTP 1.1 is RFC 2616.

The HTTP protocol is, according to the abstract, "an application-level protocol for distributed, collaborative, hypermedia information systems. It is a generic, stateless protocol that can be used for many tasks beyond its use for hypertext, such as name servers and distributed object management systems, through extension of its request methods, error codes, and headers." In practical terms, it is the mechanism by which client and server communicate when using the Web.

In the introduction to HTTP 1.1, the authors note that HTTP is a request/response protocol and describe some of the aspects of typical communications between client and server. In particular, they note that there may be several programs acting as servers and several acting as clients when web pages (or resources) are being requested and supplied.

They refer to the roles of web servers, gateways, proxies, caching, and browsers (or other user agents) as clients, servers, and sometimes both client and server at the same time. For instance, a proxy may be a client when it is requesting a page from a web server. At the same time, it may be a server for the browsers it is making requests for as it serves them the pages it receives from the web server. Also noted is HTTP 1.1's capability to support *caching*, which is the holding of recent copies of a page at a closer, more accessible location for faster retrieval.

Section 4 of the specification mentions HTTP headers, which form an important part of any communication between client and server or vice versa. HTTP headers "include general-header (Section 4.5), request-header (Section 5.3), response-header (Section 6.2), and entity-header (Section 7.1) fields," and "follow the same generic format as that given in Section 3.1 of RFC 822 [9]. Each header field consists of a name followed by a colon (":") and the field value. Field names are case-insensitive. The field value MAY be preceded by any amount of LWS [linear white space], though a single SP [space] is preferred."

Module 3 covers how to use ASP objects to show the value of request and response headers. HTTP headers can be read, modified, and created using ASP objects, and they may affect application behavior. Headers' capabilities will be discussed in detail as they are encountered and used within applications.

General Header Fields

In Section 4.5 of the HTTP specification, there are a few general header fields that apply to both request and response messages. They are listed on the following page.

Note

All HTTP 1.1 listings include both the object or message and the section of the specification where further information may be found, in this and other modules.

Cache-Control	Pragma	Upgrade
Connection	Trailer	Via
Date	Transfer-Encoding	Warning

Request Headers

In Section 5 of the HTTP specification are the request headers. One of the most important parts of a request message is the header containing the method by which data is conveyed to the server. Current allowable methods are listed here (note that the most common are GET and POST):

OPTIONS	POST	TRACE
GET	PUT	CONNECT
HEAD	DELETE	

Section 5.3 of the HTTP specification also lists allowable request header fields. The fields include data about the character set and language employed, the browser type, expiration, and other important message data. Please refer to the appropriate section of the HTTP specification at the W3C website (**http://www.w3.org/**).

Response Headers

After a server has been contacted by a client and has read and interpreted the request, it builds a response message consisting of a status line, headers, and a message body. The message body includes the HTML or XHTML that makes up the returning page, while the status line indicates the status of the request.

Status-line components (including the status code and status message) are built in the following way. The status code is a three-digit code meant to be interpreted by machines (although some are well-known to humans, such as the "HTTP 404 Not Found" code/message combination). It is followed by the status message (or reason-phrase, to be technically correct). The status message is the Not Found portion of the status line mentioned previously. There are several categories of allowable status codes based on the first digit of the code, as follows:

- **1xx: Informational** The request was received, continuing process.
- **2xx: Success** The action was successfully received, understood, and accepted.
- **3xx: Redirection** Further action must be taken in order to complete the request.

- **4xx: Client Error** The request contains bad syntax or cannot be fulfilled.
- **5xx: Server Error** The server failed to fulfill an apparently valid request.

Note

According to the specification, the status messages are recommendations and may be changed without affecting the protocol's operation. This means you can modify these messages using ASP without affecting the server's standard use of them.

Visit the World Wide Web Consortium and review the specification and the descriptions associated with the various codes, messages, and headers mentioned in this module to gain a better understanding of how they work. They will be covered in greater depth as we go along, but this book does not attempt to make you an HTTP master.

How Active Server Pages Works

Active Server Pages is popular for building dynamic website applications because it contains many prebuilt objects that make life easier for the developer and it uses VBScript for basic program structures. In this section we review ASP to provide a background for how ASP.NET works, and you'll find many of the structures written for ASP are extended by ASP.NET to resemble high-level application programming.

The built-in ASP objects make it easy to communicate with the server, to start, control, and manage the site as a persistent application, and to work with individual users during separate sessions. These objects are also available for use in ASP.NET. The highly integrated nature of ASP and HTML, VBScript/JavaScript, and databases/SQL means you must be on good terms with all of them, but if you have any programming background, you'll find the commands and syntax very easy to understand and use. If not, learning the basic structures of these languages will assist you with any other programming languages you choose to learn going forward.

ASP and HTML

If you have a working knowledge of HTML, or are proficient with a good HTML editing program such as FrontPage or Dreamweaver, you can create ASP pages the same way you would an ordinary HTML web page. In fact, for ASP 3.0 and IIS 5.0, Microsoft recommends that you create all your pages (even static HTML pages) with an .asp filename extension, because the ASP processing engine can process ordinary HTML pages nearly as fast as the web server itself.

Looking at ASP Code You can start ASP pages as web pages because there is a lot of HTML-based content in the output ASP scripts generate. For example, suppose you want to return to the user the value of a form field that was submitted. You would use something like the following:

```
<HTML>
<HEAD>
<TITLE>The Title of this Page</TITLE>
</HEAD>
<BODY>
<% Response.Write(Request.Form("fieldname")) %>
</BODY>
</HTML>
```

Notice the ASP code delimiters are slightly different from the HTML delimiters, in that they contain the % sign. This tells the ASP processing engine that there are ASP-related commands in the code, and that they need special attention.

If no delimiters are found in the code, the engine streams the code straight to the web server, so processing takes place almost as quickly as if the server processed it firsthand. Code containing ASP commands is processed line by line in the normal fashion.

Scripting with ASP

You can also use the HTML script tags (<SCRIPT>) to identify scripting elements within your pages, and these tags can be placed anywhere you want. They would look something like this:

```
<HTML>
<HEAD><TITLE>The title goes here</TITLE></HEAD>
<BODY>
<SCRIPT>
VBSCript and ASP code go here
</SCRIPT>
</BODY>
</HTML>
```

Client-Side Scripting Client-side scripting, as its name implies, is executed on the client. For routine calculations that don't require any special security measures, or for which users reading the code is not a concern, client-side scripting has the advantage of utilizing the user's processing cycles. Client-side scripting is the default when ASP scripts are embedded in web pages, but they can also be explicitly set using the RUNAT attribute, as follows:

```
<SCRIPT RUNAT="client">
```

Server-Side Scripting Server-side scripting must be explicitly set with the RUNAT attribute when using the <SCRIPT> tags. Script that is run at the server will not be seen in the finished page; rather, the user will see the results of processing. If you use the source attribute within a <SCRIPT> tag, you can include any script file you choose within the web page for processing at the server:

```
<SCRIPT RUNAT="server" SRC="mypath/myscript.asp"></SCRIPT>
```

To make the separate script file, you can use a plain text editor such as Notepad. The script file should contain only script code, not HTML commands, and the <SCRIPT> tag itself must contain no other code. The advantage here is that you can reuse the same script many times throughout your website; changing the script once changes the function of each page. It is sometimes more useful to use the server-side Include instruction. The only limitation on server-side Includes is that each block of code must be delimited, meaning you must end a block of code in the current page before you call a block of code from an external script file. This instruction will be used extensively in ASP code examples in later modules.

Built-in ASP Functions

ASP version 3.0, as installed with Windows 2000 and IIS 5.0, comes with a variety of built-in objects, properties, and methods. These provide the foundation that makes ASP work so well with HTML, VBScript/JavaScript, SQL, and Active Data Objects (ADOs). They also allow access to HTTP and the HTTP headers to make your life easy when creating dynamic web applications. Let's take a look at capturing and sending data to users first.

Capturing Data The Request object exposes collections that capture data as it travels in a stream from the browser via a hypertext link or a form submittal. Data that can be captured includes HTTP variables, cookies, query strings, and the contents of form fields (including the field names). For example, capturing data submitted by a form can be accomplished using the Request.Form(*fieldname*) object/method combination in ASP.

Sending Data The Response object allows you to insert data in the response stream heading back to a particular user, such as strings, the values of variables, cookies, and custom HTTP headers. For example, sending a message back to the user for display in a web page can be accomplished using the Response.Write(*string*) object/method combination in ASP.

Creating ASP Applications The Application object, created when the first page is requested by the client, stores variables and object references that any page in the application can access. Using the OnStart event, statements can be processed whenever the application is first opened.

Creating ASP Sessions The Session object is created whenever a user connects to your application, and it is unique for each user (the user must accept cookies for the Session object to work). It can hold variables and object references for the entire session. The session ends when the timeout period expires.

The ASP Server Object The Server object is used for instantiating Component Object Model (COM) objects, as well as translating characters into the proper format for URLs and within HMTL.

ASP and VBScript/JScript

ASP.NET applications are written using Visual Basic.NET, C#, and JScript, but traditional ASP applications are written with VBScript or JScript. By default, ASP supports both the VBScript and JScript scripting engines. You can install other scripting engines to interpret PerlScript and TCL. Microsoft also introduced Microsoft Windows Script Interfaces, a new way for scripting engine vendors to add scripting and OLE automation capabilities. According to Microsoft, any language or runtime environment, including VBA, VBScript, Perl, and Lisp, can run as a scripting engine on a Windows script host (such as Internet Explorer). ASP uses the default scripting engine, which is set in the Application Configuration dialog box shown in Figure 2-2. Since VBScript is so widely used with ASP, the remainder of this section is devoted to the VBScript language.

VBScript is a subset of the Visual Basic programming language. Rather than being compiled, it is *interpreted*, meaning it is converted into machine language on the fly as the browser or server reads it. This makes it run more slowly than a precompiled program (like any interpreted language). However, the programs are generally much shorter and tend to run quickly, so you usually won't notice the difference.

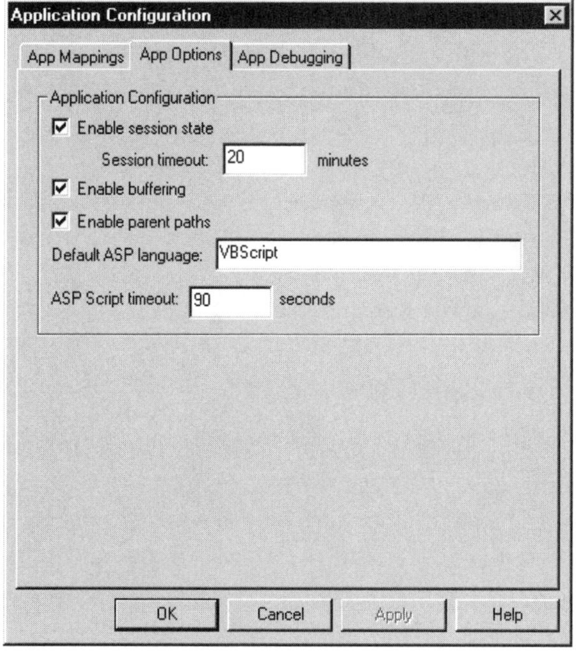

Figure 2-2 The Application Configuration dialog box

A big advantage to using VBScript is that it is similar in usage and syntax to Visual Basic. It is possible to use VBScript and JScript in the same document, although for heavy use this may not be the most efficient use of the server. Keep in mind that for each scripting engine used, ASP has to load that engine and send code to it. It's best to avoid switching in and out of ASP script in a single page. Keep your code inside one set of ASP delimiters (<% *code* %>) and you'll only have one processing job to execute. For small jobs or scripts, this may not be a problem, but for larger or more complex scripts, switching can slow things down considerably.

VBScript Basics

The 5.0 versions of Internet Explorer and Internet Information Server both support VBScript 5.0. There are several interesting new language elements in VBScript 5.0, including the Class object and Class statement, the Eval function, the Ignore Case property, the Length property, the Timer function, and the With statement. We've assembled a VBScript 5.0 appendix at the end of this book, and we'll cover commonly used and essential VBScript commands, reserved words, and structures here. For an up-to-the-minute reference, the Microsoft VBScript documentation can be downloaded at **http://msdn.microsoft.com/scripting/vbscript/download/vbsdoc.exe**.

Variables in VBScript Variants are the only data type available in the VBScript scripting engine. Because they can store many types of data, they take more room and require more processing cycles; they are not as efficient at storing or processing data, but they have some excellent advantages. For instance, inside a variant, values are stored as individual subtypes, and they automatically convert data types appropriately in most situations. You must exercise caution when ordering VBScript statements to make sure you'll get the correct result (this will be discussed in greater detail later in this module, when we discuss the VarType method).

Variables can be declared anywhere within code, simply by using the Dim statement. However, it is wise to use the Option Explicit statement (<% Option Explicit Dim var1, var2 %>) at the beginning of your code, because it forbids the use of variable names that have not been explicitly dimensioned. This means that if you accidentally include a variable that doesn't exist, an explicit error will emerge, making debugging your code a much easier job.

VBScript Features Microsoft organizes VBScript (by features included) in one section of the documentation, and we'll follow that convention. Please note, comments can be included using the REM (for "remarks") keyword or simply an apostrophe ('). Programming features include, for example, Array Handling (the first feature mentioned in the online documentation), which contains the following:

- **Array function** Array (*arglist*)
  Returns an array of Variant type, where *arglist* is a comma-delimited list of values.
- **Dim statement** Dim *varname*[([*subscripts*])][, *varname*[([*subscripts*])]] . . .
  Declares variables, including arrays.

The Set statement is used frequently as the Assignment feature, such as when you are setting a recordset equal to a particular set of records from a database table. The syntax is as follows:

- **Set statement** Set *objectvar* = {*objectexpression*}
  Makes the object equal to the object expression, where the expression results in the selection of records from a table via a database connection. Can also be used to associate a procedure reference with an event or create a new instance of a class.

VBScripts include the following *constants* and *literals* (constants are always the same value; literals describe, literally, conditions of variables):

- **Empty** Used to indicate an uninitialized value (but not Null)
- **Nothing** Used to remove an association from an object variable, as in *vRecordset* = Nothing (where vRecordset is a recordset that was associated with records from a database table)
- **Null** Used to indicate that a variable contains no valid data
- **True** Contains a value of –1 (not 1)
- **False** Contains a value of 0 (zero)

Control Flow Structures Some of the most important and frequently used VBScript structures are the *control flow* structures, such as If…Then and Do… While. You'll most likely use all of them repeatedly in your scripts.

- **Do...Loop** Do [{While | Until} *condition*] [*statements*] [Exit Do] [*statements*] Loop: This structure repeats a block of statements until a condition is true or while a condition is true, depending on how it is set up.
- **For...Next** For *counter* = *start* To *end* [Step *step*] *statements*] [Exit For] [*statements*] Next: This structure simply repeats a block of statements until the counter runs out. You can set the value the counter must reach, as well as the step size for each iteration. The step can be either positive or negative.
- **For Each…Next** For Each *element* In *group* [*statements*] [Exit For] [*statements*] Next [*element*]: This structure repeats a block of statements for each element in an array or collection. You'll use this with every collection you encounter in ASP objects.
- **If…Then…Else** If *condition* Then [*statements*] [ElseIf *condition-n* Then [*elseifstatements*]] … [Else [*elsestatements*]] End If: This structure is also

used often and specifies conditional execution of VBScript statements. You can nest them to check multiple conditions, but you should examine the Select Case structure for complex conditional checking.

- **Select Case** Select Case *testexpression* [Case *expressionlist-n* [*statements-n*]] … [Case Else *expressionlist-n* [*elsestatements-n*]] End Select: This structure is useful for checking many conditions and selecting statements to perform based on the valid condition.
- **While…Wend** While *condition* Version [*statements*] Wend: This structure can iterate through statements based on a condition, but it is more practical to use the Do…Loop structure to do this.
- **With** With *object statements* End With: This structure is new to VBScript (although it has a history in VBA and Visual Basic) and is a welcome addition to the language. It allows you to reference an object once and execute multiple statements against that object, without re-referencing the object for each statement.

Data Type Conversions VBScript can perform the normal data type conversions from variant subtypes, such as:

- **CStr function** Returns a variant of subtype String.
- **CInt function** Returns a variant of subtype Integer.
- **Cdate function** Returns a variant of subtype Date.
- **Abs function** Returns the absolute value of a number.
- **Asc and Chr functions** Asc returns the ANSI character code of the first letter in a string, and Chr returns the letter associated with an ANSI code.
- **Hex, Oct, Fix, and Int** Returns the hexadecimal, octal, and integer portions of numbers, respectively, with Fix rounding down for negative numbers and Int rounding up.

Common date/time functions in VBScript include:

- **Date** Returns the current system date.
- **Time** Returns the current system time.
- **Day** Returns a whole number representing the day of the month.

- **Month** Returns a whole number representing the month of the year.
- **Year** Returns a whole number representing the year.
- **Now** Returns both the current system date and time.

Error Handling Not surprisingly, errors sometimes occur in VBScript code. There are statements you can use to handle them (On Error Resume Next and On Error GoTo 0). On Error Resume Next enables inline error handling, so you should include one of these statements in each procedure to handle any errors that crop up. On Error GoTo 0 disables error handling.

Hint

The behavior that occurs when errors are encountered at runtime depends on the host running the code. Sometimes hosts notify users of errors and stop code execution, and sometimes they don't. Make sure to take this behavior into account when building ASP applications.

Eval, String, IO, Math, and Variant Functions The Eval function is new to VBScript among the expressions, and it removes confusion in statements such as (x=y) as to whether to perform an assignment or a comparison. In JScript the assignment operator (=) is different from the comparison operator (==), so no confusion exists. For example, you can use the Eval function as part of an If...Then structure to test whether one value is equivalent to another, whatever the subtype.

Formatting strings can be performed using several functions, among them the FormatCurrency function. This function returns a currency value that uses the currency symbol defined in the system Control Panel.

There are also several input/output functions, such as the MsgBox function. This function displays a message box with text you specify (literally or using a variable) and then waits for input from the user. It can display 16 different button combinations and will return values (from 1 to 7) indicating OK, Cancel, Abort, Retry, Ignore, Yes, or No, depending on the button types you set it to display.

Math functions included with VBScript are limited compared to other languages. One statement often employed is the Randomize statement. This function initializes the random number generator and can be used in conjunction with the Rnd function to produce random numbers. Other math functions include Tan, Cos, Sin (tangent, cosine, sine) and Exp, Log, and Sqr (exponent, logarithm, and square root).

VBScript has a fairly complete complement of operators, including addition (+), subtraction (–), multiplication (*), division (/), exponentiation (^), less than (<), greater than (>), string concatenation (&), and Boolean operators such as And and Or. These operate in the normal fashion.

Besides the string functions mentioned earlier (Asc and Chr), there are a few more you can use with VBScript. Find the number of characters in a string with the Len function, or reverse the order of characters in a string with StrReverse. Join strings in an array with the Join function, and convert case in a string with the LCase and UCase functions.

Finally, there are the variant functions, which help determine the subtype of variants. These include IsArray, IsDate, IsEmpty, IsNull, and IsNumeric, each of which returns a Boolean value as an indicator, and the VarType function, which returns a specific value indicating the subtype.

The VBScript functions listed here are only a subset of all those that are available; refer to the appendix in this book and Microsoft's online documentation for more information.

ASP.NET, ADO, ADO.NET, and Databases/SQL

ActiveX Data Objects (ADO) is used extensively with traditional ASP pages for database access, while CDO.NET (naturally) is used with ASP.NET and the .NET Framework. We'll cover ADO here to give you an idea of its capabilities; in Module 9 there is complete discussion of ADO.NET and its differences compared to traditional ADO.

ASP and Databases

Database access is one of the most important and most frequently used capabilities of ASP. Technically, the objects used to access databases aren't ASP. They are ActiveX Data Objects (ADOs), and they make it easy to connect to, retrieve, and manipulate records from a database table. As defined by Microsoft, ADO consists of a COM type library with a program ID (ProgID) of ADODB. There are seven objects in the ADO object model:

- **Command** Maintains information about a command, such as a query string or parameter definitions. Use it to execute a SQL query string on a Connection object.
- **Connection** Maintains connection information on the data provider (the database you are accessing, for example).

- **Error** Contains extended error information (as distinct Error objects in the Errors collection if two or more errors result from the same incident).
- **Field** Contains information from a single column of data in a recordset. Each Field object exists as part of the Fields collection in a recordset.
- **Property** Defined by the data provider, this is a characteristic of an ADO.
- **Recordset** A set of records from a database table or a cursor pointing to those records. You can set the properties of recordsets so that they are read-only or updateable to various degrees. If you open a recordset using the Connection object, you can open multiple recordsets on the same data provider.

In typical ASP scripts, you'll first make a connection to the data provider using a DSN or an on-the-fly connection (more on these in Module 9), then you'll execute a SQL query string against the database table or tables from which you want to retrieve records. Of course, if you are inserting records (rather than retrieving records) you may use an INSERT statement instead of a SELECT statement. Once the recordset is populated, you can begin manipulating the field values—editing, adding, or deleting records, or simply navigating records as you see fit.

ADO includes many methods specifically designed for working with records, such as:

- **AddNew** Creates a new record.
- **Delete** Deletes the current record or group of records.
- **Move and MoveFirst/Last/Next/Previous** Moves to the specified record.
- **Open** Opens a cursor and also allows you to specify the cursor type and lock type.
- **Update** Saves changes made to the current record.
- **Requery** Refreshes data in the recordset.

There are also a number of properties useful for working with records in ADO, especially BOF (beginning of file) and EOF (end of file). Among the most valuable are the following:

- **RecordCount** Returns the current number of records in a recordset.
- **PageCount** Indicates how many pages of data are in a Recordset object.

- **MaxRecords** Indicates the maximum number of records to return to a Recordset object.
- **BOF and EOF** Indicate that the current record position is either before or after the first or last record in a recordset. This comes in handy when you want to know if there were any records returned following a query string execution (recordset.EOF equals true indicates no records were returned).

1-Minute Drill

- What is the difference between HTML and HTTP?
- What is the difference between ASP and VBScript?

Ask the Expert

Question: Where do website languages and protocols come from?

Answer: Hypertext Markup Language (HTML) is a language defined by Standard Generalized Markup Language (SGML). The HTML 4.0 specification (technically just a recommendation) is a formally defined SGML Document Type Definition (DTD). The DTD defines the allowable HTML tags and attributes that produce web pages according to the current version of the HTML specification.

VBScript is a subset of the Visual Basic programming language, created by Microsoft. It acts as an interpreter for scripting code within web pages and on the server.

Active Server Pages (ASP) is also a Microsoft-created technology. ASP is, according to Microsoft, "an open, compile-free application environment in which you can combine HTML, scripts, and reusable ActiveX server components to create dynamic and powerful web-based business solutions. Active Server Pages enables server-side scripting for Internet Information Server (IIS) with native support for both VBScript and JScript."

JScript is Microsoft's version of Sun's JavaScript; Microsoft calls it "a powerful scripting language targeted specifically at the Internet, [and]

- HTML is a markup language for writing web pages that can be understood by any browser. HTTP is a protocol for sending web pages across the Internet and relaying messages from the browser to the server and vice versa.
- VBScript is one of several scripting languages that can be used to write programs either on the server or on the browser. ASP is a technology for using those scripting languages plus a built-in set of special functions to create highly interactive web pages.

the first scripting language to fully conform to ECMAScript, the Web's only standard scripting language."

SQL stands for Structured Query Language. Specifically developed for interacting with relational databases, it has a specification independent of the versions customized to work with individual vendors' RDBMS products. Versions of the language can be traced as far back as 1974; in 1986, an ANSI standard for SQL was adopted. SQL is the universal language for accessing databases and is used in all popular DBMS products.

Question: What role does each language play?

Answer: HTML is the basic construction tool for web pages today. Scripting languages such as VBScript, JScript, and JavaScript add programmatic functionality to web pages, both on and off the server. ASP is a technology rather than a programming language and provides built-in objects that enhance the developer's ability to work easily with HTML, as well as script languages, programs, components, and data sources. SQL is the language used to query and work with relational databases and other data sources.

Question: Do I really have to understand how to program them all? Aren't there automated tools that will do the programming for me?

Answer: You don't have to be an expert in programming each of these languages, and there are many tools available to make working with them easier. For example, few people still code all their HMTL by hand. Instead, they use FrontPage or Dreamweaver to do the bulk of the work. However, you should be familiar with each of them and understand their strong and weak points, as well as how they interact. Making them work together is your job.

Question: Is there any way to change HTTP headers? How does this affect the browser?

Answer: You have access to HTTP headers via the Request and Response objects, so you can view their contents. However, some of them cannot be changed directly. Instead, you might have to store their value (a cookie, for example) in a variable and then change it on the return trip (when you send a new cookie back, for example). Changing headers, such as status messages, can directly affect the browser. For example, if you change the status message to **307 – Temporary Redirect**, you can send the browser to a location different than the one requested.

Processing ASP.NET Applications

Now that we have a good idea of how ASP applications work in practice, let's talk about how ASP.NET applications work. One of the first new things you'll encounter is the *common language runtime* (CLR). As we began to discuss in Module 1, the CLR is one of the main components of the .NET Framework. When you create applications that run within it, it provides very important services that enable the .NET Framework to perform its magic. In the next section we'll discuss how it does this in depth.

Another major component of the .NET Framework is the .NET Framework class library, a set of object-oriented, reusable classes that can be used to develop complex distributed, dynamic applications with ASP.NET. Classes are the basic programming structures from which objects can be created. ASP, as we've mentioned, makes some prewritten objects available (such as the Request and Response objects), and with .NET it is easy to use the built-in classes to create your own objects of any type.

The Common Language Runtime (CLR)

Microsoft refers to the CLR as an agent that provides memory management, thread management, and remoting services. The term "agent" is a good one, because it has a multitude of duties that do not directly make your application do particular processing, but instead makes sure that the environment is "healthy" for your application. For example, the CLR manages memory. It makes decisions about what memory to allocate and when, so that you don't have to explicitly do this in your code. That makes your job easier, and, we hope, the CLR will be more efficient than you would be under any given circumstances, so your code will probably run better. It is, in effect, serving as your agent to make sure the environment in which your applications run is clean and stays that way.

Microsoft makes a distinction between code that is designed to run in the CLR (managed code) and code that is not (unmanaged code). The reason for this is so developers can use already written code within the overall .NET Framework. Although many of the benefits of using managed code are lost, the ability to reuse already written code will allow much of the existing investment in programming to remain intact, instead of being lost.

The CLR is hosted with ASP.NET so that ASP.NET may enable the use of files with an extension of .aspx, and with Web Services. Web Services are distributed, server-side application components, programs that run back on the server whose functionality is available across the Internet/Web to other servers and Web Services. Web Services communicate in XML, so any other application that understands (consumes) XML may use the data they provide. Web Services can be found and addressed directory-style with Universal Description, Discovery, and Integration (UDDI), and as applications can be called to perform their functions with Simple Object Access Protocol (SOAP). With ASP.NET, Web Services can be created in the .NET Framework and published via IIS.

Visual Basic.NET

VB.NET is Microsoft's latest version of Visual Basic, and some dramatic changes have occurred in the language. Where traditional ASP processes VBScript by default, ASP.NET uses VB.NET. The program flow structures found in VBScript are also in VB.NET, with some very useful additional capabilities. In this section we cover the object-oriented properties and features of the language.

VBScript and VB.NET

If you've already built ordinary ASP pages and have used VBScript, you'll find that almost all of what you've learned is applicable (from a programming standpoint) to VB.NET. The differences have primarily to do with the object-oriented nature of VB.NET, and even in this aspect ASP has already prepared you for the programming style you'll use. In ASP you use built-in objects; in VB.NET you can use the same built-in objects plus create and run new objects of your own. In the remaining modules of this book we'll provide many examples of VB.NET object creation and usage; for now we discuss object-oriented programming as implemented in VB.NET.

Objects and Classes

As we've mentioned, in ASP there is the Request object. To use the Request object implies that one has been generated. A Request object is automatically generated in ASP whenever a browser makes a request against a page in your ASP application.

Object Components Objects are derived from *classes*. The term class refers to programming that is designed to allow the creation of objects with various *fields*, *properties, methods, and events*, and so forth. For example, you might write program code that defines properties and methods of a class of objects resembling houses. You might define one of the properties as "address", but there would be no value attached to this property until you create an instance of the class (the object) and give it an address. Therefore the object is a real instance within the program code that in this case represents an actual house somewhere, while the class is simply the "template" from which the object was derived.

Methods for objects are a bit different than properties. For example, the Response object is always available within ASP and can be used to return output to a user. It has a Write method associated with it, and this method can be used to write text back to the user. Often you will create objects that contain not only their own properties but other data as well, and this data can be operated upon using methods available to the object.

Fields are similar to properties in that the data stored in them can be read or set. For example, if you provide a field named color for a house object, that field can have a value set in it, and the value can be read later on as necessary. Setting and retrieving values in fields is quite a bit less complex than setting and retrieving values for properties, because properties provide a great deal more control over these functions and also allow more control over what values may be set.

Events provide a triggering mechanism for objects. For example, if a value in an object is updated, you can set it so an event occurs. When the event occurs, it can then be detected by other objects so that methods may be triggered within them. For example, suppose you have an object representing a field on a form, and a name is entered using alphabetical characters. If the field is designed to represent numbers instead of letters (as the price of an item) when the user goes to the next field the event triggered by going to the next field could validate the contents of the first field. Upon determining that letters and not numbers have been entered, your field object could cause the program to display a message box to the user telling them to go back and enter the right kind of data in the field.

Other Object-Oriented Qualities

Object-oriented programming also includes the concepts *encapsulation*, *inheritance*, and *polymorphism*. Encapsulation means that we don't need to know anything about what is going on inside an object as it is executing a method or modifying a property. The method is called and the action performed, and that's all we need to know. For example, there is a Write method for the Response object, but we don't have to know how the job gets done, we just call it and it is performed, and text appears in the user's browser.

Inheritance means we can create new classes based on existing (base) classes. If we make a new class, it will inherit all the properties and methods of the existing class, plus we can give it new properties and methods that don't exist in the base class. Basically, this means that classes can serve as templates for objects of them and as templates for whole new classes (which can then be used to create instances of objects just like the base class).

Polymorphism means that methods and properties of base and derived classes can have the same name and be used in the same way, even though the actual functions happening inside the objects made from those classes may be completely different. For example, a method named GenerateShippingNumber may work to generate shipping numbers for objects named UPSShipping and FedExShipping in completely different ways, but the end result will still be a shipping number, and the way the methods are called is exactly the same.

Ask the Expert

Question: Can you describe, step-by-step, what happens when a user enters my website's URL in their browser? I'm curious about exactly what gets sent where, and how the server, the scripting engines, the database, and ASP interact.

Answer: The request goes initially to the web server. Depending on the file extension (.htm, .html, .asp, .shtml, and so on), the contents of the file are returned to the user or processed by ASP or a scripting engine. If processed by ASP, any connections to data sources are opened, and input or output is accomplished and then returned to ASP. ASP returns the processed output to the server for relay back to the user. Think of it like this:

- **HTML-only file** (including client-side scripting) Retrieved by Web Server and returned to client, finishes processing performed at client.
- **ASP file** (including HTML, ASP, and perhaps ADO and SQL) Retrieved by Web Server, sent to ASP and other scripting engines for processing, performs ADO/SQL database functions, finishes processing by ASP and other scripting engines, and returned to client.

Question: Which programming language should I use, VB.NET or JScript?

Answer: That depends on your familiarity with these languages. VBScript and JScript scripting engines each possess a standard installation of ASP, so the deciding factor will be your comfort level with either language. Their capabilities are nearly identical, so there's not much to base a decision on there.

Question: **I've heard it can be tough to use SQL, especially when you have to insert variable values in a SQL statement. Any tips to make the going easier?**

Answer: Fortunately, SQL is similar across vendors. Unfortunately, the differences seem to be in the way they handle variable insertion. My recommendation is to use the built-in SQL generators most of the popular Relational Database Management System (RDBMS) programs have and read everything you can on the specific syntax required for each program (or version).

Question: **What are the pros and cons of database programs on the market? Do I need to use SQL Server or Oracle, or can I put Microsoft Access to productive use?**

Answer: Microsoft Access 97 and 2000 are very good desktop-level RDBMS programs, useful for quickly prototyping desktop and small-scale web applications. Beyond a certain size and number of concurrent users, however, Access won't perform well, so you'll need to make sure SQL Server, Oracle, and other major RDBMS programs are in your plans. These programs are industrial-strength databases, and although they are more expensive than Access, they supply the tools, capabilities, robustness, and performance required by higher-level websites and enterprise applications.

1-Minute Drill

- Why is it important to document your code and use consistent names for your variables?
- What happens when you switch from HTML to ASP code?

- Without documentation, you may forget the purpose of the functions you wrote, and without consistent variable names it may be confusing to understand which variable holds which type of data.
- Each time you go from one type of code to another, the server must redirect processing, which consumes additional time.

Project 2-2: Create a Simple ASP.NET Application

Now it's time to tie together the loose threads of HTML, ASP, and VBScript by writing a simple application. You'll program the application with typical ASP VBScript structures and syntax to illustrate differences between ASP and ASP.NET and then complete the application properly in VB.NET. The application displays a very simple form that gathers user input and then conditionally outputs text depending upon inputs.

Step-by-Step

1. In this step you'll build an HTML page with a form that sends input to itself. The HTML form element contains the instructions to send the input to the same page. You'll use the PFE text editor to write the code. Open PFE, create a new file by clicking File | New, save it as indexm02p01.aspx, and start by entering the following code:

```
<HTML><%@ Page Language="VB" %>
<%
Dim i As Integer
Dim Choices(3) As String
%>
<html>
<head>
<title>Project 2-2</title>
</head>
```

2. The code just written starts a page using VB as the language and then goes on to dimension two variables, named *i* (of data type integer) and Choices (an array variable with four places to hold data of data type string). Following that ordinary HTML is inserted to begin the page.

3. To begin the body of the page, use the HTML body element and then begin a form element in the center of the page. This is accomplished with the following code:

```
<body>
<center>
<form method="post" action="indexm02p01.aspx">
```

4. Notice that the form element contains an action attribute whose value is the name of your file. This directs the user's input back to the same file, so you'll have to have some processing in our file (shown after a few more steps) to capture the input and process it.

5. Within the form there will be several form controls that allow users to enter their name and their choice of pets (cats are best, of course). The first control will be a text box and the second will be a drop-down menu with four choices available. You can create these controls using both HTML and VB.NET, as shown here:

```
<b> Hello <input name="YourName" type="text" value=
"<% Response.write Request.Form("YourName") %>">
Category:
     <select name="TypeOfPet">
<%
     Choices(0) = "cats"
     Choices(1) = "dogs"
     Choices(2) = "birds"
     Choices(3) = "snakes"
     For i = 0 To Choices.Length-1
          If (Request.Form("TypeOfPet") = Choices(i)) %>
               <option selected>
<%
          Else
%>
               <option>
<%
          End If
          Response.write Choices(i)
%>
          </option>
<%
     Next
%>
     </select>
</b>
```

6. Notice the first and second lines of code are actually supposed to be on the same line but have been cut to fit properly in this book. Code lines are often cut in this way in the text of the book, but the code downloaded from the website will not be separated in this way.

The first line of code sets up a form control of type *text*, and then fills it with the name the user entered, if one exists (the first time the page is opened nothing has been submitted, so nothing is written for the value). The block beginning at the word "Category:" starts another control that is a drop-down list. This is the HTML select element. The choices in the drop-down are built using a For…Next loop, and if there has been a selection the item selected will be designated as such using the If...EndIf block. Notice that the available choices have been set using "Choices(0) = cats" and so on. Each item in the array is set this way, and can then be referred to with "Choices(i)" as the For…Next loop progresses.

7. To complete the processing, your form, and the page, code in a processing block, and then the ending form, body, and html element tags, as shown here:

```
<input type="submit" name="Find" value="Find">
<p>
<%
     If (Not Request.Form("Find") = Nothing)
%>
          Hello
<%
          Response.write(Request.Form("YourName"))
%>
          , you selected:
<%
          Response.write(Request.Form("TypeOfPet"))
     End If
%>
</form>
</center>
</body>
</html>
```

The form control of type Submit creates a button on the form. This button is a control whose name and value (the label) will be submitted and stored in the Form collection of the Request object, just like all the other names and values of form controls.

8. The If…End If block checks to see if the form control named "Find" is equal to nothing, and if not writes a response back to the user that includes plain-text as well as the values the user submitted.

9. To test your mini-application, all you need to do is open Internet Explorer and browse to the file. Note that you cannot use File | Open | Browse to open the file; you must enter the correct URL for the file so it is served up by the web server.
10. Upon opening this file for the first time, the screen in Figure 2-3 is displayed.
11. This is an error message generated by ASP.NET. It tells you what the problem is, what line it was found on, and gives more detailed output from the compiler,

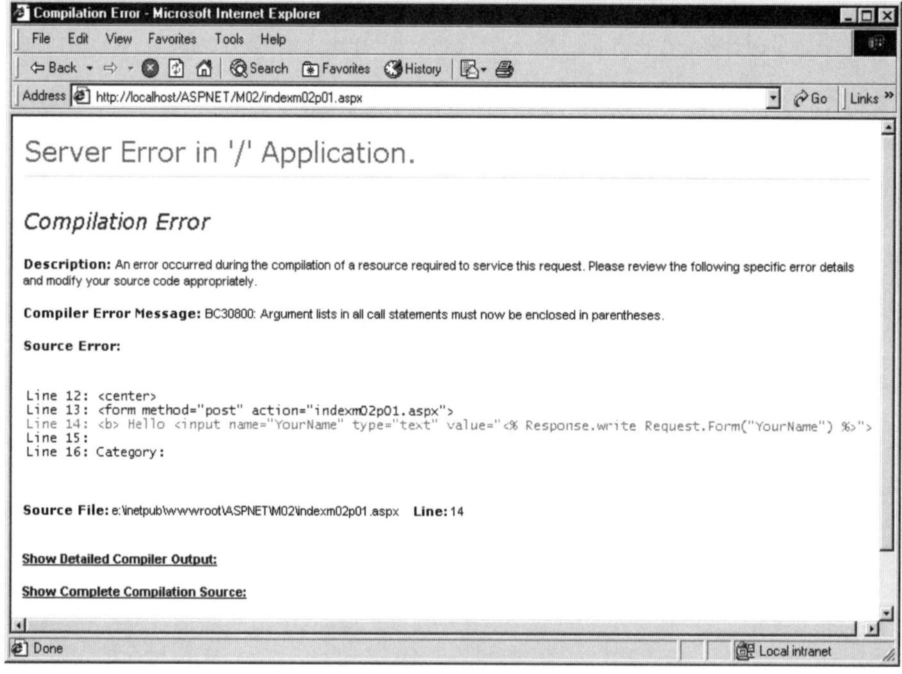

Figure 2-3 An ASP.NET error message

as well as complete compiler source code generated. Figures 2-4 and 2-5 show what is under these links (the second figure shows partial output from the complete source code).

12. The problem is you have used an old ASP-compatible method for writing responses back to the user “Response.write Request.Form(“YourName”)”. This works fine in ASP, but VB.NET requires a more formal syntax: “Response.write(Request.Form(“YourName”))” in which the argument for the Response.write method is enclosed in parentheses.

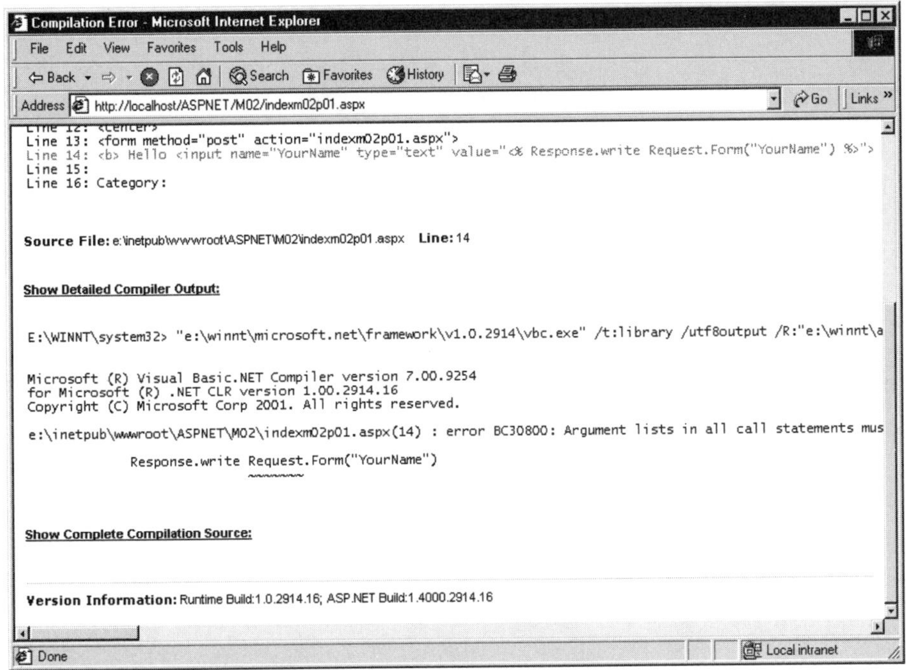

Figure 2-4 Detailed compiler output

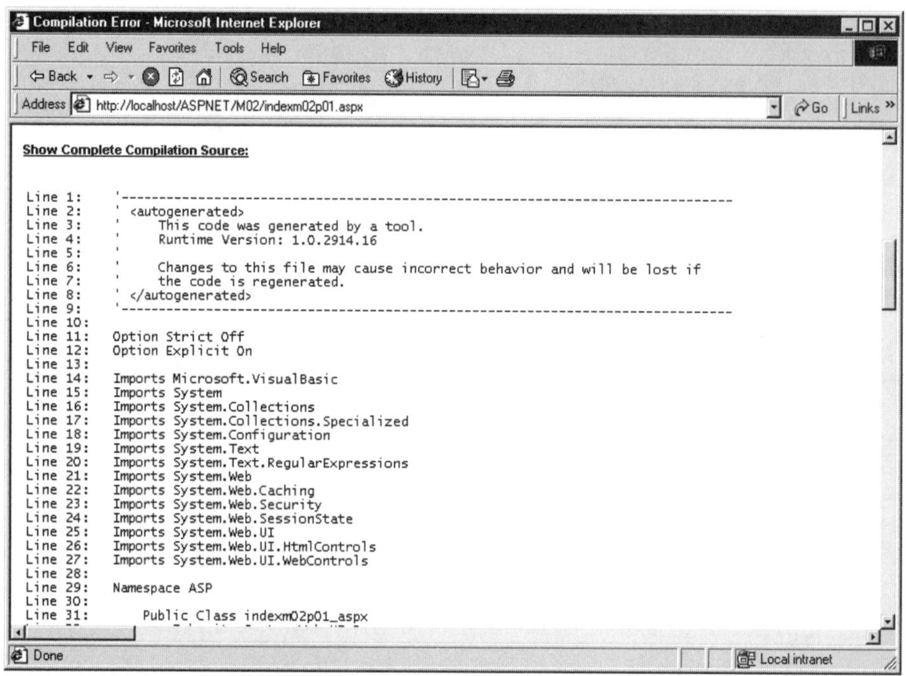

Figure 2-5 Compiler source code

13. Looking at the detailed compiler output, you'll find three other instances of this error. Changing all four instances in your source code, resaving, and refreshing the file in the browser produces the finished page, as shown in Figure 2-6.

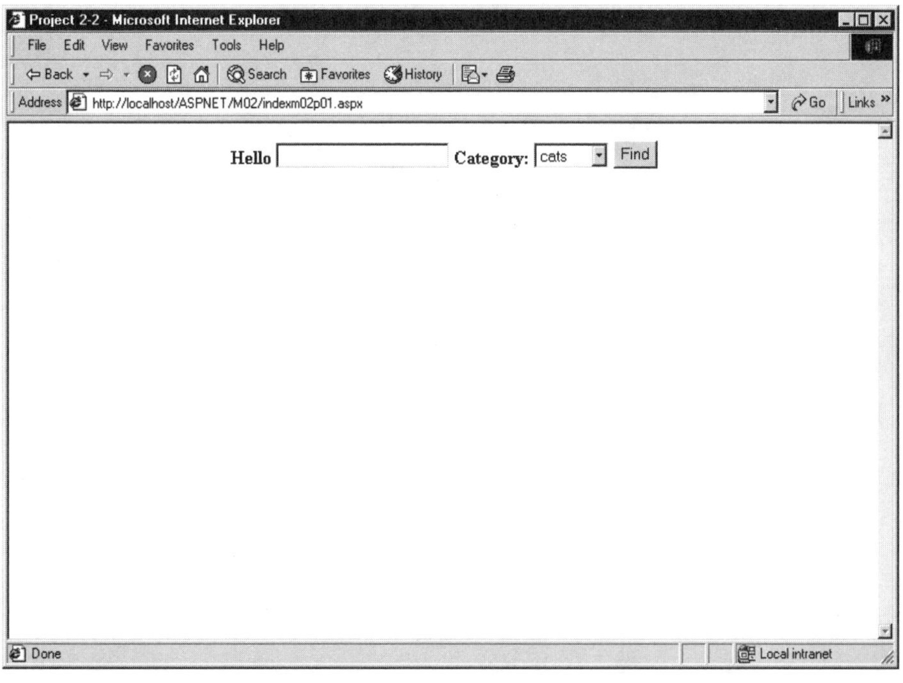

Figure 2-6 The initial ASP.NET page and form

14. Now you can enter your name and make a choice from the drop-down list. Upon doing so, you will see the output shown in Figure 2-7.

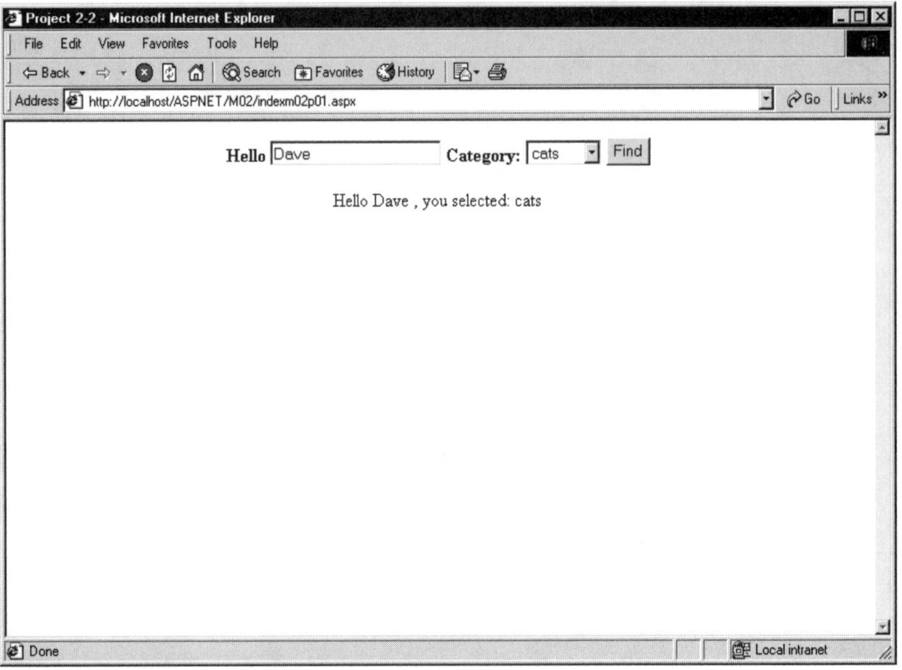

Figure 2-7 The output after submission

Mastery Check

1. What languages/technologies are commonly used to construct web pages and online applications?

   A. Hypertext Markup Language (HTML)

   B. Visual Basic Scripting (VBScript)

   C. Active Server Pages (ASP)

   D. Practical Extraction and Reporting Language (Perl)

   E. All of the above

2. Hypertext Transport Protocol defines communications between web server and web browser. What kinds of messages are included in these communications?

   A. Time and date

   B. Browser and server type and version

   C. Cookies

   D. Status and error messages

   E. Web pages

   F. All of the above

3. Delimiters are characters used to define commands in programming languages. The delimiters for HTML are _______ and _______. The delimiters for ASP code within HTML are _______ and _______.

4. Describe three common coding practices that make your code more readable, more debuggable, and less error-prone.

   ____

   ____

5. Who decides on the layout and look of a website? Who should have input?

   A. The client or manager paying for the job

   B. The users

Mastery Check

C. The designer/programmer

D. The graphic artist

E. All of the above

6. What languages are used to program ASP.NET pages?

A. eXtensible Hypertext Markup Language (XHTML)

B. Visual Basic.NET

C. C#

D. JScript

E. All of the above

7. What does the term *data type* mean? What kinds of data types are there?

A. Data type refers to the type of data a user submits, such as personal information and billing information. There are a multitude of data types, depending on how you choose to categorize submitted data.

B. Data type refers to the type of data in question, such as strings, numbers, and so forth. Depending on the data type, certain types of processing are possible. For instance, a string of data may not be added to another string, but if the data types are changed to some numerical type, then the two items of data may be added.

C. Data type is set when a variable is dimensioned, and whatever data is entered in that variable must be of that type or an error will occur. There are many data types, such as string, integer, date/time, and so forth.

D. B and C.

E. None of the above.

8. Hard-coding values into a page or into program code is a bad idea and should be avoided wherever practical because if the value is present in several places, pages, or programs, much more _________ is required to change the value.

Mastery Check

9. Describe three ways in which coding XHTML is different from coding HTML.

____

____

10. What built-in ASP objects are available? Are these same objects also available in VB.NET?

A. The Request and Response, Application and Session, and Server objects are available and can be used in VB.NET as well.

B. No ASP objects are available in VB.NET.

C. The Response.write and Request.Form objects, and they are available in ASP.NET as well.

D. All of the above.

11. What program structure would be useful for looping through a set of statements until a particular value is reached?

A. The For…Next loop

B. A Select…Case block

C. An If…End If block

D. The Do…Until loop

E. All of the above

12. What does polymorphism mean?

____

____

13. An ASP file should have the file extension _____ while an ASP.NET file should have the file extension _____.

14. Describe three things you might see when an error is generated in your code upon compiling it for the first time.

____

____

Mastery Check

15. How is your code compiled in the CLR, and when does this happen?

A. All the files in your application, including HTML files, are compiled. They are compiled the first time the application is accessed, and thereafter only the compiled resource is used. If you make a change to a file, that file will be recompiled the next time it is accessed.

B. You must explicitly compile your files, and they are compiled every time the application is run, in case you make a change

C. Only files with program code are compiled, and they are compiled each time the application is run, to speed things up.

D. None of the above.

Module 3

Programming ASP.NET with Visual Basic.NET

The Goals of This Module

- Learn VB.NET programming
- Review and understand data types
- Examine common data processing functions
- Explore built-in ASP objects
- Practice sending and retrieving data
- Explore fundamental interactivity methods in ASP.NET
- Examine the Server object
- Practice using the Server object

Microsoft's .NET Framework is the platform upon which ASP.NET applications are built. ASP.NET applications are made from Web Forms and Web Services, the Web Forms constituting the user interface (UI) or front end, and the Web Services making up the back-end. Any programming language can be used to write the commands that tell Web Forms and Web Services what to do, but only those for which there is a .NET compiler can run in the CLR as *managed code*. Managed code takes advantage of the built-in memory management, garbage collection, and other features of .NET, making the programmer's life much easier.

Of the programming languages available for .NET, Visual Basic is one of the easiest to learn and use. The syntax is pretty simple and straightforward, and the program instructions are fairly English-like. A typical ASP.NET program is created as a plain-text file, starts with a declaration of the language type, and then declares variables. Next, whatever actions are required to be performed are performed. For example, less complex applications might contain all the logic for a series of actions that takes place on a website in one "program" file, with individual HTML pages displayed at the appropriate times.

The program file could be divided up into blocks of program instructions activated when certain buttons are clicked on the screen, and each time a button is clicked control passes from the user back to the program file running on the server. When the program file gets done with its processing (looking up data in a database, calculating a result, and so on) it sends the display page to the user, with the appropriate data inserted. This back and forth interaction is very common in website applications.

Any data held by the program file during processing is best kept in variables of the correct data type, and any processing done will almost always be done with the same basic commands and processing structures found in most programming languages. In this module we discuss data types, processing structures, and built-in objects that can be used with VB.NET, and we delve deeply into objects used by almost every ASP application you'll find. The intent is to provide some background on ASP, while at the same time providing an easy introduction to objects, properties, and methods in general.

VB.NET Programming Language Structures

The first requirement for working with any kind of data is to capture that data in the appropriate container, and that's why variables exist. Although you can use data directly in your programs, as you've seen, hard-coded data is very difficult to do much with. Variables, on the other hand, can morph into other values from a starting value. And variables can be assigned a particular data type, so you'll always know what kind of data you're working with and be able to perform the appropriate operations on it.

Programming languages also contain operators and functions that work like operators. Common operators are the arithmetic operators such as plus (+) and minus (–). These can be used to perform arithmetic calculations of numbers directly but are more commonly used on the values of variables. For example, suppose your program has a block of code that looks like this:


```
Dim x as Int
Dim y as Int
Dim z as Int

x = 2
y = 3
z = x + y
Response.write("The value is " & z)
```

In this code, you dimension (create) three variables, *x*, *y*, and *z*, with data types of Integer. The Integer data type means that no decimal places are allowed. Next, you set the value of *x* and *y* to numbers. You could just as easily have retrieved these values from the user rather than hard-coded them into your program. Finally, you set the value of *z* to be the result of adding *x* and *y* together. The code that says "x + y" is called an *expression*, and when the program runs the expression is said to be *evaluated*. From that point in the program, *z* contains the value of the expression "x + y", or 5.

To see the results of your program, you must send it to the user somehow. You could store it, use it later, perform more calculations on it, or do anything else you want, but if you want to see it you must output it, so you use the built-in Response object's Write method to send it as text to the user. Notice the response you build is partly text (the part in the quotes) and partly just the plain variable *z*. The part after the code "Response.write" is also called an expression, but since it is text, it uses the ampersand (&) operator to concatenate (join together) the initial string and the value of the variable. The result is a string that reads "The value is 5", and this is sent directly back to the user as text by the Response.write object/method combination.

This little program gives up processing control once it sends its output back, and nothing else will happen until the user provides an appropriate response back to the program. If the user browses to another website and doesn't provide an appropriate response, the program will not do anything else and will eventually time out.

Generally, all programs have structures and functions like the ones just mentioned. Now its time to take a look at programming with the .NET Framework and VB.NET specifically.

ASP.NET Data Types

One of the advantages of using the .NET Framework and the CLR is that data types have been standardized across the CLR, so that no matter what language you use you can exchange values among programs easily. Microsoft calls this the Common Type System, or CTS. The standard types are listed in the center column of the Table 3-1, with their VB.NET equivalents on the left. After the table is a description of each data type.

Strings

The String data type consists of characters such as letters, digits, and punctuation symbols (period, comma, exclamation point, and so forth) that are part of the

VB.NET Type	CLR Type	Size
Boolean	System.Boolean	2 bytes
Byte	System.Byte	1 byte
Char	System.Char	2 bytes
Date	System.DateTime	8 bytes
Decimal	System.Decimal	16 bytes
Double	System.Double	8 bytes
Integer	System.Int32	4 bytes
Long	System.Int64	8 bytes
Object	System.Object	4 bytes
Short	System.Int16	2 bytes
Single	System.Single	4 bytes
String	System.String	Constrained by OS
User-defined	System.ValueType	Sum of sizes

Table 3-1 VB.NET and CLR Data Types

Unicode character set. You can find out more about Unicode and the characters it includes at **www.unicode.org**. From 0 to perhaps 2 billion Unicode characters may be assigned to a string variable. Although strings can be concatenated, and digits can be part of strings, if the data type of two sets of digits (such as 24 and 36) is a string, the program cannot add them together with a numerical operator such as +. Even though they look like numbers to you and me, they are string characters to the computer, and if you try to add them a data type mismatch error will be produced.

Numbers

Decimal, Double, Integer, Long, Short, and Single are numeric data types and can be added together, as well as have other common arithmetical calculations performed on them. Short is simply a small version of an integer taking up 2 bytes and allowing values from –32,768 to 32,767. Integer allows values from –2,147,483,648 to 2,147,483,647, and Long allows values from –9,223,372,036,854,775,808 to 9,223,372,036,854,775,807. Single, Double, and Decimal provide for decimal places, and single allows values from –3.402823E+38 to –1.401298E-45 and from 1.401298E-45 to 3.402823E+38, where E means exponent. Double allows values from –1.79769313486231E+308 to –4.94065645841247E-324 and from 4.94065645841247E-324 to 1.79769313486231E+308, while Decimal allows values from +/–79,228,162,514,264,337,593,543,950,335 with no decimal point or +/–7.9228162514264337593543950335 with 28 places to the right of the decimal (the smallest nonzero number allowed is +/–0.0000000000000000000000000001). All these numerical data types can be operated upon with arithmetical operators.

Dates

Dates have their own data type so that date and time calculations can be performed. Since dates and times are numbered differently from ordinary numbers (3600 seconds in an hour, 24 hours in a day, and so forth) a special set of operations must be available, and a special data type is required. The Date data type can be assigned any date or time from January 1, 0001 to December 31, 9999, so we shouldn't be seeing any Y2K-type problems for a long while.

Bit and Byte Types

It's very common to find values in programs that are either True or False, much like the On/Off state of bits in a microprocessor. The data type assigned to this set of values is Boolean and is often used as a flag or signal of a condition. For example, was the e-mail field filled in, Yes or No? Anytime you have either one of two values, you can use this data type to represent the values. The Byte and Char data types extend this sort of value range 0 to 255 (Byte) and 0 to 65535 (Char). The Byte data type is much like a byte of computer data, which consists of binary numbers from 00000000 to 11111111 (0 to 255 in decimal numbers).

The Object Data Type

Modern programming languages often include a data type that can automatically be any data type; for example, string, number, date, and so on. The programs automatically shift data types according to the context in which they are used. For example, suppose you dimension two variables as a data type object (or don't specify a data type at all). If you then set these variables equal to strings that happen to be digits and attempt to add these strings together, the program will automatically convert them to the appropriate type and perform the addition. The final result will automatically be a numeric data type. The Object data type fills this role in VB.NET.

Object data types are useful in some cases, but be careful. If you lose track of the data type and use it inappropriately, you'll get data type mismatch errors in your code. One place this occurs is when you insert a variable in a SQL statement. SQL statements don't perform the automatic conversion, and if the "data type of the moment" for your Object variable is incorrect, you'll get an error.

In VBScript, all variables were automatically of data type Variant, which performed the same kinds of functions as the Object data type. VB.NET does not allow the Variant data type.

User-Defined Data Types

Many programming languages and language specifications give programmers the ability to define their own data types. User-defined data types are constructed from more primitive data types cobbled together. For example, you might want a data type that is the combination of a customer's first name, middle initial, last name, and birth date. The first three members in your user-defined data type should be strings, while the last member would be a date data type. A user-defined data type's size depends on the sizes of its members, and the range of values each member can take on depends on the range of its own data type. We'll take a look at user-defined data types again when we discuss the XML-Schema specification in Module 7.

Operators

Operators are the programming language symbols that direct the program to perform an operation on multiple values. For example, suppose you have two variables named *X* and *Y* that are currently equal to 2 and 3, respectively, and you write a statement that says:

```
Z = X + Y
```

The plus sign (+) is called an operator. There are quite a few arithmetical operators, as well as operators that perform other functions (such as comparison). We'll review the available operators in the next few sections.

Note

When you add the value of one variable (in this case *X*) to another (*Y*), the variable which will contain the answer (*Z*) should be of the same data type. To ensure that VB.NET will notify you if you violate data type rules (such as trying to assign a numerical value with a decimal point to a variable whose data type is Integer) use the Option Strict statement in your code at the top of the page.

Arithmetical Operators

Arithmetical operators include the familiar addition (+), subtraction (-), multiplication (*), and division (/) operations. Division with the (/) operator may result in an answer containing a decimal place. To show an *exponent*, use the carat symbol (^) found on your keyboard on top of the 6.

Integer division can be performed with the (\) operator, but only with data types that have no decimal place, such as Int and Long. The result of integer division is simply the answer without the remainder (32 \ 6 = 5, for example, where the remainder of 2 is discarded). *Modulus arithmetic* can be performed using the Mod operator, and the result is the remainder.

Bitwise Operators

Bitwise operators convert integer numbers into binary form and then perform a comparison of the numbers to produce a result. For the And operator, the comparison produces a 1 anywhere in the binary numbers that both numbers have a 1. For example, if the first number is 6 and the second number is 10, the code might look like this:

```
X = 6 AND 10
```

The number 6 is 0110 in binary form, and the number 10 is 1010 in binary form. In this case the answer would be 2, because the binary number that results from this operation is 0010 (only the third position of each number both contain a 1), or 2 in decimal form. Other bitwise operators include Or (in which a 1 is produced if either number contains a 1 at a particular spot), Xor (in which a 1 is produced if only one but not both spots contain a 1), and Not (in which the bits of a single binary number are inverted, including the sign designating whether they are positive or negative).

Concatenation Operators

Both the plus sign (+) and the ampersand (&) can be used as concatenation operators. Concatenation simply means to join together two strings (although a number of other data types can serve as the starter values). A good example of where concatenation comes in handy is in printing names from a database. The values may have been retrieved from a database as FirstName and LastName, and you'd want to join them together with a space for printing, as follows:

```
Dim vFirstName As String
Dim vLastName As String

vFirstName = "Dave"
vLastName = "Mercer"
Response.write ("Your name is " & vFirstName & " " & vLastName)
```

To simply write out string data to the user the Response object's Write method can be used, and connecting the string portions (in quotes) with the values assigned to the variables by using the ampersand demonstrates how the ampersand works. The plus sign can also be used for this function, but it is safer to use the ampersand because an error will result if an incorrect data type is used, thereby informing you of a probable coding error.

Logical Operators

Logical operators perform their operations on expressions that result in a Boolean value (True or False). For example, you can use the And operator to produce a True result if two expressions both result in True values, as shown in this code listing:

```
Dim a As Int
Dim b As Int
Dim c As Int
Dim d As Int
Dim y As Boolean

a = 10
b = 20
c = 30
d = 40

y = b < a And c < d
```

In this case, *a* is less than *b* (True) and *c* is less than *d* (also True) so the And operator returns True, and therefore the value of *y* is now True. Logical operators also include Or (in which if either expression is True the result is True), Not (in which only one expression is required, and if it is True the result is False, and vice versa), Xor (in which if either expression but not both is True, the result is True), AndAlso (in which if the first of two expressions is False then the result is automatically False and the second expression is not checked), and OrElse (in which if the first of two expressions is True, then the result is automatically True and the second expression is not checked).

Comparison Operators

Comparison operators return True or False based on the comparison of variable values, and they can apply to numerical or sting values with equal ease. Often used in If…Then structures, the numerical comparison operators available are equal (=), inequality (<>), less-than (<), greater-than (>), less-than or equal to (<=), and greater-than or equal to (>=). If the value in variable *a* is less than the value in variable *b* and they are compared using the equals sign (as in If a = b Then) the condition will not be met because *a* is not equal to *b*, and any code inside the structure will not run.

Strings may be compared with the equal sign as well, so that if one string is the equivalent of another (If "smith" = "smith" Then, for example). Strings may also be compared using the Like operator, so that partial matches will still result in a True value. For instance, is you were to write the code

```
If "smith" like "smi*" Then
  Do something
End If
```

the condition would be met and the code contained in the structure would run.

Exception Handling with VB.NET

As we mentioned in Module 2, exception handling is an important part of a well- designed application, and it would be surprising if an application never encountered an exception while running. VB.NET goes beyond the basic exception handling capabilities provided by VBScript, and the next few sections reveal how these new capabilities work.

Structured and Unstructured Exception Handling

You want to capture errors when they occur because not doing so means the application will produce an ugly error message and will terminate. Although this may solve the immediate problem by not letting a user proceed if they have entered the wrong kind of data, it is extremely bad form. If your application is going to fail (even for a good reason) it should always fail gracefully, meaning that the user never sees technical error messages, but instead sees a message such as "Incorrect type of data, please try again". VB.NET provides for both structured and unstructured exception handling, although you cannot use both of them in the same code block.

Structured Exception Handling Structured exception handling means that you have placed markers on your blocks of code, associating them with a particular handler or handlers. The handlers are activated when the error raised matches a specific condition, so you can not only catch errors but respond to particular types of errors individually as well.

To create a structured exception handling block of code, start your code with the Try statement, and then place within the code a Catch block for code to execute if the code in the Try block generates an error. You can also use the Finally statement to run code right before the Try block is exited, and End Try exits the code block. Following is an example written in pseudocode:

```
Try
    'Here is where your normal code goes
Catch 'Here are filters for error types
    'Here is the code that runs on errors
Finally
    'Here is code that runs before Try exits
End Try
    'This exits the Try block
```

Unstructured Exception Handling Unstructured exception handling means you've placed the On Error statement at the beginning of a block of code, and any error that arises activates that statement and its associated handling code. It is the only method offered in ASP, but can be used in ASP.NET as well. Here's an ASP/ADO example of the On Error statement being used to cancel the update of a recordset if an error is thrown:

```
On Error Resume Next
    rst1.Update
    If conn.Errors.Count > 0 Then
        For Each objError in conn.Errors
            Response.Write("Error " &
            objError.SQLState & ": " &
            objError.Description & " | " &
            objError.NativeError)
        Next
            conn.Errors.Clear
            rst1.CancelUpdate
    End If
On Error GoTo 0
```

Common ASP.NET Page Syntax

It is very likely that you will be creating a good many Web Forms as you program ASP.NET applications, so we have included in this section a description of several common sections you might program into your Web Forms, and what they mean. When using Visual Studio.NET Web application templates (as we do extensively in this book) many of these Page sections will be pre-programmed for you.

However, it is still a good idea to know what they are and what they do, as you may need to change them along the way.

The @ Page Directive

The @ Page directive defines a set of attributes specific to a single page in a web application, that is, attributes for a file with a .aspx extension. To include more than one attribute (as a name=value pair) use a space separated list. Its use is allowed only on pages of this type and only once per page. Although it can be used anywhere on the page it is customary to insert it at the top of the page. Following are a few of the attributes:

- **Buffer** Specifies whether HTTP response buffering is on or off (True or False). True is the default. If buffering is on no response will be provided to the user until all processing is complete.
- **Debug** If Debug is True then the page will be compiled with Debug symbols, slowing performance but making it easier to debug your application. Turn it off when you're ready to deploy your application.
- **Explicit** If this is set to True then the Option Explicit statement is in force, meaning you must declare variables. The default is False.
- **Strict** If this is set to True then the Option Strict statement is in force, meaning you cannot perform some data type conversions implicitly. The default is False.
- **Transaction** If this is set to True transactions are supported. The default value is NotSupported. Module 11 has more information about transactions.

The @ Import Directive

The Import directive should be added to your code whenever you want to include a particular namespace in your Web Form. A namespace represents a class, for example, the System.Web.SessionState class. This and many other classes are automatically imported into pages, but if you create a custom class or want to use a pre-programmed class (from ASP.NET, for example) you should include an Imports directive for each namespace you want to add to the page.

Built-in ASP.NET Objects and Interactivity

Using a browser is pretty easy: just point and click to get to a link, or fill out a form and press the submit button to send information. Beneath the ease and simplicity, though, is a fairly complex transaction: a two-way communication between the web server and the client (the browser, or in more precise terms, the *user agent*). Understanding what's going on behind the scenes is important to your ASP.NET programming efforts, and it's also important to remember that browsers aren't the only clients that might access your website.

Let's use the example of a browser to illustrate in detail how things are done. Suppose a user opens their browser and enters your domain name in the address field. When they press ENTER, their browser makes a connection with the web server across the Internet and then requests the default page (assuming they've entered no filename after the domain name). As they traverse the website, their browser requests each page they click on by its full path and filename. Using the full path and filename is required because the web is *stateless*, which means that the web server doesn't maintain a continuous connection to each client and, therefore, doesn't know one page request from the next.

The actual content of the request may contain much more information than just the path and the filename. For instance, the request may include the time, date, accepted application file types, cookies, host IP address, browser type, connection type, and so forth.

If the requested page is available *anonymously* (meaning no username and password is required to access the page), the server will respond with similar information plus the HTML content of the page. The returned information may include date, time, server type, connection type, cookies, and so on. This response is also the source of those annoying messages such as "HTTP1.1 404 Not Found." If the request is valid, the page will be displayed; if not, the user will see the HTTP version and the appropriate error message.

The Request Object

As you've seen, all the objects built into ASP are still available, and VB.NET provides excellent tools for creating your own classes and object instances. The Request object is very commonly used in ASP scripts, so we'll examine it in detail (as well as some of the other built-in ASP objects) before we launch into a complete discussion of Web Forms in Module 4.

The request object captures data transmitted by the user to the server, and this data can be used by your application to formulate responses. When a link is clicked or a form is submitted, the request object captures all the data within the request, including the HTTP variables, cookies, query strings, security certificates, and certain properties of the request that can be used to manage communications. All this data is then immediately available to the activated ASP script.

In ASP.NET, changes have been made to the way the Request object works. In ASP, the Request object returns an array of values when a collection is accessed. In ASP.NET, the Request object returns what is called a NameValueCollection. We provide examples of the code for accessing each type of data in the following sections.

Request Object Collections

Objects commonly have collections of data associated with them, and the Request object is no exception. Collections of data can be accessed by addressing (referring to the Request object by name) the Request object and the name of the collection (for example, the Form collection) and then referring to the name of the item in the collection (a field from the form named LastName, for example). Setting a variable to be equal to the value of the data found in this object-collection field might be coded as follows:

```
Dim mystring

mystring = request.form("LastName")
```

Naturally, for this code to work the user must have entered some data in an HTML form field named LastName and hit the submit button to send this data to your script or application.

With ASP.NET and VB.NET, if there are multiple values for a single field or key, the collection can be addressed as an index that is zero-based (starts at zero) while in ASP the collection starts at one. There are other differences as well, as shown in the following code examples:

```
'For ASP.NET
Dim mystring As String
```

```
mystring = Request.Form.GetValues("LastName")

'For ASP.NET using the index, if the LastName field has more than one value

mystring = Request.Form.GetValues("LastName")(0)
mystring = Request.Form.GetValues("LastName")(1)
```


The Request object includes five built-in collections, each of which captures specific kinds of data:

- **Query string** The name/value pairs attached to the end of a requested URL, or the name/value pairs resulting from the submission of a form where the method equals GET (like this: <FORM ACTION="someaction.asp" METHOD="GET">)
- **Form** The name/value pairs resulting from the submission of a form where the method equals POST (like this: <FORM ACTION="someaction.asp" METHOD="POST">)
- **Server variables** The names and values of the HTTP header plus the names and values of several environment variables from the web server
- **Cookies** The values of all cookies sent with the user's request (by default the only cookies sent are those that are valid for the domain of the web server)
- **Client certificate** The values of the fields/entries in the client certificate offered to the server

The Request object captures all this data in these collections and then makes it easily accessible by your scripts for further processing. Nothing special is required, and as soon as the user hits the submit button the data is waiting for you to work with it just by calling the Request object.

Request Object Properties and Methods

The only property of the Request object is TotalBytes, which represents the total number of bytes in the body of the request. You probably won't be using this very frequently (unless you have an unusual application); more likely you'll be interested in the contents of each name/value pair.

The only method of the Request object is BinaryRead. BinaryRead retrieves a specified number of bytes from a request sent using METHOD="POST" and is somewhat complementary to the Form collection. Both are ways to get data from the request when the POST method is used, and use of either one prevents use of the other. This means that if you use the BinaryRead method, it will return the data it finds as a Variant array and at the same time prevent successful use of the Form collection. As its name implies, BinaryRead reads data in binary form; it is not currently used much. We'll discuss it in more depth in the Response object section (see "The Response Object") later in this module.

Note

The Form collection, if used first, will prevent subsequent use of the BinaryRead method (for a single request, not all future requests).

Referencing Items in a Collection The Request.Form collection provides a *Count* property, meaning you have access to the value representing the number of items in the collection. Using this value, you can set up a looping structure to iterate through each item in the collection. You could use the integer index method by incrementing a variable each time the loop is traversed, as shown here:

```
For intIncr = 1 To Request.Form.Count
     Response.Write (Request.Form(intIncr) & "<BR>")
Next
```

The HTML form and output results look the same as the first example, but the ASP script uses the For…Next loop to do the work. Notice that instead of using the ASP delimiters (%) to separate the ASP code from the HTML, only the actual <BR> tag is located inside quotes. This works just as well as the previous technique and relieves you of switching in and out of ASP code. (Also, you would typically want to do something more useful than simply writing back the values in the collection, such as entering them into a database—but more on that subject in later modules.)

If you'd like to gather the names as well as the values of each item in the collection, you can use the For Each looping structure, in the following fashion:

```
For Each collItem In Request.Form
     Response.Write (collItem & " = " & Request.Form(collItem) & "<BR>")
Next
```

This will display both the names of each collItem (and you can create whatever name you want for collection items, such as objItem, myItem, and so forth) and then the value associated with it (with an equal sign in between) as shown here:

```
fullname = theirname
address = theiraddress
phonenumber = theirphonenumber
```

The QueryString Collection

A query string carries names and values after a URL it is pointed at. It can be created with the hypertext link tag and looks like this:

```
<A HREF="www.mydomainname.com/
myscript.asp?fullname=Dave">
Click Here
</A>
```

The filename shows the intended script target, and the data following the question mark consists of names and values separated by the equals sign. As mentioned earlier, the contents of the QueryString collection can be retrieved from a hypertext link, or from the values submitted from a form using the GET method in the form tag. If you happen to know the names of the value pairs, you can retrieve them individually by name (or you can iterate through them using the same techniques used with the Request.Form collection). You can also simply retrieve the entire string by omitting the field or pair name (like this: Response.Write Request.QueryString).

The ServerVariables Collection

When a request is sent from the browser, certain HTTP headers are sent. When they arrive at the server, the server also generates a set of variables. Both of these sets of values are accessible through the ServerVariables collection. To view these variables, you need to modify your responding script slightly (note that this is an ASP code example), as follows:

```
<HTML>
<HEAD>
```

```
<TITLE>My Form Results</TITLE>
</HEAD>
<BODY BGCOLOR="lightblue" TEXT="black">
<CENTER>
<TABLE BORDER=1><TR><TD><B>Name</B></TD>
<TD><B>Value</B></TD></TR>
<% For Each collItem In Request.ServerVariables %>
<TR><TD><% Response.Write(collItem) %></TD><TD>
<TD><% Response.Write(Request.ServerVariables(collItem)) %></TD></TR>
<% Next %>
</TABLE>
</CENTER>
</BODY>
</HTML>
```

This script produces raw ServerVariables output in tabular format and at the top lumps together multiple-value variables. For easier reading, Table 3-2 shows a small section of the table produced to give you an idea of what server variables contain.

Using ServerVariable Values Take a look at the HTTP_REFERER value. It shows the URL and path of the file from which you were referred to the current script. You can use that value to direct the user back to the same page, depending on the conditions you find when processing the user's request (for example, a missing field in a form). Remember, more than one form could be

Name	Value
ALL_HTTP =	HTTP_ACCEPT:image/gif, image/x-xbitmap, image/jpeg, image/pjpeg, */*
HTTP_ACCEPT_LANGUAGE	en-us
HTTP_CONNECTION	Keep-Alive
HTTP_HOST	cx847962-a
HTTP_REFERER	http://cx847962-a/ASPBEG/CH03/default8.htm
HTTP_USER_AGENT	Mozilla/4.0 (compatible; MSIE 5.01; Windows NT 5.0)
HTTP_COOKIE	ASPSESSIONIDGQGQGLZQ = OODPIFCBBDGJKPJOPMBPHLPA
HTTP_ACCEPT_ENCODING	gzip, deflate

Table 3-2 The HTTP Variables, Including Cookie, User Agent, and Host

accessing the same script, so it might be important to know which one is making the call.

Another useful value is the HTTP_USER_Agent, or the type and version of the browser being used. Sniffing out this value allows you to produce and send browser-specific pages back to the user based on this value. After all, even though HTML is supposed to be platform independent, we're all still very aware of the differences between browser types and versions, and it's pretty common these days to produce several versions of a page for the various browsers being used.

In conjunction with browser type, you may want to be aware of the HTTP_ACCEPT_LANGUAGE value. This value is supplied by the user's browser and specifies what language the browser is operating in. Like providing a browser-specific version of a page to the user, you can use this value to provide a language-specific page.

The HTTP_COOKIE value contains the values of any session cookies received. This information is very useful for tracking the movement of users across the site, as well as other things like establishing sessions each time the user connects.

The Cookies Collection

Cookies are small strings of data that a web server can send to a browser and then retrieve at will. Cookies have attributes that can specify their lifetime and availability, which you would set with the Response object. The primary value in cookies is the value that can be set according to whatever scheme you choose, typically a unique identifier so you can tell one browser from others in a multitude of requests. Among the common values set in cookies are expiration date, domain and path, usernames and passwords, and just about anything else you can think of that you'd like to see the next time that browser connects.

Note

If the Expires property is not set, the cookies will expire when the browser is next closed. This property is convenient for setting cookies only for the time a user might be surfing on a given day.

Single-Value Cookies Cookies can be either single-value or multiple-value (the syntax differences are explained in the Response object cookie section later in this module), and it is often important to determine the difference and extract all the values if a cookie has more than one. You can use the simple iteration routine to collect individual values:

```
For Each collItem In Request.Cookies
   Response.Write(collItem & " = " &
Request.Cookies(collItem) & "<BR>")
Next
```

Multiple-Value Cookies Suppose one of the cookies has multiple values? You could use the HasKeys property of the Cookies collection in something like the following code to iterate through the multiple cookie values:

```
If Request.Cookies(collItem).HasKeys Then
   For Each collItemVal In Request.Cookies(collItem)
      Response.Write(collItem & "(" & collItemVal & ")"
 & " = " & Request.Cookies(collItem)(collItemVal)
 & "<BR>")
   Next
End If
```

Naturally, knowing the names and values of all cookies received in a request is the first step toward knowing what to do with the request if the functions being provided by the script depend on cookie values for conditional processing. You'll delve further into cookies and how to set their values in the upcoming Response object section (see "Writing Data to the Browser").

1-Minute Drill

- What is the syntax for iterating through a collection, and how is the name of each item in the collection arrived at?
- A cookie can have a value, but how do you set a value within a multiple-valued cookie?

The ClientCertificate Collection

The ClientCertificate collection is primarily useful for assisting you in managing website security, by allowing you to force users to provide digital

- *For Each XXX in YYY, Do Something, Next* is the syntax—where *XXX* is the name you've assigned for each item in the collection and *YYY* is the object containing the collection. The item name is simply whatever you assign.
- Assign a name to the attribute you want to attach to the cookie, and then assign a value for that attributeProd.

certificates to authenticate themselves. ASP provides a way to access the variables included with a certificate via the ClientCertificate collection, and you can use the typical iteration methods to read out these variables. Once again, modify your script to display them, as shown here:

```
<CENTER>
<TABLE BORDER=1>
<% For Each collItem In Request.ClientCertificate() %>
<TR><TD><% Response.Write(collItem & " = " &
Request.ClientCertificate(collItem)) %></TD></TR>
<% Next %>
</TABLE>
</CENTER>
```

This code, properly inserted into a normal script page, produces such data values as the certificate issuer, the subject's name and company (subject being the person who registered the certificate), public key, validity (from and until) dates, and so forth.

Tip

Your server must be set up to accept personal certificates, or submitting a request with a personal certificate on your browser produces no results.

Ask the Expert

Question: I know I can get data from a form submitted by a user. Do I have to create a form for everything?

Answer: No, you can sometimes use the QueryString method to get data more effectively by attaching the necessary values to the URL within the HTML anchor tag. And often you can simply display a button to click without field elements by using the hidden HTML form elements.

Question: What if the user modifies the form by hand? Doesn't this present a security risk?

Answer: Yes, and in the more advanced applications you'll always find extensive, server-side validation of form field values precisely because of this problem.

Question: There seem to be several ways to write the syntax for the Response object. Which is best?

Answer: It depends on what you are doing, but as a general rule you should try to avoid inserting lots of HTML and ASP blocks within each other. If you have some HTML tags that have to go back to the user with your other output, use the Write method of the Response object to output the HTML tags as text strings.

Question: There seems to be so much information coming from the user. Do I need all that information? Why are all those variables transmitted each time?

Answer: Server variables are an important part of the communication between browser and server, and maintaining the client/server relationship is their primary function. However, tapping into the values of those variables allows ASP to do some very interesting things. For example, one of the variables tells ASP what browser version is being used. This information allows ASP to programmatically assign special versions of your website pages according to browser type, meaning you can make pages that look good on a variety of browsers. That capability is covered in more detail in Module 8.

Question: I'm not quite sure I understand how cookies work. There seem to be several kinds, each with several values possible. Can you describe them in more detail?

Answer: You'll learn more about session cookies in Module 5, but for now you should know that they play an important role in establishing individual communication with a specific user. Ordinary cookies serve to identify a particular client so ASP can track site usage from click to click. You can make cookies multivalued by adding keys, and you can retrieve those values with the techniques described previously in this module.

Question: How does authentication work? Is it hard to set up certificates? Where do they come from?

Answer: You can get certificates from certificate-issuing companies such as Verisign, and there is a fairly simple procedure for placing them on your server in the IIS documentation. To authenticate themselves, users must have a personal certificate installed on their browsers. The certificate can be decoded only using a reference to other numbers stored by the certificate authority, so certificate values not meeting this requirement are considered false.

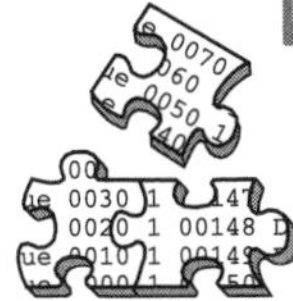

Project 3-1: Using the Request Object

The Request object is great for capturing form data for a multitude of purposes, from checking to see if a user is already in your database to validating form input to conditionally redirecting a user to setting cookies.

You'll use the Request object extensively in your applications, so let's put it to work in a simple but powerful way right off the bat, checking to make sure a submission form is properly filled out and complete prior to allowing the submission process to be completed. First you'll make a submission form in HTML, and then you'll make a script that checks the value of each field and validates it.

To make the submission form, you can use Notepad (for you hard-core HTML programmers out there) or some handy HTML-editing program like Dreamweaver or FrontPage. Remember, if you use FrontPage to create a form, you'll have to delete a few items from the form in order to use it with ASP.

Step-by-Step

Here's the HTML code for you to add to your submission form:

```
<html><head>
<meta http-equiv="Content-Language" content="en-us">
<meta http-equiv="Content-Type"
 content="text/html; charset=windows-1252">
<meta name="GENERATOR"
content="Microsoft FrontPage 4.0">
<meta name="ProgId"
content="FrontPage.Editor.Document">
<title>In Practice Submission Form</title>
</head><body bgcolor="#99FFCC">
```

```
<H2>Please register using the following form:</H2>
<form method="POST" action="--WEBBOT-SELF--">
<!--webbot bot="SaveResults"
 U-File="fpweb:///_private/form_results.txt"
S-Format="TEXT/CSV" S-Label-Fields="TRUE" -->
<table border="1" width="100%"><tr>
<td width="50%" align="right">
<b>First Name:</b></td>
<td width="50%"><input type="text"
 name="FirstName" size="20" tabindex="1"></td></tr>
<tr><td width="50%" align="right">
<b>Middle Initial:</b></td>
<td width="50%"><input type="text"
 name="MI" size="20" tabindex="2"></td>
</tr><tr>
<td width="50%" align="right">
<b>Last Name:</b></td>
<td width="50%"><input type="text"
 name="LastName" size="20" tabindex="3"></td>
</tr><tr>
<td width="50%" align="right">
<b>Address 1:</b></td>
<td width="50%"><input type="text"
 name="Address1" size="20" tabindex="4"></td></tr><tr>
<td width="50%" align="right"><b>Address 2:</b></td>
<td width="50%"><input type="text"
 name="Address2" size="20" tabindex="5"></td></tr><tr>
<td width="50%" align="right"><b>City:</b></td>
<td width="50%"><input type="text"
 name="City" size="20" tabindex="6"></td>
</tr><tr>
<td width="50%" align="right"><b>State:</b></td>
<td width="50%"><input type="text"
 name="State" size="20" tabindex="7"></td>
</tr><tr>
<td width="50%" align="right"><b>Country:</b></td>
<td width="50%"><input type="text"
 name="Country" size="20" tabindex="8"></td></tr><tr>
<td width="50%" align="right">
<b>Zip or Postal Code:</b></td>
<td width="50%"><input type="text"
 name="PCode" size="20" tabindex="9"></td>
</tr><tr>
```

```
<td width="50%" align="right"><b>Home Phone:</b></td>
<td width="50%"><input type="text"
 name="HomePhone" size="20" tabindex="10"></td>
</tr><tr>
<td width="50%" align="right"><b>Fax:</b></td>
<td width="50%"><input type="text"
 name="Fax" size="20" tabindex="11"></td>
</tr><tr>
<td width="50%" align="right"><b>Pager:</b></td>
<td width="50%"><input type="text"
 name="Pager" size="20" tabindex="12"></td></tr><tr>
<td width="50%" align="right">
<b>Mobile Phone:</b></td>
<td width="50%"><input type="text"
 name="Mobile" size="20" tabindex="13"></td></tr><tr>
<td width="50%" align="right">
<b>Email Address:</b></td>
<td width="50%"><input type="text"
 name="Email" size="20" tabindex="14"></td>
</tr><tr>
<td width="50%" align="right"><b>Website URL:</b></td>
<td width="50%"><input type="text"
 name="WebsiteURL" size="20" tabindex="15"></td>
</tr><tr>
<td width="50%" align="right">
<input type="submit" value="Register Now"
 name="B1"></td>
<td width="50%"><input type="reset"
 value="Start Over" name="B2"></td>
</tr></table>
</form>
</body></html>
```

Notice that FrontPage has inserted a few META tags that explain the generator used (FrontPage 4.0), as well as the language, content type, and character set. These won't hurt anything, but you can't use the form as is. FrontPage has inserted a reference to its own WEBBOT named SaveResults.

1. Remove the code referencing WEBBOT and replace it with the name of the script you're going to send the contents of the form submission to. The script will be named Project3-2.asp (you'll construct it in your next project). Then edit the FORM tag as follows:

```
<form method="POST" action="Project3-2.asp">
```

2. Don't forget to remove the two lines about WEBBOT that follow the FORM tag as well. These set the parameters for the FrontPage WEBBOT and are no longer needed. The finished form should be named **Project3-1.htm**, and looks like that shown in Figure 3-1.
3. Because this module is divided into separate sections for the Request and Response objects, you need to split your validator script into two parts: the part that does the data capture and validation and the part that does the responding (this will be shown in the Project 3-2 section for the Response object). An easy way to capture the correct names for fields (as well as the look and feel of the submission form) is to copy the file with a new name and then proceed to modify it in a simple text editor such as Notepad or WordPad.
4. Capture all the data sent by the user and insert it into variables. You can accomplish this simply by setting variables equal to Request.Form values,

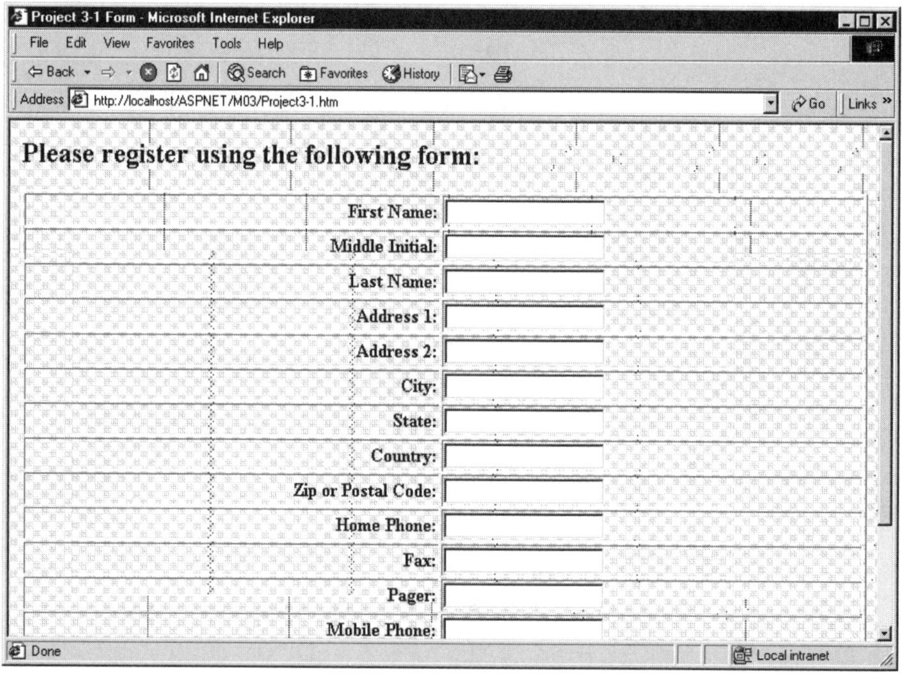

Figure 3-1 The Project 3-1 registration form

as shown in the following ASP example (please note that the HMTL tags making up the return page have been omitted):

```
<%
fname = Request.Form("FirstName")
mi = Request.Form("MI")
lname = Request.Form("LastName")
addr1 = Request.Form("Address1")
addr2 = Request.Form("Address2")
cty = Request.Form("City")
st = Request.Form("State")
cntry = Request.Form("Country")
post = Request.Form("PCode")
hphn = Request.Form("HomePhone")
fphn = Request.Form("Fax")
pgr = Request.Form("Pager")
mphn = Request.Form("Mobile")
email = Request.Form("Email")
wURL = Request.Form("WebsiteURL")
%>
```


5. Note that if you write the same code for ASP.NET using VB.NET, you would have to give the script an extension of .aspx rather than .asp, include the language declaration (since this goes at the top of all your pages, we won't mention it again), use the Dim statement to dimension all your variables because that is the default behavior (remember Option Explicit is the default), and apply data types to your variables. In this case your data type would be String. Finally, to set the variables equal to the values coming in, you need to use the GetValues method. The code to use would resemble the following:

```
Dim fname As String

fname = Request.Form.GetValues("FirstName")
```

6. Following data acquisition, you can test each value to determine whether the field contains data and whether the data is the right kind and contains the right values. Test to make sure the fields contain data. Forms that include an e-mail field usually require that you provide this data, which makes sense because that is the most common communication method on the Internet.

For the e-mail field, you can test for data with the following code (note that this is pseudocode, not real code):

```
If email = "" Then
     send an error message
Else
     keep processing
End If
```

7. For validation, check to make sure the e-mail field contains the @ sign, no spaces, and no special or escape characters that might break something. VBScript offers simple character-checking functions to assist you in this common task.

   Once you have validated the data sent by the user, it's time to do something with it. Other processing you might perform and responses you might supply are covered in the Project 3-2 section for the Response object in the next section of this module.

The Response Object

The Response object is your utility tool for responding to users' requests, but it serves other useful functions as well. For example, you can selectively direct users to other URLs or pages with the Redirect method. It also works with the buffering function (which stores the content of a returning page until all processing is complete) so you can send individual completed portions while the user is waiting for the other processing to get done.

Note

In ASP 2.0, buffering had to be explicitly set, while in ASP 3.0, buffering is the default, so you may find yourself using the buffering control functions in the Response object more frequently.

Response Object Collections

There is only one collection in the Response object, the Cookies collection, which contains the values of all cookies that are to be sent to the browser in the current response. Cookie values must be created before they are made part of the response; once they are part of the response, they are write-only, which means you can determine their names from the Response object but not their values.

Response Object Properties

The Response object has nine properties, most of them readable and editable. They are created by the server, but you can change them to suit your needs.

- **Buffer** This property can be either True or False and specifies whether output being processed will be held in the buffer until all output is ready for delivery. Because you must set this property before any other output is sent, it is usually the first line in an ASP page. As mentioned previously, buffering is True by default in ASP 3.0 and False by default in earlier versions of ASP.
- **IsClientConnected** This property is also True or False, depending upon whether the browser is still connected and loading a page. It is useful for initiating an action when the user goes to another page before finishing the current page's processing.
- **Expires** The value of this property is a number representing the minutes for which a page is valid. If the user has this page cached for less than the value of Expires, the cached page will be displayed; otherwise, a new page will be generated.
- **ExpiresAbsolute** This property is a specific date and time when the page expires, regardless of how old it is. It is expressed as a date/time value with the pound sign before and after the value.
- **Status** This property contains the status value and message that will be sent to the browser in the event of an error and can be used to indicate successful processing as well. It uses a string as the value and message.
- **CacheControl** This property controls (or at least, *should* control) whether proxy servers cache the page. Not all proxy servers honor this property. Set it to Public to allow caching and Private to disallow caching. It is also a string value.
- **Charset** This property adds the name of the character set in use to the HTTP Content-Type header and is a string value.

- **ContentType** This property can be used to set the HTTP content type for a response. If it is not used, the standard "text-html" is used. It is a string value.
- **PICS** This property, also a string, adds data to the header indicating whether the response contains content with adult themes, violence, and so forth.

Response Object Methods

The Response object is a workhorse, and it includes a number of useful methods that do the work. You've already used the Write method, and next you'll learn about the rest, including header and log methods and buffer control methods.

- **Write("string or other value")** This method is used to write a string (or other value) into the overall response and is typically inserted into the HTML code at the location where you want the response string to become part of the page.
- **Redirect("url")** This method tells the browser to load the page or URL specified (as a string). The "302 Object Moved" HTTP header is used to accomplish this action.
- **Flush()** This method forces an emptying of the buffer at the current stage of processing. It is useful for providing users a partial response, especially where the remaining processing may take quite some time, so they'll continue waiting for the rest of the page.
- **End()** This method ends processing and returns whatever has been completed so far. It is useful when some process is either taking too long or cannot be completed normally.
- **Clear()** This method simply erases the contents of the response buffer (but not the HTTP headers).
- **AddHeader("name," "content")** This method adds a custom header to the response, with *name* and *content* values, and must be processed before any page content is sent.
- **AppendToLog("logentry")** This method adds a string to the web server log entry for the response when the W3C Extended Log File Format is used.

- **BinaryWrite(SafeArray)** This method is used for writing the data contained in a Variant-type SafeArray into the output stream without character conversion occurring. As its name implies, it is useful for writing binary data such as that making up image files.

Writing Data to the Browser

You've already written data (received via the Request object's Form collection) back to the browser with the Response object. The syntax is pretty straightforward; just Request.Write and then the string, variable, or object reference you want to use as output. For example, assuming a user filled out a simple form and clicked the submit button, the following ASP code will write a message from you, the contents of a variable containing a date, and the values found in form fields back as a web page to the user (the result is shown in Figure 3-2):

```
<CENTER>
<H2><% Response.Write "Thank you for responding" %>
</H2>
Today's Date is: <% tDate = Date()
Response.Write tDate %><P>
Your personal data entries were:<BR>
<% Response.Write(Request.Form("FirstName")) %><BR>
<% Response.Write(Request.Form("Address1")) %><BR>
<% Response.Write(Request.Form("HomePhone")) %><BR>
</CENTER>
```

Note that with ASP.NET and VB.NET, the Date variable would have to be dimensioned and a data type assigned, the GetValues method used, and parentheses used with the Response object, rather than just plain quotes, as shown in the following ASP.NET code:

```
<CENTER>
<H2>
<% Language="VB"
Dim tDate As Date
Response.Write("Thank you for responding") %>
</H2>
Today's Date is: <% tDate = Date()
Response.Write(tDate) %><P>
Your personal data entries were:<BR>
```

```
<% Response.Write(Request.Form.GetValues("FirstName"))
 %><BR>
<% Response.Write(Request.Form.GetValues("Address1"))
 %><BR>
<% Response.Write(Request.Form.GetValues("HomePhone"))
 %><BR>
</CENTER>
```

Sending Cookies

Cookies are a little more complex than strings and so forth, because there are more parts to them and because they may play a special role in your interactions with users. For example, some cookies spend quite a while on the user's machine, while others last only as long as a single session. And it's up to you to make sure you give each cookie a truly unique ID so you can always be sure which user you are dealing with.

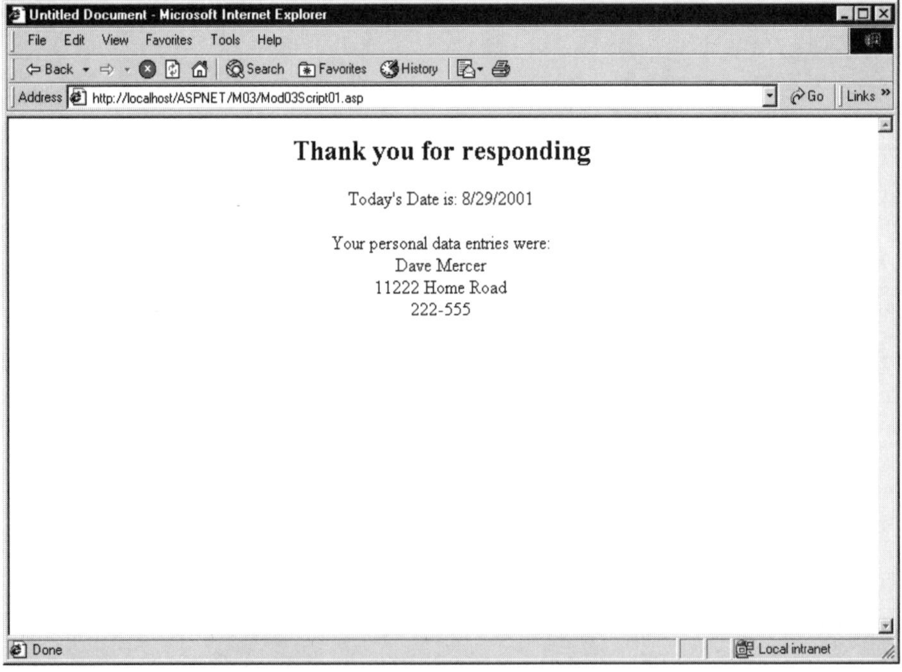

Figure 3-2 Returning Request items and the current date using Response

For example, to write a single-valued cookie named "mycookie" with the value "MyCookie" you would use this:

```
Response.Write("mycookie") = "MyCookie"
```

To write a multiple-valued cookie with a primary name of "mycookie" and two subvalues named "mycookieA" and "mycookieB" with values "X" and "Y," respectively, you would code like this:

```
Response.Write("mycookie")("mycookieA") = "X"
Response.Write("mycookie")("mycookieB") = "Y"
```

Syntax and coding are very straightforward in ASP and ASP.NET. Nothing magical; just write out a common-sense version of what you're trying to do and voilà, cookies of both kinds.

Cookie Constraints Cookies, like the values in other collections, are read- and write-only. After receiving cookie values, you can't go back and change them, and this is good practice. Explicitly setting variables to cookie values and then processing the values means you can always rest assured that what was sent with the request is still intact, no matter how much processing you've done. The same goes for any cookies you're sending out.

In practice, this means that to update cookie values, you can't just reset some of them. You've got to completely rewrite the entire cookie, substituting the new values. That means, of course, that you must capture *all* cookie values each time you want to update *any* cookie values.

Another factor that comes into play is the placement of cookie values being sent in the output stream. They are part of the HTTP header, and as such, must be created before you send any other output back to the browser. However, they can be created anywhere in your page, as long as nothing is flushed back to the browser before cookie creation is accomplished.

Hint

With ASP 3.0, buffering is set to True by default, so you can completely process everything before creating your cookies, if you prefer to do things that way. This comes in especially handy when the results of the processing affect cookie values in some way.

Writing Data with the BinaryWrite Method

As websites become more complex, interactive, and functional, you can expect to depend more heavily on methods such as BinaryRead and BinaryWrite. Dealing with binary data stored in a database, and perhaps gathering binary data occasionally, are powerful capabilities. For example, suppose you wanted to display employee pictures stored in database records. Pulling the record and outputting the bytes via BinaryWrite would do the trick.

To make the data ready for output, you would first have to construct Variant-type array (call it vArEmpImage) of the bytes pointed to by the database record. Overall, the process calls for accessing the database (perhaps selecting records by the username/password of an employer), retrieving the appropriate record of an individual employee, setting the value of vArEmpImage equal to the bytes that make up the image file pointed to by the EmployeePicture field, and then using the code as follows:

```
Response.BinaryWrite(vArEmpImage)
```

Redirecting the Browser

Have you ever been a victim of that little "prank" by which a website makes it impossible to back out using the Back button? Annoying, to say the least, but it's easy to do with browser redirection. Just make an ASP script that immediately redirects a person to another page, and each time that person hits the Back button, he or she will go to the ASP script, which immediately opens to the page the user just backed out of.

Browser redirection makes use of the "302 Object Moved" HTTP header and is the same as creating a Refresh META tag in an HTML page. The META tag would look like this:

```
<META HTTP-EQUIV="REFRESH" CONTENT="0;
URL=someotherplace.htm">
```

In this case, content is the number of seconds before the refresh takes place, and the URL is, of course, where the user will end up after the refresh. When you send the "302 Object Moved" HTTP header, you're just telling the browser to update its location—you're not actually sending a new page, so the browser then sends a request for the new page.

Note

Refer to the discussion of the Server object for information about the Transfer method in ASP 3.0. The Transfer method allows you to switch execution of processing from one page to another and is more suitable for many common tasks involving some form of redirection.

Page Buffering in ASP

Most ASP scripts that work within a single page or so of code will operate very quickly, producing results with little detectable lag or latency. But going into a database or performing complex processing can sometimes take quite a while, especially if the database must be accessed several times to complete processing.

For example, suppose you are searching for a value and, on finding no values, search again for related values in the same database. This might happen when you build a directory of listings (of whatever your clients might want to list, such as dentists in a given region) for advertising purposes.

If a user searches for a dentist within his or her city, and the search finds none that match the specific criteria used, you might set the ASP script to return to the database using broader search criteria (the entire county, for instance). However, it would be nice to return a message to the user noting that although no records were found in the initial search area, your application is in the process of searching the surrounding area as well.

This is just good business practice and encourages users to wait for the finished search, rather than skipping to the next page or even away from the website altogether. The way you make this happen is by manipulating ASP's buffering feature.

To demonstrate, suppose you code your script to process a select query of the database and no records are found. You could use the following code to send a message back to the user:

```
Response.Write("No dentists matching your
 specifications were found in the city you
 chose. We are now searching the surrounding
 area and will provide these results shortly.")
Response.Flush
```

You can also use the Response.End method to end all processing and send any buffered content to the user, or you can use the Response.Clear method to clear out the buffer. You might use these methods where partial processing has resulted in a complete response, or where partial processing has resulted in a response that must be erased (and presumably your script would then generate the correct response).

Tip

Use the IsClientConnected property of the Response object occasionally during consecutive processing efforts to determine whether the user is still connected. This prevents processing cycle waste when users get tired of waiting and click away, which can happen frequently, especially when a user has a low-speed connection. There's no point in continuing processing if the user is already gone.

Setting Page Properties

The properties possessed by a web page are defined in large measure by the content of the HTTP headers you send back with the page requested. Whether and when it is cached or expires, its MIME type and any PICs labels included can be specified using the CacheControl, Expires (and ExpiresAbsolute), Status, ContentType, and PICs properties of the Response object via the AddHeader method.

Caching Most people are familiar by now with the fact that browsers cache web pages in a temporary folder on the hard drive while they're surfing. I have a friend who, at one point, saved images from many of the sites he surfed simply by raiding his cache folder every so often. The purpose of caching, of course, is to speed up loading of pages you've recently visited. ISP proxy servers often cache as well (an important point to note for web developers, as developers like to see the new look of pages they've just updated).

While the goal of caching is admirable, the effect is to dilute the "instantly updated" quality of web material. After all, if you're looking for the latest price on an item, you don't want to be using yesterday's web page. Users can play with their cache and update settings in the browser (in Internet Explorer 5.0, look in Tools | Internet Options; clicking the Setting button brings up the Settings dialog box), but you can also manipulate caching parameters by changing various Response object properties.

For example, if you would like to instruct proxy servers not to cache a page, you can set the CacheControl property to "Private" like so:

```
Response.CacheControl = "Private"
```

Setting the CacheControl property to "Public" has the opposite effect. Again, it's wise to understand that proxy servers are not bound to honor this setting and may still choose to cache if they want.

If caching occurs, the length of time in which a page remains cached can be affected with the Expires and ExpiresAbsolute properties. Expires contains the number of minutes since page acquisition before a page should be removed from the cache, and ExpiresAbsolute gives a fixed date and time for removal. Both properties are set using the same simple syntax as the Response.CacheControl property. However, remember that the data type of Expires is a number, while the data type of ExpiresAbsolute is a date and time combination, so you must make the appropriate syntax adjustments when specifying them (no quotes for numbers, and the pound signs for dates and times).

The Status Property and Adding Headers Status messages are like the server talking to the browser, telling the browser what has happened to its request for a page. HTTP 1.1 contains quite a few built-in status messages, and you can use the Response.Status property to generate or change them. For example, if a user has not been authenticated and you want to mislead the user into thinking the wrong URL was entered, you could generate an "HTTP 404 Not Found" message with the following code:

```
Response.Status = "HTTP 404 Not Found"
```

Not only can you generate status messages, but you can send them for use in conjunction with other headers, including ones you have generated or modified yourself. Table 3-3 is a partial list of common HTTP status messages (for more information, see Module 2).

Section Reference	Meaning
400 Section 10.4.1	Bad Request
401 Section 10.4.2	Unauthorized
402 Section 10.4.3	Payment Required
403 Section 10.4.4	Forbidden
404 Section 10.4.5	Not Found
405 Section 10.4.6	Method Not Allowed
406 Section 10.4.7	Not Acceptable

Table 3-3 HTTP Status Messages

Each of the section references shown in Table 3-3 refers to areas online in which more information is available about that particular status message. The "404 Not Found" listing, for example, says that the server has not found anything matching the request and gives additional information about when and why this message is used and what it means.

Now, suppose you want to send a message back declaring that the user is unauthorized to access the page requested, and require the user to provide authentication. You can send a "401 Unauthorized" message with the Status property, and then add a header for authentication as follows:

```
Response.Status = "401 Unauthorized"
Response.AddHeader "WWW-Authenticate", "BASIC"
```

Using the ContentType Property

Content type refers to the kind of data (or file format) you are sending to the browser. The value of the ContentType property is a short text string of the form ("type"/"format"). An example would be "text/html." This example is the default for all ASP pages unless otherwise specified. Other common types are "text/text" for text files and "image/jpeg" for JPEG image files.

The technical term for these content type identifiers is *MIME-type*, or Multipurpose Internet Mail Extensions. When sending content of a type other than HTML text files, make sure you include the ContentType property *before* sending any content.

1-Minute Drill

- Name the types of responses you can produce with the Response object.
- How can you tell if a user has clicked away from your website while you are processing a request for them?

Project 3-2: Using the Response Object

You've already created an HTML submission form for users to fill out when they want to enter your application, as well as the data capture scripting and

---

- Write, Binary Write, Redirect, and flushing of processed content.
- Examine the IsClientConnected property.

Ask the Expert

Question: What does it mean if a property of an object is read-only? For instance, cookies are read-only. How can they be changed if they are read-only?

Answer: Being read-only means that the value you retrieve cannot be changed as a property of the current Request object. However, if you reset the cookie using the Reponse.Write method, you are actually destroying the old cookie and creating a new one with the same name. Doing this means that the next time you retrieve that cookie it will have the new value. Although it is read-only in the current Request object, you can still manipulate its value, but not directly.

Question: How does buffering work? Why would I use it, and what disadvantages are there to using it?

Answer: Scripts can sometimes take a while to process. Rather than have the processed contents dribble out to the user as they are processed, you can save them in a buffer on the server until they're all done. Of course, if you want the user to receive partial contents, you can use buffering, but also use the Flush method to send the currently complete results to the user. If the user has disconnected before processing is complete, you can check for that condition and use the End method to end unnecessary processing.

Question: How does caching work? Should I try to control caching?

Answer: Unfortunately, some servers are set up to cache content so they can deliver it more quickly to their users. If a user is interacting with your website, the same URL might produce a different result each time they click there. But if the server is caching, it will offer the same old page. Therefore, you should try to set caching attributes, but keep in mind that not all servers are smart enough to respect your caching settings, and it may still cause a problem.

validation scripting in the ASP script called. Now it's time to actually respond to the user. It would be easy to return the data they supplied, but how about if you return a page that lets them change the data if they desire, as well as pointing out any required fields they neglected to fill in? Here's how.

Step-by-Step

1. Open a Notepad window and write a validation routine for the e-mail field, using a conditional statement to check the incoming value of the field. You can use the Project3-1.htm file as the basis for your new file, but don't forget to save your changes with the new name in step 3.
2. If the value is null, send a message back to the user requesting that they fill in the value.
3. If the e-mail field is filled in, use a table structure (with HTML table tags) to display back to the user each value they filled in, plus the name of the field. Save the file you create as Project3-2.asp.

   Here is code similar to what you might use for these functions:

```
<%
If email = "" Then
   Response.Write("<H2>You must fill in your
 email address to submit this form</H2>")
Else
%>
<H2>Thanks!</H2>
Here is the data you filled in.
<form method="POST" action="Project1a.asp">
<table border="1" width="100%"><tr>
<td width="50%" align="right">First Name:</td>
<td width="50%">
<input type="text"
 value="<% Response.Write(fname) %>"
 name="FirstName" size="20" tabindex="1">
</td></tr><tr>
<td width="50%" align="right">Middle Initial:</td>
<td width="50%">
<input type="text"
 value="<% Response.Write(mi) %>"
 name="MI" size="20" tabindex="2">
</td></tr><tr>
<td width="50%" align="right">Last Name:</td>
<td width="50%"><input type="text"
 value="<% Response.Write(lname) %>"
 name="LastName" size="20" tabindex="3">
</td></tr><tr>
<td width="50%" align="right">Address1:</td>
```

```
<td width="50%"><input type="text"
 value="<% Response.Write(addr1) %>"
 name="Address1" size="20" tabindex="4">
</td></tr><tr>
<td width="50%" align="right">Address2:</td>
<td width="50%"><input type="text"
 value="<% Response.Write(addr2) %>"
 name="Address2" size="20" tabindex="5">
</td></tr><tr>
<td width="50%" align="right">City:</td>
<td width="50%"><input type="text"
 value="<% Response.Write(cty) %>"
 name="City" size="20" tabindex="6">
</td></tr><tr>
<td width="50%" align="right">State:</td>
<td width="50%"><input type="text"
 value="<% Response.Write(st) %>"
 name="State" size="20" tabindex="7"
></td></tr><tr>
<td width="50%" align="right">Country:</td>
<td width="50%"><input type="text"
 value="<% Response.Write(cntry) %>"
 name="Country" size="20" tabindex="8">
</td></tr><tr>
<td width="50%" align="right">Zip or Postal Code:</td>
<td width="50%"><input type="text"
 value="<% Response.Write(post) %>"
 name="PCode" size="20" tabindex="9">
</td></tr><tr>
<td width="50%" align="right">Home Phone:</td>
<td width="50%"><input type="text"
 value="<% Response.Write(hphn) %>"
 name="HomePhone" size="20" tabindex="10">
</td></tr><tr>
<td width="50%" align="right">Fax:</td>
<td width="50%"><input type="text"
 value="<% Response.Write(fphn) %>"
 name="Fax" size="20" tabindex="11">
</td></tr><tr>
<td width="50%" align="right">Pager:</td>
<td width="50%"><input type="text"
 value="<% Response.Write(pgr) %>"
 name="Pager" size="20" tabindex="12">
</td></tr><tr>
```

```
<td width="50%" align="right">Mobile Phone:</td>
<td width="50%"><input type="text"
 value="<% Response.Write(mphn) %>"
 name="Mobile" size="20" tabindex="13">
</td></tr><tr>
<td width="50%" align="right">Email Address:</td>
<td width="50%"><input type="text"
 value="<% Response.Write(email) %>"
 name="Email" size="20" tabindex="14">
</td></tr><tr>
<td width="50%" align="right">Website URL:</td>
<td width="50%"><input type="text"
 value="<% Response.Write(wURL) %>"
 name="WebsiteURL" size="20" tabindex="15">
</td></tr><tr>
<td width="50%" align="right">
<input type="submit" value="Register Now" name="B1">
</td>
<td width="50%">
<input type="reset" value="Start Over" name="B2"></td>
</tr></table></form>
<%
End If
%>
```

The ASP Server Object

The ASP Server object has a kind of catch-all role in the scheme of things. It assists with error handling, instantiating components, translating HTML tags into their proper codes for display, redirecting control, and other miscellaneous tasks. We'll discuss it here in the same fashion as the rest of the ASP objects, but first we need to lay the groundwork to make it easier to understand what the Server object does and why it is so important.

If you think about how typical application programs work, you recognize that they manage some functions and operational aspects that ordinary web pages can't. Each screen within the program may contain controls that initiate actions through what's onscreen or via menus and toolbars, and other screens within the program can directly access the values or state of those controls, dialog boxes, and menu choices when it's their turn to appear or continue your processing.

If you should call a sub-program into being, it can run within the *context* of the current screen or application program, meaning it understands what is already going on and can provide services related to your existing processing environment or state. In addition, application programs encompass error-handling capabilities that provide specialized messages (although sometimes they're not very helpful) depending on not just the error occurring but the *context* in which the error occurred.

ASP Page and Object Context

ASP contains an object called the ObjectContext object, and it is available explicitly whenever you need to reference the context of a page (to retrieve the values associated with any of the ASP objects currently in it). The benefit inherent in this kind of capability is that the object (whether it is a component of some type, a connection object, or some custom object you've instantiated) can itself remain stateless, meaning it does not have to hold its own references to the context after it finishes whatever it's doing. Instead, it can simply reference the context of a page whenever it needs to and get the latest data. The data will be unique to that page for any object created inside that page.

Note

In earlier versions of ASP the method for referencing page context was to retrieve the ScriptingContext object via the OnStartPage event, triggered when the page was executed in ASP.

On the other hand, if you instantiate objects or components outside a page (using the VBScript Set and CreateObject commands, for example) you lose page context and the isolation and scalability provided by the server. Therefore, under most circumstances it's best to use the Server.CreateObject method to instantiate objects. Here's an example:

```
Dim myObj As Object

myObj = Server.CreateObject("ProgID")
```

In ASP.NET, however, you can use another method to create objects that allows for early binding. Early binding means you can work with objects in a type-safe manner. To use early binding, you would write your code using the following syntax:

```
Dim myObj As New Object
```

Server-Side Includes

Another handy set of capabilities of IIS (and ASP) is called server-side includes. Server-side includes are directives that tell the server to perform certain actions while processing your scripts. Our first experience with one of these directives came when we were building a rather large and complex database access script. The processing had become fragmented among several sets of conditions, and it was getting difficult to make sure our conditional statements matched, even with commenting and indenting. The script was just too large.

To make it easier to read, we cut out sections of the script between conditional statements where the processing was routine and placed those sections into text files of their own. Then we inserted include directives like the following code so that the code sections would be placed in the ASP file from external files when the script was processed by the ASP engine:

```
<!-- #include file="script1.txt" -->
```

The resulting script was much easier to read and debug. As an added bonus, we could now reuse the script segment again wherever we wanted, while only having to maintain or update it in one file.

Include statements are a popular way to insert blocks of code or HTML into pages or scripts, but if you're looking for a way to simplify reading your code as you write it, Visual Studio.NET (VS.NET) includes a feature that hides unused code blocks inside an ellipsis in the Integrated Development Environment (IDE). We'll discuss the benefits of this when we use VS.NET in Module 4.

The Purpose of the Server Object

The reason there is a server object is that you need something that can perform actions for you that directly affect the server and its operating environment. The following property (only one property is available) and methods (seven of them) are designed to give you the control you need on the server side:

- **The ScriptTimeout property** Can set or return the number of seconds a page can be processed before an error is generated.
- **The CreateObject("identifier") method** Creates an instance of an object, which can be an application, a scripting object, or a component.
- **The Execute("url") method** Halts the current page's execution and executes another page, after which execution on the current page is resumed.
- **The Transfer("url") method** New in ASP 3.0, this method works like the Execute method (stopping execution of the current page and transferring execution to another page) but does not return control to the current page after the new page executes.
- **The MapPath("url") method** Returns the physical path and filename of a file or resource.
- **The HTMLEncode("string") method** Converts a string of HTML characters from ordinary characters to special characters (converts "<" to "<", for example).
- **The URLEncode("string") method** Converts a string of characters making up a URL from nonlegal characters such as "?" and " " to legal characters such as "%3F" and "+".
- **The GetLastError() method** Returns details of the last error that occurred via the ASPError object.

The ScriptTimeout Property

Among the things you want to be able to control at the server is the processing time allocated to each script. As a programmer, you are undoubtedly aware that poor programming can produce endless loops or even just excessive processing time. When you are hosting many scripts, and especially when many developers may be creating those scripts, it is important to have some kind of default timeout to halt execution and return an error message. This is the function of the ScriptTimeout property. The default is set at 90 seconds, but you can use the ScriptTimeout property to exceed that if you wish. And if you create a buggy script, the timeout will at least prevent it from running on forever.

How long does it take to process a given script? Perhaps a better question would be is the time it takes to process a script fixed and determinable, does it always fall within a certain range, or is it highly variable or even random? The answer, of course, is that your scripts will not always take exactly the same time to process (because the processing time depends partly upon the current load on the server and its resources), but they should fall within a fairly predictable range. And if they routinely exceed a reasonable amount of time, you should investigate creating faster-running components to handle some of the load.

But suppose you want to run a script beyond the default 90 seconds allowed by the server for ASP scripts? The ScriptTimeout property can be modified to enable scripts to run past the default. We've set scripts to run for as long as 15 minutes for testing purposes, but longer than that is not advisable. For one thing, you'll run into timeout functions in browsers or intermediate servers, which can be just as bad.

In any case, here is a simple bit of code that sets the processing time for a script to five minutes:

```
<% ScriptTimeout = 300 %>
```

If you use this in a script, the script will keep processing until it is done or until it hits the five-minute mark, and then generate an error message. We've found this useful when we wanted to verify that processing was producing the correct results, even when the script runs beyond the default limit. However, if your script tends to run beyond the default limit, you really need to investigate other ways of performing the processing, because even 90 seconds is an awfully long time to keep your users waiting. And by the way, even if you set processing for 10 or 15 minutes, you run the risk of the user's connection timing out.

The CreateObject Method

You can use the CreateObject method to create instances of objects within your ASP scripts, and these objects include applications (such as Excel and other Office applications), components (such as page counters, ad rotators, content rotators, and so forth), and scripting objects (such as dictionaries, file objects, and so on). Some of these components (which will be covered in more detail in Module 6) provide the capability of persisting values beyond the scope of a session or application, even saving data in separate files on the server for use at any time.

The Page Counter Component To demonstrate how object creation works, you'll create an instance of the Page Counter component. The Page Counter component counts the number of times a particular page is requested, and it saves that data in a text file on the server. Use code like the following to create an instance of the Page Counter in ASP:

```
<% Set objPageCounter =
 Server.CreateObject("MSWC.PageCounter") %>
```


Once you've created an instance of the Page Counter component, it's time to do something with it. The Page Counter component includes several methods to set the hit count, increment the hit count, and return the current hit count. They are as follows:

- **Reset()** This method sets the hit count to zero for the current page, or you can include the path to another page to set that page's hit count to zero.
- **PageHit()** This method increments the hit count for the current page.
- **Hits()** This method returns the hit count for the current page, or for another page if you include the other page's path.

In practice, if you want to use this component to track visitors to a particular page, you could use ASP code such as this (after creating the object):

```
<%
objPageCounter.PageHit()
vHits = objPageCounter.Hits()
Response.Write "You are visitor number " & vHits & "."
%>
```

The Execute and Transfer Methods

The Execute and Transfer methods allow you to do something that was impossible with earlier versions of ASP, namely, transfer control and execution from one page to another without having to use the Response.Redirect method. The big benefit is that it is totally up to you, on the server side, how you want to accomplish the transfer, and you don't have to go back to the user's browser and force it to another page to get the job done.

Tip

While Execute and Transfer are exciting and long-awaited methods, keep in mind that they don't work on previous versions. If you are using ASP 2.0 and IIS 4.0 or earlier, make sure you use the Response.Redirect method.

When you use the Execute method to transfer control to another page, execution on the current page stops and execution on the new page begins. The new page has control until execution finishes, at which time control passes back to the calling page. When you use the Transfer method, execution on the current page stops and control passes to the new page. When execution on the new page finishes, that's it. There is no further reference to the calling page unless you specifically include it (perhaps using another Transfer call).

Another big benefit of using the Execute and Transfer methods is that the page context is transferred as well. All the variables that are available from the calling page are also available within the new page, and the browser doesn't even recognize that it's working with a new page. The called pages work exactly the same as the calling pages, from the point of view of the browser.

To show how this works, let's build a few pages that transfer control back and forth a few times, while retaining the values passed to the first page by a form. Start by creating a simple form with code like this:

```
<HTML><HEAD><TITLE>Using Execute and Transfer</TITLE></HEAD>
<BODY>
<FORM METHOD=POST ACTION="index2.asp">
Enter Your Name:<INPUT TYPE="text" NAME="yourname" SIZE=20>
<INPUT TYPE="submit" VALUE="Execute and Transfer">
<INPUT TYPE="reset" VALUE="Clear">
</FORM>
</BODY></HTML>
```

Next, you'll create three scripts; one for processing the submission and two more for demonstrating the Execute and Transfer methods, respectively. For processing the submission, make a file named index2.asp, using ASP code like the following:

```
<%
vName = Request.Form("yourname")
Response.Write("Here is your original submission
 of your name: " & vName & "<P>")
Server.Execute("index2a.asp")
Server.Transfer("index2b.asp")
%>
```

This code writes back the original submission and then sends execution to the file named index2a.asp. Index2a.asp is going to again write back the original submission (even though it is another page it still has access to the original submission data in the Request.Form collection) and then return control to the calling page (index2.asp). Index2a.asp has ASP code that looks like this:

```
<%
vNamea = Request.Form("yourname")
Response.Write("This is the second page to be
executed, and here is your original submission
 of your name again: " & vNamea & "<P>")
%>
```

Notice that after index2a.asp gets done executing, it automatically returns to index2.asp at the point where it left off, and then processes the next command in line, namely the Transfer call to index2b.asp. Index2b.asp then writes back the originally submitted data and when it's done, execution dies right there. Index2b.asp looks like this in ASP code:

```
<%
vNameb = Request.Form("yourname")
Response.Write("This is the third page
 to be executed using the Transfer method
 and after showing your name here execution
 will stop: " & vNameb & "<P>")
%>
```

The MapPath Method

Files inside an ASP application (the default virtual application) can be accessed by their virtual path or URL. Sometimes, though, you need to access files by their real (actual or physical) path. The MapPath method lets you get the physical path to a file from the server, and this in turn lets you do things like read and write files (using the proper built-in objects, of course). You're probably not anxious to learn how to write files all over your server, but there are times when it is not only convenient but necessary.

For example, suppose you want to keep a set of text files related to your website outside the website itself, in a folder called WebsiteContentFiles. You might want to do this to keep them inaccessible to anyone who might try to guess their names, while making them accessible to properly authorized users via a URL (such as **http://mycomputer/webcontent**). At the same time, you might want to be able to resolve the correct physical path to them for your own management purposes. If so, you can use ASP code like the following to retrieve the physical path from the URL:

```
<%
vFilePath = "mycomputer/webcontent/webfile.htm"
Response.Write(Server.MapPath(vFilePath))
%>
```

The Response.Write method in the code just listed will display the physical path and filename of the file referenced by its URL. We'll put together a more elaborate and useful example when we get into Module 6 and begin using the FileSystemObject object and its colleagues.

The HTMLEncode Method

If you've ever written a web page about coding HTML, you may have noticed that the code to produce the greater-than and less-than signs for display in a browser does not consist simply of the intended character, but rather a special character. Special characters direct the browser to display the correct character on screen, instead of interpreting the character as the beginning of a new HTML tag.

For example, suppose you wanted to display the leading HTML tag in a page, the <HTML> tag. You would use special characters to make the browser display the greater-than and less-than signs onscreen (like this: <HTML>). Notice the use of the ampersand to start special characters and the use of the semicolon to end them.

Converting HTML Characters Sometimes, when inserting data in the output stream, you want to display characters for HTML tags instead of letting the browser interpret them, and that is where the HTMLEncode method comes into play. Suppose that you've set up a dictionary of HTML tags, and the person retrieving them can search by function to find the appropriate tag. You would want your output to consist of properly displayed HTML tags and not have the browser interpret them. You might use code such as the following to produce this result (assume you've created a search form in HTML that points to the following ASP script segment):

```
<%
vSearchFunctionText = Request.Form("searchentryfield")
%>
```

The code could then use the variable as a parameter to search your dictionary (a database) for the appropriate tag or tags. Next, you would have to include some code to process the database output and return properly encoded HTML tags for display in the browser. Getting data from a database will be covered in later modules, so assume a variable named vDatabaseOutput has been assigned a value from one of the records in the database. Subsequent code might look like this:

```
<%
Response.Write("The tag for that function is" & Server.HTMLEncode(vDatabaseOutput))
%>
```

The URLEncode Method

Another encoding situation you might encounter (and perhaps more frequently than encoding HTML for display, depending upon your line of work) is encoding URLs. These days, URLs can include some characters that are not legal within HTTP, such as spaces, exclamation point, ampersands, and so on. Using the URLEncode method on a string representing a URL will remove nonlegal characters from the string and replace them with compliant characters. For example, suppose you want to place a link in your web page that references another page whose name contains a space. Perhaps the link reads **www.e4free. com/another page.htm**. You can't send this as is because the space will not be properly recognized. In this case, you could use the URLEncode method to properly encode the URL with a plus sign instead of the space. Let's examine some code to see how you would perform this conversion:

```
 <A HREF="
<% Server.URLEncode("http://www.e4free.com/
otherpage.htm") %>
">Click here to go to another page</A>
```

As you can see, this method works in a pretty straightforward way, and the output to the server from such a link would look like this:

```
http%3A%2F%2Fwww%2Ee4free%2Ecom%2Fanother+page%2Ehtm
```

At this point, you might be asking what these percent signs and numbers are that have replaced the nonlegal characters in the URL. The percent sign is an escape character. Nonlegal characters are represented by the percent sign followed by a hexadecimal number corresponding to the ANSI number of the nonlegal character. For example, if you have an exclamation point in your URL and you use Server. URLEncode to encode it, it will be converted to %21. You can find lists and further discussion of allowed and nonlegal characters at **www.ietf.org/rfc/rfc2396.txt**, or look for a discussion of HTTP 1.1 at **www.w3.org**.

The ASPError Object

The process of creating ASP applications inevitably involves errors, so naturally there are error handling features built into ASP. The Server object has a method called GetLastError, and it provides fairly detailed information about errors encountered while processing your scripts. It works by creating and returning a reference to an object named the ASPError object.

The ASPError object has nine properties, outlined here:

- **ASPCode** This property is an integer value for the error number generated by ASP.
- **ASPDescription** This property is a string value providing a description of the error.
- **Category** This property is a string value showing the source of the error.
- **Column** This property is an integer value for the character position within the file that generated the error.
- **Description** This property is a string value consisting of a short description of the error.
- **File** This property is a string value giving the name of the file that was being processed when the error occurred.
- **Line** This property is an integer value for the line number within the file that generated the error.
- **Number** This property is a number value that shows the standard COM error code.
- **Source** This property is a string value returning the actual code that caused the error, if it is available.

IIS Error Handling

Trapping errors and generating error-specific feedback in response to them takes a little beforehand work on your part, due to the way ASP and IIS errors are processed at the server. I'm sure you recall the familiar "404 File Not Found" error message. Obviously, this message is displayed by the server when the page a user requested is not found, but the way this works may not be so obvious.

In fact, there are static HTML pages stored on the server that are mapped to each error status code returned, 404 being one of them. You can find them if you go to the folder WINNT/Help/iishelp/common (there are quite a few other interesting HTML pages stored here as well; you might want to take a minute or two and review them while you're there). Most of them (and all of the status code error pages) can be located and opened in your browser, as Figures 3-3 and 3-4 show.

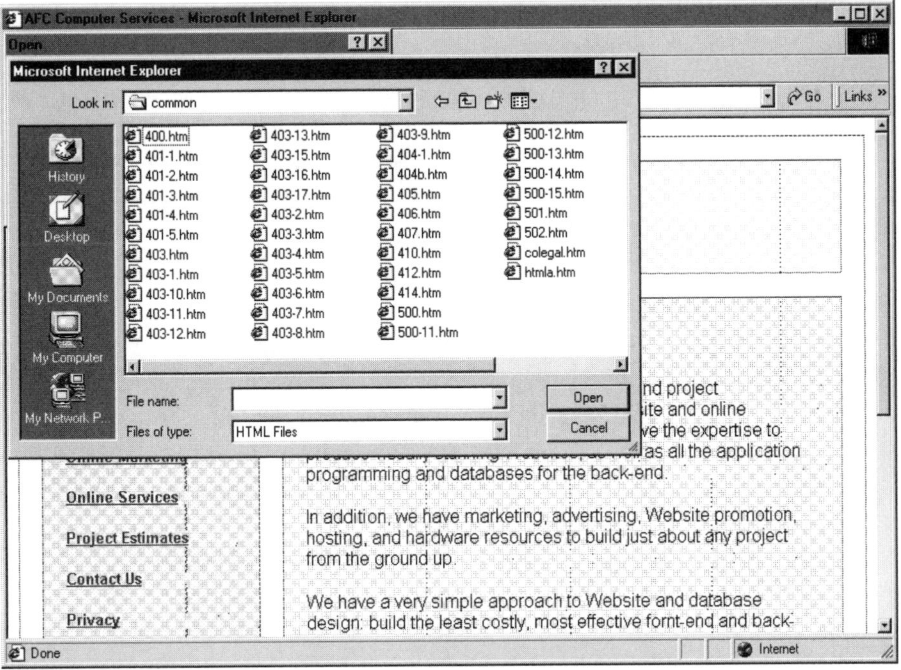

Figure 3-3 Finding error pages in Internet Explorer

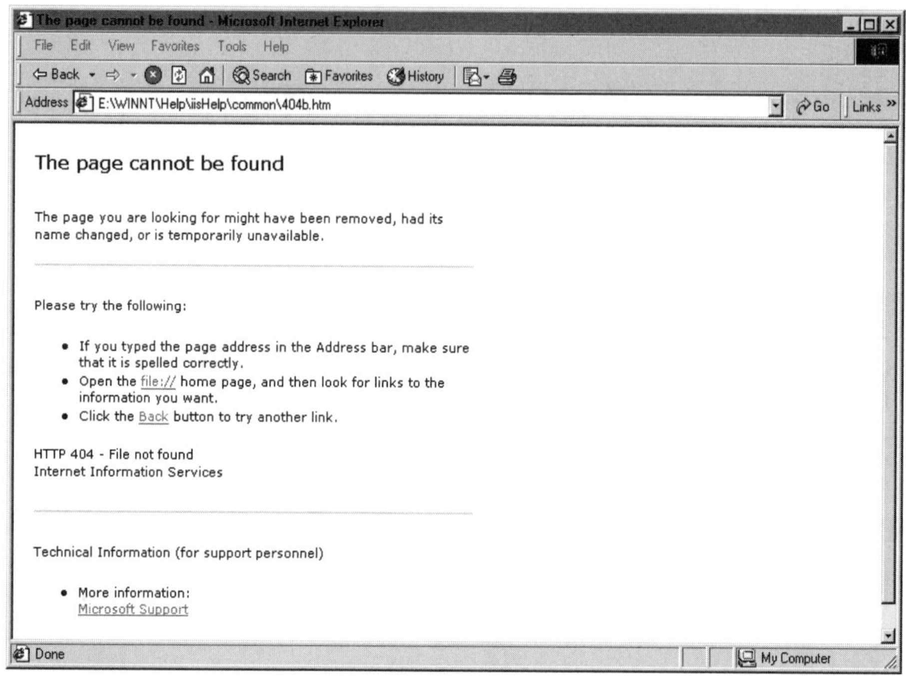

Figure 3-4 Opening the 404 File Not Found page

The 404b.htm file is depicted in Figure 3-4. This page opens automatically whenever IIS encounters this particular error, and because it is a plain HTML page you can customize it to your heart's content. Many website hosting companies and ISPs customize these with company logos and custom messages, and truthfully some of these custom error pages provide better customer service in the form of more reassuring or understandable messages.

But these status codes do not become active when an ASP error occurs, except for the 500;100 error code. This code is mapped to a URL rather than a file, and the default file there is named 500-100.asp. Notice the .asp extension. This is an ASP script, and you can replace this mapping with another pointing to a custom-made file of your own.

The really exciting part of this mechanism, however, is the fact the way this mapping works. When an ASP error occurs, the file tied to the 500;100 error is activated and it receives the entire context (references to all variables) and a reference to the ASPError object *from the page where the error occurred.*

Note

ASP error file mapping can be set for your entire application or individually by folder within an application. You can set specific messages for any part of your application or a single set of messages for the entire thing.

Remapping the 500;100 File To change the mapping of the 500;100 file, you need to use the Internet Services Manager. Open it up and find the website folder you want to change mappings for. Select that folder and then open the Properties dialog box with the Custom Errors tab showing, as in Figure 3-5.

Find and select the existing 500;100 HTTP Error, then click the Edit Properties button. The Error Mapping Properties dialog box will appear (see Figure 3-6). Also shown in Figure 3-6 is the new URL you mapped this HTTP Error to, in this example /ASPFTGU/CH04/AnError/CustomError500-100.asp.

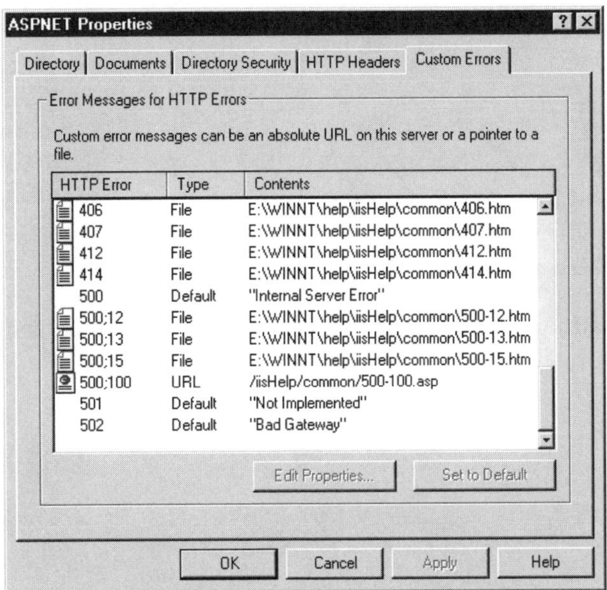

Figure 3-5 The Properties dialog box on the Custom Errors tab

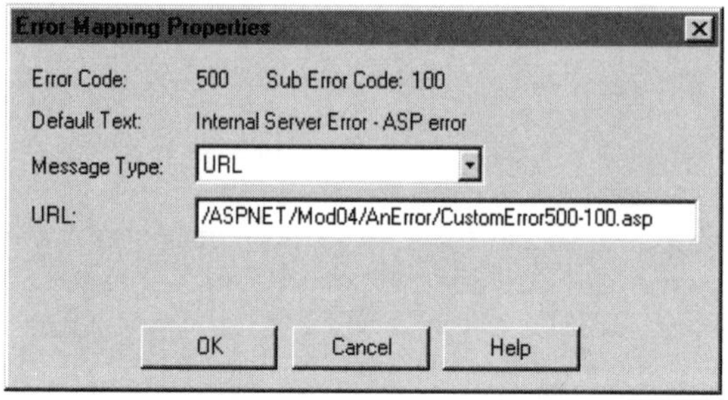

Figure 3-6 The Error Mapping Properties dialog box

Now you can place a customized error trapping script in this folder and it will be activated whenever an ASP error is generated (but only for this folder).

Trapping Errors

Now that you've set up a folder in your website for error handling, you can put a page in there to generate errors and demonstrate how they are trapped and handled. Start by making an HTML page as follows:

```
<HTML><HEAD><TITLE>Custom ASP Error Page</TITLE>
</HEAD>
<BODY BGCOLOR="white" Text="black">
Click <A HREF="errormaker2.asp">here</A>
 to generate an error.
</BODY></HTML>
```

Next, build an ASP script page that contains some broken code to trigger an error when you reference it from your hyperlink. The code in it looks like this:

```
<HTML><HEAD><TITLE>Custom ASP Error Page</TITLE>
</HEAD>
<BODY BGCOLOR="white" Text="black">
<%
Response.Send "This makes an error"
%>
</BODY></HTML>
```

Since there is no collection, property, or method named Send for the Response object, this code generates an ASP error in the 500 group, with a subgroup of 100. When this error occurs it is mapped to the 500;100 error message and control is then transferred to the custom error script you've specified in the Internet Services Manager on the server.

Note

As it mentions in the IIS help files, Internet Explorer 5.0 will replace your custom error message with its own default message if your message is less than a certain file size. Make sure your custom error script is over 512 bytes, or it will not appear in the browser.

Mastery Check

1. What are variables?

   A. Variables are temporary names for objects you have created, such as the Response object.

   B. Variables are placeholders for data that can vary as an application executes.

   C. Variables are data that varies during program execution.

   D. Variables are *x*, *t*, and *z* only.

   E. None of the above.

2. What are VB.NET data types, and how are they related to variables?

   A. The term *data type* refers to the kind of data represented within a variable, such as String, Date, Number, and so forth. VB.NET data types have names assigned to them that may not be the same as the names assigned to data types in other languages.

   B. Data types are special names for variables, such as String, Date, Decimal, and so forth.

   C. Data types are optional in VB.NET and are only applied to variables that contain more than one type of data.

   D. All of the above.

   E. None of the above.

3. Operators are programming language symbols that perform operations on variable values (or hard-coded values). The arithmetical operators include _____ to perform addition and _____ to perform subtraction. The _____ operator can also be used to concatenate strings as well as perform addition.

4. Describe how the logical operator *And* works.

   ____

   ____

Mastery Check

5. Suppose you have an And operation in which the first expression is True and the second expression is False. What answer would be produced, and what would the data type of the answer be?

   A. The answer would be True, and the data type would be Byte.

   B. The answer would be False, and the data type would be Char.

   C. The answer would be True, and the data type would be Logical.

   D. The answer would be False, and the data type would be Boolean.

   E. None of the above.

6. When you write "Request.Form("fieldname")," what does the word *Form* represent?

   A. A built-in ASP object

   B. A method of the Request object

   C. A collection of the Request object

   D. A property of the Request object

   E. All of the above

7. What object collection could you retrieve to get a cookie from the user?

   A. Request.ServerVariables("HTTP_COOKIE")

   B. Request.Cookie

   C. Both of the above

   D. Neither

8. HTML/XHTML forms are often used to collect values from the user. The ________ attribute in the ________ element contains the information necessary to tell the browser where to send the form contents.

Mastery Check

9. Describe the relationship between the Request object and the Response object and how they are used with forms to create interactivity.

____

____

10. What are properties and methods?

    A. A property is like a piece of real estate on the screen, and a method is how that property is accessed in your code.

    B. Properties and methods apply to ASP scripts, but not to VB.NET applications.

    C. Properties and methods are things that objects have. Properties are values assigned to objects, while methods are functions that can be performed with or on an object's data.

    D. All of the above.

11. What program structure would be useful for looping through a set of items in a collection?

    A. The For…Each…Next loop

    B. A Select…Case block

    C. An If…End If block

    D. The Do…Until loop

    E. All of the above

12. What does a cookie do?

____

____

13. A server-side include file makes it easy to include the same code in multiple pages. An include file would be written with the _______ directive.

Mastery Check

14. Describe how you could write code so that if processing is taking too long you could keep the processing going until it was done and then return control to the user.

____

____

15. What does the CreateObject method of the Server object do?

A. Objects are made from classes in VB.NET or are already built-in to ASP. When the CreateObject method is run, an instance of the object is created and that instance can be filled with data or otherwise used in any way its programming calls for.

B. Before you can make objects appear onscreen, you must create classes for those objects, and the CreateObject method runs a wizard that automatically creates those classes.

C. Only the server can create objects, and that is the purpose of the CreateObject method. All objects running on the server are created using the CreateObject method, from which all classes are derived.

D. None of the above

Module 4

Web Forms and ASP.NET

The Goals of This Module

- Learn the ASP.NET interaction model
- Learn how events and the DOM work
- Review the fundamentals of user-interface design
- Examine event-based application design
- Learn about the Web Forms code model
- Practice using an IDE (VS.NET)
- Build several simple Web Forms
- Build a validation routine for a Web Form

While ASP is useful for developing interactive web applications, ASP.NET takes application development to the next level, with all the tools and capabilities necessary to build complete applications, regardless of whether they are Web based or not. The built-in ASP components are useful, but an entire interactive model called Web Forms has been developed by Microsoft to support the user interface. Web Forms encompasses the built-in ASP objects and adds quite a few more objects and capabilities for total application control.

In this module we will demonstrate project building using Visual Studio.NET (VS.NET), and show the basics of building an application using Web Forms, ASP.NET, and VB.NET. Our use of ASP code examples will continue to diminish, except where it is necessary for backwards compatibility.

Web Forms

Web Forms is the name Microsoft gives to specially designed ASP.NET HTML pages that include forms and the back-end processing that supports them. They use common ASP techniques plus added capabilities to make a coherent framework for web applications. Users can use the forms to interact with your application, and the back-end processing can provide the appropriate outputs to the user. Ordinary static HTML web pages may still be useful for much of the content displayed on your site that doesn't change much.

Programming Web Forms

Web Forms, on the other hand, are a programmable interface, with objects, properties, and events at your disposal. If you've ever done any work with applications such as Microsoft Access or any of the Visual programming languages, you've probably seen the capabilities we're referring to here. For example, in Microsoft Access 97 and 2000, to create a database application you create the tables, queries, forms, and reports that make up the application, and also special forms that serve as navigational aids for the user (essentially, the user interface). In design mode, you create forms, add controls to access data within tables/queries, and add command buttons for specific functions. If you right-click a button you've added and open up its properties box, you can attach code to events, so that when the button is clicked its onclick event is activated and the code you've entered runs. This visual programming paradigm is very popular, and Microsoft has made every effort to bring it to web application programming, although some of the fundamentals are new and different.

The Stateless Nature of the Web

As we'll discuss further in Module 5, the Web is *stateless*. What this means is that there is no preservation of variable values or the current state of a web page when request and responses to and from the web server are made. Naturally this makes it difficult to interact properly with users, and many methods around this problem have been developed, some of which work quite well. Web Forms allow developers access to some methods that preserve values in controls, and ASP.NET contains objects especially designed to provide control for management of state as individual user sessions and as overall applications. Together, these capabilities make it possible to develop web applications with as much flexibility as ordinary desktop applications.

Web Forms Capabilities

The front-end Web Forms pages are made from HTML just like any other pages, so they can be created to run properly on any browser or made browser-specific if you want to use features of a particular browser (such as Internet Explorer). The workings of a Web Form can be programmed in any CLR-supported language (we will use VB.NET) and will run quickly because they are compiled.

Web Forms Structure

Web Forms consist of the front-end *page* (a file ending in .aspx with HTML and connector code that makes up what is displayed to the user) and back-end logic that responds to user inputs. The interesting thing is that the back-end code can be part of the page file (activated only when the user makes a response) or in separate files altogether, known as *code-behind* files.

The Web Forms Code Model

A model, in this context, means a way of thinking about how various parts of the whole work together. The Web Forms code model breaks the overall functionality of the application into two major portions, display and data processing. Display occurs when a web page is first requested, although some processing may occur to decide what version of the page to display for the client (browser) in use. Processing occurs when some kind of input has been offered by the client other than another page request, and the application must perform some functions before again returning the appropriate display.

Although it's easy to mix display code (usually HTML) with processing code (ASP, VBScript, VB.NET, SQL, and so forth) and this model was followed in many ASP scripts and applications you'll run across, it's really best to make the effort to separate the two kinds of code from each other. Otherwise, it will be much harder to reuse code for other purposes, and it will be much harder to debug and modify effectively.

The Class File If you store your code separately, it will be in a processing code file, also known as the code-behind file we spoke of. Still, the display code file (an .aspx file) and the processing code file (perhaps .aspx.vb if you are using VB.NET) form a single unit for the server to work with, in the form of a page class file. ASP.NET dynamically creates a new class based on the display and processing code, and then compiles it. This new class is based on the ASP.NET page class but is extended by the controls and processing code you've added. When the page is requested, it works like a little executable program that simply outputs HTML. Although you create it like a traditional HTML page and ASP script, it becomes a compiled, executable program on the server.

1-Minute Drill

- What are the two main parts of the Web Forms code model?
- What happens to your Web Forms files when they are compiled?

Web Forms Processing

We've already discussed how ordinary web pages work with the server to perform normal website functions. A user may request a page (or otherwise interact with the web server) by entering a URL in the address area of the browser and pressing Enter, by clicking a link, or by clicking the submit button on a form. In each case, a request is sent to the server, and the server responds by either outputting web pages directly, or by passing the content of the request to a program, and then the program performs whatever processing is required

---

- The HTML web page file on the front end and the file containing the programming on the back end.
- They are used to create a new class derived from the Page class.

and still outputs web pages. Each time a request/response cycle happens, it is called a *round trip*.

Round trips not only take a fair amount of time, they also place a load on the server and eliminate information from the last request/response cycle. Unfortunately, while things such as validating data entered by a user into a form can often be done on the browser with JavaScript, the only way to get a fresh look at data in a database or perform some types of processing is to make a round trip to the server. Therefore, minimizing round trips is a common objective during your design. That said, with generally faster connection speeds, more powerful servers, and technologies such as ASP.NET, the disadvantages are rapidly dwindling as the need for application-like behavior increases.

Minimizing Round Trips

On many occasions a single access to a database can provide enough data (in the form of a recordset) for a user's needs at a given point in application use. Through data-binding, the status of any data in a recordset, as well as changes made by the user, can be maintained while avoiding excessive trips to the server and connections to the database. Another way Web Forms helps minimize round trips is that the available server controls only change state or raiser events in response to explicit user actions. For example, it would be wasteful to cause a trip to the server to activate a drop-down menu each time the user runs the mouse over an area on the menu but does not actually click the menu choice.

Web Forms Viewstate The current status of a Web Forms page and its controls is called the *viewstate*. This means all the choices the user has made, all the data the user has entered, and so forth. The Web Forms framework saves this information with each round trip so that it can be faithfully recreated upon each round trip, sparing you lots of hard programming work explicitly saving these details.

Web Forms and Events

Most programmers and programming languages are evolving towards the object-oriented programming (OOP) paradigm; the new edition of Visual Basic (VB.NET) is just one example. Part of the reason for this is the ability of objects to trigger events when their state changes or when external actions affect them. One of the easiest interactions to understand between object and events is the onclick event that occurs when a user clicks a button on a form. Clicking the button activates the onclick event, which in turn can then pass the event to another object, run some code, or both. Events can, of course, also be completely ignored, conditionally processed, and so forth. This mechanism is extremely useful in modern programming because you never know what the user might click or do next, or what might happen on the Internet that affects your web application. For example, if you are running a sweepstakes, you want to notify the user when the entry deadline has passed, even if they haven't completed their entry form, so they can't enter after a certain point.

Ordinary HTML Events

Ordinary web pages are made from HTML or XHTML, both of which include the Document Object Model (DOM). The DOM is another model, and it represents a particular way of thinking about web pages and the objects on them. As we mentioned in our short discussion of HTML/XHTML, the tags that make up objects on a web page (such as the <IMG> tag) create *elements* (in this case an image on a web page) when rendered, and the parts inside an HTML element (such as the name or ID) are called *attributes*. These are equivalent in the DOM to objects, so that an image on a web page can be thought of as an object in its own right. The attributes of an element are equivalent to the properties of an object, and the intrinsic events of an HTML element are the same as the events to which those objects respond.

The DOM sets up a hierarchy of objects on a web page. The window in which the page is displayed is the top level or parent object, and the page itself is the next lower level, while a form (if present) would be the next lower level, and a control on the form would be the next lower level, and so forth. Lower level objects are called child objects, and higher level objects are called parent objects (they are parents of their own children and children of their parent objects).

The DOM is only a model; to implement it requires that programmed support for the intrinsic events be built into browsers displaying web pages. Fortunately, such support is built into many versions of Internet Explorer and Netscape Navigator. One example of this support is your ability to write scripts that dynamically change the properties of objects displayed on the page (the page is called the document object in the DOM).

Suppose you want to change the background color of the page in response to the user placing the mouse over a certain image. You could write a JavaScript function such as the following to perform this action:

```
<html>
<head>
<title>Untitled Document</title>
<meta http-equiv="Content-Type" content="text/html;
 charset=iso-8859-1">
<script language="JavaScript">
function changecolor() {
document.bgColor = "#FF0000"
}
</script>
</head>
<body bgcolor="#FFFFFF">
<img src="Back8.png" width="80" height="30"
 onmouseover="changecolor()">
</body>
</html>
```


This combination of script and HTML takes advantage of the onmouseover event associated with the image element. When the event is triggered, the function will run, in this case changing the background color of the document (page) object. Remember, the background color is an attribute of the BODY element, and as such it can be changed as a property of the BODY object in the DOM.

There are a number of events that occur on ordinary web pages (onmouseover, onclick, onload, and so forth), and the DOM provides what is called an *event flow architecture* for them. Events in the DOM start at the top level object, flow down to the object where the event actually occurred, and then flow back up to the top. During this flow the events may be captured, bubbled, or cancelled according to your programming. The reason for this expanded architecture is to allow developers the greatest amount of programming flexibility. More information can be found at the World Wide Web Consortium's site (**www.w3.org**) under the heading DOM Level 2.

Web Forms Events

You have access to all the objects and events associated with ordinary HTML forms and controls when you use Web Forms, of course, but there are some additional processing steps and events at your disposal as well. The primary difference is that the Web Forms framework uses these objects and events just a little differently, and they require a round trip to the browser, rather than occurring exclusively on the browser. Although they require a bit more overhead to perform, they perform many valuable functions that make your web applications work more like desktop applications. For example, you can create your own event-handling methods that are activated and run on the server whenever a particular event is triggered. Often, events will be triggered explicitly as part of the user interaction coded into prebuilt server controls that you can simply drag and drop into your Web Forms when using VS.NET, much the same way you would when using a Visual programming tool. This eases the programming burden considerably.

Like any system of events, there is a particular flow during which events take place automatically. When a page is loaded, the onload event occurs for the document object, and any code attached to it runs. This happens regardless of what the user does. The Web Forms Page model also includes events that occur automatically, but back at the server. For example, the pageload event happens when the page is loaded, and it may check to see whether the page is being loaded for the first time, set the configuration of all controls on the page (including whatever changes the user made the last time around), and perform data binding as necessary. Once everything is properly set, the Web Form is transmitted to the user.

Creating Web Forms Event Handlers

To work with events programmatically, meaning to capture events and process your own code in response to the events' action, you may need to build event-handling methods and bind events to them. Your first step toward doing this is to find out the name or names of the events that are supported (that is, are intrinsic to) the server controls you are using to raise the events, such as buttons, input boxes, check boxes, and so forth). You also need to use the correct signature for the event to be handled. While many events have the same signature, some require a specific event-handling class.

Coding Event-Handling Methods

Server controls, as the name implies, run on the server. They have their own name (actually, the ID attribute is used, as it is always unique), and they are coded in a similar fashion to ordinary HTML form controls. You can connect their intrinsic events to methods using much the same syntax, such as the following:

```
<asp:Button id="MyButton" runat="SERVER"
 OnClick="TheMethod" />
```

To make it work properly, you'll have to use a signature such as this:

```
Private Sub TheMethod(ByVal sender As Object,
 ByVal e as EventArgs)
```

Next, you could write code that creates the event-handling method. This code is just like any other code but is called an event handle because it runs in response to the event being raised. You might write something such as the following as your method:


```
<%@ Page Language="VB" %>
<%@ Import Namespace="System.Collections" %>
<HTML>
<HEAD>
<SCRIPT RUNAT="SERVER">
Protected Sub MyButton_Click(Source As Object, e As EventArgs)
MyLabel.Text = "OnClick Event has been activated"
End Sub
</SCRIPT>
</HEAD>
<BODY>
<FORM RUNAT=SERVER>
<asp:Button id=MyButton runat="server"
Text="Activate Event"
onclick="MyButton_Click" />
<br />
<asp:Label id=MyLabel runat=server />
</FORM>
</BODY>
</HTML>
```

Ask the Expert

Question: We seem to be taking a big step away from hand-coding web pages and forms for user interactions. How much of the traditional ASP is left, and where is ASP.NET taking us?

Answer: The original ASP provides many capabilities on the back end to assist with the processing of forms, the main user interaction in many web applications. ASP.NET takes this a large step further down the road, not only compiling the forms and back-end processing into a class file, but also providing many new tools and controls to make the job of programming web applications easier.

For example, the inclusion of validation controls makes it much easier to perform common validation functions, rather than having to rely on JavaScript on the client side. Although client-side operations take less time and processing overhead (for the server), it is a sad fact that in order to properly secure your applications, validation must be done on the server side as well to prevent malicious users from jamming up your application with inappropriate or lengthy data streams.

Because so many tools and templates for building web applications are already in VS.NET and because the tools make it easy to work in a visual mode already familiar to many designers, using VS.NET will only become more and more desirable.

Building Interactive Applications with VS.NET

We've discussed installing VS.NET in Module 1, so for this exercise we'll start VS.NET and proceed from there. When we reach Project 4-1, we'll build a Web Form step-by-step, but before we do we'll discuss the user interface and tools available in VS.NET so you'll be comfortable with them. When you start VS.NET initially, you should see a screen resembling the one shown in Figure 4-1.

Solutions and Projects in VS.NET

As you've seen, an application consists of more than just a single file full of code; oftentimes there are files for displaying data, files for processing data, files holding references to databases, and so forth. To use VS.NET effectively, one of the first steps you'll perform is to create a container for all the files, folders, references, and other resources that make up your overall solution to the problem at hand. VS.NET offers two types of containers: solutions and projects. A solution typically contains one or more projects, and the projects contain files, folders, and references (called items) supporting a particular part of the overall application. In addition, a solution may contain items called miscellaneous files that are not relevant to any particular project or that must be available to several projects across the solution.

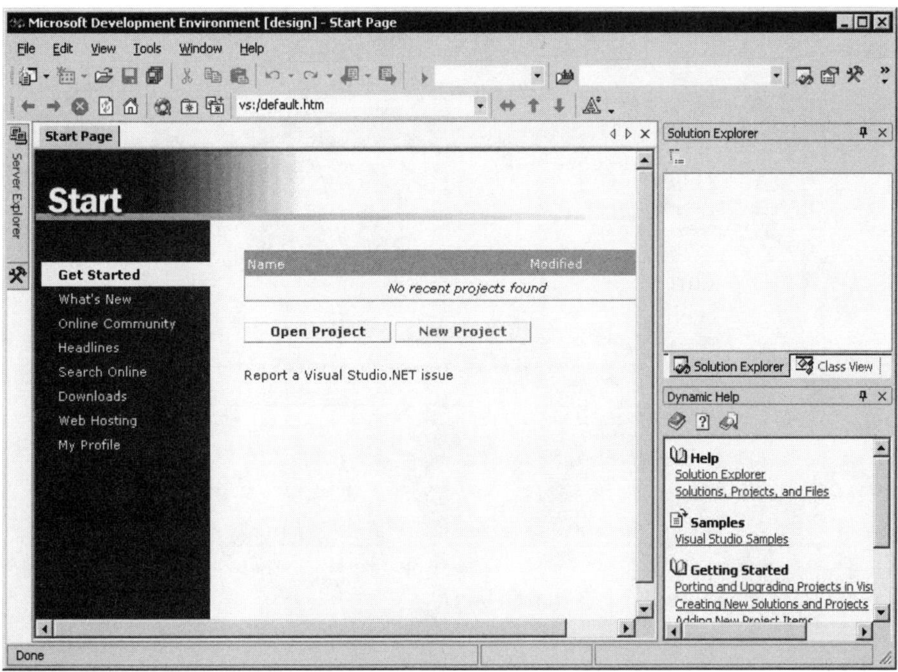

Figure 4-1 The opening screen of VS.NET

Web projects maintain actual files in a physical directory on the development machine (published later to the production server, if you are going live with the application). The directory in which the files are kept is referred to as the project directory.

Creating Solutions

To create a new solution, you create a new project, and doing so automatically creates a new solution container to hold the project. Click File | New | Project to open the New Project dialog box (Figure 4-2). In the Project Types box on the left, choose Visual Studio Solutions, name your solution ReminderForm (Figure 4-3), and click OK to save it in the default location. When you finish, you'll see the ReminderForm solution in the Solution Explorer pane in VS.NET, with the note (0 projects) attached to it. Obviously, there are no projects or items inside the solution yet.

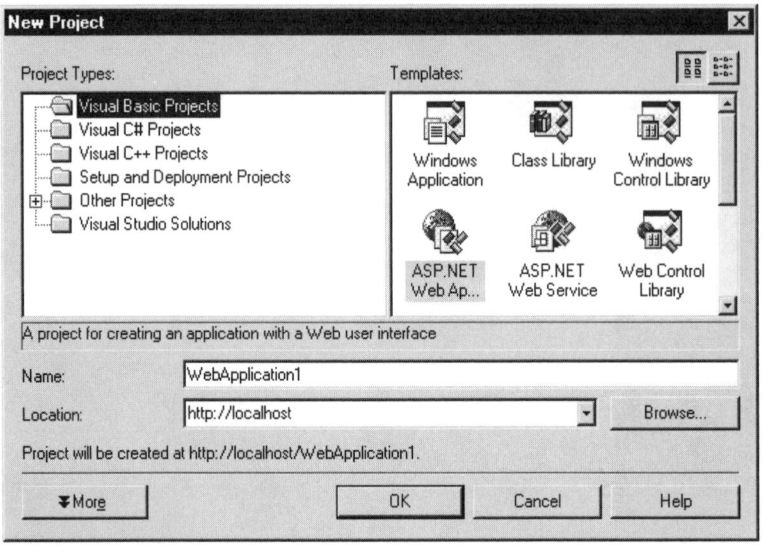

Figure 4-2 The New Project dialog box

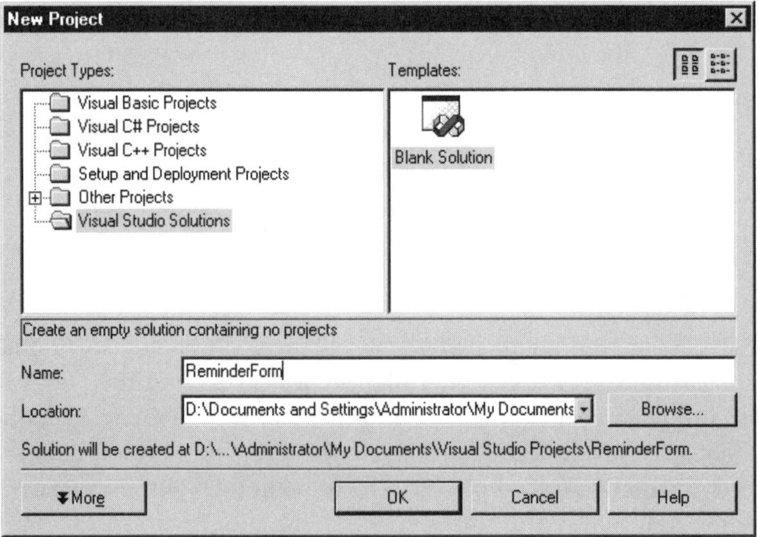

Figure 4-3 Saving the new solution

Creating Projects

To create a project to go into the solution you just created, you can either right-click the solution and choose Add | New Project, or go to the File menu and choose Add Project | New Project. When the New Project dialog box opens, make sure Visual Basic Projects is selected on the left side under Project Types, and choose ASP.NET Web Application from the Templates section on the right. Name the project ReminderForm and click OK. The files and folders created for the project will go into the default location, which in this case will be **http://localhost**. The end result will be one project listed in your solution, a number of files listed as being in the project, and a Web Form page shown in the main document window in Design view (see Figure 4-4).

Solution Explorer

Solution Explorer is one of the tools VS.NET provides to make it easy for you to manage your solutions and projects. It shows the files, folders, and other objects

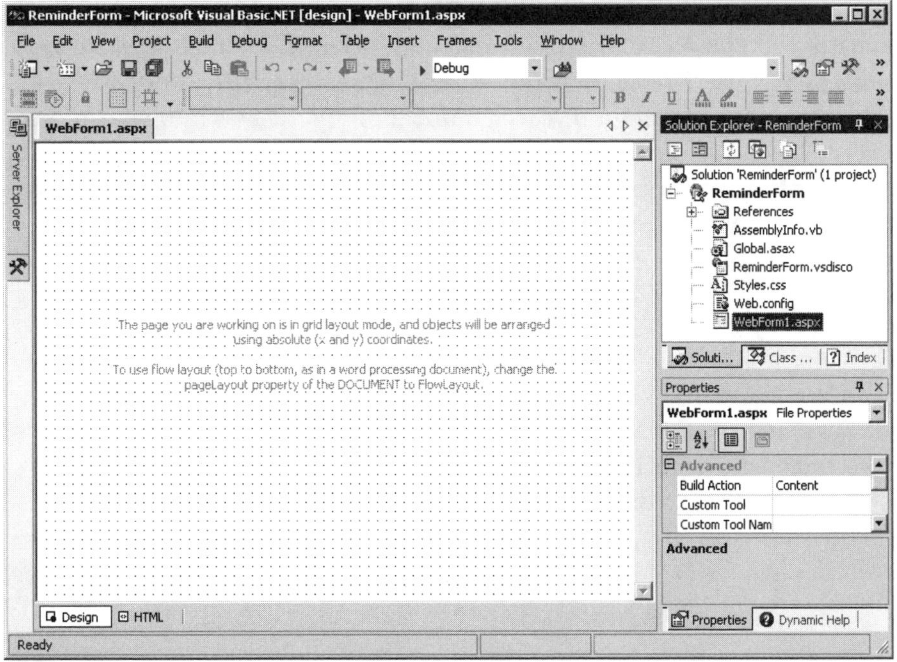

Figure 4-4 The project, files, and document in the ReminderForm solution

that make up your solution or are related to your solution; if you click any one of them, the Properties box just below Solution Explorer shows you detailed information about them. If you've ever built applications with Microsoft Office products such as Access, you know how convenient easy access to properties is.

The ReminderForm project file is the parent of the other files making up the project. The other files include:

- References
- AssemblyInfo.vb
- Global.asax
- ReminderForm.vsdisco
- Styles.css
- Web.config
- WebForm1.aspx

Solution Explorer provides a convenient way to track and manage the resources of your project while remaining unobtrusive in the upper-left corner of VS.NET. Clicking View on the menu reveals a number of other views into your project, such as Class View, Server Explorer, Resource View, and so on. The idea of all these tools is to give you easy access to what you need while at the same time giving you enough space to actually work on a document.

Creating a Web Form

Once your new project has been fully created, you should see the document named WebForm1.aspx in the document window on the left side. The best way to design your Web Form is with the document in GridLayout mode, as mentioned on the document itself. To change from GridLayout mode to FlowLayout (if you wish) and set other settings, right-click the document and choose Properties from the shortcut menu. You'll see the Document Property Pages dialog box shown in Figure 4-5.

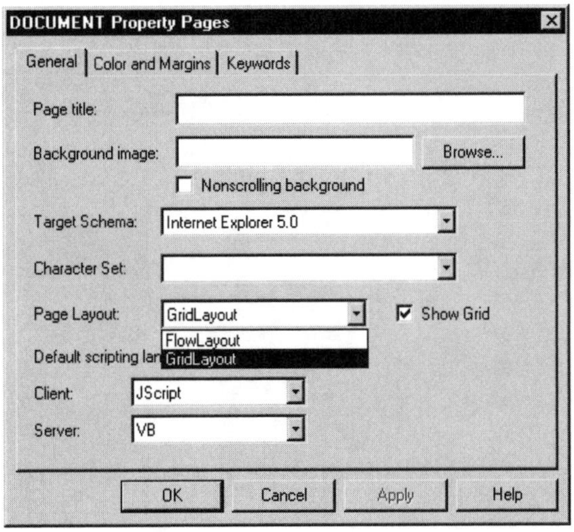

Figure 4-5 The Document Property Page dialog box

The Document Property Page Dialog Box

The document window provides a working space that allows web developers to easily create and place web page elements for both static and dynamic pages as part of an overall web application. In GridLayout mode, items added to the page are positioned exactly in pixels via X and Y coordinates. The X coordinate is measured from the left to the right in pixels, and the Y coordinate is measured from the top to the bottom in pixels. Using GridLayout makes it much easier to size and align objects on the screen correctly. Whether or not the grid shows onscreen can be toggled via the Show Grid radio button on the dialog box.

The title of the page, any background image, client and server default languages, colors and margins, and keywords can all be set with this dialog box. For example, set the document so it has a title of Reminder form, a color of light blue (#ccffff in HTML color codes), and keywords of "Birthdays, Holidays, Meetings, Appointments". Click OK, and the document should change to a light blue color. To see the actual changes in the HTML, go to HTML Source view by clicking the HTML tab at the bottom of the document. You'll see HTML code like the following:

```
<%@ Page Language="vb" AutoEventWireup="false"
 Codebehind="WebForm1.aspx.vb"
```

```
 Inherits="ReminderForm.WebForm1"%>
<!DOCTYPE HTML PUBLIC "-//W3C//DTD HTML 4.0
 Transitional//EN">
<HTML>
<HEAD>
<meta name="keywords" content="Birthdays,
 Holidays, Meetings, Appointments">
<title>Reminder Form</title>
<meta name="GENERATOR"
 content="Microsoft Visual Studio.NET 7.0">
<meta name="CODE_LANGUAGE"
 content="Visual Basic 7.0">
<meta name="vs_defaultClientScript"
 content="JavaScript">
<meta name="vs_targetSchema"content="
http://schemas.microsoft.com/intellisense/ie5">
</HEAD>
<body MS_POSITIONING="GridLayout" bgColor="#ccffff">
<form id="Form1" method="post" runat="server">
</form>
</body>
</HTML>
```

Notice the code in ASP.NET delimiters that begins the page, specifying the language for this page as well as a "code-behind" page named "WebForm1.aspx.vb". Also, notice that a form has already been added to the page in HTML, even though it is not yet visible as an object on the document in Design view.

Adding Controls to Your Web Form

To create your form, you can add controls to the form from the toolbox, accessible by clicking View | Toolbox. The toolbox contains a number of tabs (such as Web Forms and HTML), each of which drops down when clicked to reveal control choices such as Label, Text Box, and Text Area. Clicking one of the choices allows you to draw the control onto the document, after which you may inspect and change its properties individually. You are able to add controls to the document only within the form area in the HTML.

To inspect and change properties of a control after you've added the control to the document, just click the control to select it and then review the properties listed in the Properties pane in the lower-right corner. The properties listed match the attributes of the HTML element represented by the control. For example, a text box has the properties name, value, size, and maxlength and so forth, all corresponding to those same attributes for the INPUT element (when set as a text field) found in HTML.

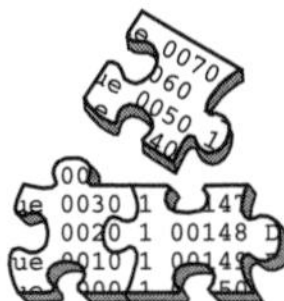

Project 4-1: Build a Web Form Application

4

In this project you'll be making a form that allows the user to enter contact information, as well as a few items of information the user would like to be reminded of by date. The form will collect and validate the data, a small application on the server will process it to generate a list of reminder dates, and the data will be presented to the user for final review. You'll build the actual reminder application in later modules.

Step-by-Step

You already have a Web Form under construction; now you can concentrate on the actual elements of the form and what you want it to do. First, you want to collect enough information so that you can provide the user with a reminder, plus establish an account on your online service system. For that, you'll need a number of text boxes for name, address, phone numbers, e-mail address, and so forth. Since this is a free service, there's no need to collect billing information.

1. Add a heading to the form that identifies it to the user. Switch the form to FlowLayout mode by right-clicking the form and opening the Document Property Pages dialog box, then changing the small drop down in the center. This lets you add text and other common web page items easily, just like you would in any HTML editor. Write a nice heading, such as "Please enter your data here". You might like to resize the text a bit larger so it's easier to read and change the font to something easier to read as well (size 4 and Arial Black is used in Figure 4-6). You can find the tools for changing font characteristics on the Formatting toolbar. The formatting toolbar should be open by default, but if it isn't go to View | Toolbars and choose the Formatting toolbar. While you're there you'll see the other toolbars available as well.
2. Next, switch back to GridLayout by clicking View | Property Pages, opening the Document Property Pages dialog box, and reselecting GridLayout. Begin your form by adding a table to the page under your heading by clicking View | Toolbox. The toolbox will appear (by default on the left side of the work area). Click the Web Forms tab to open the list of Web Forms controls available. Click the table button from the list and draw a table in the center of the form.

3. Now that you've drawn a table, right-click it to open the Table Property Pages dialog box, then change the background color of the table to a nice light blue and close the dialog box.

4. You can use the Table menu choice to find choices for inserting and deleting rows in the table. Add or subtract rows and columns (put the cursor in the row or column you want to affect) until you have 8 rows and 2 columns. Put text labels (you can write text in, rather than use label controls) in the left-hand column for First Name, Last Name, Address, City, State, Zip, E-mail, and Phone, and add TextBox controls from the Web Forms tab of the Toolbox to the right-hand column. Resize the table until it matches the edges of the text and text fields using the cursor, and move the table to the center of the page to arrange it nicely. It might help to turn on Snap To Grid by choosing Format | Snap To Grid. This will make everything automatically align with the Grid markers (you can also turn the grid markers on or off using the menu choice just above Snap To Grid). Your form should resemble the one in Figure 4-6.

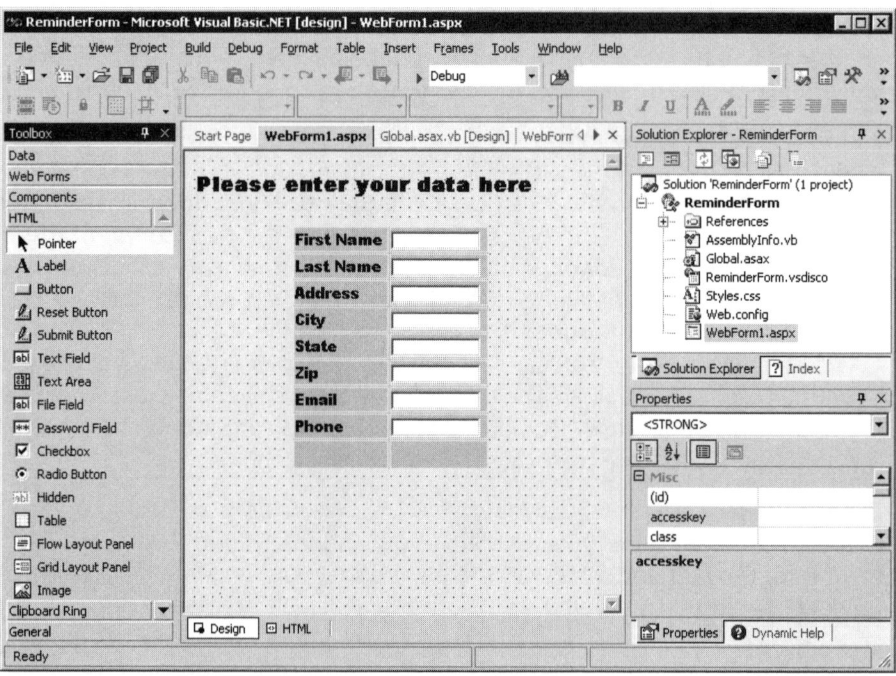

Figure 4-6 The form under construction

5. To use the text fields, you need to name them properly, so right-click the first one and select Properties from the drop-down menu. On the lower right of your screen you'll find the Properties pane, and you should see the ID property immediately. Enter a descriptive name for your fields in the ID property without spaces or special characters. For example, name the First Name field FirstName. Name the E-mail text box UserEmail.

6. The purpose of this application is to allow the application to record enough information so that the application can later remind the user of birthdays via phone or e-mail. Modify the table by adding rows, columns, headings, and text boxes until it looks like the one shown in Figure 4-7. For the drop-down box, use the HTML control (click the HTML tab of the toolbox) for Dropdown list and add it next to the words "Notify By". Name it Notification Method and right-click it to open its Property Pages dialog box. Enter the choices **Phone** and **E-mail** in both the Text and Value areas as Options for the drop-down box (you'll have to enter **Phone** in each box and then click Insert; do the same for E-mail, as shown in Figure 4-8).

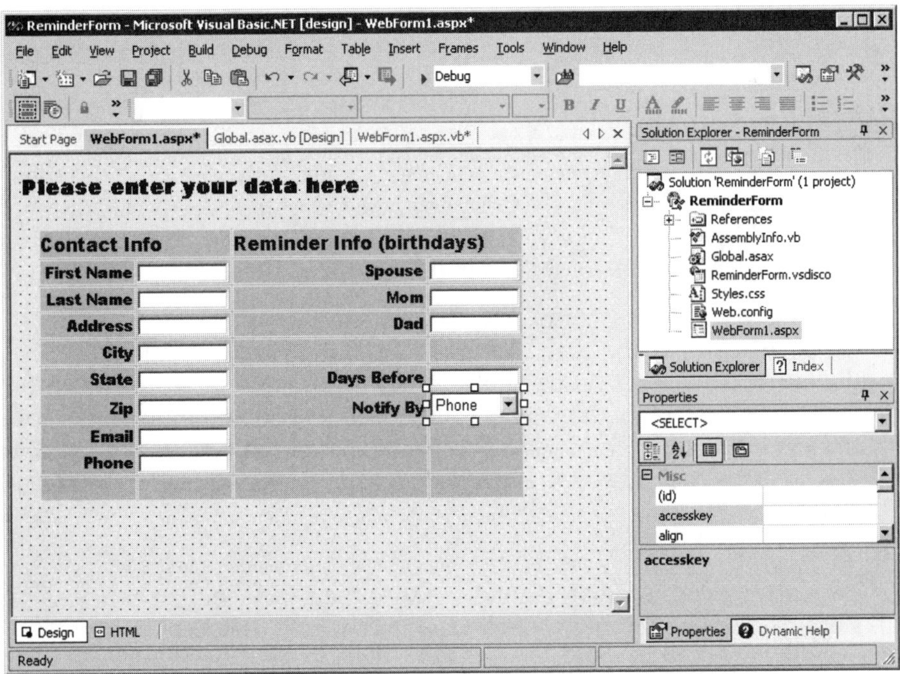

Figure 4-7 The form with reminder info areas added

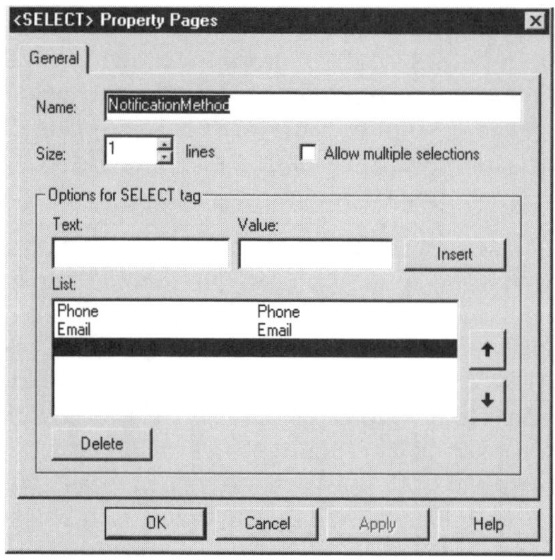

Figure 4-8 The <SELECT> Property Pages dialog box

7. Now you're ready to add the controls that validate data entered into the form. The form must ensure that data is entered into several fields (first and last names, phone number, e-mail address, at least one birthday, and the number of days before the birthday to make the notification). The form will also check to ensure that a valid e-mail address format has been used and that the birthdays are properly formatted as dates.

8. Click the Web Forms Controls tab on the toolbox and select RequiredFieldValidator, then drag and drop it next to the required fields. In the ControlToValidate property of each validator, enter the name of the text field it will validate; in the Text property of each validator enter an asterisk (*); and in the ErrorMessage property enter an appropriate message to the user, such as **First name is required**. Your form should now resemble Figure 4-9.

9. To check that the user has entered a workable e-mail address, add a RegularExpresionValidator control next to the E-mail field. In its ControlToValidate property, enter **UserEmail**; in its Text property, enter an asterisk (*); in its ErrorMessage property, enter **Your e-mail address must contain an asterisk and an extension**; and in its ValidationExpression property, click the ellipsis (you may have to click in the property first) to

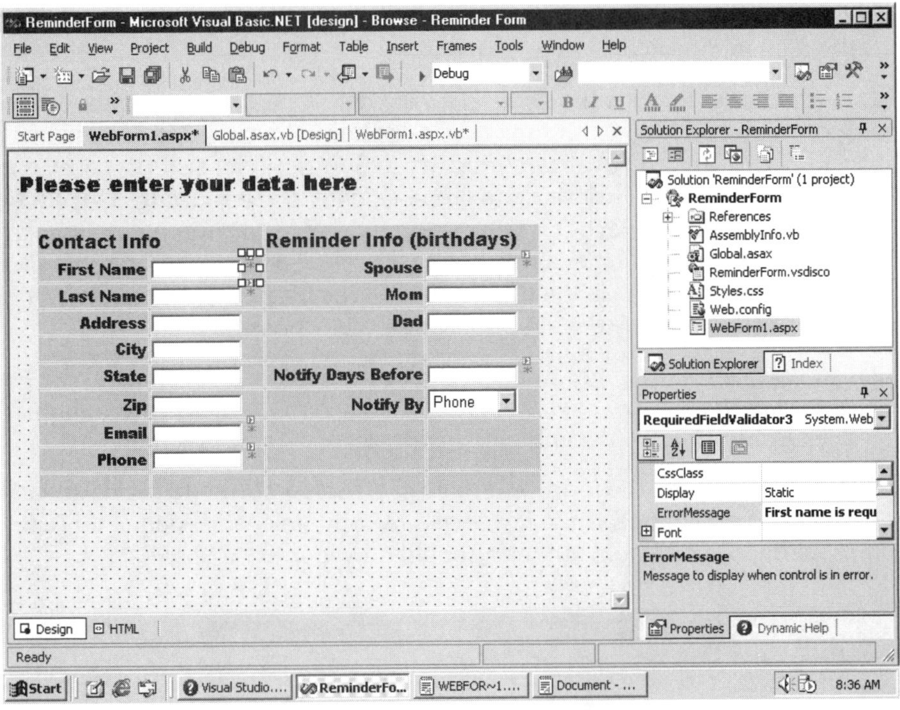

Figure 4-9 The form with required field validators in place

display the Regular Expression Editor dialog box and choose Internet E-mail Address from the list. The dialog box is shown in Figure 4-10.

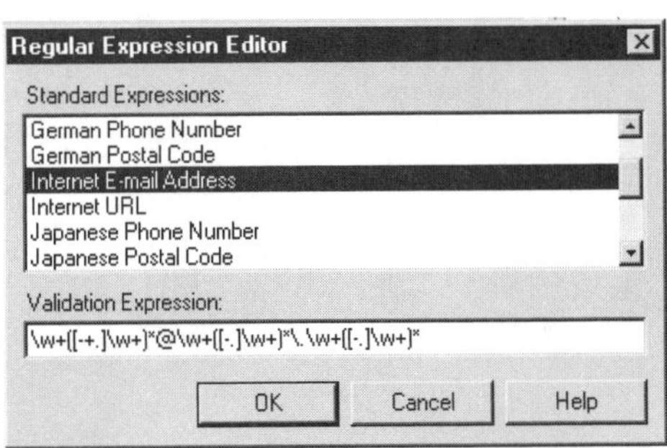

Figure 4-10 The Regular Expression Editor dialog box

10. You can also set the Display property of the control to Dynamic. This makes the asterisk display only as necessary.

11. To check that the user has entered a valid date for a birthday, at least in the Spouse text field, add a CompareValidator control next to the Spouse text field. Set its ControlToValidate property to Spouse; in its Text property, enter an asterisk (*); in its ErrorMessage property, enter **Date must be formatted properly**; in its ValueToCompare property, enter a minimum date such as **01/01/1900**; in its Operator property, choose Greater Than from the drop-down list (accessible via the ellipsis); in its Type property, choose Date from the drop-down list; and in its Display property, choose Dynamic.

12. To display error messages to the user cleanly, add a ValidationSummary control to the last row of your table (you may have to merge the cells of this row by selecting the entire row and selecting Table | Merge Cells).

13. In order to submit the form, you must give users a button to click. Add a Button control in one of the lower cells of your table, and change its Text property to Send Info. Your form should now look like Figure 4-11.

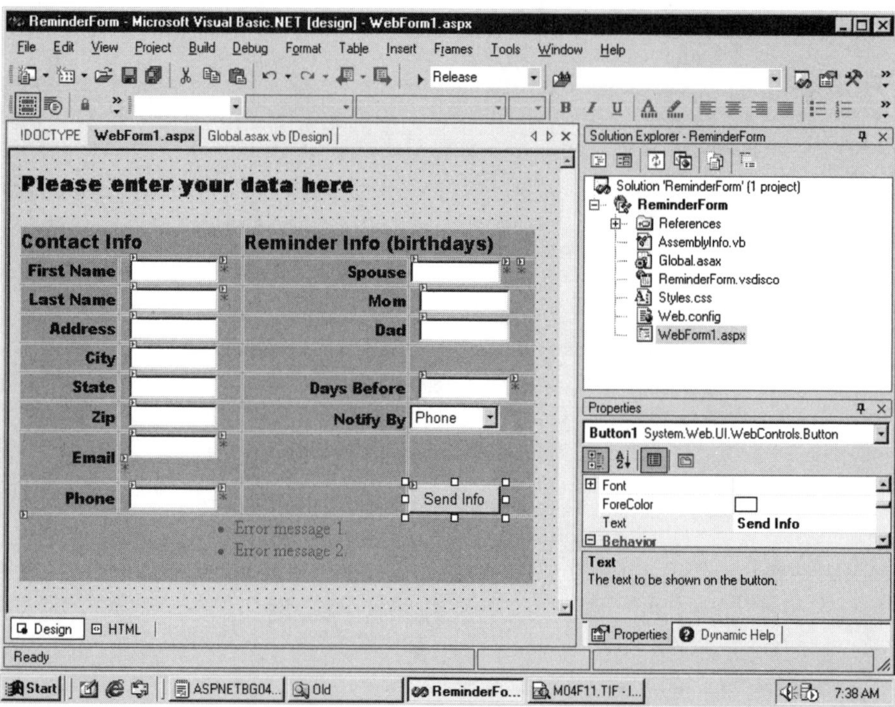

Figure 4-11 The finished form in Design view

14. To compile and check the form as a user would, right-click the form name in Solution Explorer (at the top right of your screen) and choose Build and Browse from the shortcut menu. This will compile the form and its associated controls and display it in Browser view, as shown in Figure 4-12. Try entering a few items of information and enter an e-mail address and birth date incorrectly. You should see the appropriate responses in the browser window, in the area where you put the ValidationSummary control, similar to Figure 4-13.

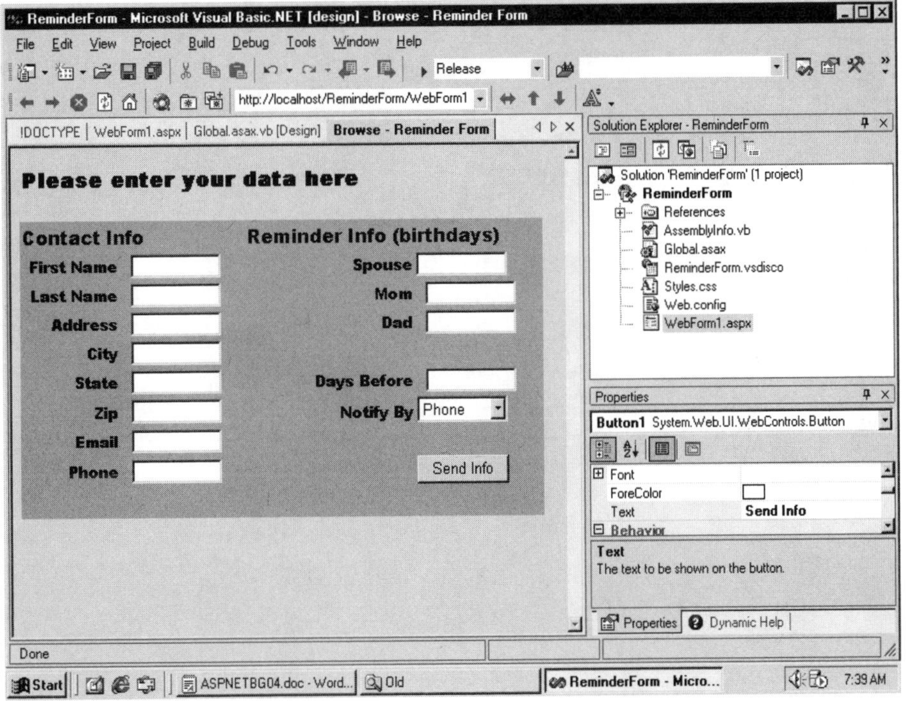

Figure 4-12 The finished form in Browser view

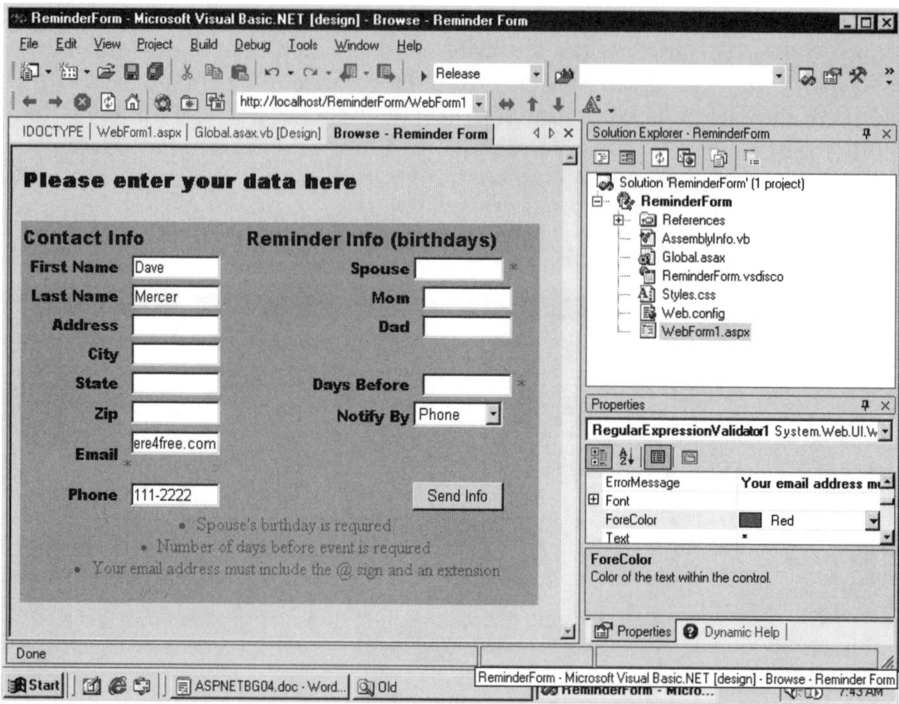

Figure 4-13 The form with an error message displayed

Mastery Check

1. What does a Web Form consist of, essentially?

A. An HTML web page with HTML form controls built-in

B. An HTML web page with an HTML form and JavaScript to handle the processing

C. An HTML web page with an HTML form and a back-end page with programming for processing on the server

D. A server-based programming page only

E. None of the above

2. What does the term *stateless* mean for websites?

A. There are no geographic boundaries for websites.

B. An ordinary website does not track variables, values, or conditions of controls every time a request/response is performed.

C. The browser does not record what items the user clicked.

D. The browser records what items the user clicked, not the server.

E. None of the above.

3. Web Forms and their back-end processing pages are _________ into a class based on the ASP.NET _________ class. Because it is _________ it runs much faster than traditional scripting and HTML pages.

4. Describe how an easy method of making ASP pages with HTML can hinder code reuse and readability when inappropriately applied to larger, more complex pages.

____

____

Mastery Check

5. What is a round trip, and why should they be reduced whenever practical?

   A. A round trip is one processing cycle, and extra processing cycles take CPU time.

   B. A round trip is one request/response cycle, and it can take too long to go back to the server.

   C. A round trip is one request/response cycle, and the request object is not always available.

   D. None of the above.

6. What does the term *viewstate* mean?

   A. The current condition of controls on the browser

   B. The content currently displayed in the browser

   C. The content currently cached on the server

   D. The content in transit from the server to the browser at any given time

   E. None of the above

7. What files are created automatically when you create a new project using the web application template in VS.NET?

   A. A Web Form file, a code-behind file, a global file, and a styles file

   B. A class file

   C. An .aspx file named WebForms1.aspx

   D. None of the above

8. You can view your files in _______________ in VS.NET, and view the properties of each control in the ____________ pane.

Mastery Check

9. Describe how you would change from GridLayout view to FlowLayout view on your Web Forms page.

____

____

10. What property of a Web Forms control would you set to specify its name?

A. The Name property

B. The ID property

C. Both the Name and ID properties

D. None of the above

11. What type of control would you add to your Web Form to ensure that a particular field is filled in?

A. A Web Forms RequiredFieldValidator control

B. An HTML RequiredFieldValidator control

C. A FieldRequiredValidator control

D. You would write a script in the text field control

E. None of the above

12. What does the Text property do for Web Forms validation controls?

____

____

13. You can add rows or columns to a table on a Web Form by choosing ____________________ from the menu.

Mastery Check

14. Describe three properties of the CompareValidator control that affect the data type, value, and error message displayed when the control operates.

____

____

15. How would you perform test validation on your form after you've built it?

A. Right-click the form in Solution Explorer and select Build and Browse from the shortcut menu, then enter values and see if the validation routines work properly.

B. Save the form, open the browser and browse to the form, then enter values and see whether it works as designed.

C. Click Test from the menu and an automatic testing routine will take place.

D. A and B.

E. None of the above.

Module 5

ASP.NET Configuration, Scope, and State

The Goals of This Module

- Learn about website application configuration and state
- Understand where and how ASP.NET configuration is stored
- Review ASP.NET configuration parameters
- Modify a Web.config file
- Learn the concepts of scope
- Examine ASP.NET Application and Session Objects
- Learn how ASP.NET state is maintained and managed
- Review the properties of the httpApplicationState class
- Create and configure an ASP.NET application with sessions

If you've used many common desktop applications such as Microsoft Word or Excel, you know that you can set up these programs just the way you like them. These settings are usually called something like Options or Preferences. Setting options or preferences *configures* the program, and the program will remember your settings each time you start using it.

You can configure ASP.NET applications in a similar manner, although instead of setting usage options you will typically be configuring the environment in which the application runs. Configuration for ASP.NET applications defines their capabilities on the server, such as authentication and authorization, use of cookies, and developer's capabilities (such as debugging).

Along with configuration, the scope of ASP.NET components affects the capabilities of your application as well. For example, suppose your application allows users to place orders. The information they enter for an order is of interest only to them, and no other users need to know what is in their order. However, if in the process of placing an order the number of products available in inventory decreases, *all* other users placing orders need to know this. The scope of information about a specific order should be limited to that user, while the scope of information about inventory should be application-wide (global).

Another example of the need for global scope is when a particular function must be available to all users. Suppose you have a function that calculates a size dimension for a product you're selling, and this function is required in 17 different parts of your application. Rather than recoding the function 17 times across the application, you can make it available globally so that if there is ever a change to the way the calculation is performed, you only have to change it in one place.

The term *state* refers to the current condition of an application, and each of its parts (services, Web Forms, and so on) can have an individual state as well. Since the Web is by nature stateless and the user interface (a Web Form) is separate and disconnected (between requests) from the application it runs on (the server), maintaining state information from request to request and from user to user requires the use of special capabilities. Some of the same capabilities that allow functions and values to be limited to a single page or accessible across the application or session are also useful in maintaining state.

Any good application development platform makes it easy to control configuration, scope, and state, and ASP.NET is no exception. There are some unusual aspects in the way ASP.NET handles these things, and this module covers these subjects in depth.

ASP.NET and Configuration

We began our discussion of application configuration for ASP applications in Module 3. This type of configuration is a bit simpler to perform than ASP.NET configuration, because many of your options can be set with dialog boxes. In ASP.NET, configuration parameters are stored separately in a file, and you have access to more options, although with greater flexibility comes a bit more complexity. In the following section we cover more of ASP configuration, and then we move on to ASP.NET configuration.

ASP Applications

Upon installation of Windows 2000, IIS, and ASP, a default website is created, and it is set up as a web application (see Figure 5-1). On the Default Web Site Properties dialog box, in the Home Directory tab, the name given this application is Default Application. Within the default application on the root folder you can also set up virtual applications in subfolders. Virtual applications are able to access (see) variables in the default application, but not vice versa.

However, if a virtual application happens to store a variable with the same name as an existing variable in the default application, it can only see its own variable (for that name), while other virtual applications in the default application can still see the original global variable for that name. It's probably best in most situations to use different names for variables in the default and related virtual applications. This is an example of how scope is limited depending on which application is looking for a particular variable value.

Configuring ASP Applications

As we discussed in Module 3, for ASP applications the Internet Services Manager can be used to create virtual applications, remove virtual applications, and set properties for virtual applications (and the default application as well). In ASP applications, Application and Session objects are created when a page is first requested, and the Request and Response objects operate within their individual sessions as well as within the overall application. The Server, Application, Session, Request, and Response objects all work together to provide true application-style functionality at your website.

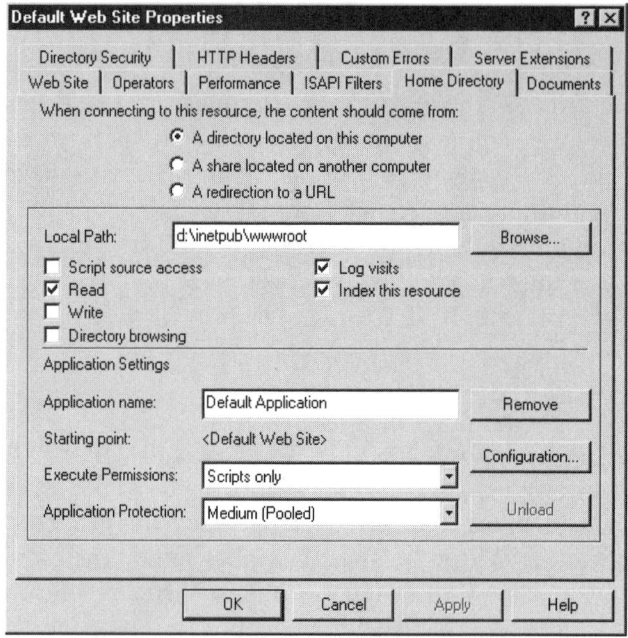

Figure 5-1 The Default Web Site Properties dialog box

ASP.NET Applications

ASP.NET applications are configurable as well. To create an ASP.NET application you can use an existing directory in the Default website directory, or make a new one within the directory. Just right-click the directory in Internet Services Manager and choose New. Put an ASP.NET page (with .aspx as the file extension) and then request the page with your browser. A new ASP.NET application will automatically be created.

The administrator of an application can control the resources available to an application, determine the version of assemblies the application uses (assemblies will be discussed in greater detail in Module 7), and tell the application where other applications and objects reside. Developers can also exercise control over how the application runs, including whether it uses cookies, the type of error messages displayed, and so on. Configuration settings can be defined and changed easily, without hurting running applications.

ASP.NET applications are configured with special XML files. The files conform to the XML format so that they can be easily parsed and edited with common XML tools. XML files are human-readable, meaning you can open ASP.NET configuration files up in any simple text editor (such as Notepad) and read through them to gain an understanding of their settings. In XML, the main parts of a document are called elements, and any special options associated with those elements are called attributes. In ASP.NET configuration files there are elements such as session state (covers the current configuration of a session), and session state has an attribute name Timeout (contains the setting for how long a session will be maintained while unused or idle before the session is destroyed). All main configuration sections are XML elements, and all the properties are XML elements. We'll cover XML in greater depth in Module 7.

Note

Although the XML elements and attributes in an ASP.NET configuration file resemble HTML, they are not the same. In XML, the names of elements and attributes must be written in the proper case as shown in the examples, and all elements must be properly closed. Essentially, the files must be well-formed XML documents.

ASP.NET Web.config Files

In ASP.NET, application configuration information is stored in files named Web.config. Each folder from the root website on down contains Web.config files, and they can all have different or separate settings. The settings in the top folder are applied to all folders below it, so that the only settings that need to be applied to subfolders are those specifically applicable to them or in conflict with the settings inherited from folders above. When the application runs, configuration settings for each resource on the site are calculated and cached and then applied to that resource whenever it is requested. Web.config files are protected from improper HTTP requests by a setting in the web server that sends an HTTP 403 (access forbidden) if a user requests the file directly.

Note

A machine configuration file, named C:\WINNT\Microsoft.NET\Framework*version*\CONFIG\Machine.config, contains ASP.NET configuration settings for your web server as a whole. Of course, if your drive letter or any other parts of the address differ, that part of the file address would also be different. For example, on one of our computers the appropriate drive letter is D.

An Example Web.config File

In this section is an example of a complete Web.config file that was automatically generated for the ReminderForm application we developed in Module 4. In a typical file you wouldn't necessarily keep all the comments found in this one, but they are good as examples and explanations.

```
<?xml version="1.0" encoding="utf-8" ?>
<configuration>
 <system.web>
<!--  DYNAMIC DEBUG COMPILATION
Set compilation debug="true" to insert debugging
 symbols (.pdb information) into the compiled page.
 Because this creates a larger file that executes
 more slowly, you should set this value to true only
 when debugging and to false at all other times.
 For more information, refer to the documentation
 about debugging ASP.NET files.
-->
  <compilation defaultLanguage="vb" debug="true" />
<!--  CUSTOM ERROR MESSAGES
Set customErrors mode="On" or "RemoteOnly" to enable
 custom error messages, "Off" to disable. Add <error>
 tags for each of the errors you want to handle.
-->
  <customErrors mode="RemoteOnly" />
<!--  AUTHENTICATION
This section sets the authentication policies of the
 application. Possible modes are "Windows", "Forms",
 "Passport" and "None"
-->
  <authentication mode="Windows" />
<!--  AUTHORIZATION
This section sets the authorization policies of the
 application. You can allow or deny access to
 application resources by user or role. Wildcards:
 "*" mean everyone, "?" means anonymous
 (unauthenticated) users.
-->
  <authorization>
   <allow users="*" />
<!-- Allow all users -->
<!--  <allow
        users="[comma separated list of users]"
```

```
            roles="[comma separated list of roles]"/>
        <deny
            users="[comma separated list of users]"
            roles="[comma separated list of roles]"/>
-->
  </authorization>
<!--  APPLICATION-LEVEL TRACE LOGGING
Application-level tracing enables trace log output
 for every page within an application. Set trace
 enabled="true" to enable application trace logging.
 If pageOutput="true", the trace information will be
 displayed at the bottom of each page. Otherwise, you
 can view the application trace log by browsing the
 "trace.axd" page from your web application root.
-->
  <trace enabled="false" requestLimit="10"
 pageOutput="false" traceMode="SortByTime"
 localOnly="true" />
<!--  SESSION STATE SETTINGS
By default ASP.NET uses cookies to identify which
 requests belong to a particular session. If cookies
 are not available, a session can be tracked by
 adding a session identifier to the URL. To disable
 cookies, set sessionState cookieless="true".
-->
  <sessionState
     mode="InProc"
     stateConnectionString="tcpip=127.0.0.1:42424"
     sqlConnectionString="data source=127.0.0.1;
     user id=sa;password="
     cookieless="false"
     timeout="20"/>
<!--  PREVENT SOURCE CODE DOWNLOAD
This section sets the types of files that will not
 be downloaded. As well as entering a httphandler
 for a file type, you must also associate that file
 type with the xspisapi.dll in the App Mappings
 property of the web site, or the file can be
 downloaded. It is recommended that you use this
 section to prevent your sources being downloaded.
-->
  <httpHandlers>
    <add verb="*" path="*.vb"
 type="System.Web.HttpNotFoundHandler,System.Web" />
```

5

```
    <add verb="*" path="*.cs"
 type="System.Web.HttpNotFoundHandler,System.Web" />
    <add verb="*" path="*.vbproj"
 type="System.Web.HttpNotFoundHandler,System.Web" />
    <add verb="*" path="*.csproj"
 type="System.Web.HttpNotFoundHandler,System.Web" />
    <add verb="*" path="*.webinfo"
 type="System.Web.HttpNotFoundHandler,System.Web" />
  </httpHandlers>
<!--  GLOBALIZATION
This section sets the globalization settings of the
 application.
-->
  <globalization requestEncoding="utf-8"
 responseEncoding="utf-8" />
</system.web>
</configuration>
```

Notice that all of the configuration information is placed between the beginning and ending <configuration> tags. Configuration is the root XML element for the document. If you need to read settings from inside your ASP.NET application once it has started running, there are methods available to do so. For example, a session can be configured as "cookieless" by setting the *session state* element's *cookieless* attribute to a value of True, meaning it won't automatically issue and retrieve cookies to manage state. (We'll get into this later in this module, in the section entitled "Maintaining State with Cookies.") To access the value of the session state element's cookieless attribute, you might use code such as the following:

```
Dim ssCookieless As Boolean

ssCookieless = Session.Cookieless
```

ASP.NET Configuration Section Handlers

ASP.NET has a number of built-in configuration section handlers like session state (and you can even program your own if you like). Table 5-1 briefly notes these handlers and their functions.

Section	Function
appSettings	Configures custom settings for an application.
authenticate	Configures ASP.NET authentication support.
authorization	Configures ASP.NET authorization support.
browserCaps	Configures browser capabilities component settings.
compilation	Contains compilation settings.
customErrors	Defines custom error messages.
globalization	Configures globalization settings.
httpHandlers	Maps incoming URL requests to IHttpHandler classes.
httpModules	Adds, removes, or clears HTTP modules.
httpRuntime	Configures ASP.NET HTTP runtime settings.
identity	Controls the application identity of the application.
machineKey	Configures keys to use for encryption and decryption of forms authentication cookie data.
pages	Identifies page-specific configuration settings.
processModel	Configures ASP.NET process model settings on IIS web server systems.
securityPolicy	Defines valid mappings of named security levels to policy files.
sessionState	Configures session state HttpModule.
trace	Configures ASP.NET trace service.
trust	Configures the code access security permission set used to run a particular application.
webServices	Controls settings of ASP.NET web services.

Table 5-1 Configuration File Section Handlers

The Session State HttpModule In the example configuration file, you may have noticed the session state settings; following is the complete set of attributes and value available for this handler:

- **Mode** This attribute specifies where to store session state information and may be set to Off (no session stored), Inproc (stored locally), StateServer (on a remote server), and SqlServer (on a SQL Server).
- **Cookieless** This attribute specifies whether or not to use cookies to maintain state, and may be set to True (no cookies) or False (use cookies).

- **Timeout** This attribute specifies the number of minutes before a session is abandoned because it is idle.
- **ConnectionString** This attribute specifies the server and port for storing session state remotely.
- **SqlConnectionString** This attribute specifies the connection string to a SQL Server.

1-Minute Drill

- Name three configuration settings that can be set for ASP.NET applications.
- What configuration setting makes ASP.NET sessions use cookies?

ASP.NET and State

Beyond the Request and Response objects, the next two most important objects in ASP are the Application and Session objects, because with them you can manage state. These objects do much of the work that allows you to set up your website as a real, application-style program, rather than just dynamic pages.

As a website application developer, one of your primary concerns is managing how your application deals with visitors. A prerequisite to dealing effectively with visitors is knowing who they are and the status of their overall interaction with your application. The ASP Application and Session objects provide the information you need to continually gauge their status and create appropriate responses/processes to their inputs and actions.

Visitor Status and State

The concept of *state* may seem a little fuzzy, so let's see if we can't clarify it with an example or two. Suppose you run a convenience store and people show up, buy things, and leave without you ever knowing who they are. Although you could sell products this way, suppose someone came into the store and claimed

---

- The browserCaps handler configures settings for the Browser Capabilities component, the compilation handler configures compilation settings, and the customErrors handler defines custom error messages.
- Setting the session state handler's cookieless attribute to False makes sessions use cookies and is the default (it does not need to be changed for sessions to use cookies).

they'd been there an hour ago and bought a product that is now on sale, and they want a discount. If you had no way to tell that this was true, you could call your situation stateless. Every visitor to your store is for all intents and purposes anonymous. On your website, even if you have hit tracking statistics, you can't be sure it's the same computer hitting your site each time, much less the same person.

On the other hand, suppose each person swipes a club card when they enter your store (not just when they make a purchase) and your closed-circuit camera watches them as they browse through your store. If you can make a connection between who they are and what they do when in your store, you are cognizant of state. This puts you in a much better position to deal effectively with your customers. It works the same on the Web. If they must log in when they enter your site, or if you can capture a long-duration cookie, you can reference data from all their previous visits. Even if they don't have a cookie already set from a previous visit, you can still manage all their interactions if they'll let you set a cookie for the duration of their current visit.

ASP contains two state-related objects (Application and Session) because there are basically two kinds of state we want our web application to be cognizant of at all times. One is the state of an individual user's visit, and the other is the state of all current users' visits. Two things happen when your web application is used. Whenever the first page of your ASP web application is requested for the first time, the Application object is created, and whenever an individual user first requests a page an individual Session object is created.

So, for example, if a person is on your site filling out a survey and they submit their survey answers, you may want to provide the number of other folks who are currently also filling out and submitting survey forms as well as the average responses. Therefore, you would need to know both the individual answers as well as the overall answers. Typical web applications are constantly using variables like these, and the Application and Session objects make ideal places to store these types of variables across multiple page requests or an entire application in operation.

ASP: Maintaining State with Cookies

Whenever a visitor to your site first requests a page, ASP attempts to set a special cookie that lasts only the length of their visit (until they go to another site or close their browser). You've seen it in the HTTP headers in Module 2; it's called ASPSESSIONID. It only lasts the current session because it has no expires date, and it isn't visible in the Request or Response Cookies collections.

ASP generates this cookie automatically to support state within your application for each user session. Of course, if their browser doesn't allow cookies (if it's too old or they've disallowed cookies in their Options), you won't be able to track interactions with them, and you'll be less capable of dealing effectively with them.

Tip

The automatically created ASPSESSIONID cookies only provide state for the current session, not multiple sessions over time. You'll want to set up longer duration cookies with the Request and Response Cookies collections, with an expiration date fairly far into the future, to track users across several sessions.

State Maintenance in ASP.NET

ASP.NET has a richer set of tools than ASP for maintaining state, and it makes it easy to manage the tradeoffs inherent in state maintenance for online applications. The tradeoffs have to do with security, server usage, and privacy, as well as convenience for developers. And keep in mind that state maintenance not only refers to values generated during a user's session with an application; state also refers to things like the current status of a control on a form, such as a choice that has been selected in a drop-down list, or text that has been entered in a text box. Ideally, your application could keep track of all these things in a way that is transparent to the user.

State Maintenance Methods

The current status of things (state) is more difficult to maintain because the client and server are separated, and as we've said, the Web is stateless. The things a user is doing to a form are unknown to the server, at least until the form is posted. And once it's posted, all the values that were in it are lost and must be recreated on the browser if the same form is returned to the user after that transaction.

By the same token, what is happening back at the application on the server (if other users have logged in and are changing global values in some way, for example) is unknown to the client, at least until the page is refreshed.

To maintain state, state information must be kept somewhere, and to update the client and server with state information from each other requires some type of communication between the client and server. The trouble is, storing state information takes space and retrieval time (both CPU processing and database retrievals, in some cases), while communications between client and server take time. Also, some methods of storing state information are very insecure, because they involve putting the stored values right in the HTML a user could read (and change) by saving the page to their desktop and opening the source code in their browser.

In the end, if you want to preserve state information each time the server or the client state changes, you have to recreate the values (or the form) at each end. The ASP.NET page framework can automatically save and recreate page/form/control state, and also has built-in tools for saving values and datasets. In addition, ASP.NET works well with the traditional methods for saving and renewing state information. For each of these methods, the main tradeoff is security for scalability and vice versa. Storing data on the client is very scalable but insecure, while storing data on the server is very secure but hard to scale. Following is a list of methods, starting with client-side storage:

- **Cookies** Stored on the client, cookies are small strings (often limited to 4K) of text with a name and a value. Multiple cookies can be stored, but they are relatively insecure (since users can find, read, and alter them). Cookies can be stored as a text file or in the active memory of the client (usually a browser). As an application developer, you can use the Response object to read and write cookies (and thereby maintain state information across page requests, form posts, and so on), so long as the user's browser is set to accept them. Cookies are also useful because they can be set to last for the life of the session or for a very long time. Another advantage of using cookies is that the client must send data back to the server that created the cookie, preventing other servers from improperly requesting cookie data.

- **Hidden fields** Stored on the client, hidden fields are HTML form controls that are not displayed to the user, although again the user can see them if the source code is examined. An example of using a hidden field would be after a database request is made to retrieve a user's account information, the user ID might be stored as the value of a hidden field. This way, when the user edits their own account record, their user ID number is passed back to the server along with their edits when they post the form, thereby giving the server the information it needs to look up and change that record in the database. The main disadvantages are that the information is not secure and a form post is required. Also, hidden fields contain only a single, text value.

- **Query strings** Query strings are small text strings formed as name/value pairs that are attached to the end of the URL and sent with page requests, such as when a link is clicked or a URL is entered in the address bar. Query strings are not secure and can be easily seen by simply looking at the address bar of the browser. In addition, they are limited in size. A query string starts after the URL following a question mark. It is a series of names followed by an equal sign and the value associated with the name. They can be retrieved and parsed easily with the Request object and are available in the Querystring collection. The following code example shows their structure (where firstname is the name of the name/value pair and Dave is the value):

```
http://www.e4free.com?firstname=Dave&lastname=Mercer
```

- **View State property** This property is part of the controls on Web Forms, including the page itself. When Web Forms are used, this property automatically saves the current state of the control (and sends it to the server as part of the posted form request) so that the state can be recreated the next time the Web Forms page is generated on the client. As a developer you can also explicitly save any information you'd like within the View State property of a particular control so that it is available in the page when it is recreated. View State values are stored in hidden fields on the form, but they are hashed and compressed to make them much more secure than the plain-text values in ordinary hidden fields. You must place a form control on the server (<form runat="server">) to make View State work. To write and read View State values you would use code such as the following (although you probably wouldn't do so in the same block of code):

```
Dim vUserID as Long

ViewState("userID") ="80352" 'writes the userID

vUserID = CLng(ViewState("userID")) 'reads the userID
```

- **Application State object** This object runs on the server and stores state information on the server. While it is more secure because it is on the server, it also makes it harder to scale up your applications to many users because so many server resources are involved. It is actually an instance of the HttpApplicationState class, and in ASP it is called the Application object. You can use it to store application-specific values and data that must be accessible to every page in every session. The values are stored with a name and a value (a name/value pair). Note that if the server crashes, application values will be lost (unlike properly transacted information stored in a database) and the global nature of the values applies to a single application on one server, not on several servers connected together. Applications are automatically started when the first user requests a page inside the application, and they end after the timeout period for the last user.

- **Session State object** This object runs on the server and stores state information on the server. While it is more secure because it is on the server, it also makes it harder to scale up your applications to many users because so many server resources are involved. It is actually an instance of the HttpSessionState class, and in ASP it is called the Session object. You can use it to store session-specific values and data that must be accessible to every page inside a particular session across multiple page requests or form posts. The values are stored with a name and a value (a name/value pair). Sessions are by default created and maintained with special cookies, and if the cookies are not accepted sessions can still be maintained by adding session ID data to the end of the URL. Sessions are automatically started when a user requests the first page inside an application, and they end after the session timeout period expires (or the session is explicitly ended by the application).

- **Databases** Information in databases is stored on the server, and the variety of data types and sizes, as well as the sophisticated processing available, makes databases a valuable and often used method of storing data for state management as well as many other purposes. However, database reads make heavy use of server resources and are not appropriate under many circumstances. That said, there are times when there are few viable alternatives to using database reads. Typically, this approach is used in combination with other methods (such as storing user ID data in cookies, hidden fields, or session objects) to provide an overall managed state environment. Since the contents of the database may be changing dynamically, the results of a database read can be used to trigger conditional processing in your application (for example, if a product is found to be out of stock during the ordering process, your application can note this upon completion of an inventory read and suggest that the user try another product). Finally, some data *must* survive sessions and applications and must be available for other business processes, such as order fulfillment. In these cases, data must be written to a database or some other long-term storage system.

1-Minute Drill

- What method would you use to store state information for a session that starts and stops several times over the course of several days, if the information stored is larger than 4K?
- What method would you use to store the state of a control on a Web Form as the user fills out the form?

The ASP global.asa and ASP.NET global.asax Files

Both ASP and ASP.NET provide methods for detecting and working with the beginning and end of applications and sessions. Since they often involve setting, retrieving, and changing variables that are global in scope, the code you write is placed in a file called global.asa (ASP) and global.asax (ASP.NET), respectively.

ASP.NET and ASP global files (there must be only one of each, and they must be named exactly as just shown) can coexist independently in your application if you like, but they do not interact with each other. Note that having one or both of them is entirely optional; if you don't have them, Application and Session objects will still be created and be accessible, but you won't be able to run code when they start. These files are placed in the root directory of your application.

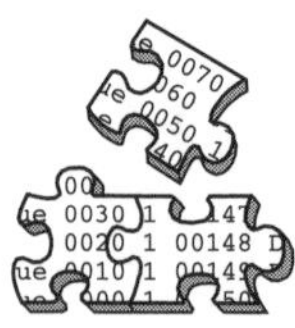

Project 5-1: Creating An ASP global.asa File

For your next exercise, you'll create a global.asa file in the default root directory of your website, and you'll put some example objects and variables in it. The global.asa file is at the root of our default directory because its role is to manage

---

- Database storage is a good method for storing state (and other) data between sessions where the size of the data is larger than 4K. Using an application object for storing this information would make it hard to scale up the application to many users, and using cookies may not work with larger data sizes.
- The View State method would be convenient for storing this type of information, as state would be maintained across form posts.

the operating environment of our application. Although you don't have to have a global.asa file in your application to run ASP code, and although you're starting with a very simple global.asa file, you'll find that this file can be used for many important management tasks and can become fairly complex.

Step-by-Step

1. In the global.asa file, you'll use the MyInfo component (we'll delve into components more later, in Modules 7 and 8) and a simple variant containing a string. To create the global.asa file, you can simply open Notepad and begin writing code like this:

```
<OBJECT ID="objMyInfo" RUNAT="server" SCOPE="Application"
PROGID="MSWC.MyInfo">
</OBJECT>
<SCRIPT Language="VBScript" RUNAT="server">
Sub Application_onStart()

objMyInfo.vDailyBanner = "The Big News Today is..."

Dim vMyVar
vMyVar = "Some text stored in the Application"
Application("storedtext") = vMyVar

End Sub
</SCRIPT>
```


2. In the start of the global.asa file, you place your <OBJECT> tag to instantiate the MyInfo component. Whenever your application starts it will build the MyInfo component with an ID of "objMyInfo". Next, insert some script to run at the server that includes a subroutine triggered when the onStart event occurs for the Application object. You can add properties to the instance of MyInfo you've created by simply naming them and adding values, as in the line that starts objMyInfo.vDailyBanner. This line creates a property named vDailyBanner and sets it equal to a string of text whenever the application starts. You can find the properties and their values in an XML file under your WINNT/system32/inetserv folder, named MyInfo.xml (but it won't be there until you run the component at least once).

3. The next step is to create a variable named vMyVar and then fill it with a short string. Then you can add the contents of this variable to the application under the name storedtext using the line Application("storedtext") = vMyVar.

4. Next, end the subroutine and end the script section, and you're good to go. You now have data in your global.asa file that is available globally but can be changed (in the MyInfo component), and you also have a simple variable (vMyVar) that can be read out.

5. To see how these objects and variables can provide their data or allow their data to be changed, use a couple of simple ASP files to retrieve and change them. First, use Notepad to create the following file and name it index.asp:

```
<HTML>
<HEAD><TITLE>Showing Application Variables</TITLE></HEAD>
<BODY>
<H2>The Daily Banner Headlines</H2>
<%
objMyInfo.vDailyBanner = "My Personal News is"
vDayBan = objMyInfo.vDailyBanner
Response.Write(vDayBan) & ": "
vMVr = Application.Contents("storedtext")
Response.Write(vMVr) & "<BR>"

%>
</BODY>
</HTML>
```

6. The first line of ASP scripting writes a new value to vDailyBanner property of the MyInfo object named objMyInfo. This new value is then available to any other pages that reference the value of that object, unless they change it themselves, in which case the value they insert is then available to all other pages. In practical terms, if there is a value that simply accumulates for all users referencing it (such as total number of visitors to a given page), this would work well.

7. The next lines collect the value of the of the vDailyBanner property from the objMyInfo object and write it back to the user, demonstrating that the value has been set and referenced. Following that, you also gather and write back the value of the "storedtext" variable from the Contents collection of the Application object.

8. If there were more than one variable in the Contents collection of the Application object, you could use code such as the following to iterate through those variables and write out their names and values:

```
For Each collItem in Application.Contents
Response.Write "The variable name is '" & collItem & "'and the value in it is: "
vMVr = Application.Contents(collItem)
Response.Write(vMVr) & "<BR>"
Next
```

The ASP.NET global.asax File

In ASP.NET, a single application consists of the files, pages, handlers, modules, and executable code within a single virtual directory structure, and the global.asax file contains code that can execute in response to a number of events, including the start and end of the application or individual sessions. Note that if you make changes to global.asax while an application is running, the ASP.NET Framework will detect the change and end and restart the application, thereby destroying all current state information.

Like the ASP global.asa file, the ASP.NET global.asax file provides access to the Application_onStart and Application_onEnd, Session_onStart and Session_onEnd events, in ASP.NET called Application_Start, Application_End, Session_Start, and Session_End events. Placing code between the beginning and end of subroutines based on these events causes that code to run when these events occur.

Here is an example of a global.asax file, with some pseudocode indicating where to place code running in response to application and session events:

```
<script language="VB" runat="server">
Sub Application_Start(Sender As Object,
 E As EventArgs)
  Place code that runs when
  your application starts here
End Sub

Sub Application_End(Sender As Object,
 E As EventArgs)
  Place code that runs when
  your application ends here
End Sub

Sub Session_Start(Sender As Object,
 E As EventArgs)
  Place code that runs when
  a session starts here
End Sub
```

```
Sub Session_End(Sender As Object,
 E As EventArgs)
  Place code that runs when
  a session ends here
End Sub

Sub Application_BeginRequest(Sender As Object,
 E As EventArgs)
  Place code that runs when
  a page request is started here
End Sub

Sub Application_EndRequest(Sender As Object,
 E As EventArgs)
  Place code that runs when
  a page request ends here
End Sub

Sub Application_Error(Sender As Object,
 E As EventArgs)
  Place code that handles
  errors here
End Sub
</script>
```

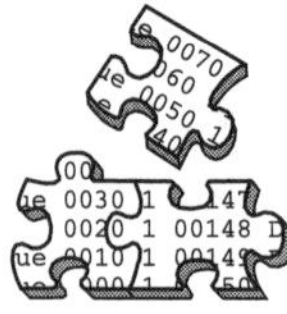

Project 5-2: Using the Application Object

The Application object is very useful for holding variables and values that are accessible to every page/user in an application, and at some point you may like to have an easy way of finding out what these variables/values are and removing some of them. As the application manager, it's easy to create a page for yourself that lets you see what is currently available as items in the Application object.

Step-by-Step

1. Open VS.NET and start a new project by clicking the New Project button in the Start Page pane. The New Project dialog box will open. Choose the ASP.NET Web Application template and enter **AppManagementPage** in the Name area of the dialog box (but leave the Location area set to your local host computer's name, in this case http://localhost). Click OK.
2. A blank Web Forms page should open up and the Solution Manager should list all the typical files in your new project (global.asax, Styles.css,

Webform1.aspx, and so on). You will add labels, a drop-down box, and a submit button to the Web Forms page, and the page will display the contents of the Application object and let you remove items from the list (from the Application object). All controls you add to the form will be positioned as shown in Figure 5-2.

3. Add two labels to the form from the Web Forms toolbox. Modify the Text property of the label at the top of the page to read Item Removed and List Rebuilt, set Fore Color to red, and name it (in the ID property) ResponseLabel. Change the text in the bottom label to read List of Items in Application Object in a green font. Set the Visible property of the top label to False.

4. Add a ListBox control to the form (from Web Forms) and size it as shown. Name it (in the ID property) AppValues.

5. Add a Button control from the Web Forms toolbox and set its Text property to Delete. Name it cmdButton1. Save the form (see Figure 5-3).

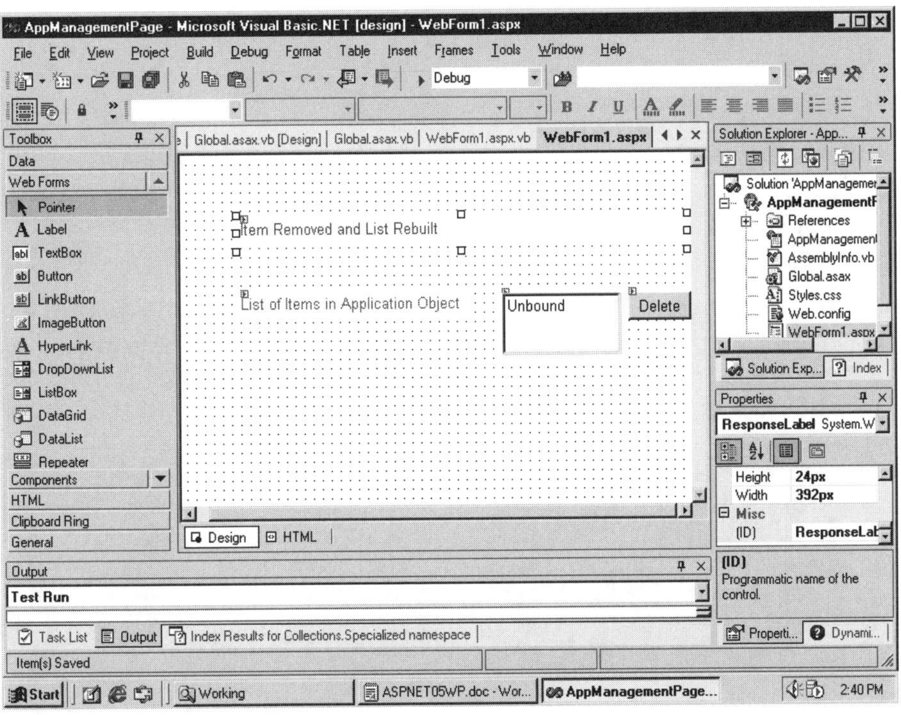

Figure 5-2 The Web Form in Design view

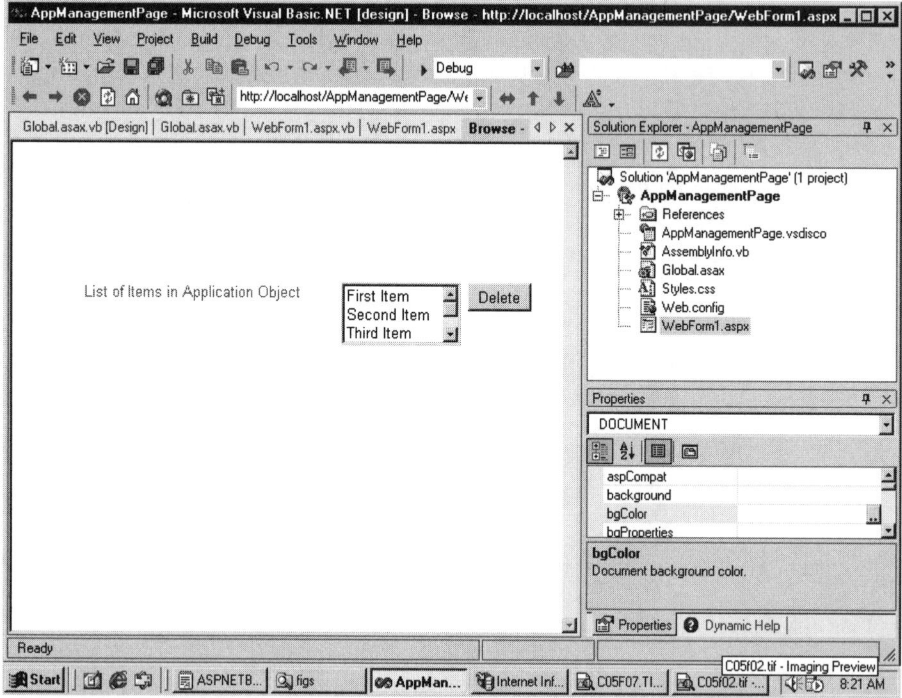

Figure 5-3 The layout of the Web Form

6. Double-click the global.asax file in the Solution Explorer pane, and then click the link that appears on the file to go into Code View. Add the following code right before the Sub Application_BeginRequest code:

```
Sub Application_Start()
  Application("FirstItem") = "First Item"
  Application("SecondItem") = "Second Item"
  Application("ThirdItem") = "Third Item"
  Application("FourthItem") = "Fourth Item"
  Application("FifthItem") = "Fifth Item"
End Sub
```

This code creates five items in the Application Object when the application starts.

7. Go back to the Web Forms page and double-click it. This takes you to the code-behind file named WebForms1.apsx.vb. In this page, add the following code to the Page Load event handler:

```
Private Sub Page_Load(ByVal sender As System.Object,
  ByVal e As System.EventArgs) Handles MyBase.Load

Dim collitem As String
Dim appValuesName As String
  If Not IsPostBack Then
    For Each collitem In Application
      Me.AppValues.Items.Add(New
 ListItem(Application(collitem), collitem))
    Next
  Else
    appValuesName =
 Request.Form.GetValues("AppValues")(0)
     Application.Lock()
     Application.Remove(appValuesName)
     Application.UnLock()
     AppValues.Items.Clear()
     For Each collitem In Application
       Me.AppValues.Items.Add(New
 ListItem(Application(collitem), collitem))
     Next
       ResponseLabel.Visible = "True"
  End If
End Sub
```


8. This code runs each time the page is loaded (the first time it is requested and then each time it is posted to itself). It dimensions the variables, checks to see if this is the first time or a postback, fills the AppValues control with the list of items from the Application object, removes items from the Application object if the page has been posted, rebuilds the list, and finally sets the Visible property of the top label to True.

9. Note that you don't have to use the Application.Contents collection in ASP.NET (as you would in ASP); you can simply use Application and the name of the item. And the Application_onStart event becomes just Application_Start in ASP.NET.

The Application Object

The Application object has no properties, but it does have collections, methods, and events. It provides a global storage space for variables (all of type Variant, with subtypes for each data type) that can house text, numbers, dates, arrays, and pointers to COM objects. Within the root folder of an application, you will place a special file named global.asa. This file has several functions, including initialization of Application and Session variables. We'll discuss (and provide examples of) global.asa as we progress through the chapter.

Scope

As we discussed earlier, web applications often need data available encompassing all current users as well as individual users. If you've ever programmed, you understand the concept of global (public) and local (private) scope. Global variables make their values available to everything in an application, while local variables are only available within their own procedure.

In a similar fashion, data residing in the Application object is available across the entire web application, while data residing in an individual Session object is only available to that individual session. Data in variables dimensioned while a script or procedure runs is available only as long as processing is occurring on that page. As we mentioned earlier, the Application object is created once as soon as the first user requests a page, and Session objects are created for the first and every subsequent user. Session objects are closed when users leave the site or close their browsers, while the Application object only closes after all active Sessions are closed or the server is shut down.

The Application Object's Events

Events are like triggers. They are a way of defining things that can happen to objects. For example, you are probably familiar with the onClick event for buttons in many programming environments. It occurs whenever the user clicks a button. The Application object is associated with two events, providing a means of initiating actions whenever an application starts or ends. The events are as follows:

- **onStart** This event occurs when the application starts and before the first requested page is executed or any sessions are created.

- **onEnd** This event occurs when the application ends and after any sessions have ended.

We'll put these two events to work in a global.asa file (we'll outline what this file does shortly) to set up some objects and variables in the Application object, and we'll also use similar events to do the same kinds of things with the Session object.

Application Object Collections

The Application object offers two collections:

- **Contents** This collection consists of the variables in the Application object that are not specified using the <OBJECT> tag.
- **StaticObjects** This collection consists of the variables in the Application object specified using the <OBJECT> tag.

Application Object Methods

The Application object also includes several methods that are very handy for managing the Contents collection. As you've seen, you can add variables to the Contents collection by giving them a name and a value (like this: Application ("variablename") = value). Suppose you want to get rid of a variable? There are a couple methods you can use to do that (Remove and RemoveAll).

Another issue arising with Application variables because of their global nature is who has control. If user1 accesses the value of a variable and after some processing tries to reset the value, what happens if user2 tries to do the same thing at the same time? The Application object has two methods that help you manage concurrency in a simple but effective way.

Here are the methods of the Application object:

- **Contents.Remove("variablename")** This method lets you remove a variable by name.
- **Contents.RemoveAll()** This method lets you remove all the variables in the Contents collection.

- **Lock()** This method lets you lock the Application object so that only the current page can access the Contents collection.
- **Unlock()** This method unlocks the Application object.

Removing variables is pretty straightforward; just write Application. Contents.Remove and give the variable name, or simply use the RemoveAll method to remove all variables. Of course, it helps to know the name of the variable if you want to remove a specific one. Locking the Application object is also pretty straightforward, but like any system of locking and unlocking, it is possible to get users into a situation where each is waiting for the other to release a variable, so it's important to always use the Lock and Unlock methods together and only perform actions on one variable at a time.

Here's an example of removing variables and locking/unlocking the Application object. First you'll create a simple form for entering new variables' names and values, and then you'll create a script to respond to the request. Use the following code to create the form (name it something like "index.htm"):

```
<HTML><HEAD><TITLE>Showing Application
 Variables</TITLE></HEAD>
<BODY>
<H2>Creating Messages Accessible to Everyone</H2>
<B>Add a variable and value
 to the Application object</B><P>
<FORM ACTION="index2.asp" METHOD=POST>
<TABLE><TR><TD>
Name Your Variable:</TD><TD><INPUT TYPE="text" SIZE=20
NAME="newvariable"></TD></TR>
<TR><TD>Enter Your Value:</TD><TD>
<INPUT TYPE="text" SIZE=50 NAME="newvalue"></TD></TR>
<TR><TD><BR></TD><TD><INPUT TYPE="submit" VALUE="Add
 Variable and Value">
<INPUT TYPE="reset" VALUE="Clear"></TD></TR></TABLE>
</FORM>
</BODY></HTML>
```

The HTML code builds a simple page and puts a form inside a table to arrange it nicely on the page. The form contains two text boxes, one for the name of the variable and one for the message you want to insert into the variable. Naturally, each text box has a distinct name so the script on the other end can process them into the new variable. The web page is shown in Figure 5-4.

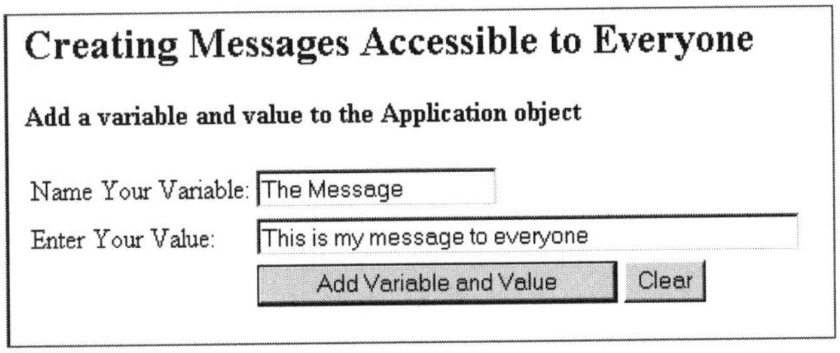

Creating Messages Accessible to Everyone

Add a variable and value to the Application object

Name Your Variable: The Message
Enter Your Value: This is my message to everyone
[Add Variable and Value] [Clear]

Figure 5-4 Your HTML form for creating a new Application variable

Now build a script that creates the new variable and then shows you that it has been created by telling you what the name is and what the value is. Use the following code (name the file index2.asp):

```
<HTML><HEAD><TITLE>Showing Application
 Variables</TITLE></HEAD>
<BODY>
<H2>The New Application Variable and Its Value</H2>
<%
vNewVariable = Request.Form("newvariable")
vNewValue = Request.Form("newvalue")
Application.Lock
Application(vNewVariable) = vNewValue
Application.Unlock
For Each collItem in Application.Contents
      If collItem = vNewVariable Then
            Response.Write "Your new variable is
 named '" & collItem & "' and the value in it is: "
            vNVal = Application.Contents(collItem)
            Response.Write(vNVal) & "<BR>"
      End If
Next
%>
</BODY></HTML>
```

The responding script starts with ordinary HTML code to create a page, then sets a couple variables (vNewVariable and vNewValue) to the value of the text boxes coming from the form. Once these values are set, the application is locked. The new variable is created, the new value is added; following these actions the application is unlocked. Following that, the ASP script iterates through the Application Contents collection until it finds the one whose name matches the name given by the user (using a For Each...Next loop and the If...Then conditional processing). The next lines respond to the user with the name of the variable and the value assigned by the user.

The Application object is very useful for holding variables and values that are accessible to every page/user in an application, and at some point you may like to have an easy way of finding out what these variables/values are and removing some of them. As the application manager, it's easy to create a page for yourself that lets you see what is currently available and remove those you'd like to remove.

Making an Application Management Page

Making an Application Management page means you'll be creating a page that gives you abilities other users might not have. In this case, you're going to make the management page display all current variables and easily remove those you choose. Create a new file and call it appman.asp. The code looks like this (see Figure 5-5 for a view of the Application Management page in the browser):

```
<HTML><HEAD><TITLE>Application Management</TITLE>
<META http-equiv="Content-Type"
 content="text/html; charset=iso-8859-1">
</HEAD>
<BODY BGCOLOR="#EEFFFF">
<FONT SIZE="+2" face="Arial, Helvetica, sans-serif">
<b>An Application Management Page</b></FONT>
<HR ALIGN="left" WIDTH="50%">
<TABLE BORDER=1 cellpadding=10><TR><TD COLSPAN=2 ALIGN=center>
<B>Current Variables and Values</B></TD></TR>
<TR><TD><B>Variable</B></TD><TD><B>Value</B></TD></TR>
<% For Each collItem in Application.Contents
vVVal = Application.Contents(collItem)
Response.Write "<TR><TD>" & collItem & "</TD>"
Response.Write"<TD>" & vVVal & "</TD></TR>"
Next
%>
</TABLE>
<br>
<FORM METHOD="POST" ACTION="appman1.asp">
Remove Value from Application
```

```
<SELECT NAME="select" size="1" MULTIPLE>
<%
For Each collItem in Application.Contents
     Response.Write "<OPTION>" & collItem & "</OPTION>"
Next
%>
</SELECT>
<INPUT TYPE="submit" VALUE="REMOVE">
</FORM>
<HR WIDTH="50%" ALIGN="left">
</BODY></HTML>
```


The page that actually does the removing (named appman1.asp) will have a section in it (inside the typical HTML code) that looks like this (see Figure 5-6 for a page view of the response):

```
<%
Application.Lock
Application.Contents.Remove(Request.Form("select"))
Application.Unlock
%>
The variable has been removed. Click
<A HREF="appman.asp">here</A> to go back
 to the Application Management page.
```

The main Application Management page begins with a table listing all current Application variables and their values. This table list includes variables

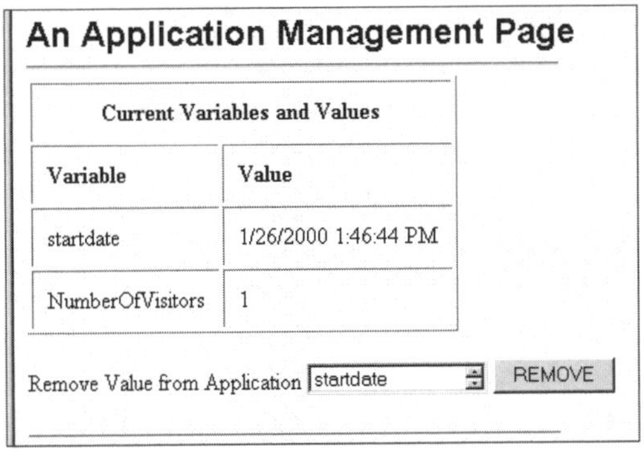

An Application Management Page

Current Variables and Values	
Variable	**Value**
startdate	1/26/2000 1:46:44 PM
NumberOfVisitors	1

Remove Value from Application [startdate] [REMOVE]

Figure 5-5 The Application Management page

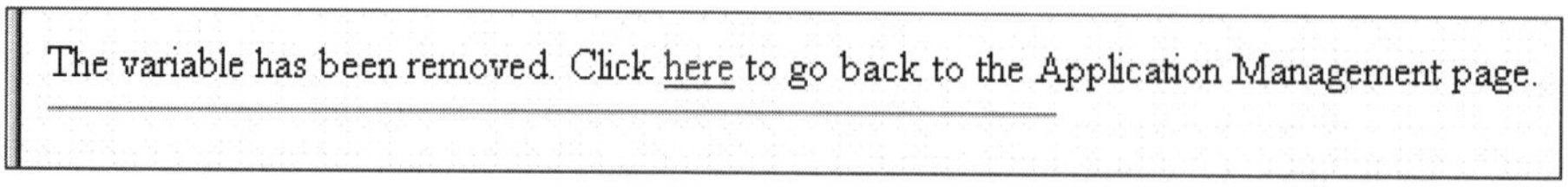

The variable has been removed. Click here to go back to the Application Management page.

Figure 5-6 The removal response

that were initialized when the application was first started as well as any variables that have been added by users along the way. Each variable/value row of the table was created using the familiar iteration procedure through each item in the Application.Contents collection.

Below the variable/value table is a control comprised of a drop-down box or menu that contains, as the name of each option, the names of each variable in the Application.Contents collection.

When the REMOVE button is clicked, the name of that option is sent back to the appman1.asp script. The appman1.asp script locks the application, removes the variable named in Request.Form("select"), and unlocks the application. It then displays a message to the user that the variable has been removed as well as a link pointing back to the Application Management page (appman.asp). When the user returns to the Application Management page, the table list and drop-down menu are refreshed.

ASP Sessions

Like the Application object, the Session object exists to make variables available and to perform functions such as initializing those variables when a session is started. The primary difference between a session and an application is that the application is global, while the session is local to its user. Variables found in the session are accessible only by the user who started the session.

ASP creates sessions by default whenever a user first requests a page (and does so automatically for each user who requests a page). Upon reflection, you will see that this implies some exchange of identifying information between the server and the user, so the server can recognize each individual user from the others. The identifying information that is passed is a special cookie, as we mentioned previously. If cookies are disabled, you can use the URL method of attaching identifying information to page requests.

Sessions in ASP.NET

In ASP.NET, sessions are created in a manner similar to ASP sessions, using a 120-bit string that is unique and very difficult to generate maliciously. ASP.NET sessions can maintain state information across page requests via the cookie or URL methods, depending on how you configure the session state handler.

Enabling and Disabling ASP Sessions

Processing cookies each time a page is requested consumes server resources and can be disabled if you choose. If you happen to know that some of your pages perform actions that require no sessions to get the job done, you can turn off sessions for those pages with a processing directive, like so:

```
<% ENABLESESSIONSTATE=False %>
```

You can also turn off sessions for the entire application by going into the Internet Services Manager, opening the Web Site Properties dialog box, and changing the Enable Session State setting. To perform this action, start the Internet Services Manager, open the Default Web Site Properties dialog box, and click the Home Directory tab. Next, click the Configuration button to open the Application Configuration dialog box, shown in Figure 5-7. Now you should be able to enable or disable session state by checking or unchecking the check box, and you should also be able to change the default session timeout.

The Session Object

Like the Application object, the Session object has several events associated with it that allow you to initiate actions when a session starts or ends. Sessions start with the first page requested and end under the following circumstances:

- The session times out before the page is loaded (the default is 20 minutes, as you can see in Figure 5-7).
- The Session.Abandon method is called.

You can set the timeout period at the Application Configure dialog box, or you can set it for individual pages using the Session.Timeout property. Either way, it provides a convenient way of managing user sessions within your application.

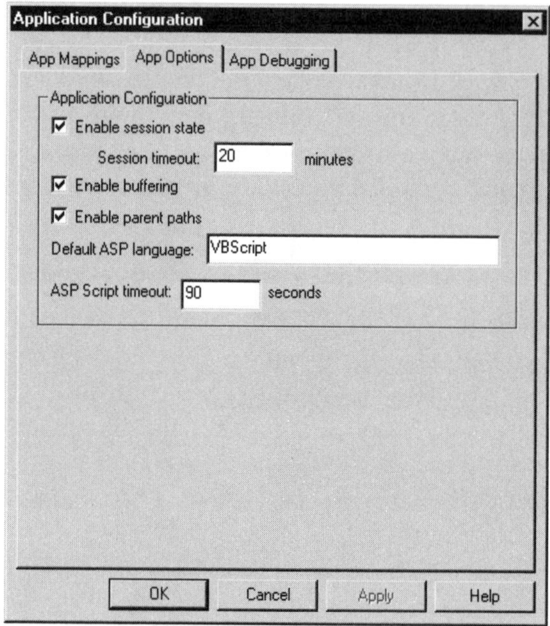

Figure 5-7 The Application Configuration dialog box

Session Event Handlers

The two session event handlers are onStart and onEnd. They work in the same fashion as the Application object onStart and onEnd events and are utilized from the global.asa file. To illustrate how they work, let's build in a useful little function that counts the total number of visitors to the site during the current run of the application. Start by making some modifications to the global.asa file, with code like this inserted into the Application_onStart subroutine to initialize the global counter variable:

```
Application("NumberOfVisitors") = 0
```

This just adds a variable named "NumberOfVisitors" to the Application.Contents collection when the application starts and sets the value to zero. To make the counter variable count, you'll also need to add some code to the global.asa file such as the following:

```
Sub Session_onStart()
Application.Lock
nVisitors = Application("NumberOfVisitors") + 1
Application("NumberOfVisitors") = nVisitors
Application.Unlock
End Sub
```

This code locks the application, increments the counter variable's value by 1, and then unlocks the application. Lastly, you'll make a page (named sessionman.htm) for users that tells them the current total number of visitors, using code like this:

```
<HTML><HEAD><TITLE>Session Events</TITLE></HEAD>
<BODY>
<FONT SIZE="+2" face="Arial, Helvetica, sans-serif">
<b>Your Session</b></FONT><P>
There are currently
<%
objVarVal = Application("NumberOfVisitors")
Response.Write(objVarVal)
%>
 visitors in this website.<BR>
</BODY>
</HTML>
```

This code retrieves the current value of the "NumberOfVisitors" variable and displays it on the page, inside a text message describing the value they are seeing.

Session Properties

The Session object includes four properties:

- **CodePage** This property sets the code page as a number representing the character set that will be used in the browser when displaying the page. For example, ANSI code page 1252 is used to display pages in American English.
- **LCID** This property sets the locale identifier. Each locale has a unique identifier number that refers to such things as the type of currency symbol to use with a page.
- **SessionID** This property contains the session identifier number (of type *long*) that is generated by the server upon creation of the session.

All SessionIDs are unique within an instance of the Application object but may be used repeatedly across consecutive instances of an Application.

Knowing the SessionID of a user will come in very handy as your applications get more complex, and it can also be useful to know the code page and LCID they are using. Let's make our user session page display these values.

Create a new asp page and call it session2.asp (place it in any website folder and it will run), and put code like the following in it (inside the usual beginning and ending HTML tags):

```
<FONT SIZE="+2" face="Arial, Helvetica, sans-serif">
<b>Your Session Properties</b></FONT><P>
<TABLE><TR>
<%
vCodePage = Session.CodePage
vLCID = Session.LCID
vSessionID = Session.SessionID
vTimeout = Session.Timeout
Response.Write "<TD>The Code Page you are
 using is: </TD><TD><B>" & vCodePage & "</B></TD></TR>"
Response.Write "<TD>Your Locale Identifier is: </TD>
<TD><B>" & vLCID & "</B></TD></TR>"
Response.Write "<TD>Your Session ID is: </TD><TD>
<B>" & vSessionID & "</B></TD></TR>"
Response.Write "<TD COLSPAN=2>Your Session will time
 out in <B>" & vTimeout & "</B> minutes with no
 further use.</TD></TR>"
%>
</TABLE>
```

This code lays the variables and their values out in a borderless table by setting the value of variables equal to the value of the Session Properties for code page, LCID, SessionID, and Timeout, as shown in Figure 5-8.

Session Collections

Like the Application object, the Session object has two collections: the Contents collection and the StaticObjects collection. The Contents collection contains all the variables and their values that are generated in a given session but are not defined by the <OBJECT> tag. The StaticObjects collection contains all the variables that are generated in a given session and are defined by the <OBJECT> tag.

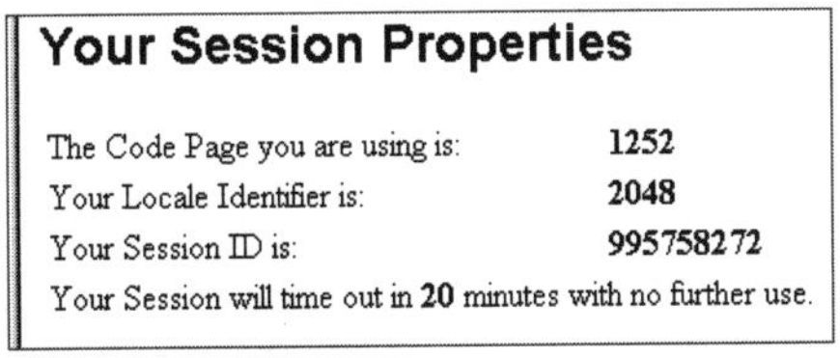

Your Session Properties

The Code Page you are using is:	**1252**
Your Locale Identifier is:	**2048**
Your Session ID is:	**995758272**

Your Session will time out in **20** minutes with no further use.

Figure 5-8 Session Properties displayed

The values in the variables can be read using any of the methods we discussed for the Application object, and the values in the Contents collection can be changed, while the values in the StaticObjects collection remain static (no surprise there).

Session Methods

Finally, the Session object also has methods for removing variables and for ending the session. They are as follows:

- **Contents.Remove("variablename")** This method removes the variable you have named.
- **Contents.RemoveAll()** This method removes all variables from the Contents collection.
- **Abandon()** This method ends the current user session and destroys the Session object when the page has finished executing.

The usage of the Contents.Remove and Contents.RemoveAll methods is the same as for the Application object, while the code for using the Abandon method is simply:

```
<% Session.Abandon %>
```

Note

Making a call to the Session.Abandon method works, but only after the calling page finishes executing. To ensure that it works properly, make it the last call on a page, or exit the page after the call.

Ask the Expert

Question: I'm a little unclear about when I need to use Application, Session, and Request events. When should I use these events, and why?

Answer: The global.asa or global.asax files are optional, and your application does not necessarily have to use the Application, Session, or Request events to perform its functions. However, you have the option of using these files and events because they can make it easier for you to develop a good application and for the application itself to work properly.

For example, suppose you want to display a message of the day whenever a new user logs on to your application. You could keep the message for the day in a database and place code in each page that forms a database connection, retrieves the information, and then displays it. This would work, but the application would pay a heavy price in terms of database reads.

Alternatively, you could set some code that retrieves the message for the day when the Application_onStart event is triggered and set some code in the Session_onStart event that checks to see whether it is time to retrieve a new message of the day. The message of the day could be kept in the Application object and refreshed only when a day or more has passed, instead of each time a page is requested, thereby significantly reducing the number of database reads.

Question: Sounds good. What are some other uses for Application, Session, and Request events?

Answer: The Application object is useful for storing data that is changed by all users across an application, and the Session object is useful for storing data that pertains uniquely to an individual user. Suppose you are running a website that tracks user responses to a survey and displays updated results to all users in real time. You could use a variable in the Application object to store this data and have code in the application change the value of this global variable whenever an individual user submits new responses to the survey. Likewise, the Session object might be used to keep track of an individual user's preferences during their session, as opposed to the preferences of all other users who happen to be logged on at that time.

Project 5-3: Using the Session Object with ASP.NET

The ASP objects we have covered so far, although we are not getting much into common components or databases, can still provide enough functionality to do some interesting things, so this section will go a little further than we have with other project sections. All the code in this project will be done in ASP.NET.

You're going to make a rudimentary shopping-cart application with a management area to place products online and check current orders; a process for users to become shoppers; and the capability for users to add items to their baskets, remove items from their baskets, calculate their total at any time, and place their orders. It won't be secure (or very fancy, either) but we'll get to those things in later modules.

Note

After you've read this code from beginning to end and tested it out, you'll notice that it doesn't save the contents of the variables (products or orders) from one running of the application to the next, a major weak point. Another limitation of this shopping-cart application is that it allows only one product to be ordered per order. We'll examine how to save the contents of variables across sessions and application instances in the modules on components (as well as add more than one product to an order) and how to insert values directly into a database in Modules 9 and 10 on Active Data Objects .NET (ADO.NET).

Step-by-Step

You're going to make a new project called ShoppingCart in VS.NET and use a global.asax file similar to the one you created earlier in this module. The website will be called the Ecommerce Adventure.

1. To create the code for the global.asax file, open the file in code view and insert the following three event handlers:

```
Sub Application_Start()
  Application("numberofsessions") = 0
  Application("numberoforders") = 0
  Application("numberofproducts") = 0
End Sub
Sub Session_Start()
  Session("numberofproductsincart") = 0
  Session("pcounter") = 0
```

```
  Application.Lock()
  Application("numberofsessions") =
 Application("numberofsessions") + 1
  Application("numberoforders")
 = Application("numberoforders") + 1
  Application.UnLock()
End Sub
Sub Session_End()
  Application.Lock()
  Application("numberofsessions")
 = Application("numberofsessions") - 1
  Application.UnLock()
End Sub
```

2. The handler for application starts and adds three items (numberofsessions, numberoforders, and numberofproducts) to the Application object, and all are set equal to zero. The handler for session adds two items (numberofproductsincart and pcounter) to the Session object and increments the number of sessions and the number of orders stored in the Application object up by one each. (The pcounter item is simply for generating a new number in sequence for each product added to the user's shopping cart). The session end handler decrements the number of sessions stored in the Application object.

3. To build the shopping-cart manager's screen (named SCManager.aspx), start with the form automatically added to the project WebForm1.aspx (in the Solution Explorer pane) and rename it as you would any ordinary file by clicking it twice slowly and then entering the filename.

4. Add Labels, ListBoxes, and TextBoxes from the Web Forms toolbox until the form resembles that shown in Figure 5-9. Only the large boxes next to Choose Action and Product List are ListBoxes (named "choice" and "ProductsList" in their respective ID properties). Add the choices for the ListBox named choice by entering them manually in the Items collection property of the ListBox (click Add and enter **No Choice**, **Add Product**, and **Delete Product** in the dialog box that appears when the ellipsis is clicked in this property field). Name the text boxes **NumberOfCustomers**, **NumberOfOrders**, **NumberOfProducts**, **ProductName**, **ProductNumber**, and **ProductPrice** according to the labels next to them. Enter a capital **P** as the Text property of the TextBox named ProductNumber. Note that there are two labels in red near the top of the form; the second label (with the word "None" showing) must be named ResponseLabel. Figure 5-9 shows the Manager form under construction.

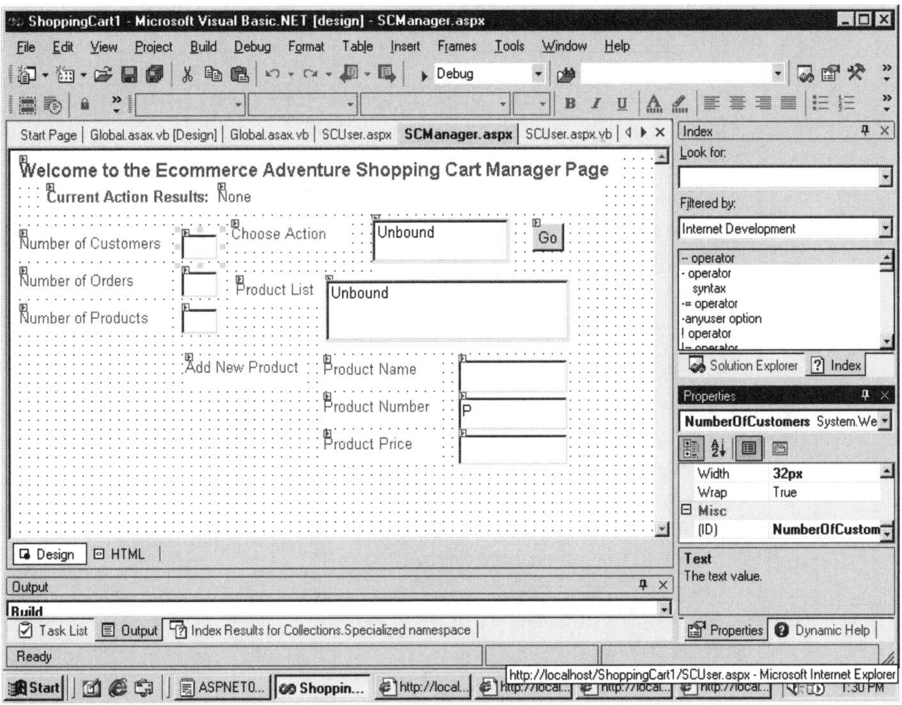

Figure 5-9 The SCManager.aspx form in Design view

5. The purpose of this form is to tell the manager how many customers are currently online, how many orders are in progress, and how many products are currently residing in the application. The form also lets the manager add and delete products to the list in real time. To make the form work, add code such as the following to the Page_Load event handler in the code-behind page (double-click the Web Form to show the code behind page). Make sure to put your code between the Sub and End Sub code of the Page_Load handler.

```
Dim collitem As String
Dim productsListName As String
Dim productsNumber As String
Dim choiceClicked As String
  NumberOfCustomers.Text
 = Application("numberofsessions") - 1
```

```
 NumberOfOrders.Text
= Application("numberoforders") - 1
 NumberOfProducts.Text
= Application("numberofproducts")
 If Not IsPostBack Then
   For Each collitem In Application
     If Left(collitem, 1) = "P" Then
       Me.ProductsList.Items.Add(New
ListItem(Application(collitem), collitem))
     End If
   Next
 Else
   choiceClicked
= Request.Form.GetValues("choice")(0)
   Select Case choiceClicked
     Case "No Choice"
       ResponseLabel.Text = "No Action Taken"
       NumberOfCustomers.Text
= Application("numberofsessions") - 1
       NumberOfOrders.Text
= Application("numberoforders") - 1
       NumberOfProducts.Text
= Application("numberofproducts")
     Case "Delete Product"
       productsNumber
= Request.Form.GetValues("ProductsList")(0)
       Application.Lock()
       Application.Remove(productsNumber)
       Application("numberofproducts")
= Application("numberofproducts") - 1
       Application.UnLock()
       ProductsList.Items.Clear()
       For Each collitem In Application
         If Left(collitem, 1) = "P" Then
           Me.ProductsList.Items.Add(New
ListItem(Application(collitem), collitem))
         End If
       Next
       NumberOfCustomers.Text
= Application("numberofsessions") - 1
       NumberOfOrders.Text
= Application("numberoforders") - 1
       NumberOfProducts.Text
= Application("numberofproducts")
```

```
        ResponseLabel.Text = "Product Deleted"
      Case "Add Product"
        productsListName
= Request.Form.GetValues("ProductName")(0)
& " - " & Request.Form.GetValues("ProductPrice")(0)
        productsNumber
= Request.Form.GetValues("ProductNumber")(0)
        Application(productsNumber)
= productsListName
        Application.Lock()
        Application("numberofproducts")
= Application("numberofproducts") + 1
        Application.UnLock()
        ProductsList.Items.Clear()
        For Each collitem In Application
          If Left(collitem, 1) = "P" Then
            Me.ProductsList.Items.Add(New
ListItem(Application(collitem), collitem))
          End If
        Next
        NumberOfCustomers.Text
= Application("numberofsessions") - 1
        NumberOfOrders.Text
= Application("numberoforders") - 1
        NumberOfProducts.Text
= Application("numberofproducts")
        ResponseLabel.Text = "Product Added"
    End Select
  End If
```


6. To use the form, the manager only needs to make a choice of what type of action to take and click the Go button. The code determines whether a postback is occurring, and if not, simply fills out the list of application items. An application and a session are started (but notice the counting of sessions and orders showing on the management form are decremented by one to account for the manager's own session). If a postback is not occurring, the form collects the value of the "choice" ListBox and uses the Select Case structure (the syntax is equivalent in VB.NET and VBScript) to decide which action to take.

7. If the action to take is Delete Product or Add Product, products are added to or deleted from the Application object as items whose name is the ProductNumber value (and must start with a *P*, which is why *P* is the default

Text property for the ProductNumber Text field). For all actions, the ProductsList ListBox is cleared and refilled, the number of customers, orders, and products is rechecked, and the ResponseLabel Text property is reset.

8. To create the SCUser.aspx form, you can click on the SCManager.aspx file and copy and paste it. A copy of the file will be created in your project. Rename it SCUser.aspx, and modify it so it resembles the form shown in Figure 5-10.

9. For the Full Name and Email Address fields, name them **FullName** and **EmailAddress** in their ID properties. These fields don't do anything in this example, but they represent contact and billing information that would ordinarily be collected in a shopping cart application. Numerous other fields

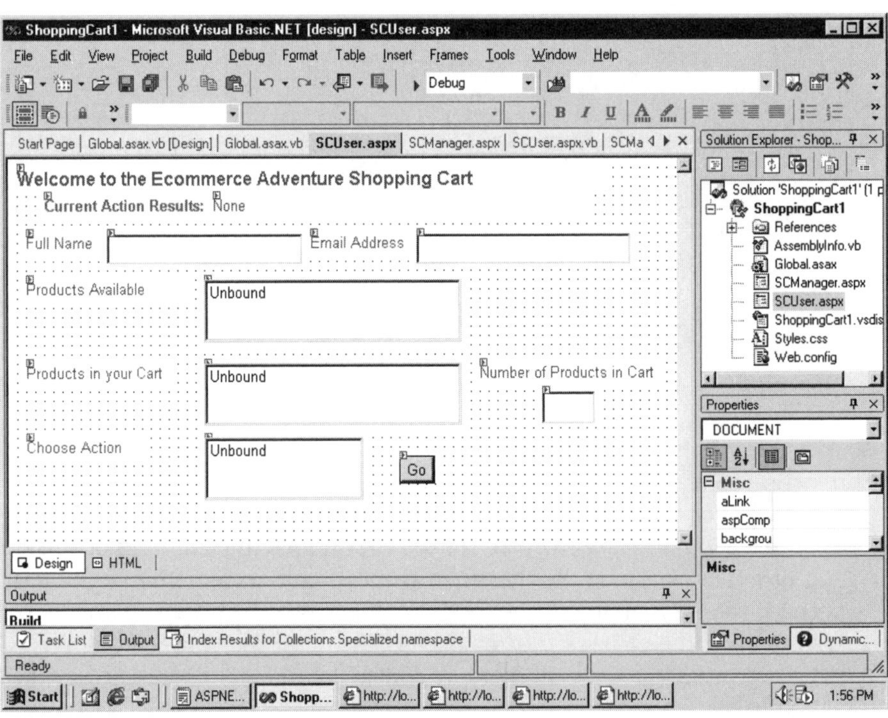

Figure 5-10 The SCUser.aspx form in Design view

like them would be added, and their contents would probably be validated before submission.

10. The label showing the word "None" must still be named ResponseLabel, and it will serve the same function in this form. The ListBox next to Products Available is the same one as in the SCManagers form, named ProductsList2 on this form. It gets filled with available products (stored as items in the Application object) the same way the one on the Managers form does. The ListBox at the bottom also works the same way as the "choice" ListBox on the manager's form, but the choices are different (Empty and Quit is added).

11. The ListBox in the middle, next to Products in your Cart, is named ProductsIn Cart. The text box to the right of that is named NumberOfProductsInCart. These show the products that are part of the Session object for this customer (remember, each person who logs on has a unique session generated) and the incremented number of products for the customer.

12. To make the form work, use the following code (place it in the code-behind page):

```
Dim collitem As String
Dim productAdded As String
Dim productDesc As String
Dim choiceClicked As String
NumberOfProductsInCart.Text
 = Session("numberofproductsincart")
If Not IsPostBack Then
  For Each collitem In Application
    If Left(collitem, 1) = "P" Then
      Me.ProductsList2.Items.Add(New
 ListItem(Application(collitem), collitem))
    End If
  Next
Else
  choiceClicked = Request.Form.GetValues("choice")(0)
  Select Case choiceClicked
    Case "No Choice"
      ResponseLabel.Text = "No Action Taken"
      ProductsList2.Items.Clear()
      For Each collitem In Application
```

```
        If Left(collitem, 1) = "P" Then
          Me.ProductsList2.Items.Add(New
ListItem(Application(collitem), collitem))
        End If
      Next
      NumberOfProductsInCart.Text
= Session("numberofproductsincart")
    Case "Delete Product"
      productAdded
= Request.Form.GetValues("ProductsInCart")(0)
      Session.Remove(productAdded)
      Session("numberofproductsincart")
= Session("numberofproductsincart") - 1
      ProductsList2.Items.Clear()
      For Each collitem In Application
        If Left(collitem, 1) = "P" Then
          Me.ProductsList2.Items.Add(New
ListItem(Application(collitem), collitem))
        End If
      Next
      ProductsInCart.Items.Clear()
      For Each collitem In Session
        If Left(collitem, 1) = "P" Then
          Me.ProductsInCart.Items.Add(New
ListItem(Session(collitem), collitem))
        End If
      Next
      NumberOfProductsInCart.Text
= Session("numberofproductsincart")
      ResponseLabel.Text = "Product Deleted"
    Case "Add Product"
      productAdded = "P" & Session("pcounter")
      productDesc = Application
(Request.Form.GetValues("ProductsList2")(0))
      Session(productAdded) = productDesc
      Session("numberofproductsincart")
= Session("numberofproductsincart") + 1
      Session("pcounter") = Session("pcounter") + 1
      ProductsList2.Items.Clear()
      For Each collitem In Application
```

```
        If Left(collitem, 1) = "P" Then
          Me.ProductsList2.Items.Add(New
ListItem(Application(collitem), collitem))
        End If
      Next
      ProductsInCart.Items.Clear()
      For Each collitem In Session
        If Left(collitem, 1) = "P" Then
          Me.ProductsInCart.Items.Add(New
ListItem(Session(collitem), collitem))
        End If
      Next
      NumberOfProductsInCart.Text
= Session("numberofproductsincart")
      ResponseLabel.Text = "Product Added to Cart"
    Case "Empty and Quit"
      Session.RemoveAll()
      Session.Abandon()
      Application.Lock()
      Application("numberoforders")
= Application("numberoforders") - 1
      ResponseLabel.Text = "Cart Emptied. Goodbye."
      ProductsList2.Items.Clear()
      For Each collitem In Application
        If Left(collitem, 1) = "P" Then
          Me.ProductsList2.Items.Add(New
ListItem(Application(collitem), collitem))
        End If
      Next
      ProductsInCart.Items.Clear()
      For Each collitem In Session
        If Left(collitem, 1) = "P" Then
          Me.ProductsInCart.Items.Add(New
ListItem(Session(collitem), collitem))
        End If
      Next
      NumberOfProductsInCart.Text
= Session("numberofproductsincart")
  End Select
End If
```

Figure 5-11 shows the Manager's page with a few products added, and Figure 5-12 shows the user's page with a few products in the cart.

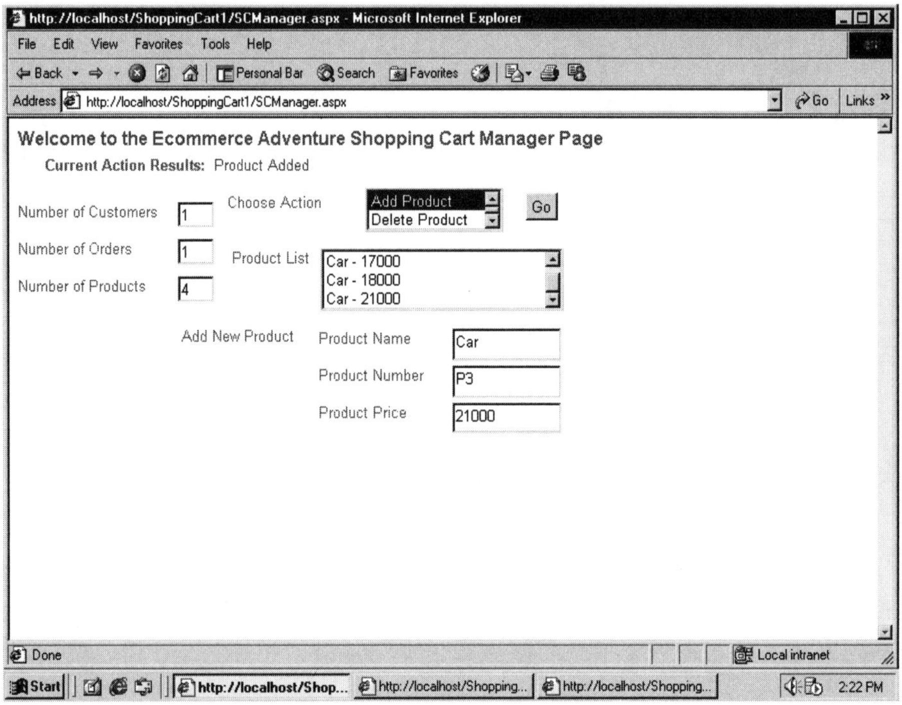

Figure 5-11 The Manager's page

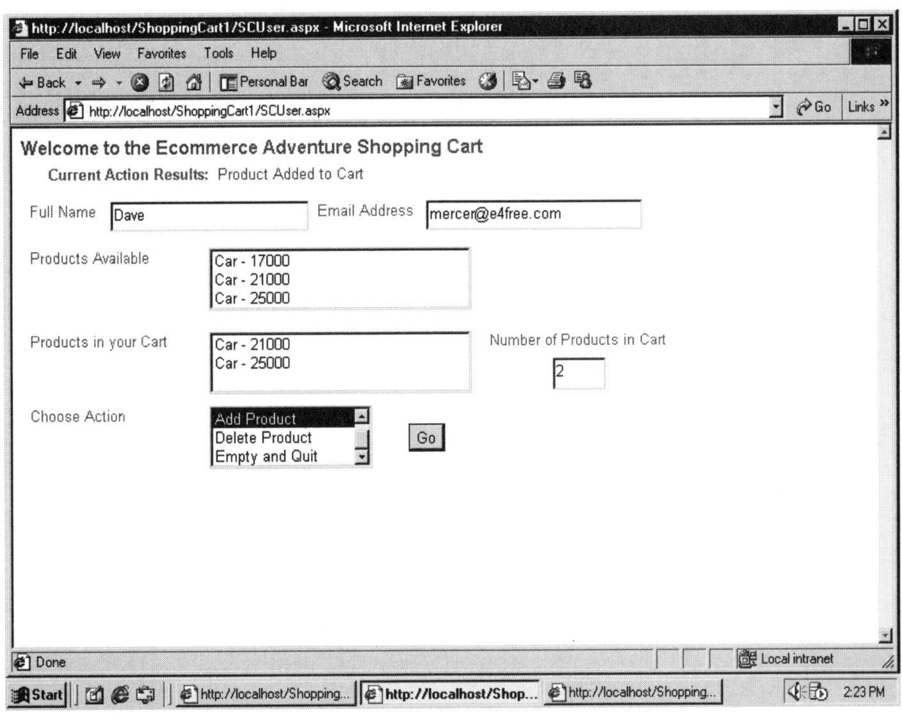

Figure 5-12 The User's page

Mastery Check

1. What is the difference between an ordinary ASP or ASP.NET application and a virtual one?

   A. A virtual application resides on several distributed servers.

   B. A virtual application has no user interface.

   C. A virtual application is a separate application running in a subfolder off the root folder of the default Website.

   D. None of the above.

2. What does scope mean, in the context of ASP?

   A. Defines the audience for your script.

   B. Allows every script to see the variables of every other script.

   C. Defines which variables can be seen by which scripts.

   D. None of the above.

3. What is the difference between application and session scope?

   A. Only application managers can use application scope.

   B. Only users can use session scope.

   C. Application scope maintains variables that can be seen by any script running within the application, while session scope maintains variables that can be seen only by scripts running within the session of that individual user.

   D. There is no functional difference.

4. By what mechanism does the global.asa file permit you to run code when your applications and sessions start or finish?

   A. Global parameters

   B. Scope settings

Mastery Check

C. Cookies

D. Events

5. How does your ASP application identify an individual user and establish a session?

A. The user must log in.

B. By the user's IP address.

C. Using a session cookie.

D. None of the above.

6. The code to add a variable to the application is:

____

____

7. The code to abandon a session is:

____

____

8. The code to remove all variables from a session is:

____

____

9. What is the scope of variable values contained in the default application and in virtual applications?

A. Virtual applications can see variables in the default application unless they happen to have the same names, but the default application cannot see variables in virtual applications.

B. Virtual applications cannot see variables in the default application unless they happen to have the same names, but the default application can see variables in virtual applications.

Mastery Check

C. Virtual applications cannot see variables in the default application and the default application cannot see variables in virtual applications.

D. Virtual applications may not have variables; only the default application may have variables, and the scope of variables in the default application is global.

E. None of the above.

10. Configuration in ASP.NET is managed using _____ files. Your computer, individual applications, and even individual pages may each have their own configuration defined in these files.

11. How are ASP.NET configuration files created, and in what format are they written?

____

____

12. What configuration section handler of an ASP.NET configuration file controls the applications browser capabilities, and what section controls Web Services?

A. The clientConnection and servicesWeb sections, respectively.

B. The browserCaps and webServices sections, respectively.

C. These configuration settings are controlled in the application, not in the configuration file.

D. None of the above.

13. What methods can ASP.NET use to manage state?

A. Cookies

B. URL extensions

C. TelNet sessions

D. Only A and B above

E. A, B, and C above

Mastery Check

14. What happens when you make changes to an ASP.NET global.asax file while your application is running?

A. The changes will be added to the application only when the application is shut down, thereby preserving any state information stored in Application and Session variables.

B. The changes will be added to the application the first time the server detects there are no open sessions, thereby preserving state information but updating the application as soon as practical.

C. The changes will be detected and the entire application shut down and restarted, destroying any current state information.

D. None of the above.

15. What practical differences are there in the way ASP and ASP.NET make use of the Application and Session objects and their event handlers in the global.asa and global.asax files?

A. The state attribute must be set for ASP.NET applications, but this is not necessary (or possible) for ASP applications.

B. There is virtually no practical difference.

C. ASP.NET does not use Application and Session objects, so the comparison is not valid.

D. None of the above.

Module 6

ASP.NET Objects and Components

The Goals of This Module

- Learn the relationships between the members of the Scripting Object Model
- Create and use the Dictionary object
- Create a FileSystemObject object and navigate the file system with it
- Create Drive, Folder, and TextStream objects and list their properties
- Set up the Ad Rotator component and associated image files
- Review the Browser Capabilities component and capabilities storage text file
- Link content into web pages using the Content Linking component
- Review the Counters components methods for general tracking

If you've already done application programming, you're probably used to being able to read and write files from and to the drives. If you've done JavaScript and VBScript programming in web pages, you may have noticed that these capabilities are absent. Naturally, because JavaScript and VBScript run upon download, these capabilities have been left out so that malicious programmers cannot write web pages that destroy user's machines upon downloading a web page.

Built-in ASP and ASP.NET objects such as the Request and Response objects and objects included in the Scripting Runtime Library are not the only objects or components available to ASP. ADO and ADO.NET objects are extremely useful for accessing and working with databases, and we'll cover them in great detail in Modules 8 through 10. Other types of components are referred to as server components, and they are installed as part of the basic installation of ASP, ASP.NET, and IIS in Windows 2000.

On the server, however, there are times when you'll want to have the capability to read from or write to the drives. This module covers the objects available to ASP and ASP.NET that allow these functions to be performed. ASP.NET goes beyond using objects and components that are built-in or available from third parties. With ASP.NET, you can program your own components and deploy them with your applications.

The Scripting Object Model

Active Server Pages 3.0 (and ASP.NET) supports the use of objects installed on the server to enhance the capabilities inherent in ASP. The Request and Response objects are built-in (or intrinsic) objects. Components are objects as well. In fact, there are objects for manipulating the file system, for managing common website tasks, and even for changing registry settings and uploading files. Think of objects as reusable application program components that provide specific functionality in a way that is easy to use inside your ASP and ASP.NET applications, without having to reinvent the wheel.

An *object model* is simply a description of how available objects fit together and are related to one another in function. There are three objects that are available via the Scripting Runtime Library:

- **The Dictionary object** This object can store name/value pairs you can create, set, and retrieve.

- **The FileSystemObject object** This object gives you access to the underlying file system (via drive, folder, and file objects) on the server and in IE 5.0 on the client as well.
- **The TextStream object** This object lets you create, read, and write to text files.

These objects bear a relationship to each other (the object model), wherein the FileSystemObject is a kind of parent object capable of instantiating Drive, Folder, File, and TextStream objects, and the Dictionary object serves them both. Together they comprise the set of objects that are available in the Scripting Runtime Library.

Ask the Expert

Question: I've heard of object models before, but I'd like a better explanation of what they are and what they apply to. Can I create my own? Under what circumstances are they useful, and how can they help me?

Answer: Object models are first and foremost models, like any other kind of model. At the most basic level, all models are conceptual representations of things, some more realistic than others. For example, a model railroad contains itty-bitty railroad cars, people, tracks, and so forth, hooked together in a representation of a real railroad.

In programming, models are often used to represent how ideas or structures are related to each other. The relationship of database data in tables can be depicted via lines going from one table to the next (and we'll show examples of this in later chapters). For the Scripting Library objects, the relationships are relatively simple: primarily, which objects can create or navigate to others and what collections they have.

Question: The FileSystemObject object seems to possess many of the capabilities of a File Manager-type program. Can I develop my own with ASP.NET? If I am in the server anyway, why do I need these capabilities in ASP.NET?

Answer: It is very common to develop online applications for clients, and it is also very common that clients want certain management-type functions automated. This means that you will probably be developing a set of functions for the client's users and another set of functions for client employees who will be managing the application.

Within your user functions, FileSystem capabilities will likely be hidden or tightly controlled to keep users from breaking your server. Within client-employee management functions, FileSystem capabilities will probably be more flexible with a lesser amount of control, although you will probably build in enough control to prevent breaking the server unless the client employee is warned first.

Either way, it is likely that much of the use and management of your applications will be online, rather than directly at the server. Therefore, you or your clients need the capability to get in and work with the file system from a browser.

Creating Objects

Whenever you need to use a component, you can create an instance of it using either the Server.CreateObject method or the <OBJECT> tags. Depending upon how it will be used, there are several issues you need to take into consideration. These issues affect the scope and performance of your objects.

More About Scope

Objects created using either method have, by default, page-level scope. They are available while the page is executing ASP and are eliminated once the page execution is finished and the results are sent to the client. To set scope to the session or application level, you can simply insert the attribute SCOPE= "APPLICATION" into your <OBJECT> tags (when creating instances of that object within the global.asa file). There is an example of this practice in Module 5.

Note

There are differences in the way the Server.CreateObject method and <OBJECT> tags work. When an object is created with Server.CreateObject, it is instantiated immediately. When an object is created with the <OBJECT> tags, it is not created until first called within the script. Also, you have the ability to remove objects from the session or application if you used the Server.CreateObject method to make them, but you don't have this option if you used the <OBJECT> tags.

Performance and Threading Models

The performance and scalability of your application depends in part on how you instantiate components and partly on their *threading model*. Threads are a basic unit of instructions that the processor (CPU) can carry out to accomplish whatever task is required by the operating system and application programs running on it. Think of each thread as a set of instructions representing a task or program. Many threads can run at the same time, each one competing for processor time and carrying a priority. The threading model used by a component can affect its ability to get its job done.

There are five threading models in Windows 2000:

- **Single-threaded** One process at a time can use the component.
- **Apartment-threaded** Multiple processes can use the component but can use only one thread.
- **Neutral-threaded** Multiple processes can use the component on any of its threads.
- **Multiple- or free-threaded** Multiple processes can use the components on different threads.
- **Both-threaded** The component can be simultaneously apartment- and free-threaded.

With page-level scope, apartment-threaded and neutral-threaded components will work best; with session- and application-level scope, both-threaded components will perform best. Microsoft recommends using page-level scope wherever possible, so most of your work will probably be with apartment-threaded components (there aren't many neutral-threaded components out yet).

Creating Scripting Runtime Library Objects

In the next section, you'll be creating Scripting Runtime Library objects individually and demonstrating the types of ASP or ASP.NET code to use to work with them. The code should work whether you use it with ASP or ASP.NET. In Project 6-1, we'll demonstrate a few of them in an ASP.NET application. We'll also list all the <OBJECT> tag attributes that can be set, just for good measure. You can see what the opening ASP page looks like in Figure 6-1.

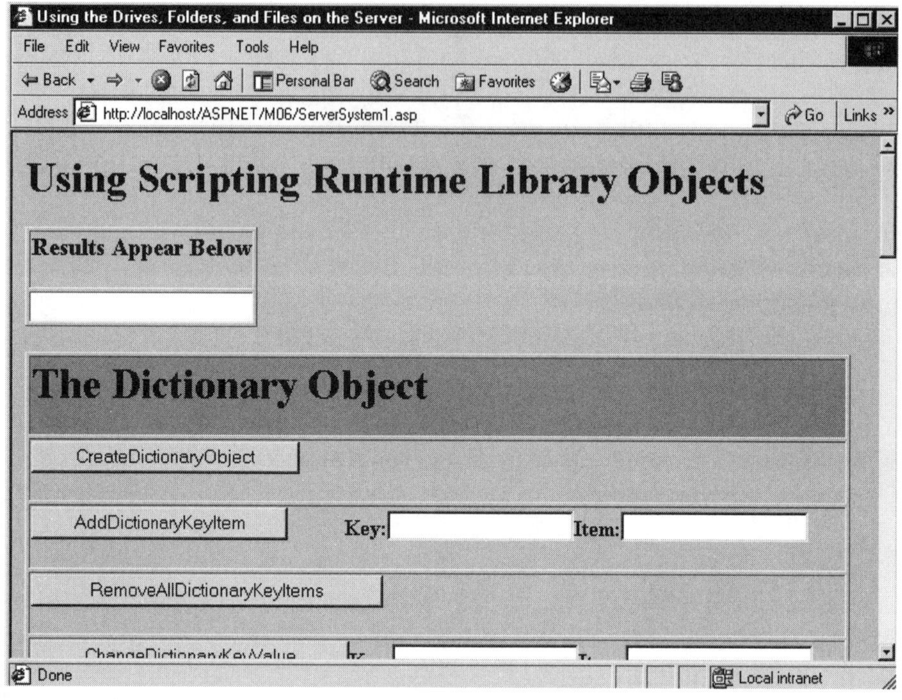

Figure 6-1 The opening ASP file system management page

Note

The code shown in the remainder of this module can be used in either ASP or ASP.NET. In ASP, you would develop web pages to display the results (the spaghetti code model), but in ASP.NET, you would separate the code from the pages using the code-behind model. Either way, the results will be the same. We won't show the separate models in this and later modules, as we've been over that ground extensively in previous modules.

The Scripting.Dictionary Object

The Dictionary object is designed to allow you to create a container for name/value pairs of your choosing. If you want to allow the user to generate their own sets of name/values, the Dictionary object comes in quite handy, as opposed to name/values derived from Form elements, where the names of the name/value pairs are hard-coded.

Dictionary Object Properties and Methods

The Dictionary object has the following properties:

- **CompareMode** This property works for VBScript only and sets or returns the string comparison mode for the names (keys) you create.
- **Count** This property returns the number of names currently in the dictionary.
- **Item(*key*)** This property sets or returns the value of an item (value) for a specified key (name).
- **Key(*key*)** This property sets the value of a name (key).

The Dictionary object has the following methods:

- **Add(*key.item*)** This method adds a key (name) and item (value) to the Dictionary.
- **Exists(*key*)** This method returns True if the specified key (name) exists and False if it does not exist.
- **Items** This method returns an array containing the items in a Dictionary.
- **Keys** This method returns an array containing the keys in a Dictionary.
- **Remove(*key*)** This method removes an individual name/value pair designated by the key you specify.
- **RemoveAll** This method removes all the name/value pairs in the Dictionary.

Creating a Dictionary Component with Page Scope

You can create an instance of the Dictionary object using VB.NET, VBScript, or JScript with the Server.CreateObject method or by using <OBJECT> tags in the global.asa or global.asax file. For example, if you want to build a Dictionary object inside an application on a page, you could use the following code:

```
<OBJECT RUNAT="SERVER" SCOPE="PAGE"
 ID="objDictionary"
 PROGID="Scripting.Dictionary"></OBJECT>
```

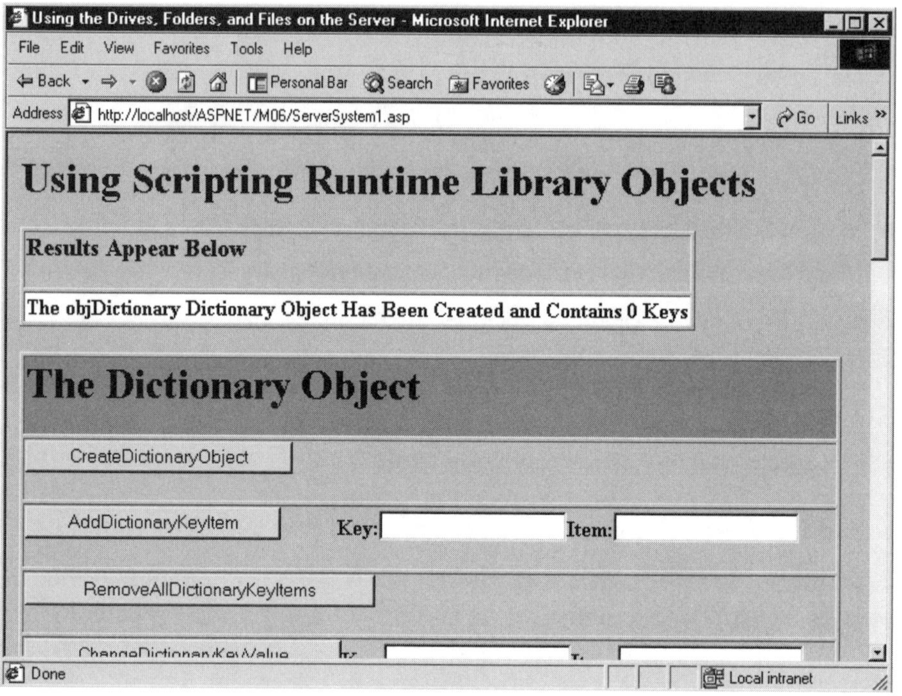

Figure 6-2 Dictionary object created with zero keys

Notice the ID parameter. The name in this code is objDictionary, but of course you can use any name you like. Using the <OBJECT> tags is permissible, but you can't set the scope higher than page level or an error will be generated. Figure 6-1 showed an example web page (with buttons for creating a Dictionary object, both from inside a page and accessing it from the global.asa file). Figure 6-2 displays the message you receive when you create a Dictionary object within the ASP page. Notice that it lists the current number of keys.

Listing Dictionary Names/Values

Name/value pairs in the Dictionary object are called keys and items, respectively. In the next code segment, you're going to create an instance of a Dictionary object with session-level scope (so it will retain values across successive pages in our application) in the global.asa or global.asax file:

```
<OBJECT ID="objDictionarySes" RUNAT="server"
 SCOPE="Session" PROGID="Scripting.Dictionary">
</OBJECT>
```

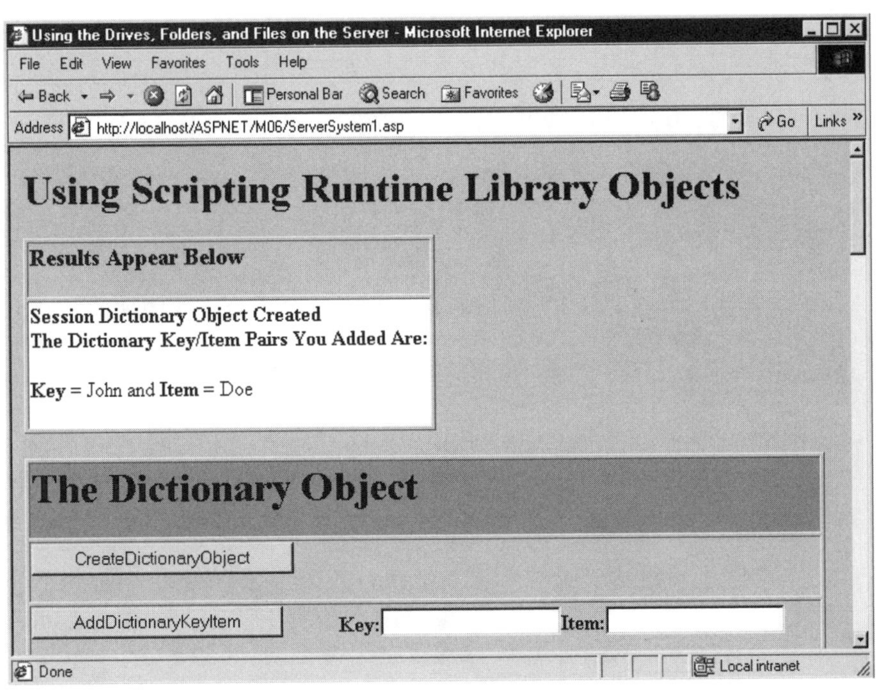

Figure 6-3 Global Dictionary object created with key/item

Next, you'll put together some code to access that Dictionary object from your application. This code will dimension a few variables (for holding name/value pair data, a counter, and a reference to the Dictionary object), set the value of some of those variables to the values received from the requesting form page, and iterate through the name/value pairs created (as shown in Figure 6-3):

```
Dim vKey
Dim vItem
Dim arKeys
Dim arItems
Dim intI
Dim objDictionaryS
Set objDictionaryS = Session("SessionDictionary")
vKey = Request.Form("key")
vItem = Request.Form("item")
objDictionaryS.Add vKey, vItem
arKeys = objDictionaryS.Keys
arItems = objDictionaryS.Items
Response.Write "<B>Session Dictionary
```

```
 Object Created</B><BR>"
Response.Write "<B>The Dictionary Key/Item Pairs
 You Added Are:</B><P>"
  For intI = 0 to objDictionaryS.Count - 1
   Response.Write "<B>Key = </B>" & arKeys (intI)
   Response.Write " and <B>Item =
 </B>" & arItems (intI) & "<BR>"
  Next
```

As an experiment to try on your own, add a name/value pair to the Dictionary object and then try to add the same name to the dictionary again. You should get an error message stating that that key already exists.

Removing Dictionary Name/Value Pairs

There is a built-in Remove method you can use to remove name/value pairs from the Dictionary object. Figure 6-4 shows it removing key/value pairs. When

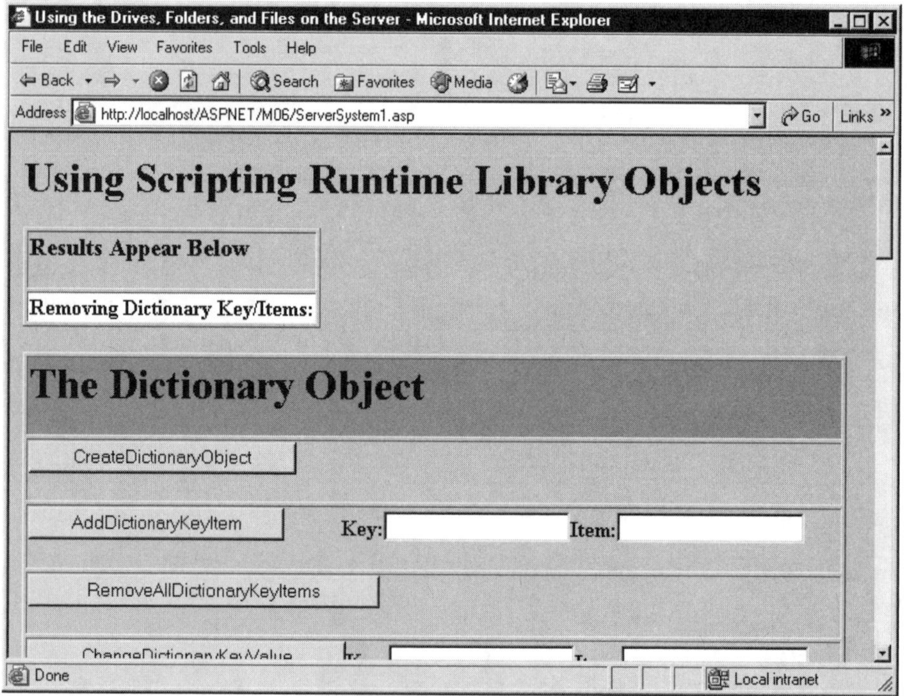

Figure 6-4 Removing key/value pairs from the Dictionary object

referencing the session-level Dictionary object created in global.asa from your page, you need to also set the session-level Dictionary equal to the object in your page for the change to take effect, as shown in the following code in line 3:

```
Set objDictionaryS = Session("SessionDictionary")
objDictionaryS.RemoveAll
Set Session("SessionDictionary") = objDictionaryS
```

Changing Dictionary Object Names/Values

Once created, Dictionary object names and values can be changed at the page level. You might want to do this so that a particular user can play a game with other users online, such as some kind of simple word game wherein one user creates a name/value pair, another user changes that name/value pair, and the first user tries to guess what was changed.

These kinds of changes can be made with code such as the following, as shown in Figure 6-5:


```
Set objDictionaryS = Session("SessionDictionary")
vKey = Request.Form("key")
vItem = Request.Form("item")
objDictionaryS.Item(vKey) = vItem
Set Session("SessionDictionary") = objDictionaryS
Response.Write "<B>Dictionary Key Item Value Has
 Been Changed To:</B><P>"
arKeys = objDictionaryS.Keys
arItems = objDictionaryS.Items
      For intI = 0 to objDictionaryS.Count - 1
            Response.Write "<B>Key = </B>"
 & arKeys (intI)
            Response.Write " and <B>Item = </B>"
 & arItems (intI) & "<BR>"
      Next
```

This code references the session-level Dictionary object, sets the value of a couple variables according to Form elements in the requesting page, changes the value of existing Dictionary object name/value pairs, and then lists the name/value pairs for review to show the changes made.

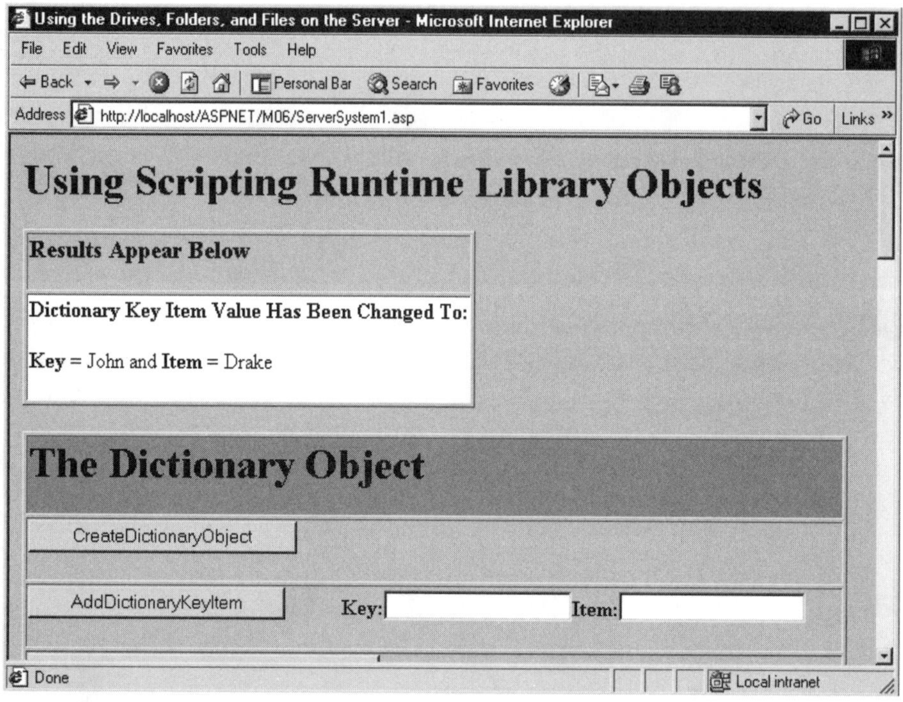

Figure 6-5 Changing item values for a Dictionary object

1-Minute Drill

- The Dictionary object contains name-value pairs. What is the Dictionary object name for a name?
- What is the Dictionary object name for a value?

The Scripting.FileSystemObject Object

Using the FileSystemObject object improperly can potentially damage your system because the FileSystemObject object can access and make changes to any folder or file on your system.

- Key
- Item

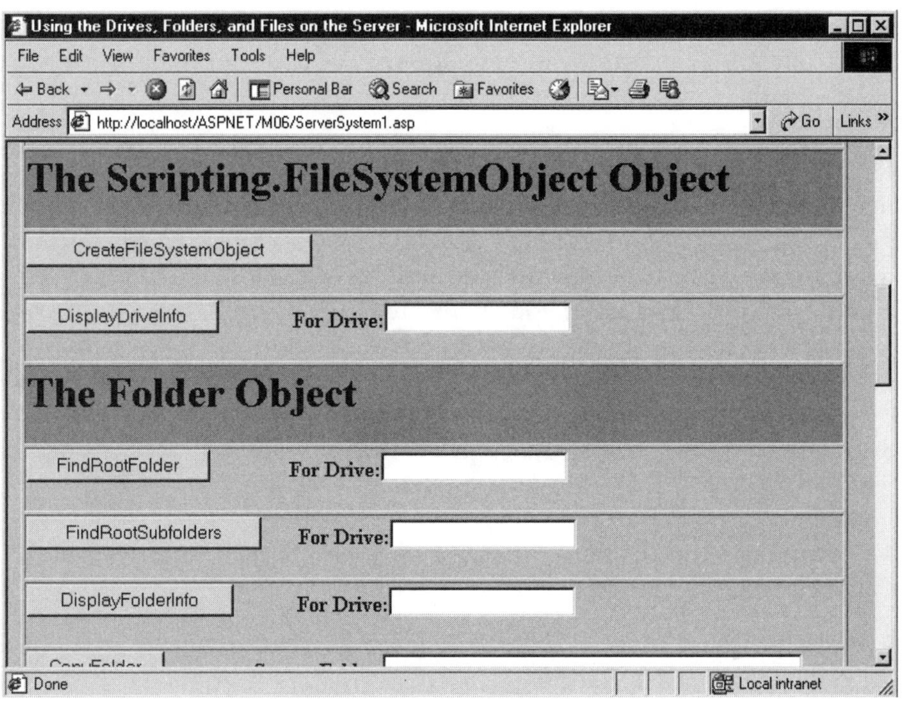

Figure 6-6 The FileSystemObject section

Keeping this caution in mind, the FileSystemObject object and its subsidiary objects are among the most valuable tools in your toolbox, precisely because of their power. The demonstration ASP page with buttons for creating and displaying info about the FileSystemObject object is shown in Figure 6-6.

Just remember, any access you provide to the server's drives, folders, and files could really screw up your operations, so be extremely careful what you do. Although in our examples we allow the user to choose any folder or file for modification, this is one time when it might be best to hard-code in folder and file references as constants, rather than provide unlimited access through variables. That way, the user can't just do anything they want (read or write to any file or folder), and you still avoid the drawback of having to change every coded reference when files or folders change.

FileSystemObject Properties

The FileSystemObject object provides only one property, Drives, and this property returns a collection of all the drives available on the system along with any network drives mapped to it. You can set an object of your choice equal to this property, and the Drives are accessible through the Drive object properties and methods (in the next section).

FileSystemObject Methods

The FileSystemObject has quite a few methods, some pertaining to drives, some pertaining to folders, and some pertaining to files. There are a number of ways to navigate to and alter folders and files, and they are useful under different circumstances. For instance, if you happen to have the entire path to a file you might want to use the FileSystemObject to retrieve and modify it. Alternatively, if you happen to be in the folder already, you might want to use the Folder object to reference and change the file. It just depends on where in the file system you are and what information you happen to have available. In any case, here are the methods of the FileSystemObject:

- **DriveExists(*driveletter*)** This method returns True if the drive letter specified exists and False if not.
- **GetDrive(*driveletter*)** This method returns a Drive object equivalent to the drive letter specified.
- **GetDriveName(*driveletter*)** This method returns the name of the drive specified by driveletter as a string.
- **BuildPath(*path,name*)** This method adds the file or folder specified by name to the current path and adds a separator character ("\") as necessary.
- **CopyFolder(*source,destination,overwrite*)** This method copies a folder from one location (the source) to another (the destination), overwriting by default unless the overwrite parameter is explicitly set to False.
- **CreateFolder(*foldername*)** This method creates a folder named foldername at the path specified in foldername.
- **DeleteFolder(*folderpathname,force*)** This method deletes a folder residing at folderpathname, and can even delete read-only folders if the overwrite parameter is set to True.

- **FolderExists(*folderpathname*)** This method returns True if the folder specified in folderpathname exists and False if not.
- **GetAbsolutePathName(*path*)** This method returns a path based on the current folder's path and the path specified.
- **GetFolder(*folder*)** This method returns a folder object equivalent to the folder specified.
- **GetParentFolderName(*path*)** This method returns the name of the parent folder for the folder or file specified in path.
- **GetSpecialFolder(*folder*)** This method returns a folder object equivalent to the special folder specified, such as a Windows folder, a System folder, or a Temporary folder.
- **MoveFolder(*source,destination*)** This method moves a folder specified in source (the complete path including folder name) to the location specified in destination (the complete path including folder name).
- **CopyFile(*source,destination,overwrite*)** This method copies a file specified in source to the location specified in destination, overwriting any existing file with the same path and name unless the overwrite parameter is set to False.
- **CreateTextFile(*filepath,overwrite,unicode*)** This method creates a text file specified in filepath, overwriting an existing file of the same path and name unless the overwrite parameter is set to False and as ASCII unless the optional unicode parameter is set to True.
- **DeleteFile(*filepath,force*)** This method deletes the file specified in filepath, even read-only files if the force parameter is set to True.
- **FileExists(*filepath*)** This method returns True if the specified file exists.
- **GetBaseName(*filepath*)** This method returns the name of the file specified in filepath, removing the drive, folder, and extension data.

- **GetExtensionName(*filepath*)** This method returns the extension for a given file.
- **GetFile(*filepath*)** This method returns a File object equivalent to the file specified in filepath.
- **GetFileName(*path*)** This method returns the name portions of the path and filename specified by path.
- **GetTempName** This method generates a random filename for use when generating temporary files or folders.
- **MoveFile(*source,destination*)** This method moves a file specified in source to the location specified in destination.
- **OpenTextFile(*filename,iomode,create,format*)** This method either creates or opens a text file named filename (depending upon whether the create parameter is set to True), using an iomode for reading, writing, or appending and formatted as ASCII, Unicode, or system default format.

Creating a FileSystemObject Object

The following code can be used to create a FileSystemObject object and iterate through the drives available on your local machine:

```
Dim objFileSysOb
Dim collObj
Set objFileSysOb =
 Server.CreateObject("Scripting.FileSystemObject")
Response.Write "<B>The FileSystemObject Has Been
 Created and the Server Drives Are:</B>"
   For Each collObj in objFileSysOb.Drives
      Response.Write "<BR>Drive = " & collObj
   Next
```

The code dimensions a couple variables, sets objFileSysOb to a server-created FileSystemObject object, and then writes back an iterated list of all the drives on the server (see Figure 6-7).

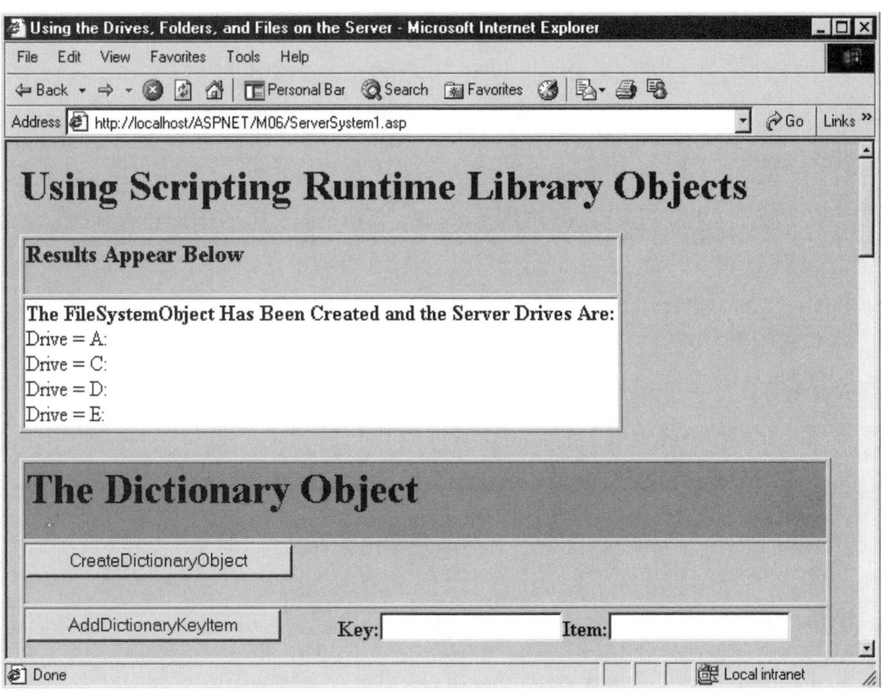

Figure 6-7 All the drives on the server

6

The Drive Object

Once you've created a FileSystemObject object, you can easily get your hands on a Drive object, and then you can start retrieving information about the available drives. Drive objects have the following properties:

- **AvailableSpace** This property returns the amount of space available on the drive.
- **DriveLetter** This property returns the drive letter.
- **DriveType** This property returns the drive type as unknown, removable, fixed, network, CD-ROM, or RAMDisk.

- **FileSystem** This property returns the file system type of the drive as FAT, NTFS, or CDFS, as long as the type is recognizable.
- **FreeSpace** This property returns the total free space available on the drive.
- **IsReady** This property returns True if the drive is ready and false if not.
- **Path** This property returns the drive letter specification for the drive (C:, for instance).
- **RootFolder** This property returns a Folder object equivalent to the root folder for the drive.
- **SerialNumber** This property returns the serial number that identified the disk volume.
- **ShareName** This property returns the network name for a shared drive.
- **TotalSize** This property returns the total size of the drive.
- **VolumeName** This property sets or returns the volume name for local drives.

Iterating Drive Properties

You can set up a listing of all available drives and their properties with the drive object using code such as the following:

```
Dim vDrive
vDrive = Request.Form("drive")
Set objFileSysOb =
 Server.CreateObject("Scripting.FileSystemObject")
Response.Write "<B>The Drive Info Is:</B><P>"
Response.Write "Drive Letter =
 " & objFileSysOb.GetDrive(vDrive).DriveLetter
 & "<BR>"
Response.Write "Drive Type =
```

```
 " & objFileSysOb.GetDrive(vDrive).DriveType
 & "<BR>"
Response.Write "File System =
 " & objFileSysOb.GetDrive(vDrive).FileSystem
 & "<BR>"
Response.Write "AvailableSpace = " &
objFileSysOb.GetDrive(vDrive).AvailableSpace & "<BR>"
Response.Write "Free Space =
 " & objFileSysOb.GetDrive(vDrive).FreeSpace
 & "<BR>"
      Response.Write "Is Ready =
 " & objFileSysOb.GetDrive(vDrive).IsReady
 & "<BR>"
Response.Write "Path =
 " & objFileSysOb.GetDrive(vDrive).Path
 & "<BR>"
Response.Write "Root Folder =
 " & objFileSysOb.GetDrive(vDrive).RootFolder
 & "<BR>"
Response.Write "Serial Number
 = " & objFileSysOb.GetDrive(vDrive).SerialNumber
 & "<BR>"
Response.Write "Share Name =
 " & objFileSysOb.GetDrive(vDrive).ShareName
 & "<BR>"
Response.Write "Total Size
 = " & objFileSysOb.GetDrive(vDrive).TotalSize
 & "<BR>"
Response.Write "Volume Name
 = " & objFileSysOb.GetDrive(vDrive).VolumeName
 & "<BR>"
```


This code dimensions a variable named vDrive to hold a drive letter specification supplied by the user and sets it equal to that value using the Request object. It then creates a FileSystemObject and retrieves a Drive object and corresponding drive properties with the FileSystemObject.GetDrive(vDrive).*property* references. Figure 6-8 shows the resulting list of Drive properties.

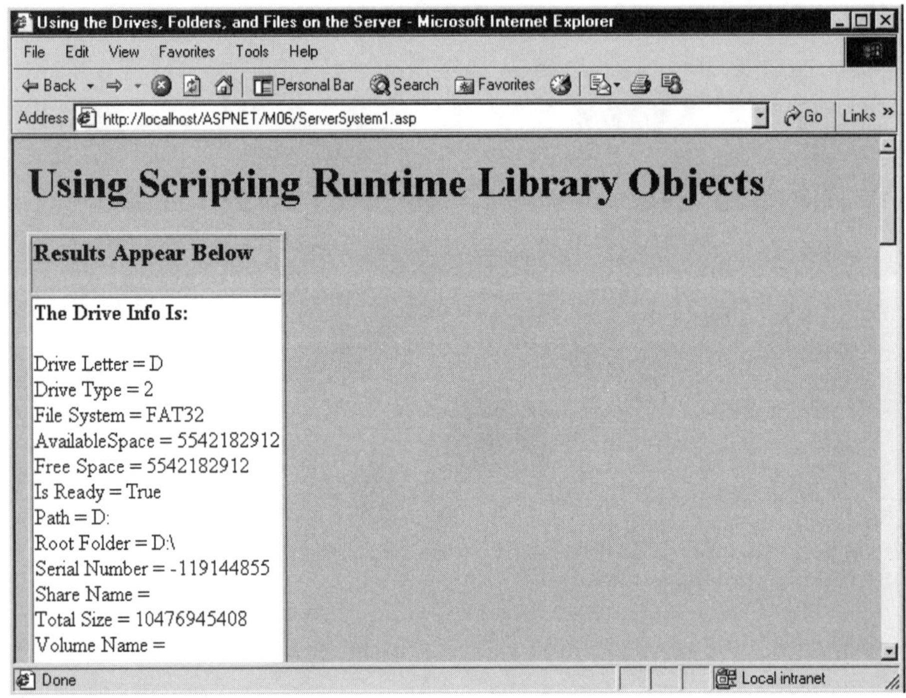

Figure 6-8 Drive properties listed

1-Minute Drill

- List three Drive object properties.
- List three types of Drive objects.

The Folder Object

Although you can get folder and files with the FileSystemObject, the Folder object can also be used to retrieve and work with files. You can use the Folder object's Subfolders property to retrieve a Folders collection and the Files property to retrieve a Files collection, and you can even create text files with the Folder object.

- Available space, drive letter, drive type
- Removable, fixed, CD-ROM

Folder Object Properties

The Folder object exposes the following properties:

- **Attributes** This property returns attributes such as normal, read-only, hidden, system, volume, directory, archive, alias, and compressed.
- **DateCreated** This property returns the date and time the folder was created.
- **DateLastAccessed** This property returns the data and time the folder was last accessed.
- **DateLastModified** This property returns the date and time the folder was last modified.
- **Drive** This property returns the drive letter for the folder.
- **Files** This property returns a Files collection of the File objects equivalent to all the files in the folder.
- **IsRootFolder** This property returns True if the folder is the root folder of the drive.
- **Name** This property sets or returns the name of the folder.
- **ParentFolder** This property returns a Folder object equivalent to the parent folder for the current folder.
- **Path** This property returns the absolute path for the current folder.
- **ShortName** This property returns the DOS version of the folder name.
- **ShortPath** This property returns the DOS version of the path for the folder.
- **Size** This property returns the size for the files and folders in the current folder.
- **Subfolders** This property returns a Folders collection for all the folders in the current folders.
- **Type** This property returns a description of the current folder as a string, if the description is available.

Folder Object Methods

Once you have a Folder object available, you can directly copy, move, delete, and so on without having to specify a full path because you're already there. You can also create a text file. The methods to accomplish these actions are as follows:

- **Copy(*destination,overwrite*)** This method copies the current folder to the location specified in destination, overwriting an existing folder of the same name unless the overwrite parameter is set to True.
- **Delete(*force*)** This method deletes the current folder and its contents; if the force parameter is set to True it will delete even read-only folders.
- **Move(*destination*)** This method moves the current folder to the location specified in destination but will generate an error if there is already a folder in that location with the same name.
- **CreateTextFile(*filepath,overwrite,unicode*)** This method creates a text file using the specified file path and name, overwriting existing files of that name if the overwrite parameter is set to True; it also overwrites files in the Unicode format if unicode is set to True.

Finding the Root Folder Being able to locate and return a reference to the root folder is often a useful ability, and the following code does just that:

```
vDrive = Request.Form("drive")
Set objFileSysOb =
 Server.CreateObject("Scripting.FileSystemObject")
Response.Write "<B>The Root Folder Is:</B><P>"
Response.Write "Root Folder =
 " & objFileSysOb.GetDrive(vDrive).RootFolder
 & "<BR>"
```

The code uses the already dimensioned vDrive variable to retrieve and hold the Drive specification supplied by the user, and then looks up the root folder (see Figure 6-9) for the specified drive using the RootFolder property for that drive from the FileSystemObject object.

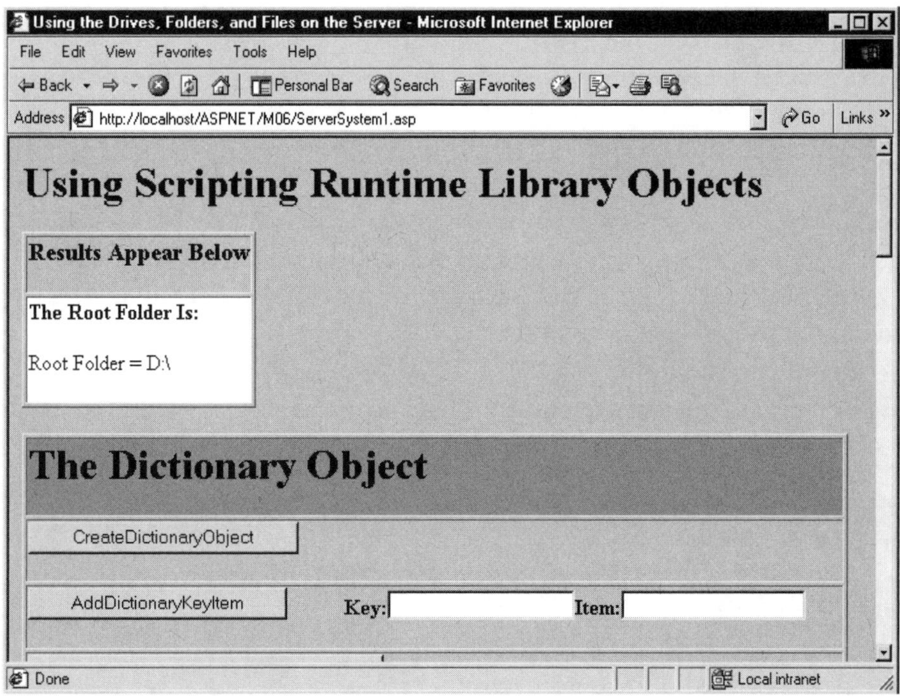

Figure 6-9 Finding the root folder

Finding Subfolders from a Root Folder Our next code example retrieves subfolders from the root folder for a drive and then lists them, another nice capability. Notice that in the following code, you need to set a reference to the Root Folder object and then retrieve the subfolders from that, rather than doing all the referencing in one step, as in previous examples:

```
Dim colFolder
Dim colSubFolders
Dim colSubFolderItem
vDrive = Request.Form("drive")
Set objFileSysOb =
 Server.CreateObject("Scripting.FileSystemObject")
Set colFolder =
```

```
 objFileSysOb.GetDrive(vDrive).RootFolder
Set colSubFolders = colFolder.SubFolders
Response.Write "<B>The Root Subfolders Are:</B>"
For Each colSubFolderItem in colSubFolders
      Response.Write "Root SubFolder =
 " & colSubFolderItem & "<BR>"
Next
```

Also, notice in the code that we dimensioned a few additional variables to handle the extra collections we're using, such as Folder and SubFolders. Figure 6-10 shows the listed subfolders.

Displaying Folder Information Each folder in the collection has its own set of data values, including date created, date last modified, size, type, path,

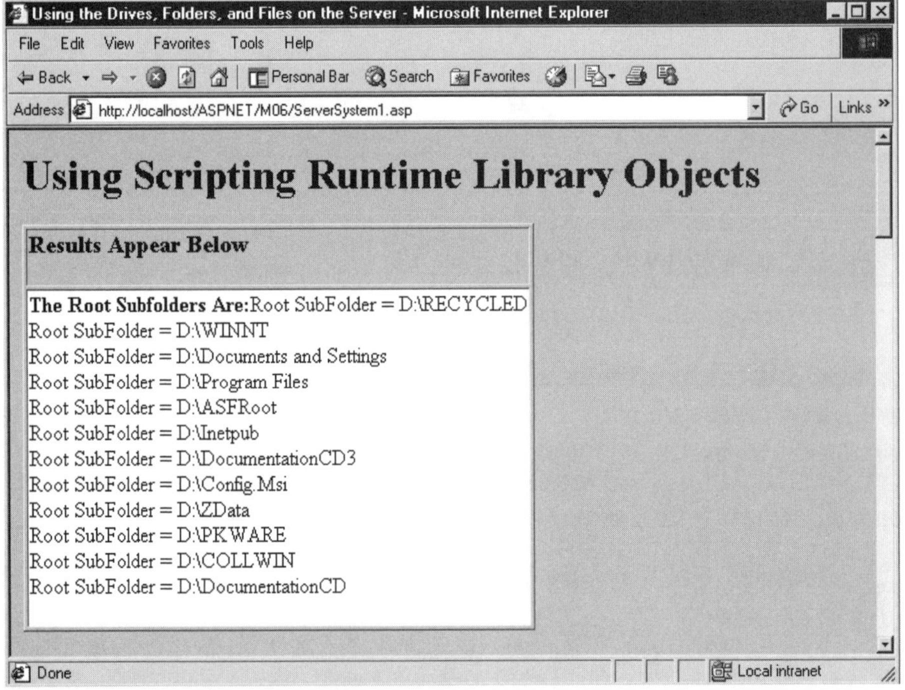

Figure 6-10 The subfolders of the D: drive root folder

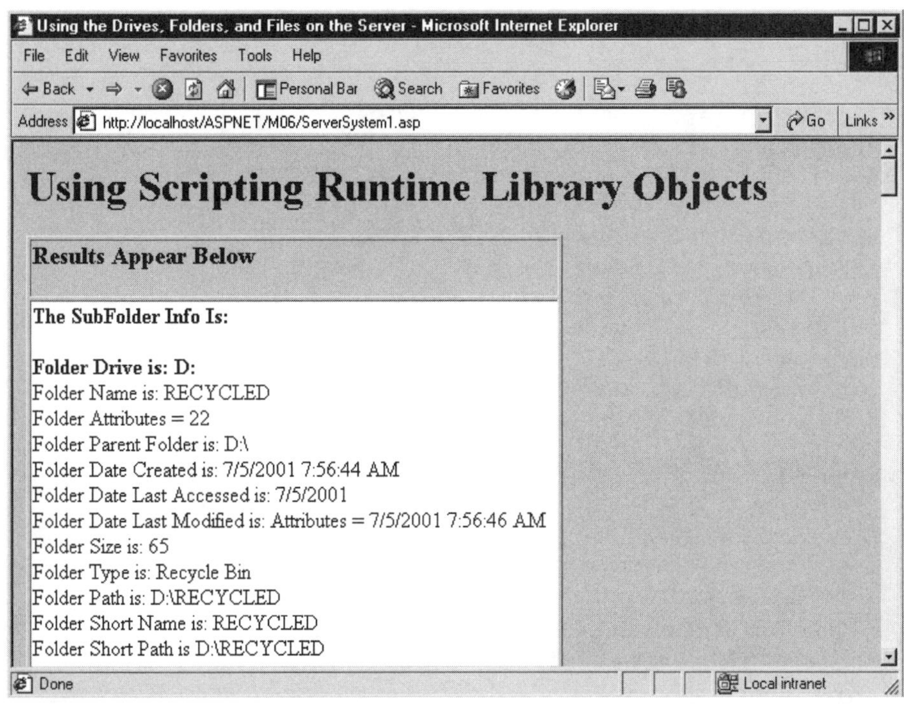

Figure 6-11 Folder info for the D: drive

and so forth. These values can be displayed using a reference to the subfolder and the usual For Each…Next loop, as shown in Figure 6-11 and the code here:

```
Dim vSubFolder
vDrive = Request.Form("drive")
vSubFolder = Request.Form("subfolder")
Set objFileSysOb =
 Server.CreateObject("Scripting.FileSystemObject")
Set colFolder =
 objFileSysOb.GetDrive(vDrive).RootFolder
Set colSubFolders = colFolder.SubFolders
Response.Write "<B>The SubFolder Info Is:</B><P>"
For Each colSubFolderItem in colSubFolders
      Response.Write "<B>Folder Drive is:
 " & colSubFolderItem.Drive & "</B><BR>"
```

```
   Response.Write "Folder Name is:
" & colSubFolderItem.Name & "<BR>"
   Response.Write "Folder Attributes =
" & colSubFolderItem.Attributes & "<BR>"
   Response.Write "Folder Parent Folder is:
" & colSubFolderItem.ParentFolder & "<BR>"
   Response.Write "Folder Date Created is:
" & colSubFolderItem.DateCreated & "<BR>"
   Response.Write "Folder Date Last Accessed is:
" & colSubFolderItem.DateLastAccessed & "<BR>"
   Response.Write "Folder Date Last Modified is:
" & colSubFolderItem.DateLastModified & "<BR>"
   Response.Write "Folder Size is:
" & colSubFolderItem.Size & "<BR>"
   Response.Write "Folder Type is:
" & colSubFolderItem.Type & "<BR>"
   Response.Write "Folder Path is:
" & colSubFolderItem.Path & "<BR>"
   Response.Write "Folder Short Name is:
" & colSubFolderItem.ShortName & "<BR>"
   Response.Write "Folder Short Path is:
" & colSubFolderItem.ShortPath & "<BR>"
   Response.Write "Folder is Root?
" & colSubFolderItem.IsRootFolder & "<P>"
```

Copying, Moving, and Deleting Folders With a reference to a particular folder, you can then copy, move, and delete folders (very carefully, of course) as shown in the following three code examples (and in Figure 6-12):

```
Dim vSFolder
Dim vDFolder
Dim vOverwrite
Dim colFolderName
vSFolder = Request.Form("Sfoldername")
vDFolder = Request.Form("Dfoldername")
vOverwrite = Request.Form("overwrite")
Response.Write "<B>The Folder Has Been
 Copied To:</B><P>"
Set objFileSysOb =
 Server.CreateObject("Scripting.FileSystemObject")
Set colFolderName =
 objFileSysOb.GetFolder(vSFolder)
colFolderName.Copy vDFolder,vOverwrite
Response.Write vDFolder
```

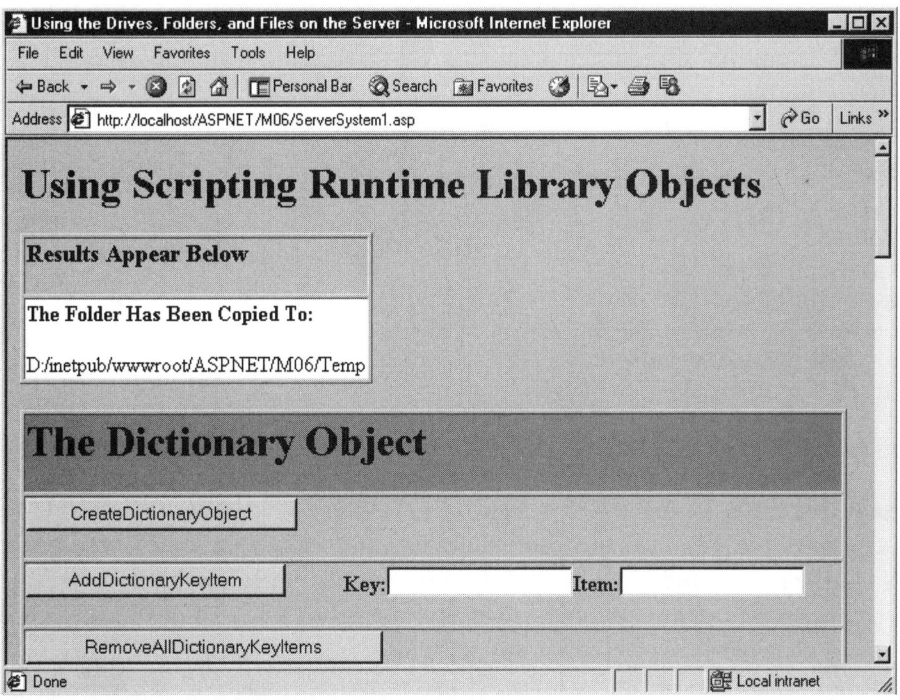

Figure 6-12 Copying a folder

Notice we first dimension more variables to retrieve the source folder, destination folder, and overwrite parameters from the user, then create a FileSystemObject object to get to the correct folder object (specified in vSFolder). The last step is to use the Copy method of the Folder object with the VDFolder and VOverwrite parameters to perform the copy, and use the Response object to tell the user what has been copied.

For moving a folder, the code is very similar:

```
vSFolder = Request.Form("Sfoldername")
vDFolder = Request.Form("Dfoldername")
Response.Write "<B>The Folder Has Been
 Moved To:</B><P>"
Set objFileSysOb =
 Server.CreateObject("Scripting.FileSystemObject")
Set colFolderName =
 objFileSysOb.GetFolder(vSFolder)
colFolderName.Move vDFolder
Response.Write vDFolder
```

For deleting a folder the code is also very similar, the primary difference being the addition of the force parameter (also retrieved from the user with the Request object and the vForce variable):

```
Dim vForce
vSFolder = Request.Form("Sfoldername")
vForce = Request.Form("force")
Response.Write "<B>The Following Folder
 Has Been Deleted:</B><P>"
Set objFileSysOb =
 Server.CreateObject("Scripting.FileSystemObject")
Set colFolderName =
 objFileSysOb.GetFolder(vSFolder)
colFolderName.Delete vForce
Response.Write vSFolder
```

Showing Files in a Folder Naturally, having a reference to a folder is just a starting point. The next obvious thing you want to be able to do is access the files in the folder, and one of the first requirements for doing that is to be able to list those files. This example (illustrated in Figure 6-13) shows how to list all

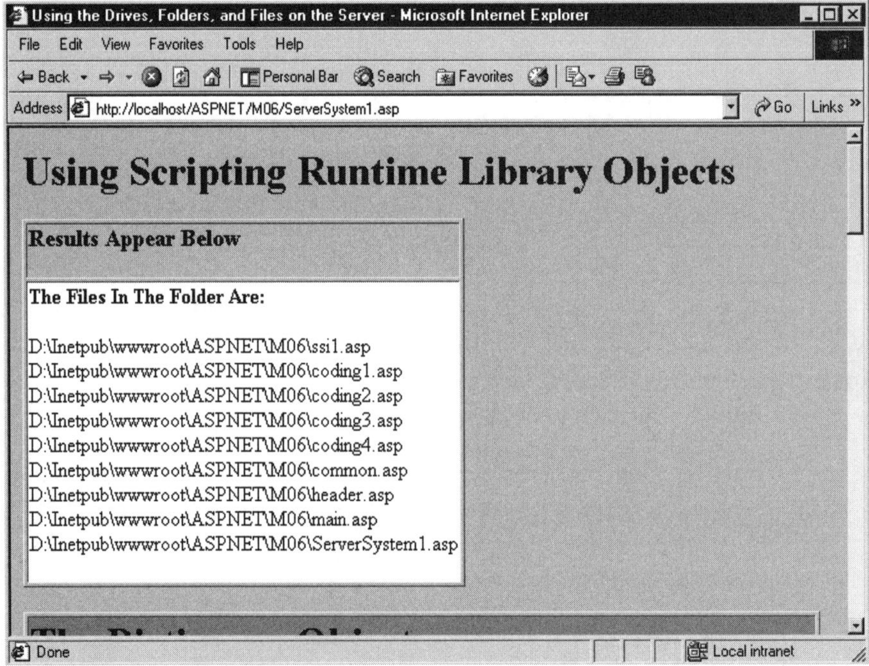

Figure 6-13 Listing the files in a folder

the files in the folder using a couple variables and the standard For Each… Next loop:

```
Dim vFileItem
Dim vFiles
vSFolder = Request.Form("Sfoldername")
Set objFileSysOb =
 Server.CreateObject("Scripting.FileSystemObject")
Set colFolderName =
 objFileSysOb.GetFolder(vSFolder)
Set vFiles = colFolderName.Files
Response.Write "<B>The Files In The Folder Are:</B><P>"
For Each vFileItem in vFiles
    Response.Write vFileItem & "<BR>"
Next
```

The vFiles variable is actually a collection of files that can be listed using the For…Next loop, using the Response object to write out the name of each file.

Creating Text Files In Figure 6-14, the rest of the Folder section of the ASP demonstration page is shown; as you can see, it provides the opportunity to create text files. To create a text file, you need to provide the correct folder name to create the file in, the name of the file you want to create, whether or not you want to overwrite an existing file of the same name, and whether or not you want the file to have the Unicode format. The following code example shows how to retrieve these values from a user and specify them to create a text file; the results are shown in Figure 6-15:

```
Dim vFilename
Dim vUnicode
vFilename = Request.Form("filename")
vSFolder = Request.Form("Sfoldername")
vOverwrite = Request.Form("overwrite")
vUnicode = Request.Form("unicode")
Set objFileSysOb =
 Server.CreateObject("Scripting.FileSystemObject")
Set colFolderName = objFileSysOb.GetFolder(vSFolder)
colFolderName.CreateTextFile
 vFilename,vOverwrite,vUnicode
Response.Write "<B>The Text File
 You Created Is:</B><P>"
Response.Write vSFolder & vFilename
```

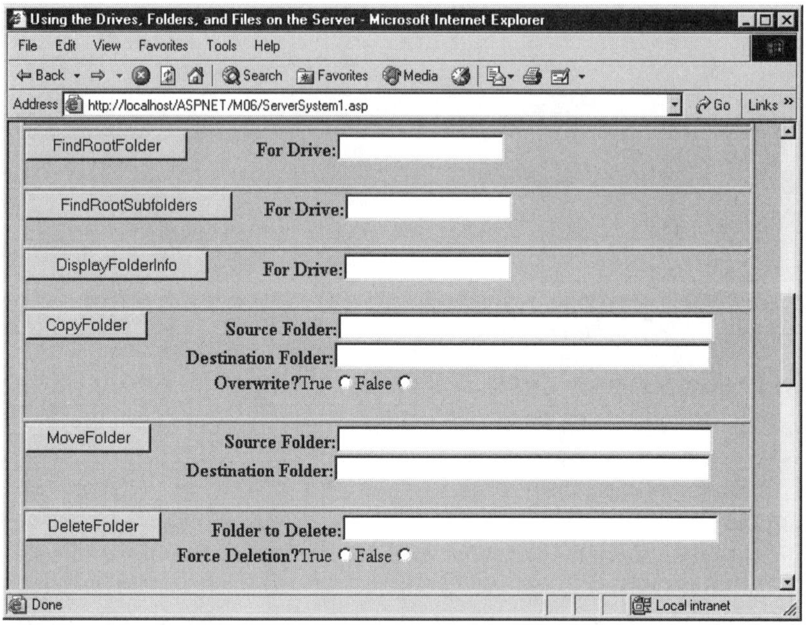

Using the Drives, Folders, and Files on the Server - Microsoft Internet Explorer
File Edit View Favorites Tools Help
Address http://localhost/ASPNET/M06/ServerSystem1.asp
FindRootFolder For Drive:
FindRootSubfolders For Drive:
DisplayFolderInfo For Drive:
CopyFolder Source Folder:
Destination Folder:
Overwrite?True False
MoveFolder Source Folder:
Destination Folder:
DeleteFolder Folder to Delete:
Force Deletion?True False
Done Local intranet

Figure 6-14 The remainder of the folder section controls

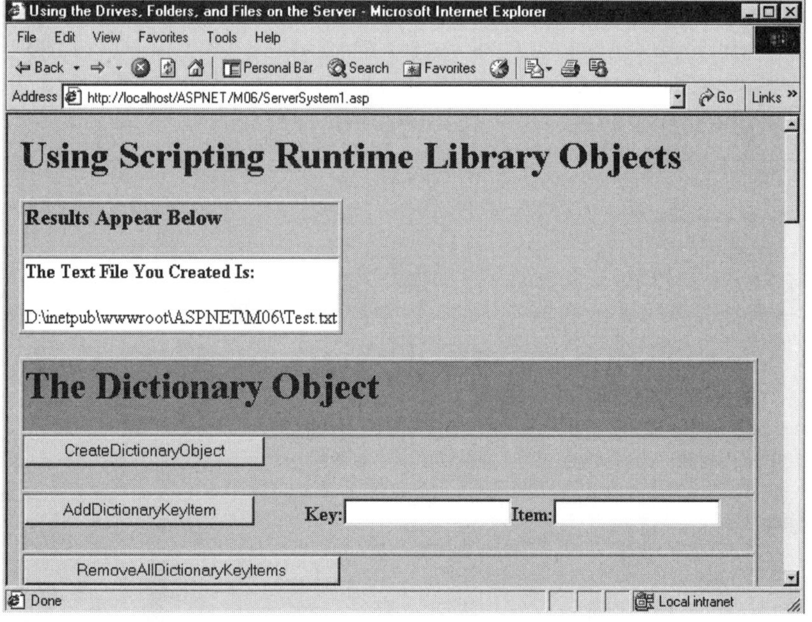

Figure 6-15 Creating a text file

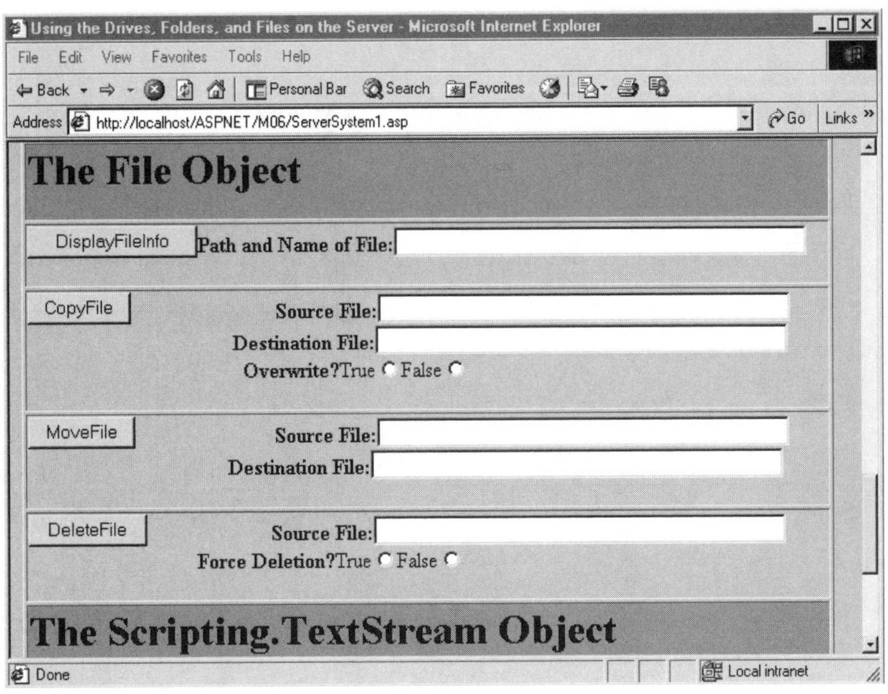

Figure 6-16 The File Object section

6

The File Object

The File object is the next-to-last object in the hierarchy of file system objects and has properties and methods quite similar to the Folder object. The File object creation and manipulation area of our ASP page is shown in Figure 6-16. You can display file information such as date created and last modified, size, and so forth, and you can copy, move, and delete files. You can also create text files or open them as TextStream objects.

File Object Properties

The File object has the following properties:

- **Attributes** This property returns attributes such as normal, read-only, hidden, system, volume, directory, archive, alias, and compressed.
- **DateCreated** This property returns the date and time the file was created.

- **DateLastAccessed** This property returns the data and time the file was last accessed.
- **DateLastModified** This property returns the date and time the file was last modified.
- **Drive** This property returns the drive letter for the file.
- **Name** This property sets or returns the name of the file.
- **ParentFolder** This property returns a Folder object equivalent to the parent folder for the current file.
- **Path** This property returns the absolute path for the current file.
- **ShortName** This property returns the DOS version of the filename.
- **ShortPath** This property returns the DOS version of the path for the file.
- **Size** This property returns the size of the file in bytes.
- **Type** This property returns a description of the current file as a string, if the description is available.

File Object Methods

The File object also has methods similar to Folder methods, as listed here:

- **Copy(*destination,overwrite*)** This method copies the current file to the location specified in destination, overwriting an existing file of the same name unless the overwrite parameter is set to True.
- **Delete(*force*)** This method deletes the current file and its contents and if the force parameter is set to True will delete even read-only files.
- **Move(*destination*)** This method moves the current file to the location specified in destination but will generate an error if there is already a file in that location with the same name.
- **CreateTextFile(*filepath,overwrite,unicode*)** This method creates a text file using the specified file path and name, overwriting existing files of that name if the Overwrite parameter is set to True and in the Unicode format if unicode is set to True.

- **OpenAsTextStream(*iomode,format*)** This method opens a file in the specified mode (reading, writing, appending), depending on the value of the iomode parameter and as ASCII, Unicode, or system default, depending on the value of the format parameter.

Displaying File Information Once you have a reference to a file, you can display data about that file with code such as the following:

```
Dim vFilePathname
Dim colFileName
vFilePathname = Request.Form("filepathname")
Set objFileSysOb =
 Server.CreateObject("Scripting.FileSystemObject")
Set colFileName =
 objFileSysOb.GetFile(vFilePathname)
Response.Write "<B>The File Info Is:</B><P>"
Response.Write "<B>File Name is:
 " & colFileName.Name & "</B><BR>"
Response.Write "File Drive is:
 " & colFileName.Drive & "<BR>"
Response.Write "File Attributes =
 " & colFileName.Attributes & "<BR>"
Response.Write "File Parent Folder is:
 " & colFileName.ParentFolder & "<BR>"
Response.Write "File Date Created is:
 " & colFileName.DateCreated & "<BR>"
Response.Write "File Date Last Accessed is:
 " & colFileName.DateLastAccessed & "<BR>"
Response.Write "File Date Last Modified is:
 Attributes = " & colFileName.DateLastModified & "<BR>"
Response.Write "File Size is:
 " & colFileName.Size & "<BR>"
Response.Write "File Type is:
 " & colFileName.Type & "<BR>"
Response.Write "File Path is:
 " & colFileName.Path & "<BR>"
Response.Write "File Short Name is:
 " & colFileName.ShortName & "<BR>"
Response.Write "File Short Path is:
 " & colFileName.ShortPath & "<P>"
```

6

In this code, you're pulling the file starting with the FileSystemObject object, so the user must supply the entire path to the file. Once you have a

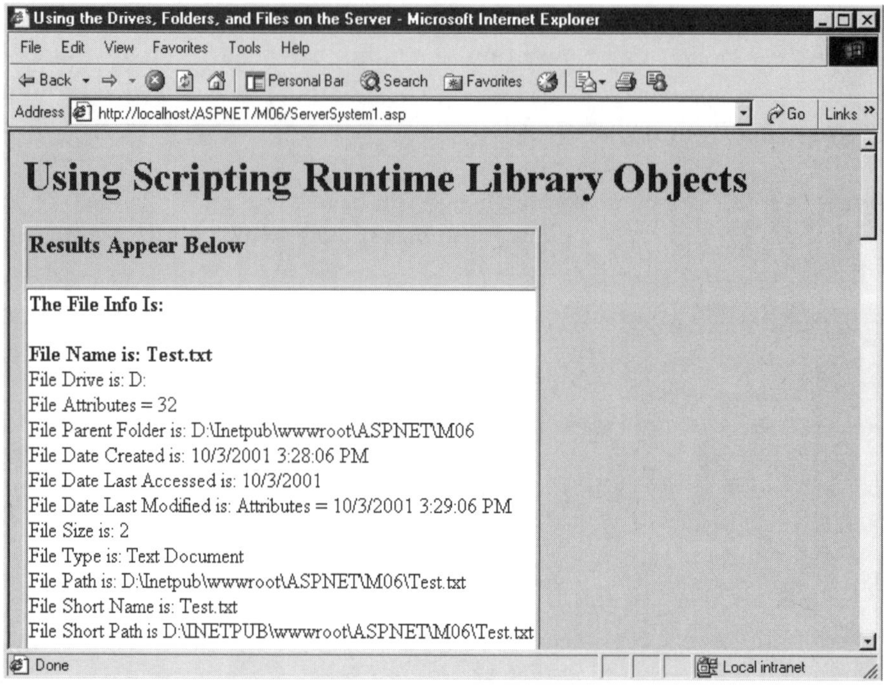

Figure 6-17 File info displayed

reference to the file, you can use the Response object and the File properties to display each individual property of the file, as shown in Figure 6-17.

Copying, Moving, and Deleting Files Files can be copied, moved, and deleted just like folders, and the following code examples demonstrate how to do this, starting with copying a file:

```
Dim vSFile
Dim vDFile
vSFile = Request.Form("Sfilename")
vDFile = Request.Form("Dfilename")
vOverwrite = Request.Form("overwrite")
Response.Write "<B>The File Has Been
 Copied To:</B><P>"
Set objFileSysOb =
 Server.CreateObject("Scripting.FileSystemObject")
Set colFileName =
 objFileSysOb.GetFile(vSFile)
```

```
colFileName.Copy vDFile,vOverwrite
Response.Write vDFile
```

You need to know the name of the file to copy, where to copy it to, and whether or not to overwrite it, so you first retrieve these values from the user and then use them with the File object and the Copy method to perform the job. Figure 6-18 shows how this works.

The code for moving a file is very similar:

```
vSFile = Request.Form("Sfilename")
vDFile = Request.Form("Dfilename")
Response.Write "<B>The File Has Been
 Moved To:</B><P>"
Set objFileSysOb =
 Server.CreateObject("Scripting.FileSystemObject")
Set colFileName =
 objFileSysOb.GetFile(vSFile)
colFileName.Move vDFile
Response.Write vDFile
```


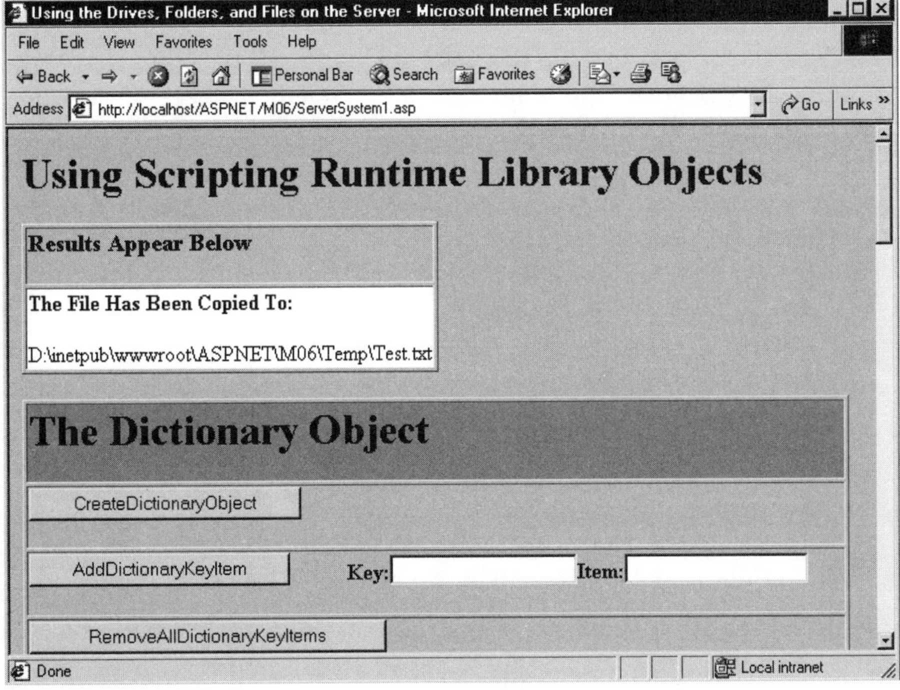

Figure 6-18 Copying a file

To delete files, you can use code like this:

```
vSFile = Request.Form("Sfilename")
vForce = Request.Form("force")
Response.Write "<B>The Following File
 Has Been Deleted:</B><P>"
Set objFileSysOb =
 Server.CreateObject("Scripting.FileSystemObject")
Set colFileName =
 objFileSysOb.GetFile(vSFile)
colFileName.Delete vForce
Response.Write vSFile
```

Here you retrieve a File object from the FileSystemObject object and get the filename to delete from the user, as well as the value of the force parameter; then you perform the action on the File object.

The Scripting.TextStream Object

Although TextStream objects are separate entities, they can only be created using the CreateTextFile, OpenTextFile, and OpenAsTextStream methods of the FileSystemObject object, the Folder object, and the File object. Any of these objects can use CreateTextFile, while only the FileSystemObject can use the OpenTextFile method, and only the File object can use the OpenAsTextStream method. Figure 6-19 shows the TextStream object section of our ASP page.

TextStream Object Properties

The TextStream object exposes the following properties to tell us about itself:

- **AtEndOfLine** This property returns True if the file pointer is at the end of a line in a file.
- **AtEndOfStream** This property returns True if the file pointer is at the end of the file.
- **Column** This property returns the column number of the current character.
- **Line** This property returns the line number for the current line.

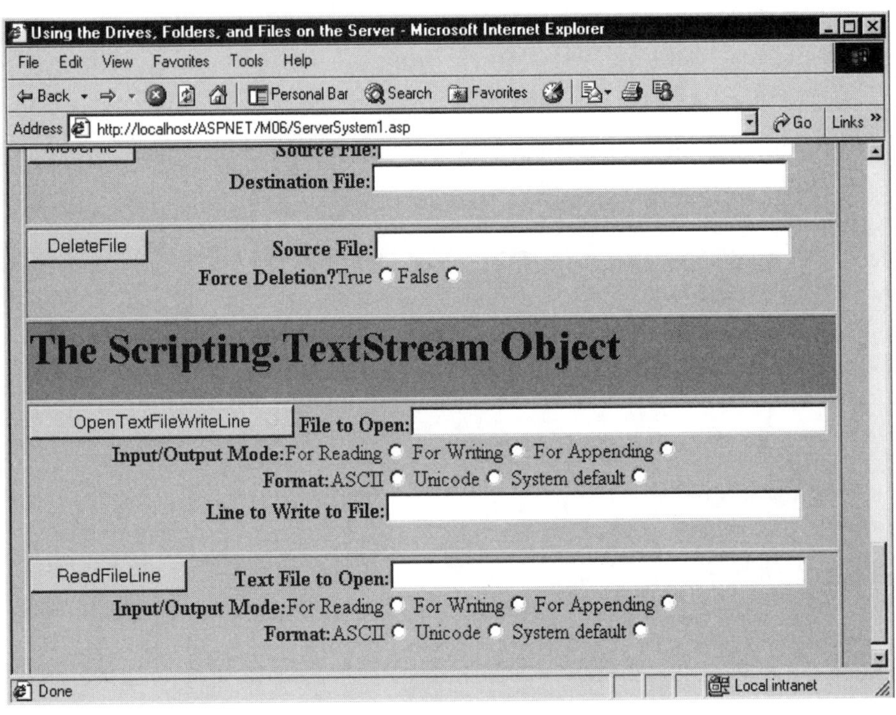

Figure 6-19 The TextStream object section

TextStream Object Methods

The TextStream object supplies methods for navigating files as well as reading from and writing to files:

- **Close** This method closes the current file.
- **Read(*numberofcharacters*)** This method reads the specified number of characters from a file.
- **ReadAll** This method reads all the characters in a file.
- **ReadLine** This method reads a line from a file as a string.
- **Skip(*numberofcharacters*)** This method skips over the specified number of characters while reading.
- **SkipLine** This method skips the next line while reading.

- **Write(*string*)** This method writes a string into a file.
- **WriteLine** This method writes a string (if specified) and a newline character to a file.
- **WriteBlankLines(*number*)** This method writes the specified number of newline characters to a file.

Creating and Writing to a File The File object can be used to create a new file as a TextStream object, and then the TextStream object can be manipulated with the WriteLine method to insert a line within that new file all at once, as the following code (and Figure 6-20) shows:

```
Dim vIomode
Dim vFormat
Dim vLinetowrite
Dim objTextStream
vSFile = Request.Form("Sfilename")
vIomode = Request.Form("iomode")
vFormat = Request.Form("format")
vLinetowrite = Request.Form("linetowrite")
Response.Write "<B>The Line You Have
 Written Is:</B><P>"
Set objFileSysOb =
 Server.CreateObject("Scripting.FileSystemObject")
Set colFileName = objFileSysOb.GetFile(vSFile)
Set objTextStream =
 colFileName.OpenAsTextStream(vIomode, vFormat)
objTextStream.WriteLine vLinetowrite
Response.Write vLinetowrite
```

Again, you retrieve the name of the file to create, its iomode, and format from the users via some variables you dimension, and then you retrieve a File object from the FileSystemObject and create a new text file as a TextStream object with the OpenAsTextStream method. Finally, you write a line to the new file with the WriteLine method.

Reading a Line from a File To read a line from a file, all you have to do is get a reference to that file and then use the ReadLine method to retrieve the line and show it to the user. Of course, you have to ask how the file should be opened, but in practice you might not leave that up to the user. However, for

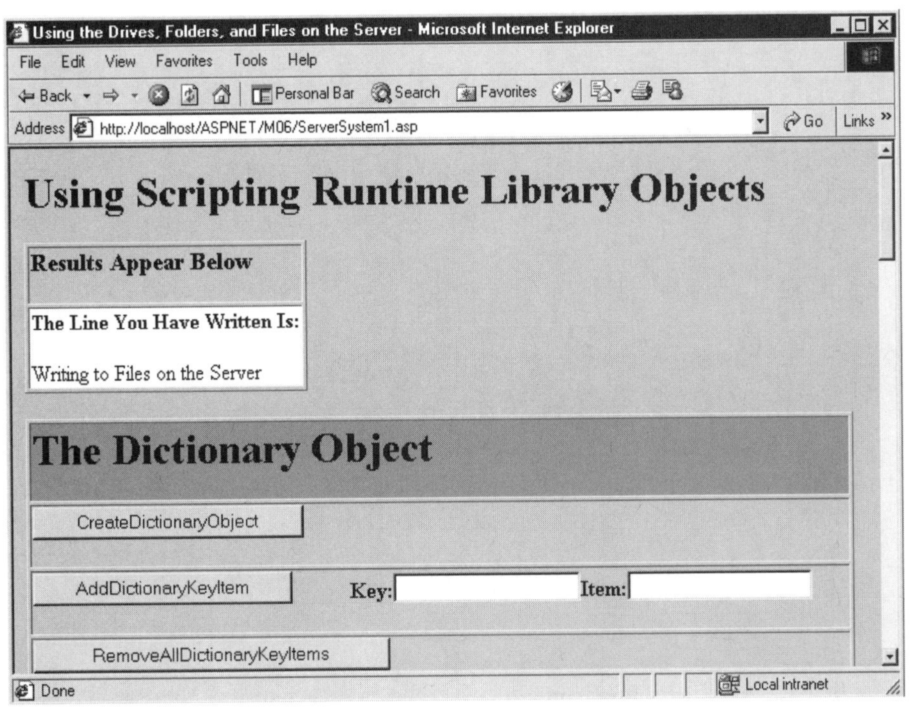

Figure 6-20 Creating a TextStream object and writing a line

demonstration purposes we show how it could be done here, and Figure 6-21 shows the results:

```
Dim vReadline
vSFile = Request.Form("Sfilename")
vIomode = Request.Form("iomode")
vFormat = Request.Form("format")
Response.Write "<B>The First Line
 in the File Is:</B><P>"
Set objFileSysOb =
 Server.CreateObject("Scripting.FileSystemObject")
Set colFileName =
 objFileSysOb.GetFile(vSFile)
Set objTextStream =
 colFileName.OpenAsTextStream(vIomode, vFormat)
vReadline = objTextStream.ReadLine
Response.Write vReadline
```

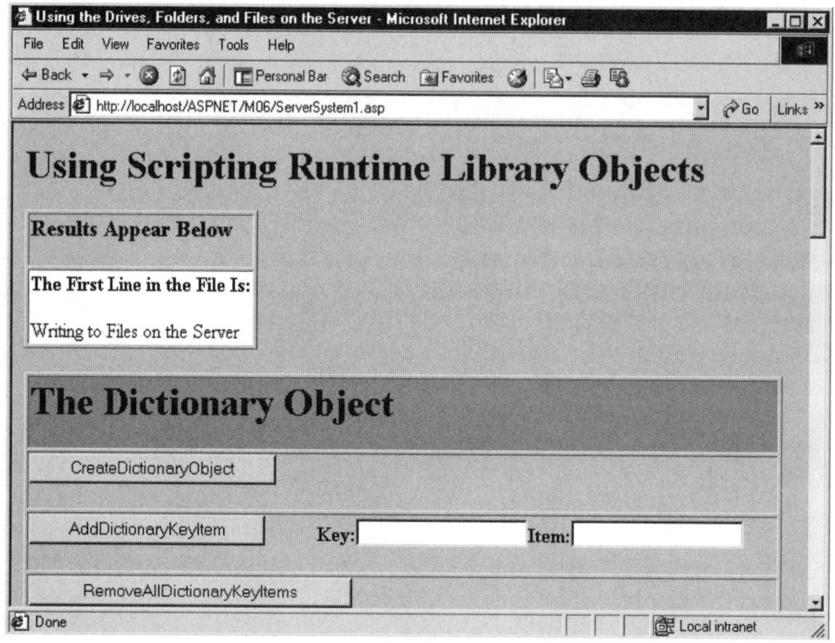

Figure 6-21 Reading a line from a file

Project 6-1: Using File System Objects

In the following example, we'll use VS.NET to create a new project for working with File System objects. Much of the code works exactly the same in ASP.NET as in ASP, so we'll build the project using Web Forms in ASP.NET. Basically, the Web Form offers the capability to list all drives on the server and to show drive info (such as free space, volume name, and so on) in a ListBox.

Step-by-Step

1. Create a project in VS.NET using the Web Application template (as we have done before) and name it FileSystemObjects.

2. On the Web Forms1.aspx page, place a label (from the Web Forms toolbox) at the top of the form and name it ResponseLabel. Place another label below it (the name is not important) and set its Text property to Actions. Place a ListBox next to the Actions label and add two items to its Items collection: List Drives and Show Drive Properties. Set the List Drives item so that it is automatically selected (Selected=True) when the Web Form opens for the user at run-time. Place a button on the form and change its Text property to Go. Finally, place an empty ListBox on the form and name it FSODrives. Change the look and position of the controls until they resemble Figure 6-22.

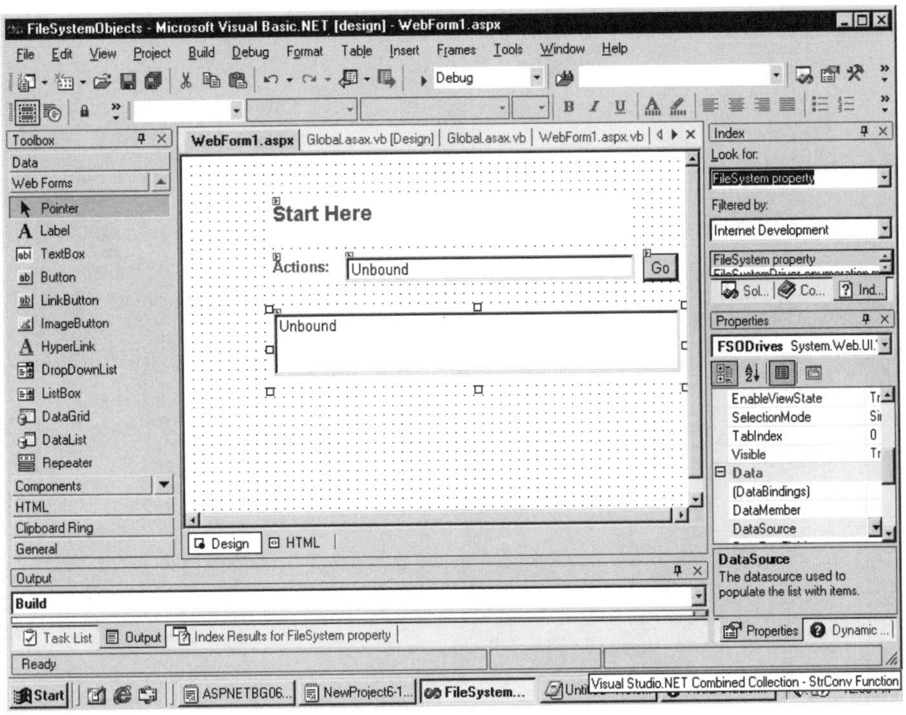

Figure 6-22 The form in Design view

3. Double-click the Web Form in Design view to open up the code-behind page, and enter the following code in the Page_Load event:

```
Dim objFileSysOb As Object
Dim collDrives As Object
Dim collObj As Object
Dim strCollObj As String
Dim strDriveInfo As String
Dim choiceClicked As String

If Not IsPostBack Then
  ResponseLabel.Text = "Please choose an
 action and click the button."
Else
```

```
  choiceClicked = Request.Form.GetValues("choice")(0)
  Select Case choiceClicked
    Case "List Drives"
      objFileSysOb =
 Server.CreateObject("Scripting.FileSystemObject")
      collDrives = objFileSysOb.Drives
      FSODrives.Items.Clear()
      For Each collObj In collDrives
        strCollObj = collObj.DriveLetter
        Me.FSODrives.Items.
Add(New ListItem(strCollObj))
      Next
      ResponseLabel.Text = "Drives Letters are listed"
    Case "Show Drive Properties"
      objFileSysOb =
 Server.CreateObject("Scripting.FileSystemObject")
      collDrives = objFileSysOb.Drives
      For Each collObj In collDrives
        If collObj.DriveType = 2 Then
          strCollObj = collObj.DriveLetter
          FSODrives.Items.Clear()
          strDriveInfo = "For Drive " & strCollObj &
 " the File System type is " & collObj.FileSystem
          Me.FSODrives.Items.Add(New
 ListItem(strDriveInfo))
          strDriveInfo = "For Drive " & strCollObj &
 " the Free Space on the drive is " & collObj.FreeSpace
          Me.FSODrives.Items.Add(New
 ListItem(strDriveInfo))
          strDriveInfo = "For Drive " & strCollObj &
 " the Path for the drive is " & collObj.Path
          Me.FSODrives.Items.Add(New
 ListItem(strDriveInfo))
          strDriveInfo = "For Drive " & strCollObj &
 " the Serial Number is " & collObj.SerialNumber
          Me.FSODrives.Items.Add(New
 ListItem(strDriveInfo))
```

```
            strDriveInfo = "For Drive " & strCollObj &
" the Total Size of the drive is " & collObj.TotalSize
            Me.FSODrives.Items.Add(New
ListItem(strDriveInfo))
            strDriveInfo = "For Drive " & strCollObj &
" the Volume Name is " & collObj.VolumeName
            Me.FSODrives.Items.Add(New
ListItem(strDriveInfo))
          End If
        Next
        ResponseLabel.Text = "Drives info is:"
    End Select
End If
```

4. The Dim statements dimension the appropriate variables, and the If IsPostBack structure separates the initial page loaded from those loaded upon subsequent requests.

5. The choiceClicked variable picks up the value of the choice the user makes regarding listing all the drives or showing drive information for selected drives. The Select Case structure provides a holding area for the code that will run depending on the choice the user makes.

6. The first Case area holds statements that pick up the drive letters and insert them as items in the FSODrives ListBox.

7. The second Case area examines each drive to determine the type (if the type = 2 then the drive is a Fixed drive, and if the drive is type = 2 then the properties of the drive are captured by the strCollOb variable and become part of a statement that is entered as an item in the FSODrives ListBox).

8. Before each ListBox is filled, the items in it (if any) are cleared, otherwise the ViewState property of the control will continue to hold previous items as well as any new items added. The ResponseLabel's Text property shows an appropriate response for each case after completion. The finished form in action is shown in Figure 6-23.

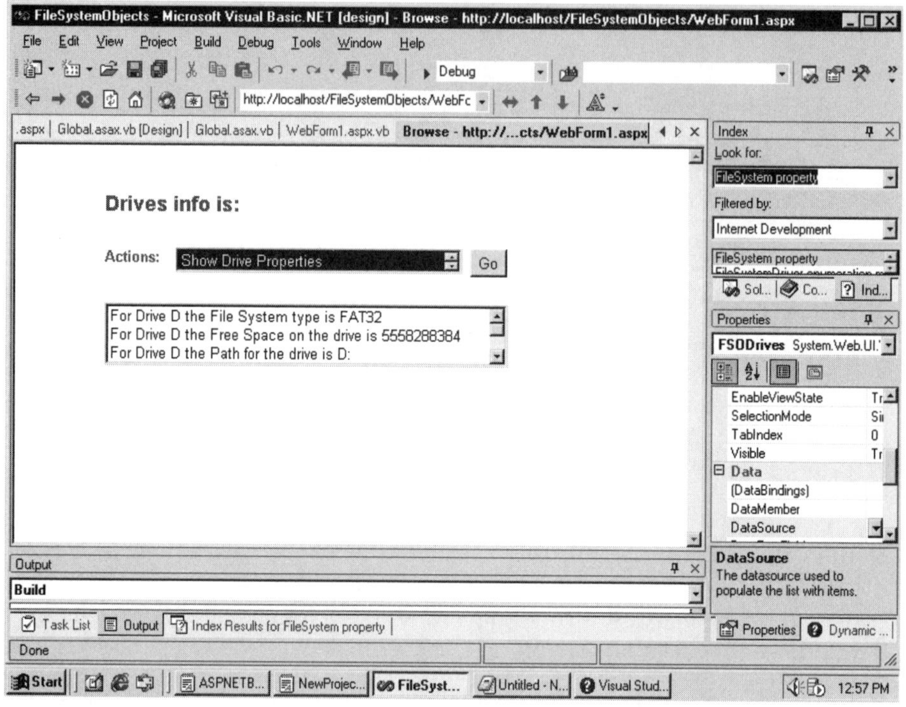

Figure 6-23 The finished form in action

Active Server Components and Controls

Server components are very handy for performing functions that would otherwise take quite a bit of programming to accomplish with ASP, and they run more quickly than plain script. In fact, it's important to use them under the appropriate circumstances, because not only do they run more quickly, they can also save you a fair amount of development time. Also, they've been tested and debugged, and you can feel confident that they will work as advertised.

Server components have DLL files, and the ones we discuss in this module should already be installed and registered. Later, we'll discuss third-party components you can buy, install, and register. By the way, you can also make and install your own components and sell them to the public if you like.

Naturally, the first server components to be written were aimed at the most common or frequently used functions for website applications. For example, the Page Counter component counts (and records) the number of times a given page has received a hit, and it can do so for any page on your site. Tracking the number of hits a page receives provides information that can be used to analyze the layout of a website, and this capability has been around in various incarnations for a long time. Building this functionality into an ASP server component was an obvious step.

In ASP.NET, some functions of server components have been built into server controls. For example, in the AdRotator control, the functions that the Ad Rotator components perform are easily available as a Web Forms control that can be added to your page by clicking and dragging.

Creating Server Components with ASP

There are two methods you can use to create server components for your ASP pages:

- The Server.CreateObject method
- The <OBJECT> tag set

These methods are identical to the process for creating Scripting Runtime Library objects, so there's no need to rehash much here. Either method works fine, but only the <OBJECT> tag method within the global.asa (or global.asax) file will create objects with application- or session-level scope.

Checking Object Instantiation

If you attempt to create a component and it isn't installed or registered, or if it is not created for any reason, your application will be damaged and perhaps unable to perform its function. Fortunately, there is a way to check whether the object exists: the IsObject function. It can work for you like this (the following example is pseudocode):

```
On Error Resume Next
Set objComponent =
```

```
 Server.CreateObject("MSWC.ServerComponent")
If IsObject(objComponent) Then
  On Error Goto 0
Else
  Response.Write "No data available.
 Please try again later."
End If
```

To use this pseudocode you would have to substitute a valid component ID, but the remaining code could be used as is. The first action is to shut off normal error handling. Next, the code instantiates the component and checks to see whether it was actually created. If so, normal error handling is turned back on and you can insert whatever scripting you'd like. If not, an error message is sent back to the user via the Response.Write method. You might also provide a Back button to take the user back to the previous page at that point.

The components we cover in this module should already be properly installed and registered, so we won't bother with the details of those processes here. When we get to the installation of third-party components, we'll walk you through the installation and registration process to give you a feel for what you'll encounter if you buy and install non-Microsoft components.

The Ad Rotator Component

While click-through rates for banner ads seem to be steadily dropping, chances are you'll sometimes find it necessary to include ads in your pages, and the Ad Rotator component's functions makes doing so pretty easy. My feeling is that you'll get more mileage from building target-specific ads (or even small sections or come-ons) into a page rather than building typical banner ads. In any case, since the Ad Rotator component has the capability to display different ads each time the page receives a hit, you can use it to produce any kind of rotation schedule you like for any image size you like.

The Schedule File

The Ad Rotator component depends on a file called the schedule file to know what ad images to display, what links to attach to them, and how frequently each one should come up. The schedule file also contains data that can send information to a redirection file (discussed in the next section) so the links can be properly formatted. Here's the schedule file for this example. Note the asterisk separating the first block of text from the rest of the file. We'll discuss the purpose of the asterisk in just a few more paragraphs:

```
REDIRECT AdRotator/RedirectionFile/RedirectFile.asp
*
AdRotator\banner1.gif
http://www.e4free.com
E4free.com
1
AdRotator\banner2.gif
http://www.acs-isad.com
Advanced Computer Services Webhosting
1
AdRotator\banner3.gif
http://www.zipwell.com
Zipwell Online Webhosting
1
```


Notice the first line uses the REDIRECT command to redirect the contents of the file to another file that will properly insert links and images for you. We'll cover this other file (called the redirection file) in a moment. First, let's talk about the other things that can be included in the schedule file.

Although you're only using the REDIRECT command in this example, there are some other commands you can use in the schedule file:

- **Width(*pixels*)** This command sets the width of the displayed ad in pixels. If it is not included, the default of 440 pixels is used.
- **Height(*pixels*)** This command sets the height of the displayed ad in pixels, and the default of 60 pixels is used if it is not included.
- **Border(*pixels*)** This command sets the width of the border around the image in pixels. You can set it to 0 so no border will show.

Now, about the asterisk. After you enter these lines, you include an asterisk (*) as a separator character before the individual settings for each ad are entered. Each ad setting consists of the following:

- **imageURL** This setting points to the location of the ad image. It can be on your server or at another location entirely (for example, the website of the advertiser).
- **advertiserLink** This setting points to the place to which the user is taken when the image is clicked. If no link is specified, a hyphen should be inserted here.

- **Text(*string*)** This setting makes your page display a line of text as an alternative if the image will not display.
- **ImpressionRatioNumber** This setting is simply a number that, when added to all the other ImpressionRatioNumbers for ads in the schedule file, represents the percentage of time this particular ad will appear on the page. For example, you have three ads in this schedule file, each of which has been assigned a 1 for its ImpressionRatioNumber. Adding these numbers together totals 3, and 1 divided by the total (3) gives 0.33 or 33 percent, so each ad will appear 33 percent of the time. By the way, there is no set order in which the ad images will appear. The Ad Rotator component generates a random selection process but ensures that each ad shows up the appropriate number of times.

The Redirection File

The redirection file can be any valid script/file that produces the redirection effect. For this example, you'll use an ASP script using the Response.Redirect method to perform the redirection action. Your example file looks like this:

```
<% Option Explicit
Dim vSendToURL
vSendToURL = Request.QueryString("url")
Response.Redirect vSendToURL
%>
```

The sole function of this redirection file is to capture the selected redirection URL and image URL from the current schedule file ad settings. As you can see, you only capture the redirection URL in your example, as the image files are located on your own server. It is often more efficient to allow advertisers' image files to remain on their own servers and just get a reference to them from the schedule file.

Ad Rotator Methods and Properties

The Ad Rotator component has a single method and three properties, as follows:

- **GetAdvertisement(*scheduletextfile*)** This method gets the currently selected image and URL settings (based on the impression ratio) from the schedule text file and in the process creates the appropriate HTML tags to encase the image file path and name and the redirection URL.

- **Border** This property allows you to set the size of the border around the image. If it is not specified, either the default or the BORDER command setting in the header of the schedule file will be used.
- **Clickable** This property is either True or False and tells the component whether the image will function as a hyperlink (using the advertiser URL specified in the schedule file). If unset, this property defaults to True.
- **TargetFrame** This property contains the name of the frame in which to display the image. It can also be set to the standard HTML frame names such as _child, _self, and _blank.

The ASP.NET AdRotator Server Control

In VS.NET, there is a server control you can use with a Web Forms application, and it performs much the same functions as the Ad Rotator component. There is a twist, however; you use an XML file to assign locations for image files to be rotated and the URLs to direct users to. We'll cover XML in much greater detail in Module 7; for now we'll use the XML file creation wizard in VS.NET to introduce us to this interesting language specification.

Creating a Web Form with an AdRotator Server Control

The process used to create a web page (using the Web Forms template) is much the same as any other Web Forms page with a "front" page made of HTML and Web Forms controls and a "code-behind" page for VB.NET programming. Just drop the AdRotator control onto the page, create (or find) some images to rotate, and store them in a folder on the site. The difference is, you're required to create an XML file to store image file locations and URLs that the control works with to carry out its functions.

Fortunately, VS.NET has a set of dialog boxes that helps you create the XML file, based on a template in the XML Designer. Just choose Add New Item from the Project menu and select XML file from the Templates window. Give the new item a unique name, and then select Ad Rotator Schedule File from within the TargetSchema property of the item. Modify the file until it looks something like the following (adding your own information for the image URL, navigate URL, and so forth):

```
<?xml version="1.0" encoding="utf-8" ?>
<Advertisements xmlns="http://schemas.
```

```
microsoft.com/AspNet/AdRotator-Schedule-File">
<Ad>
  <ImageUrl>images/banner1.gif</ImageUrl>
  <NavigateUrl>http://www.e4free.com</NavigateUrl>
  <AlternateText>To e4free</AlternateText>
  <Keyword></Keyword>
  <Impressions>10</Impressions>
</Ad>
<Ad>
  <ImageUrl>images/banner2.gif</ImageUrl>
  <NavigateUrl>http://www.e4free.com</NavigateUrl>
  <AlternateText>To e4free</AlternateText>
  <Keyword></Keyword>
  <Impressions>20</Impressions>
</Ad>
<Ad>
  <ImageUrl>images/banner3.gif</ImageUrl>
  <NavigateUrl>http://www.e4free.com</NavigateUrl>
  <AlternateText>To e4free</AlternateText>
  <Keyword></Keyword>
  <Impressions>30</Impressions>
</Ad>
</Advertisements>
```

Notice that the file starts with a heading tag and then progresses to a set of beginning and ending advertisement tags, following into individual <Ad> tags, each of which contains the URL for an image, the URL the user will be redirected to, alternate text, keywords, and finally, a value for impressions. The image URL tells the control where the image resides (often they are somewhere else on the Internet), the navigation URL instructs the control where to send the user if they click on the image, and the alternate text is displayed for users who have graphics turned off (or whose browsers are incapable of graphics). The keyword is not for search engine support but instead serves as a filtering mechanism so ads may be displayed by category. The impressions value is not to limit the number of impressions but is instead for setting a relative ratio for displaying ads. Other than using an XML file to hold these values, the AdRotator control works in the same way as the Ad Rotator Component.

Project 6-2: An Example of Rotating Ads in ASP

It's very common to have rotating ads on your website. In fact, you can pay lots of money to third-party companies for ad rotation services, so perhaps it would be a good idea to develop the capability for yourself. In this project, you'll put together a very rudimentary ad rotation service.

Step-by-Step

The following code is similar to previous pages you've done for server components and objects. It brings up a button you can use to initiate rotating ads, and after the first page load it will rotate the ads randomly each time the button is pressed:

```
<%
Option Explicit
Dim btnClicked
%>
<html><head><title>Using IIS Server
 Components</title>
<meta http-equiv="Content-Type"
 content="text/html; charset=iso-8859-1">
</head>
<body bgcolor="#77FF77">
<H2><font size="6">Using ASP Server
 Components</font></H2>
<TABLE border=1>
<TR><TD><H3>The Ad Rotator Component</H3></TD></TR>
<TR><TD bgcolor="white">
<%
btnClicked = Request.Form("btnval")
Select Case btnClicked
  Case "RotateAd"
    Dim objAdRotator
    Dim vAd
    Set objAdRotator =
 Server.CreateObject("MSWC.AdRotator")
    vAd = objAdRotator.GetAdvertisement
```

```
("AdRotator\AdRotatorTextFile.txt")
    Response.Write vAd
End Select
%>
</TD></TR></TABLE>
<P>
<TABLE border=1><TR><TD bgcolor="#00CC99">
<H3><font size="6">The Ad Rotator
 Component</font></H3></TD></TR><TR>
<TD><FORM METHOD=POST ACTION="ServerComponents1.asp">
<INPUT TYPE="submit" NAME="btnval" VALUE="RotateAd">
</FORM></TD>
</TR>
</TABLE>
</BODY></HTML>
```

1. Figures 6-24 and 6-25 show the Ad Rotator component in use in Internet Explorer 5.0, before the button is pressed and after the button is pressed. When the button is pressed, the proper case is selected and an Ad Rotator component is instantiated.
2. Next, a variable is set to the value of the GetAdvertisement method for the Ad Rotator component, returning the proper HTML string.
3. Finally, the contents of the variable are inserted into the proper area of the page with the Response.Write method.

The Browser Capabilities Component

Another very useful capability to add to your website applications is the ability to detect a user's browser type. From the early days of the web, we've all been told what a wonderful thing it is that the Web and HTML are platform- independent, but the reality is slipping ever closer to the proprietary, platform- dependent nature of traditional application programs. Every new version of browser seems to add new, nonstandard features that other browser brands don't (and won't) support, and it's not uncommon to code several versions of a page to be compliant with the majority of browser types currently in use.

Adding the Browser Capabilities component means you can at least detect and respond with appropriate web pages to most of the browsers out there. Although it won't rewrite your pages for you yet, the time is approaching when you'll be able to build in the logic to automatically redefine your web pages on the fly to be compliant with whatever browser the user happens to be using. This kind of user-based response system will make the Web much more user friendly, so expect developers to adopt these capabilities very rapidly as they become more mainstream.

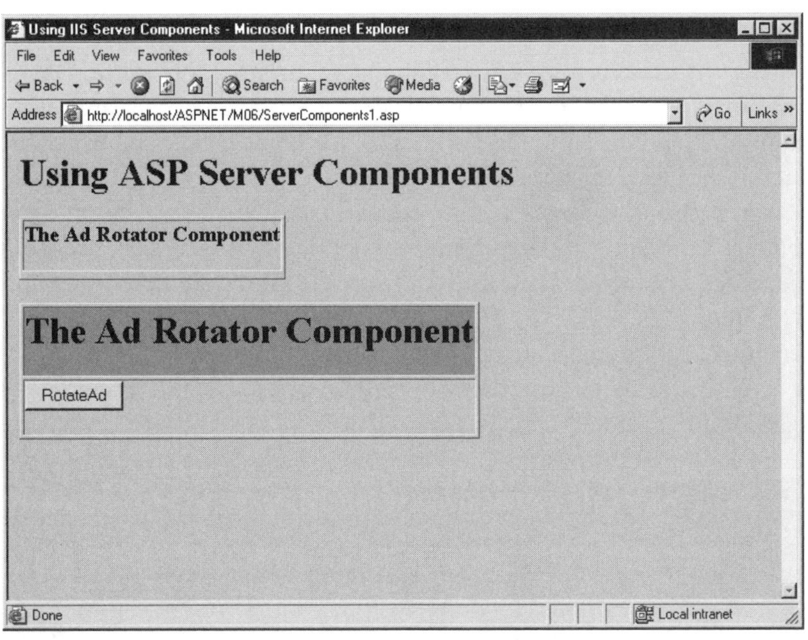

Figure 6-24 The Ad Rotator component in the browser before instantiation

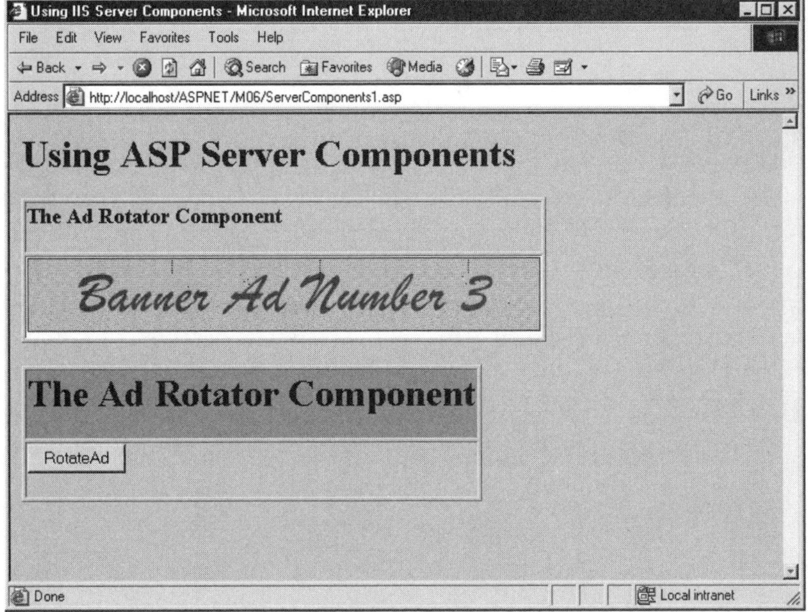

Figure 6-25 The Ad Rotator in use

The browscap.ini File

On your server, there is a file named browscap.ini, probably in the WINNT\System32\inetsrv folder. If you're not sure where it is, use the search function in Windows Explorer to find it by name. This file holds the capabilities of browsers for which it has been most recently updated. To keep up with the capabilities of new browsers and versions as they appear, you'll want to perform regular maintenance to this file and make sure it is updated often. There are websites where updated versions of browscap.ini are made available, including Microsoft's own website.

Like other text files holding data for use by a component, the browscap.ini file has its own special syntax and data elements. Here's a small section from the browscap.ini file installed with Windows 2000:

```
;;;;;;;;;;;;;;;;;;;;;;;;;;;;;;;;;;;;;;;; IE 5.0
[IE 5.0]
browser=IE
Version=5.0
majorver=5
minorver=0
frames=True
tables=True
cookies=True
backgroundsounds=True
vbscript=True
javaapplets=True
javascript=True
ActiveXControls=True
```

Comments can be added anywhere with the semicolon, as you can see on the first line, and individual browser sections are headed by the name and version of the browser encased in brackets, as shown on the second line. Following that, each property defined by this file has its own line with the name of the property set equal to the value of the property for this browser/ version. Although several of the values are strings, most of them are simply True or False Boolean values. These initial sections are called the parent browser sections, and they are followed by smaller sections that contain properties of specific minor versions or nongeneric versions for that browser type.

Displaying Browser Capabilities

Any ASP page can display the user's browser capabilities using the code shown after this paragraph, and if you can capture browser capabilities with an ASP page, you can easily redirect users to an appropriate version of the file to which they are connecting. Here's the example ASP page code:

```
<%
Option Explicit
Dim btnClicked
%>
<html><head><title>Using IIS Server Components</title>
<meta http-equiv="Content-Type"
 content="text/html; charset=iso-8859-1">
</head>
<body bgcolor="#77FF77">
<H2><font size="6">Using ASP Server
 Components</font></H2>
<TABLE border=1>
<TR><TD><H3>The Browser Capabilities
 Component</H3></TD></TR><TR><TD bgcolor="white">
<%
btnClicked = Request.Form("btnval")
Select Case btnClicked
  Case "DisplayBrowserCapabilities"
    Dim objBrowserCap
    Dim colBrowserCap
    Set objBrowserCap =
 Server.CreateObject("MSWC.BrowserType")
    colBrowserCap = objBrowserCap("browser")
    Response.Write "<B>Your Browser Is
 " & colBrowserCapcolBrowserCap =
objBrowserCap("Version")
    Response.Write colBrowserCap & "</B><BR>"
    colBrowserCap = objBrowserCap("majorver")
    Response.Write "<B>The major version is
 " & colBrowserCap & "</B><BR>"
    colBrowserCap = objBrowserCap("minorver")
    Response.Write "<B>The minor version is
 " & colBrowserCap & "</B><BR>"
    colBrowserCap = objBrowserCap("frames")
```

```
   Response.Write "<B>It is " & colBrowserCap & "
 that your browser supports frames</B><BR>"
   colBrowserCap = objBrowserCap("tables")
   Response.Write "<B>It is " & colBrowserCap & "
 that your browser supports tables</B><BR>"
   colBrowserCap = objBrowserCap("cookies")
   Response.Write "<B>It is " & colBrowserCap & "
 that your browser supports cookies</B><BR>"
   colBrowserCap =
 objBrowserCap("backgroundsounds")
   Response.Write "<B>It is " & colBrowserCap & "
 that your browser supports background sounds</B><BR>"
   colBrowserCap = objBrowserCap("vbscript")
   Response.Write "<B>It is " & colBrowserCap & "
 that your browser supports VBScript</B><BR>"
   colBrowserCap = objBrowserCap("javaapplets")
   Response.Write "<B>It is " & colBrowserCap & "
 that your browser supports javaapplets</B><BR>"
   colBrowserCap = objBrowserCap("javascript")
   Response.Write "<B>It is " & colBrowserCap & "
 that your browser supports javascript</B><BR>"
   colBrowserCap = objBrowserCap("ActiveXControls")
   Response.Write "<B>It is " & colBrowserCap & "
 that your browser supports ActiveX controls</B><BR>"
      End Select
%>
</TD></TR></TABLE>
<P>
<TABLE border=1><TR><TD bgcolor="#00CC99">
<H3><font size="6">The Browser Capabilities
Component</font></H3></TD></TR><TR>
<TD><FORM METHOD=POST ACTION="ServerComponents2.asp">
<INPUT TYPE="submit" NAME="btnval"
 VALUE="DisplayBrowserCapabilities">
</FORM></TD>
</TR>
</TABLE>
</BODY></HTML>
```

This page dimensions a couple of variables and then uses one to create a Browser Capabilities component instance. Next, it makes a variable equal to the "browser" property value and writes that back to the user, then it makes the variable equal to the "version" property value and writes that back to the user, and so forth until it has gone through most of the properties available.

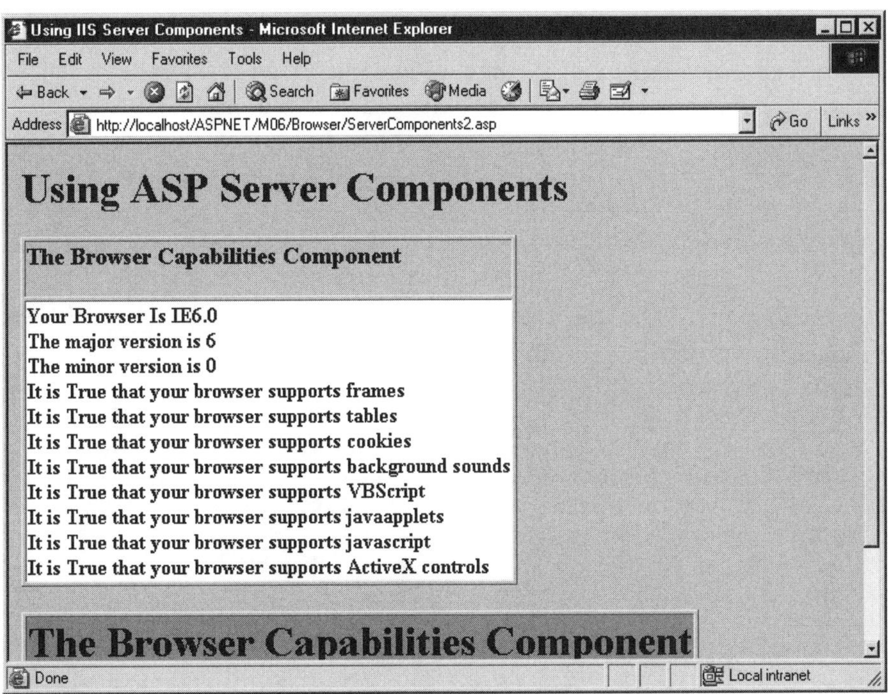

Figure 6-26 Browser capabilities listed

In order to make the installed browscap.ini file work with the version of IE installed (version 6.0), it was necessary to add the appropriate text to the browscap.ini file. For this exercise, the IE 5.0 section was simply copied and updated to 6 in every place a 5 was found. You can see the results in Figure 6-26.

Displaying Browser Capabilities in ASP.NET

Browser capabilities can also be displayed in ASP.NET, with a somewhat different syntax. The type HttpBrowserCapabilities is used to create an object collecting browser capabilities, retrieving them using the Browser collection of the Request object. Once this object is created (either in the global.asax file or in a code-behind page), these values are accessible as with any other Web Forms page.

Creating a Web Form to Display Browser Capabilities

To capture and make browser capabilities available for use, simply create a Web Forms page, as you have done many times now. To the Web Form, add a label to tell the user what they are working with, and add a ListBox control from the Web Controls section of the toolbox. Name the ListBox BcapList. Then add code such as the following to the code-behind page:

```
Dim strBCap As String
Dim browserCap As HttpBrowserCapabilities

browserCap = Request.Browser
BCapList.Items.Clear()
strBCap = "Type = " & browserCap.Type
Me.BCapList.Items.Add(New ListItem(strBCap))
strBCap = "Name = " & browserCap.Browser
Me.BCapList.Items.Add(New ListItem(strBCap))
strBCap = "Version = " & browserCap.Version
Me.BCapList.Items.Add(New ListItem(strBCap))
strBCap = "Major Version = " & browserCap.MajorVersion
Me.BCapList.Items.Add(New ListItem(strBCap))
strBCap = "Minor Version = " & browserCap.MinorVersion
Me.BCapList.Items.Add(New ListItem(strBCap))
strBCap = "Platform = " & browserCap.Platform
Me.BCapList.Items.Add(New ListItem(strBCap))
strBCap = " Is Beta = " & browserCap.Beta
Me.BCapList.Items.Add(New ListItem(strBCap))
strBCap = " Is Crawler = " & browserCap.Crawler
Me.BCapList.Items.Add(New ListItem(strBCap))
strBCap = " Is AOL = " & browserCap.AOL
Me.BCapList.Items.Add(New ListItem(strBCap))
strBCap = " Is Win16 = " & browserCap.Win16
Me.BCapList.Items.Add(New ListItem(strBCap))
strBCap = " Is Win32 = " & browserCap.Win32
Me.BCapList.Items.Add(New ListItem(strBCap))
strBCap = "Supports Frames = " & browserCap.Frames
Me.BCapList.Items.Add(New ListItem(strBCap))
strBCap = "Supports Tables = " & browserCap.Tables
Me.BCapList.Items.Add(New ListItem(strBCap))
strBCap = "Supports Cookies = " & browserCap.Cookies
Me.BCapList.Items.Add(New ListItem(strBCap))
strBCap = "Supports VB Script = " & browserCap.VBScript
Me.BCapList.Items.Add(New ListItem(strBCap))
strBCap = "Supports JavaScript =
 " & browserCap.JavaScript
Me.BCapList.Items.Add(New ListItem(strBCap))
strBCap = "Supports Java Applets =
```

```
 " & browserCap.JavaApplets
Me.BCapList.Items.Add(New ListItem(strBCap))
strBCap = "Supports ActiveX Controls =
 " & browserCap.ActiveXControls
Me.BCapList.Items.Add(New ListItem(strBCap))
strBCap = "CDF = " & browserCap.CDF
```

1-Minute Drill

- How are click-throughs enabled with the Ad Rotator component?
- In the browscap.ini file, what delimiters contain the browser name?

The Content Linking Component

Those of us born back in the age of books are familiar with the traditional, linear way of reading through material from front to back, starting with the table of contents. For those born into the information age, the table of contents may seem somewhat archaic, approaching obsolescence. For myself, it's hard to imagine reading material without a table of contents, and so it's not surprising that I've created hypertext classroom materials (static web pages) that include tables of contents.

A table of contents is actually metadata about the contents of a work (whether book, magazine, website, or whatever) that provides an easy way to skim and find information of interest. The purpose of the Content Linking component is to create an easy-to-access table of contents as well as a set of navigable links through that content. The Content Linking component has a set of methods (listed next) that allow you to not only find out how much content (how many files) you're dealing with, but to return a description and link to each, as well as move among the pages with ease.

Now, you might think the average person could just as easily use the Back and Forward buttons on their browser to perform these actions, and in many cases you'd be right, but there are also many circumstances in which you'll find it convenient to control the movement of a user through your site. The Content Linking component offers that kind of control.

- The URL is specified after the path and name of the image file.
- "[" and "]"

The Content Linking List File

Like the other components you've encountered, the Content Linking component depends on an external file kept on the server for its list of navigable content. A typical Content Linking list file will be a text file that looks somewhat like the following example:

```
ScannerClass/Section1.html   Scanner Class Introduction
 Includes introduction, Image acquisition, Digitizing
ScannerClass/Section1-Software.html
 Scanner Software Includes software for scanners
ScannerClass/Section1-ColorPrinters.html
 Color Printers Includes color printer data
ScannerClass/Section1-BuildingQuality.htm
 Getting Good Results   Tells how to properly scan
ScannerClass/Section1-Shopping.html
 Shopping for Scanners What to look for when shopping
```

Although it may not be easy to tell from the file just listed, the Content Linking list file is just a plain text file, each line of which includes three things: the relative URL of the content page of interest, the display text, and a comment describing the content. Each of the three line sections must be separated by a tab character (not spaces). Wherever the file is saved, the URL must, of course, be appropriate to point to the content files.

The Content Linking Component Methods

The Content Linking component has no properties, only the following methods:

- **GetListCount(*contenttextfile*)** This method returns the number of file listings in the content text file.
- **GetListIndex(*contenttextfile*)** This method returns the index number of the current page in the content text file.
- **GetNextURL(*contenttextfile*)** This method returns the URL for the next page in the content text file list.
- **GetNextDescription(*contenttextfile*)** This method returns the description for the next page in the content text file.
- **GetPreviousURL(*contenttextfile*)** This method returns the URL for the previous page in the content text file.

- **GetPreviousDescription(*contenttextfile*)** This method returns the description for the previous page in the content text file.
- **GetNthURL(*contenttextfile*, *number*)** This method returns the URL for the page indicated by number in the content text file.
- **GetNthDescription(*contenttextfile*, *number*)** This method returns the description for the page indicated by number in the content text file.

Project 6-3 Using the Content Linking Component

The Content Linking component is useful for creating tables of contents and providing navigation links across the site. This example uses a mechanism similar to that used in previous examples to provide the user with the ability to activate an instance of the Content Linking component. It also displays a series of links to content listed in the Content text file. Here's an easy exercise to do on your own.

Step-by-Step

Navigation buttons on each page can be created using the GetNext and GetPrevious methods of the Content Linking component. Here's the example code:

```
<%
Option Explicit
Dim btnClicked
%>
<html><head><title>Using IIS Server
 Components</title>
<meta http-equiv="Content-Type"
 content="text/html; charset=iso-8859-1">
</head>
<body bgcolor="#77FF77">
<H2><font size="6">Using ASP Server
 Components</font></H2>
<TABLE border=1>
<TR><TD><H3>The Content Linking
 Component</H3></TD></TR><TR><TD bgcolor="white">
<%
btnClicked = Request.Form("btnval")
```

```
Select Case btnClicked
  Case "DisplayLinkList"
    Dim objContent
    Dim intI
    Dim intC
    Dim vURL
    Dim vDesc
    Set objContent =
 Server.CreateObject("MSWC.NextLink")
    intI = 1
    intC =
 objContent.GetListCount("ScannerContent.txt")
    Response.Write "<OL>"
    For intI = 1 to intC
      vURL =
 objContent.GetNthURL("ScannerContent.txt", intI)
      vDesc =
 objContent.GetNthDescription("ScannerContent.txt", intI)
      Response.Write "<LI><B><A HREF= """
      Response.Write vURL
      Response.Write """>"
      Response.Write vDesc
      Response.Write "</A></B>"
    Next
      Response.Write "</OL>"
End Select
%>
</TD></TR></TABLE>
<P>
<TABLE border=1><TR><TD bgcolor="#00CC99">
<H3><font size="6">The Content
 Linking Component</font></H3></TD></TR><TR>
<TD><FORM METHOD=POST ACTION="ServerComponents3.asp">
<INPUT TYPE="submit" NAME="btnval"
 VALUE="DisplayLinkList">
</FORM></TD>
</TR>
</TABLE>
</BODY></HTML>
```

1. This code creates an instance of the Content Linking component and iterates through all the pages of content listed in the Content Linking list file with a numbered list (the <OL> and <LI> tags).

2. For each content file listed, it retrieves the URL and the description with the GetNthURL and GetNthDescription methods, using the counter intl to count each time through the loop. The variable intC is just used to hold the number of items in the list, which it retrieves with the GetListCount method. Figure 6-27 shows the linked list of files onscreen.

The Content Rotator Component

The Content Rotator component is similar to the Ad Rotator component in that it displays selected content according to a preset ratio (not a schedule or timetable). Like the Ad Rotator component, it uses a schedule file to list the content to be included in the rotation, but the only thing you can set (other than the content to display) is the rotation ratio. Again, you simply use a number to indicate the ratio, based on the total of all included numbers for each set of content you wish to display.

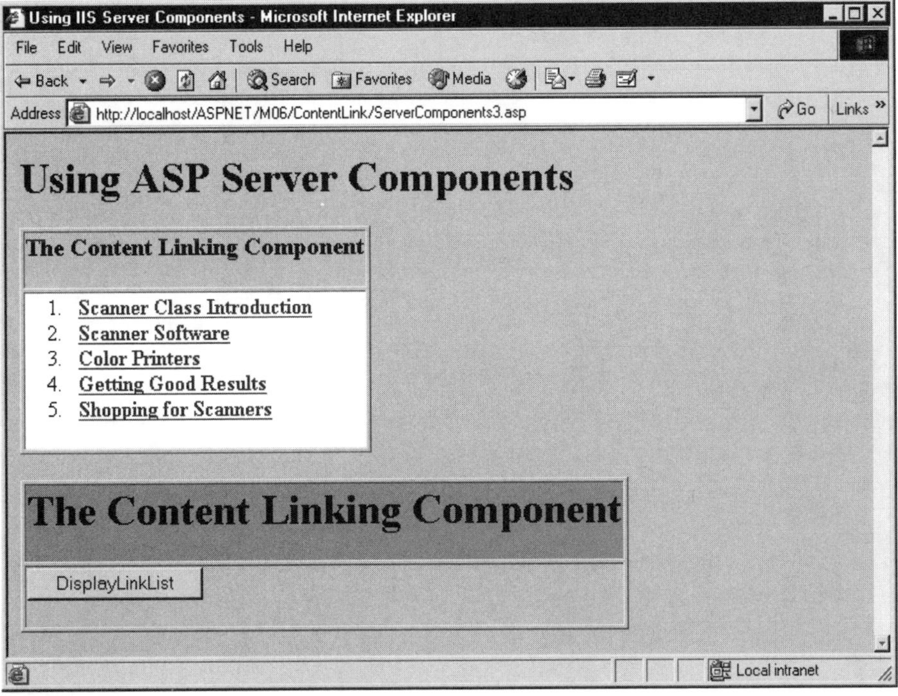

Figure 6-27 Results of the Content Linking component

Content Rotator Methods

The Content Rotator component has two methods:

- **GetAllContent(*contentlistfile*)** This method displays all the content entries in the schedule file.
- **ChooseContent(*contentlistfile*)** This method retrieves the next selected content listing from the schedule file according to the ratio you set.

The Content Rotator Schedule File The Content Rotator schedule file does not display content on a schedule, as its name implies, but rather displays content according to the ratio you've set. Each content item starts with two percent signs (%%) and then the schedule ratio number. Following that are some comments (following two slashes) and then the lines of content, which can be whatever you like until the next set of percent signs are encountered:

```
%% 1 //This text will display
 five percent of the time
For excellent web hosting and construction services,
please visit
 <A HREF="www.dynworks.com">Dynworks</A>

%% 3 //This text will display
 fifteen percent of the time
For unique Web graphics design and artistry,
please visit <A HREF="www.e4free.com/afc">
AFC Computer Services</A>

%% 5 //This text will display
 twenty-five percent of the time
For full-featured application services
 please visit <A HREF="www.servata.com">
Servata Online Applications</A>

%%11 //This text will display 55 percent of the time
For free wireless application services please visit
<A HREF="www.e4free.com">E4free</A>
```

Rotating Content

This example uses code like the other examples you've used for working with components, and after the initial page load you'll be able to rotate content each

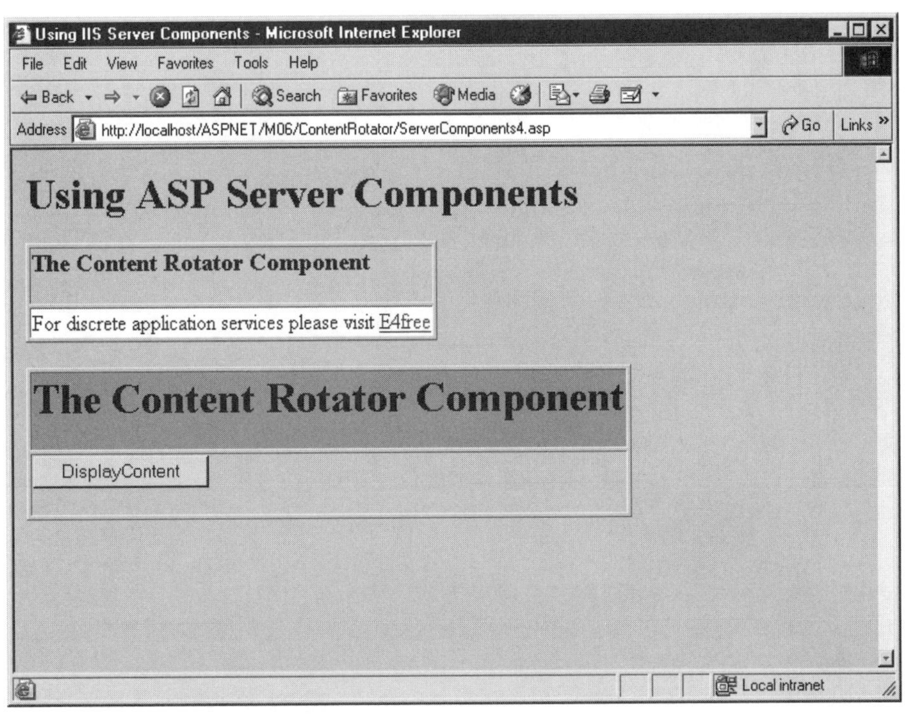

Figure 6-28 Rotating content

time you click the button provided, as shown in Figure 6-28. The example code is as follows:

```
<%
Option Explicit
Dim btnClicked
%>
<html><head><title>Using IIS
 Server Components</title>
<meta http-equiv="Content-Type"
 content="text/html; charset=iso-8859-1">
</head>
<body bgcolor="#77FF77">
<H2><font size="6">Using ASP Server
 Components</font></H2>
<TABLE border=1>
<TR><TD><H3>The Content Rotator
 Component</H3></TD></TR><TR><TD bgcolor="white">
```

```
<%
btnClicked = Request.Form("btnval")
Select Case btnClicked
     Case "DisplayContent"
          Dim objContentRotator
          Dim vCont
          Set objContentRotator =
 Server.CreateObject("MSWC.ContentRotator")
          vCont =
 objContentRotator.ChooseContent("ContentRotator.txt")
          Response.Write vCont
End Select
%>
</TD></TR></TABLE>
<P>
<TABLE border=1><TR><TD bgcolor="#00CC99">
<H3><font size="6">The Content Rotator
 Component</font></H3></TD></TR><TR>
<TD><FORM METHOD=POST
 ACTION="ServerComponents4.asp">
<INPUT TYPE="submit" NAME="btnval"
 VALUE="DisplayContent">
</FORM></TD>
</TR>
</TABLE>
</BODY></HTML>
```

1-Minute Drill

- What method is used to get the number of files in the content linking text file?
- What notation is used to specify the percentage of time content items are rotated?

- GetListCount
- %% and then the number

Ask the Expert

Question: It sounds like these components are actually little programs that run on my server. Is this the case? How many can I run? Should I pay for them or create them myself? Where can I get them?

Answer: Yes, you're right. Components are compiled programs that run on your server when they are instantiated using one of the two methods described at the beginning of this module. Since they are compiled, they run faster than script would, and since they are prebuilt and pretested, the bugs have been worked out. You don't have to buy the ones discussed in this module (or in the beginning of the next module), but typically you would buy components made by third parties, unless they are giving away time-limited demos or "light" versions.

You can run as many as your system resources will allow, meaning you are constrained by the amount of memory and processor capability, just as with any other programs. You can find third-party components on most websites related to ASP, and we'll cover some of them in the next module.

Question: These components make use of text files on the server. Is this a security risk? Will people be loading things on my server and perhaps compromising security?

Answer: Users of your site will be activating components via ASP; as long as those script files are secure, there's not much more they can do than overload your system if too many of them hit your site at once. However, if you happen to be developing sites for other people, it is probable they will want to manage their site from their location. This means you will have to allow access to some sensitive areas on your server, so it is a good idea to build management pages for them that will allow them to do what they need to do without having full access to the server. Since you're going to be developing management pages, take the time to set up appropriate users and groups, and limit the actions client-users can take on your server. It's worth the effort to preserve your peace of mind.

More Active Server Components

A good place to look for third-party components is **www.15seconds.com**, a website devoted to the construction of ASP websites and ASP applications. If you visit **www.15seconds.com/component/default.htm**, you'll find tons of free, shareware, and commercial components for evaluation and operational use, as well as plenty of reviews and documentation. You can also find many other sites where ASP is the main topic of discussion and where third-party components are available. Simply go to your favorite search engine and enter "Active Server Pages," "ASP Components," "Microsoft IIS Server Components," and so forth.

More Microsoft IIS Server Components

There are some issues concerning third-party components (such as installation, registration, documentation, and support) that will be covered later in this module. For now, let's just jump right into the rest of the installed components and their usefulness. In addition to what we have covered in other chapters, the following server components are also available with a standard installation of Windows 2000:

- The Counters component, for counting anything you want to track
- The Page Counter component, for tracking page hits
- The Permission Checker component, for checking authorization levels
- The Tools component, a set of ASP tools for common functions
- The Logging Utility component, for managing log files

These components should already be installed and ready for use when you install IIS 5.0.

The Counters Component

The Counters component is a single component that can be used to easily create any number of individual counters for an application. Since you create the Counters component from within the global.asa file, these counters are accessible from any page in your application, but by the same token this component does not scale very well. However, it is easy to use and can be quite helpful in a pinch.

Each counter you create holds a number (an integer) in a text file named counter.txt. Please note that this text file is not updated until the application ends or the server is stopped. It is not a good reference for existing counter values in real time.

Counters Component Methods

The Counters component has methods for creating counters and retrieving their values, as well as incrementing or setting values and removing counters altogether (there are no properties). The methods are as follows:

- **Get(*counter*)** This method returns the current value of whatever counter you specify. If the counter doesn't exist, it creates it and returns zero as the value.
- **Increment(*counter*)** This method increases the value of the specified counter by one. If the counter doesn't exist, it also creates the counter and sets the value to 1.
- **Remove(*counter*)** This method removes the specified counter.
- **Set(*counter*, *value*)** This method sets the value of the specified counter to *value*. If the counter doesn't exist, it also creates the counter and sets the value to *value*.

Third-Party Components for ASP

Microsoft is not the only company making components that will work with ASP—in fact, Microsoft promotes the production of components by third parties as a means of expanding the appeal of ASP and IIS. You can find third- party components by going to your favorite search engine and entering the phrase "ASP Components," or go to one of the well-known ASP developer sites such as **www.15seconds.com**, **www.4guysfromrolla.com**,**www.aspwatch.com**, or **www.activeserverpages.com**.

There are many third-party components available, and one very appealing function that several components can perform is file uploading and downloading. Microsoft makes a component of this type called the Posting Acceptor (you can find it at **microsoft.com/windows/software/webpost/post_accept.htm**), but for this exercise we'll use a third-party component called ActiveFile made by Infomentum (**www.infomentum.com**).

Getting and Installing Third-Party Components

The component we're using for this section is easy to get and easy to install. If you go to the Infomentum home page and choose ActiveFile, you'll find a selection on the menu offering a free demo version that is fully functional for the trial period. Like the other file upload components available, ActiveFile is compliant with RFC 1867, and version 2.2 can not only upload and download files, but also automatically allows users to browse for the files they want to upload. In addition, ActiveFile 2.2 has an extensive set of methods and properties to make it easier to detect Macintosh files, work with compressed files, make directories, and check file types.

Installing ActiveFile 2.2 is easy. The installation follows a standard installation process. Some third-party components can only be installed manually, meaning you have to put the files in the correct folders yourself and make changes to the registry. Manual installation can be time consuming and just a bit technical, so it's best to avoid it if possible.

ActiveFile Methods and Properties

The ActiveFile component has quite a few objects, properties, and methods available, but we're only going to cover a couple of them here. For a more detailed explanation and graphical guide, take a look at the Component Manual at **www.infomentum.com/activefile/doc**. For this example, you'll be using the Post object and the FormInputs object (which is a collection of the Post object). The only method you'll use is the Upload method of the Post object, and the only properties will be the Name and Value properties of the FormInputs object. Let's review the code and see what's happening:

```
<%
Option Explicit
%>
<html><head><title>Using Third-Party
 IIS Server Components</title>
<meta http-equiv="Content-Type"
 content="text/html; charset=iso-8859-1">
</head>
<body bgcolor="#77FF77">
<H2><font size="6">Using Third-Party
 ASP Server Components</font></H2>
<TABLE border=1>
<TR><TD><H3>The ActiveFile Component</H3></TD></TR>
<TR><TD bgcolor="white">
<%
```

```
Dim Post
Dim FormInput
Set Post = Server.CreateObject("ActiveFile.Post")
Post.Upload "E:\Inetpub\wwwroot\ASPNET\M06
\ThirdPartyComponents\Temp"
For Each FormInput in Post.FormInputs
     Response.Write FormInput.Name
 & " = " & FormInput.Value & "<BR>"
Next
%>
</TD></TR></TABLE>
<P>
<TABLE border=1><TR><TD
 bgcolor="#00CC99" COLSPAN=3>
<H3><font size="6">The ActiveFile
 Component</font></H3></TD></TR><TR>
<TD><FORM METHOD=POST ACTION="ServerComponents10.asp" enctype="multipart/form-data">
Upload this File:</TD><TD>
<INPUT TYPE="file"
 NAME="UploadedFile" SIZE="20"></TD><TD>
<INPUT TYPE="submit" NAME="btnval"
 VALUE="PostFile"></TD></TR>
</FORM>
</TABLE>
</BODY></HTML>
```


In this script, you're not allowed to use the Request object's methods to capture any values from the form, so you remove the references to the name of the submit button that activate the Select…Case statement. In doing so, you also remove the entire Select…Case structure. What's left is an ASP script that instantiates the ActiveFile component when called, uploads whatever file you've chosen, places it in the folder you've chosen, and responds with a notice saying what was uploaded. Checking the specified folder shows that the file was actually uploaded. Note that if you use the browse function, it will insert the entire physical path and the filename, but you can also use the relative path and filename and it will work just as well.

The ActiveFile product seems to work quite well with the installation of the OS currently being used, and having this capability working will add some nice application functions to your site. For example, not only can you upload files, but you can place them into a database as well. Therefore, you can allow your users to upload and post images as well as text (or other binary file types).

Ask the Expert

Question: **Microsoft has provided a number of installed components, and these components provide quite a few basic functions that come in handy in applications. I can also program my own components or make scripts that do the required functions. How can I tell when it's time to buy third-party components?**

Answer: Buying third-party components is a decision you can make based on money, time, and projected future usage. For example, suppose you have plenty of money, but little time. You might want to buy third- party components to speed up your development process. By the same token, if you have little money but plenty of time (and enough programming expertise), you might want to create your own components. An added benefit of creating your own components is that you can then sell them to other folks, although you should understand that this is essentially a business itself (meaning that while it's easy to create components, you should not assume that it will be equally easy to market and sell them competitively). Lastly, if you expect to use many variations of the component in your future applications, it may be better to develop your own so that you have the source code and can modify them as you please.

Question: **The Permission Checker and Logging Utility components seem to perform functions that only an administrator can usually perform. Why are they included?**

Answer: Sometimes you want to automate administrative functions, and these components will assist you with that effort. The Permission Checker component is useful for checking conditions to allow or disallow access to resources based on permissions. You can always assign guests a particular status at login, thereby relieving yourself of manually managing permissions for each and every user. The Logging Utility component provides similar management capability based on application conditions.

Mastery Check

1. What is an object model?

   A. A model of the functions each object performs in your application

   B. A model of the objects users are allowed to interact with

   C. A description or illustration of the relationships of objects to each other

   D. None of the above

2. What does the Dictionary object contain, and how can they be changed?

   A. Variables, and they can be changed by assigning new values.

   B. Name-Value pairs, and they can be changed by using Dictionary object properties.

   C. Folder objects, and they can be changed by removing them.

   D. The Dictionary object contains nothing that can be changed.

3. In the File object, what attributes (in what order) can be set when using the CreateTextFile method?

   A. Filepath, overwrite, unicode

   B. Filename, filesize, filepath

   C. Filepath, filename, filesize

   D. Overwrite, unicode, filesize

   E. None of the above

Mastery Check

4. Which Scripting Library objects can be used to create text files?

A. Only the File object

B. Only the Textstream object

C. Only the FileSystemObject, Folder object, and File object

D. All of them

E. None of them

5. Working with files sometimes requires navigating within them to find and edit particular sections of text. To move from one line to the next within a file, you would use the _______ method of the __________ object. To write a blank line into a file you would use the _________ method of the _________ object. To determine what column you are in within a text file, you would use the ________ property of the _______ object.

6. What capabilities does the Ad Rotator component offer?

A. It stores banner ads for display.

B. It provides a means of accessing banner ads for scheduled rotation display.

C. It provides a means of accessing banner ads for random rotation according to a set percentage for display.

D. None of the above.

7. Why is the Browser Capabilities component so important, and where is the content it uses kept?

A. It detects browser types, providing a means to display customized web content based on browser type and version. The content it uses to accomplish this is kept in a text file named browscap.ini.

B. It can automatically refer to a browscap.ini file located on the sites of the major browser manufacturers, and ensures that your content is always compatible with the latest browser types and versions.

Mastery Check

C. It checks the browser you currently have installed to make sure it is the most up-to-date version, so your pages will always be compatible with the latest browser types and versions.

D. None of the above.

8. How does the Content Linking component perform its job?

A. It links the content of your web site for you, without the traditional hyperlinks.

B. It refers to a content linking text file for information about path, name, and description of the files in your web site, and uses methods and properties to assist the user in navigating the site.

C. It links the content of your site with the content of other sites automatically, generating more traffic through reciprocal links.

D. None of the above.

9. What is one of the primary advantages of using the Content Rotator component?

A. You can set the rotation schedule and forget it, meaning you have less management to do.

B. You can rotate text and hyperlinks across your pages according to the percentage paid for by advertisers.

C. Rotating content in 3D is a cool effect to add to your site.

D. Rotating content in 3D is hard to do manually, and the Content Rotator does it for you.

10. When an object is created with the Server.CreateObject method, the object is instantiated ____________, and when an object is created using <OBJECT> tags, the object is instantiated ______________________.

Mastery Check

11. What method of the FileSystemObject object would be used to find out the extension of a file?

A. FindExtension(filename)

B. FindExtensionName(filename)

C. GetExtensionName(filepath)

D. None of the above

12. In ASP.NET, there is an Ad Rotator ___________ in the _________. You can set the images it displays and the number of impressions each should receive with an ___ file.

13. What does the ParentFolder property of the Folder object do?

A. Returns a Folder object representing the parent folder of the current Folder object

B. Creates a Folder object that is a child folder of the current Folder object

C. Navigates to the parent folder of the current Folder object

D. None of the above

14. What capability of a given browser might be critical to know if you are trying to decide how to manage state in your web application?

A. Major Version

B. Supports cookies

C. Whether the browser was a version of Netscape or Internet Explorer

D. None of the above

15. What function in VBScript can be used to determine whether an object exists?

A. IsObject(objectname)

B. Object(nameofobject)

C. IsNull(objectlocation)

D. None of the above

Module 7

Web Services and ASP.NET

The Goals of This Module

- Discuss the differences between applications and services
- Learn about XML
- Build a simple XML DTD
- Learn about SOAP
- Learn about WDSL
- Learn how to construct efficient Web Services
- Build a simple Web Service
- Practice using prebuilt Web Services

If you've followed the development of the Internet over the past decade or so, you've probably encountered statistics about growth in the number of Internet users. Early numbers, when depicted graphically, showed an exponential increase taking place. Common sense tells us that, as enticing as exponential growth appears, it's always bound to come to an end. Growth in the number of Internet users in the form of human beings will stabilize and eventually come to resemble normal population growth.

But human beings are not the only users of the Internet. Software applications can also use the Internet. For example, suppose you want to be notified whenever your stock price hits a particular mark. You could assign a person to check every hour or so, but a much more practical method would be to simply turn on an application and instruct it to check every so often and, upon finding the appropriate stock price to send you an e-mail or call your cell phone.

In order to do this, the application would have to be hosted on a server connected to the Internet constantly and contain programming logic enabling it to check stock prices (most likely from another application that generates stock prices for anonymous or subscription access), evaluate what it finds, and send an e-mail or make a call upon the appropriate condition. Essentially, you'd need an application that ran all the time and had the ability to perform independent actions.

While this example is very simple, it demonstrates the enormous power inherent in the combination of distributed, hosted, connected applications. Not only can they provide services directly to humans, they can communicate, collaborate, and accomplish tasks together, either in ad hoc groups or as groups of dedicated applications.

Web Services Development

Web Services is the term currently being used to describe hosted applications because many of them are hosted on the same servers used for websites, and their function is to provide services to (in most cases) any user, human, or machine across the Internet (but this doesn't mean that users can't be restricted, just as in any online situation). The development process is just about the same as for any type of programming: determine the desired result, figure out what inputs are required, generate the logic to perform the processing, and finally, do the coding.

Web Services are typically smaller, self-contained applications that perform specific functions rather than all-encompassing programs that do everything in one large, complex package. This is because they are hosted on servers connected to the Internet, and modular development makes more sense.

Another feature of Web Services is that they are quite a bit like functions: you can feed them inputs as arguments, and they return a result. However, before you can build Web Services, you need to become familiar with the format of the results produced and how messages are passed and procedures called with Web Services. There are a variety of languages, specifications, protocols, and so forth used, including Web Services Description Language (WSDL), Simple Object Access Protocol (SOAP), and eXtensible Markup Language (XML). We'll start by discussing XML as it is the foundation for WSDL and SOAP.

1-Minute Drill

- What is a Web Service?
- How can Web Services be accessed?

What Is eXtensible Markup Language (XML)?

XML is a very hot topic these days because it provides an excellent format for packaging and communicating data between humans, machines, or both. It is important to note that XML *is not a language*. It is a standard format for writing your own languages. These languages resemble HTML in that they are made up of elements and attributes surrounded by angle brackets (<,>), so they tend to be easy to read and to write by hand. Both HTML and XML are subsets or applications of SGML (Standard Generalized Markup Language). Technically, XML is an application profile written with and conforming to SGML.

The World Wide Web Consortium (W3C) developed XML 1.0 with the design goals that it be usable on the Internet, provide support for many applications, be compatible with SGML, be easy to use, have no optional features, be human-readable, and be concise.

- Web Services are applications that are designed to accept input from clients on the Web and return output in a particular format to the calling client. In the same way that you might create a function in a programming language and then call that function from within your program, you can create Web Service functions, host them on your website, and then call them from your web application.
- Web Services can be accessed using HTTP, SOAP, WSDL, and XML. These are standard specifications and protocols, so Web Services can easily be made available no matter what the operating system or platform.

XML can easily be used to make data available in a consistent way to people and to servers, so industry groups are developing XML applications suitable for the special terms and definitions that are used within their industries.

XML Entities

XML entities are like XML "pages," in the same way that plain-text HTML files are web pages. XML documents are composed of one or more entities (the recommendation refers to entities as storage units) containing parsed or unparsed data. The parsed data includes text and markup. The markup tags describe the layout and structure of the document. An XML processor reads XML documents and typically provides the results to an application. Microsoft's Internet Explorer 5.0 supports XML 1.0 processing as well as namespaces and the DOM and includes an engine for processing eXtensible Style Sheets (XSL), an XML version of Cascading Style Sheets (CSS).

The XML Document Structure

XML documents have two structures, one logical and the other physical. All the files or entities that make up the XML document, even though they might be physically separated, are included in the finished XML document. Logically, the document consists of elements, attributes, and so on, much like an HTML document, although XML documents can contain declarations, processing instructions, and so forth, more like a traditional executable application. Well-formed XML documents are created from well-formed subunits, including entities, elements, and so forth.

Note

Well-formed is a term used often in XML; it means that all XML structures conform to the basic structural rules of XML.

An XML document may have three parts: a *prologue*, a *body*, and an *epilogue*. The prologue and epilogue are optional. The prologue may contain comments, version information, processing instructions, and a reference to a specific XML Document Type Definition (DTD), while the epilogue may contain comments and processing instructions. The body consists of one or more elements (defined by the DTD), forming a hierarchical tree structure and possibly containing character data. In the body, elements are very similar in structure, appearance, and function to HTML in web pages. Note that since XML allows authors to create their own markup languages, the names and meanings of the elements and attributes depend on what the author created. This means that while XML documents are bound to be similar in structure, there is no requirement that the elements and attributes be similar.

The next example shows how some elements may be constructed and arranged in the body of an XML document:

```
<haircare_products>
 <haircare_conditioner brand="AuNatural">
  <color>Light Gray</color>
  <price>17.95</price>
  <conditioner_name>Brilliant Gray</conditioner_name>
 </haircare_conditioner>
</haircare_products>
```

Notice the hierarchical structure of the starting and ending tags. Each element is started by its own tag, and if it contains subelements, they all start and end within their parent element's tags.

In XML, elements may contain:

- Other elements (just as the HTML BODY element contains other HTML elements such as the P and BR elements)
- Character data
- Character references
- Entity references
- Processing instructions
- Comments
- CDATA (character data) sections

Elements are defined with angle brackets (< >), and both the starting and ending tags are required, unless the element is an empty element, in which case it has no content and must still have either a starting/ending tag combination or contain the slash (representing the ending tag) inside itself. A starting tag might be <haircare_products>, an ending tag might be </haircare_products>, and an empty-element tag might be <haircare_products></haircare_products> or <haircare_products/> (with the slash marking the end inside the same tag).

Writing XML DTDs

There are several ways to work with XML. First, you can write well-formed XML documents, just like you would write an HTML document. Writing XML documents of this type is fine, but the system or client that reads them will have no idea what the elements and attributes mean. To apply meaning to XML elements and attributes, you can build an XML DTD or XML Schema. XML DTDs, as the name implies, *define* properties (such as data types and allowable values) for XML elements and attributes. XML Schemas provide even greater support for data types and allowable values, as well as allow for a database-like structure.

There is a language for writing conforming DTDs. It uses a number of common characters, such as the exclamation point, parentheses, asterisks, angle brackets, and so forth to define elements for an XML application that are required, optional, limited, have certain attributes, and other specific properties.

Well-Formed and Valid XML Documents *Well-formedness* is a concept often used in relation to XML documents, and it means that the document contains only one root element and none of the document's elements overlaps. Just being well-formed is not enough, though. A document can be well-formed and still be meaningless within the concepts the data it contains imply. Therefore, DTDs and schemas are used to supply the rules by which a document should live. An XML document is considered *valid* if it has a DTD or schema and if it complies with the rules (constraints) expressed in the DTD. The reference to the DTD must appear before the first element in the document.

In order to write conforming XML DTDs, there are some rules to follow about the construction of elements, their attribute lists, and the way they are interpreted. For example, there can only be one document element, called the *root element*, and all other elements in the document are contained inside the root element. In addition, there can be no overlapping elements, meaning all elements in an XML document must be properly nested. Where an element is nested inside another element, the nested element is called the *child element*, and the element in which the other is nested is called the *parent element*.

Project 7-1: Create an XML DTD

This project walks through the creation of an external XML DTD file. You will write a DTD that declares elements and attributes.

Step-by-Step

1. You can use Notepad to create both the external DTD file and the XML document, and Internet Explorer (4.0 and above) to view your processed XML document. Start this project by opening Notepad.

2. In Notepad, you should be at a blank, new file. If not, click File | New. Save the file in your ASP.NET web folder with a name you'll remember. For this example, use "Project7-1.dtd".

3. Sometimes you'll want to place some comments at the beginning of the file so it will be easier to understand what you're working on. Your comments would perhaps be something like this:

```
<!-- Client version 1.0 DTD
This DTD is for creating XML documents about clients.
Copyright Dave Mercer 2001, 2002
-->
```

7

4. Now you can begin declaring the elements and attributes of your DTD. To define elements, begin with the word ELEMENT (after a less-than sign and the exclamation point) and then put the name of the element. The name of the element must conform to XML naming rules, meaning it can't start with "xml" (in either upper- or lowercase) and it can't start with a number. The element definition for your first element would start like this:

```
<!ELEMENT Clients
```

5. The next thing in the first element definition is the content model. Element content refers to the data an element may contain and it comes in four types: empty, any, mixed, and children. Since the Clients element is going to be the main element in any XML documents you produce, give it the content model designation ANY and close it off with the greater-than sign, like this:

```
<!ELEMENT Clients ANY>
```

6. There are no attributes for the Clients element, so you can go on to the next elements in your DTD. The next is Client, signifying a single client. The Client element may include the client's name as PCDATA, but each client would also have to be associated with attributes for contact and billing information, such as phone number, e-mail address, street address, and so forth. In addition, each client should have a unique ClientID number. First, write the Client element as follows:

```
<!ELEMENT Client (#PCDATA)* )
<!ATTLIST Client
   client          ID        #REQUIRED
   phone           CDATA     #IMPLIED
   email           CDATA     #REQUIRED
   fulladdress     CDATA     #IMPLIED >
```

7. Following its name (Client) is the content model. The content model is written within parentheses, spelling out a mixture of PCDATA in parentheses. This qualifies as a content model of MIXED. Notice that whenever the content model is mixed, #PCDATA must appear first in the list, and all components of the content model must be inside parentheses with the zero or more indicator following. After the declaration of the element, there is an attribute declaration list, and each attribute that the element may have is listed, along with its data type and whether or not it is required or implied. Now that a DTD has been written, an XML document based on it can be validated against it.

XML Namespaces

When you create a DTD upon which to base your XML documents, you write the reference to the DTD in your XML documents before elements appear so that the XML processor reading your document will know where to find the appropriate definitions for your elements. However, what if your document is based partially upon your own DTD and partially upon a DTD written by someone else? This is permissible, but there's potential for a conflict in the names of elements because you could make an element with the same name as an element in someone else's DTD. The solution is *namespaces*. You've already encountered namespaces in VS.NET; now we'll give a more complete definition.

The W3C has a recommendation addressing this issue, called "Namespaces in XML." A *namespace* is the set of names used for elements and so forth, and this recommendation sets in place standard rules for building and referring to

XML namespaces so as to eliminate confusion about the source and meaning of a particular element name.

To make each namespace truly unique (even when the names for two different namespaces may be identical) a URL must be supplied to point to the namespace applied to a particular element. The following code shows an example of a namespace declaration and why it is unique:

```
<haircare_conditioner xmlns:haircare='http://hair.org/schema'>
</haircare_conditioner>
```

In this code, the haircare_conditioner element is defined in the schema located at **http://hair.org/schema**. The namespace declaration starts with xmlns, followed by a colon, the name of the namespace (haircare), and the URL for that namespace.

Multiple namespaces can be used with a single XML document, as shown in the following code:

```
<?xml version="1.0"?>
<haircare_products
 xmlns:developmentdate="http://hair.org/date"
xmlns:releasedate="http://haircompany.com/date">
<haircare_conditioner name="Brilliant Gray">
<developmentdate:date>Jan 1, 2001</date>
<releasedate:date>Mar 1, 2001</date>
</haircare_conditioner>
</haircare_products>
```

A single element can also have multiple namespaces applied within it to use for child elements from a number of namespaces, as shown in the following code:

```
<?xml version="1.0"?>
<hair:haircare_conditioner
 xmlns:hair='urn:beauty.products:hair'
 xmlns:sku='urn:sku.numbers'>
    <hair:brand>Brilliant Gray</hair:brand>
    <sku:code>518613557</sku:code>
</hair:haircare_conditioner>
```

Note

Because the colon is used to separate parts of an XML namespace declaration, authors should not use colons in XML element names.

XML Elements and Attributes: Logical Structure

XML documents may contain elements and attributes. Elements are delimited by starting and ending tags, and they may be empty (containing no content) or nonempty (containing content). All elements have names, and the term for element names is Generic Identifier (GI). Elements may (but are not required to) have one or more attributes, and each attribute *must* have a name and a value.

The order of attributes in a tag is not significant, and no attribute may appear in a tag twice. Possible attribute values may be arbitrarily restricted, and the values given must conform to the possible value types listed in the DTD (if there is one). Also, no less-than (<) signs may appear in attribute values. Element and attribute names may not include some reserved characters (X, x, M, m, L, l). Element names in starting and ending tags must match any given element.

XML Processors

An XML document contains whatever tags the author decided to include, but it does not contain information for display purposes. The first part of reading and displaying XML documents is called processing, in which the document is read, parsed, checked for well-formedness, and checked for validity. The job of doing this falls on the XML processor. There are a number of XML processors available, including the Microsoft XML processor and the Simple API for XML (SAX).

Note

XML processors often work in the background for an application such as Internet Explorer or Microsoft Word and can perform their functions for any application (such as a web server or a database), not just one in which the final output is human-readable.

XML processors fit into two categories: validating and nonvalidating. *Validating* processors detect any well-formedness errors and deviations from the rules and constraints built into the DTD or schema for an XML document.

Nonvalidating processors check only for well-formedness. In general, the specification that provides for the capability of reviewing and validating XML documents and providing programmatic access to the structure, markup, and content within them is called an Application Programming Interface (API).

Displaying XML Documents with XML Transformations

Once an XML document is read, it may be used by a machine to perform functions or transformed for display to a person—often in a browser, but just as likely in some other format such as a cell phone. Since the author of the document does not necessarily know how the document is going to be displayed, an XML Transformation language is used to transform the document depending upon the client that is reading it.

The crucial difference is that XML documents must be transformed before they are displayed in a browser like an HTML document. In fact, much of the power of XML derives from the fact that XML documents can be transformed from XML into whatever other format is required, making XML the ideal standard from which to provide data to humans and machines. So, a single XML document may be transformed to XHTML for display in a browser, to a compressed or clipped version of HTML for display on a cell phone or in a PDA, or to some database format or proprietary format for use by a machine- driven application where there is no human interaction at all.

Transforming XML documents into an appropriate format for use with a particular application can be done by writing a document-specific transformation routine into the application, but there is a better way. The W3C has developed *eXtensible Stylesheet Language* (XSL) to provide a standard way of performing transformations.

XSL documents are well-formed and valid XML documents, and as with XML, XSL requires a processor to perform transformations. The processor takes an XML document and its accompanying XSL stylesheet and builds the finished product from them. The finished product, of course, is the web page, PDA display, speech, paginated document, and so forth that the stylesheet maker desired. Because the platform on which the XML document is to be displayed or rendered can be detected by the server providing the document, it is relatively easy to ensure that any given platform receives the appropriate XML document and an XSL stylesheet.

1-Minute Drill

- How is XML like HTML?
- How is XML unlike HTML?

WSDL and SOAP

When developers create Web Services, it is often with the idea in mind to publish these services and make them available to all or some users, either on a subscription basis or anonymously at no charge. Essentially, what this means is there must be some way for people or machines on the Internet to discover Web Services at will, learn enough about them to know whether they might provide the desired data and data processing (an important capability of Web Services is that they can not only process data, but that they can combine it with proprietary or specialized real-time data), strike a bargain for using the services if the services are offered on some type of for-pay arrangement, and finally, use the services as necessary. WSDL and SOAP are two pieces of the puzzle; WSDL lets users read descriptions of the services, and SOAP allows users or their machines or applications to use the services.

WSDL

Web Services Description Language (WSDL) is an XML-based language that provides elements and attributes to describe Web Services available at a particular site. For example, if you built a number of popular Web Services and hosted them at your site, you would want to list them in some kind of registry or directory and make descriptions of them available in case someone wanted to subscribe to one of them. Rather than make users come to the site and read through the descriptions, you would probably use something like WSDL to make machine-readable descriptions available, so the user's agents could discover your services and determine which services it might want to employ.

- Like HTML, XML uses the greater-than and less-than signs to denote tags. Also, XML elements are enclosed by starting and ending tags, and XML elements may have attributes consisting of a name/value pair.
- Unlike HTML, XML is a markup language formatting specification, not a markup language per se. Where HTML elements and attributes are predefined, XML allows authors to define their own elements, attributes, and other items by writing DTDs or schemas. Also, while HTML is very flexible in structure (upper- or lowercase characters may be used to write HTML tags, for example) XML is very strict.

Universal Description, Discovery, and Integration (UDDI)

If you built the services yourself, you'd know where they were and what they do. If not, there is a mechanism to ease the discovery and description process: Web Services directories can provide one area in which the developer can list information about the Web Services available on the site. UDDI specifications (find out more at **www.uddi.org**) form a standard set of instructions for the publishing and discovery of Web Service.

Adding Web References

In VS.NET (and .NET in general), when you write an application using managed code, you'll add web references that give you a connection to Web Services via a proxy class. What this proxy class does is serve as a local representation for the method in your code, so that you can code up your application just like normal, and at runtime the proxy class handles all the communications across the Internet to and from the Web Service.

To add a web reference (as you will do in Project 7-3), you open a browser-type interface that searches the URL you enter for WSDL documents. Using the WSDL documents it finds, it makes available any methods that are exposed by the Web Service.

Web Service Discovery

In order to be discovered, a WSDL document must be available. Of course, you may not want to create such a document if you want to keep the service for private, internal use only. However, if you do wish to make it public, you can create a discovery file, perhaps something like the following:

```
<?xml version="1.0" ?>
<disco:discovery
 xmlns:disco="http://schemas.xmlsoap.org/disco"
 xmlns:wsdl="http://schemas.xmlsoap.org/disco/wsdl">
<wsdl:contractRef
 ref="http://AServer/Name.asmx?WSDL"/>
</disco:discovery>
```

VS.NET automatically creates a discovery file with a .vsdisco file extension when you build a Web Service from the ASP.NET Web Service template.

Simple Object Access Protocol (SOAP)

Writing VB.NET applications has made it clear that creating functions and objects in code is a common way to encapsulate programmatic functionality into an easy-to-use structure that can be called from just about anywhere in the application, depending upon the scope of the function or object. The environment or platform on which the application runs provides the capability to make the calls, but suppose you'd like to make a call to a function or object residing on another machine somewhere else on the Internet, perhaps even running on another platform?

SOAP is one of the more popular mechanisms used to wrap calls to objects for delivery and receipt over the Internet. It is an XML-based protocol that is designed for providing all the information necessary to make and receive calls to objects across the Internet. The latest specification (SOAP 1.2, a working draft dated July 9, 2001, at **www.w3.org**) says SOAP is "a lightweight protocol for exchange of information in a decentralized, distributed environment. It is an XML-based protocol that consists of four parts: an envelope that defines a framework for describing what is in a message and how to process it, a set of encoding rules for expressing instances of application-defined data types, a convention for representing remote procedure calls and responses, and a binding convention for exchanging messages using an underlying protocol."

Ask the Expert

Question: What is so important about Web Services?

Answer: In the early days of programming, people were pretty satisfied to write programs that could accept certain pieces of data, process them correctly and efficiently, and produce a certain output format. However, it quickly became apparent that developers were writing code to do the same thing over and over, across industries and even inside the same companies.

In theory, this practice represents wasted effort, as there is no reason why the exact same function should ever be rewritten. In practice, rewriting code is very common for a variety of reasons. For example, sometimes a function that works well in a particular language can't be incorporated into an application written in another language or for another platform. Also, there is the problem of how to determine exactly what the function of a particular piece of code really is. Two functions written in different languages for different platforms and different purposes might produce exactly the same results given the same inputs, but it can be extremely difficult to verify—perhaps more difficult to verify than to simply rewrite.

The concept of Web Services includes features and capabilities designed to minimize the difficulties in reusing code. For one thing, Web Services are available to any application on the Internet, and as Application Service Providers and Internet access in general become more ubiquitous, it becomes easier and easier to simply connect to Web Services rather than rewrite all the necessary code from scratch. And since there are machine-readable discovery and description documents available, the process of doing so is also made much easier.

A special capability of Web Services makes them even more valuable. The fact that they are on the Web means that they can maintain real-time connections to data as it is generated, instead of canned values (like the old desktop applications). For example, instead of containing tax tables published last year by the IRS, a Web Service can query another Web Service hosted by the IRS before computing your taxes. It could even perform a query of the IRS Web Service for tax tables and a query of your stock broker's Web Service for the current value of your stock portfolio, resulting in the most up-to-date and accurate return possible. The ability to use real-time information from any available source on the Internet is one of the key features that makes Web Services valuable.

Question: **Why does XML seem to play such a big role in all this? XML isn't even a language!**

Answer: XML seems to be the one language specification everyone is rallying around, when it comes it data exchange. Whether it's for building the markup language for a particular industry, for creating a protocol for accessing objects, or just something to describe Web Services, XML seems to be the format of choice.

Of course, just because everyone is using XML doesn't mean that there still aren't battles being fought over which XML language to use for a particular purpose. It's just that, as the primary format for structuring these language, XML seems to be the main choice.

Web Services Background

A Web Service is created by writing a bit of code that may be accessed across the Web, meaning that it simply waits until it is called, performs the processing you've programmed, and returns the result. The common language runtime (CLR) provides support for creating and exposing Web Services. Web Service files in ASP.NET have an .asmx file extension, and the code-behind files have an .asmx.vb file extension. These file types can be a standalone service or can be included as part of a Web Forms application.

Web Service files can be created manually, as the following simple text file shows:

```
<%@ WebService Language="VB" Class="Hi" %>
Imports System
Imports System.Web.Services
Public Class Hi :Inherits WebService
<WebMethod()> Public Function Hi() As String
Return("Hi")
End Function
End Class
```

In this example, the language is first set to VB, a class is established, both System and System.Web.Services are imported, and the WebMethod itself is set as a String. The function is named Hi() (you can name the function anything you want, of course), and the processing it performs is shown in the Return line (it returns a string with the value "Hi").

To make the service available, you could name the file Hi.asmx and put it on a web server. If you then browsed to that server location, the methods would be made available.

Project 7-2: Create a Web Service

For this project, you'll walk through the process of creating a Web Service using VS.NET. Your Web Service will return a set of six random Lotto numbers between 1 and 60, with the numbers changing each time the service is accessed.

Step-by-Step

1. Create a new project using the Web Service template. Open VS.NET, click File | New | Project. When the dialog box opens, make sure Visual Basic Project

is selected, then select the ASP.NET Web Service icon to use the Web Service template, name your project LottoService, and click OK to create the new project. Figure 7-1 shows what your screen should look like.

2. VS.NET will automatically generate the necessary files and references in your project to support your Web Service. The main file is Service1.asmx and, like a Web Form, it has a code-behind file, in this case named Service1.asmx.vb. Before you open the code-behind file, there is code to modify in the .asmx file itself. However, to get to this code you must right-click the file (in Solution Explorer) and select Open With from the shortcut menu. A dialog box will open offering several choices. Choose Source Code (text) Editor.

3. Already present in the file should be the following code:

```
<%@ WebService Language="vb"
 Codebehind="Service1.asmx.vb"
 Class="LottoService.Service1" %>
```

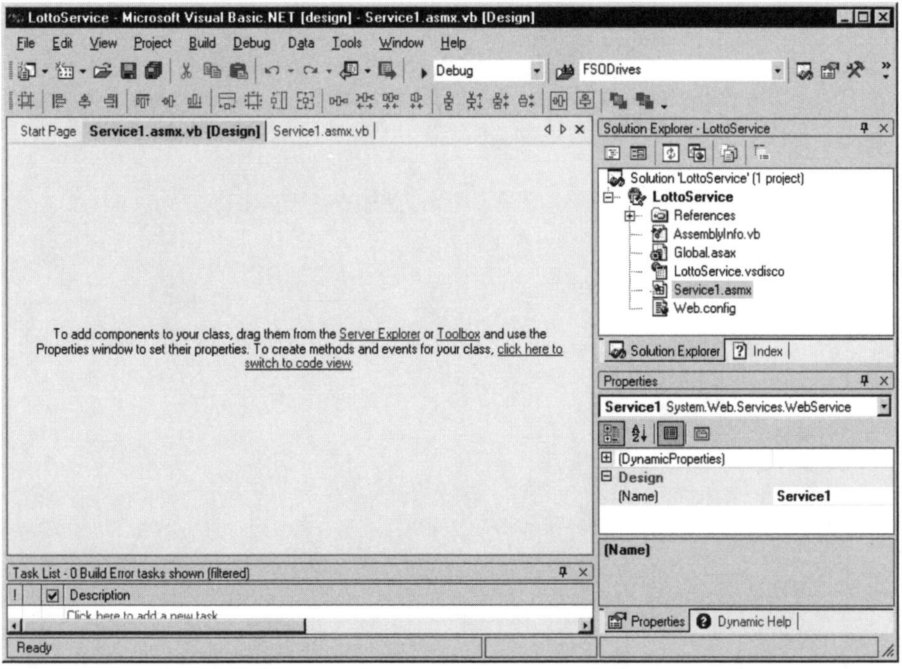

Figure 7-1 The LottoService project

4. If you change the name of your class later, make sure to return to this area of the .asmx file and change the name here as well.
5. To set the namespace for the service (this must be done to differentiate it from other Web Services that may happen to have the same name) you must open the code-behind file, in this case named Service1.asmx.vb. You can double-click the Design view of this file, or follow the link present on the Design view. Either way, you'll get into the code in the code-behind file.
6. Change the line of code in the code-behind file that says "Public Class Service1", such that it resembles the following (your namespace will have a different URL that reflects your deployment server):

```
<WebService(Namespace:="http://localhost/Lotto/",
 Description:="Provides Lotto Numbers.")>
Public Class Service1
```

7. This change allows you to set the class as a Web Service(exposed to other Web Service or applications), set a particular namespace for it, and give it a description).
8. To add the processing for your Web Service, add the following code (Figure 7-2 shows the code-behind file) to the code-behind file in the Web Method section to create the method that will run when the service is called:

```
<WebMethod()> Public Function MakeNumbers() As String
  Dim i As Int16
  Dim i2 As Int16
  Dim vArrNum As Int16
  Dim arrRandomSeq(5) As Int16
  Dim vFlag As Int16
  Dim vLottoNumbers As String
  vFlag = 0
  i = 1
  i2 = 0
  Randomize()
  arrRandomSeq(0) = Int(60 * Rnd() + 1)
  Randomize()
  For i = 1 To 5
    vArrNum = Int(60 * Rnd() + 1)
    For i2 = 0 To 5
      If arrRandomSeq(i2) = vArrNum Then
        vFlag = 1
      End If
    Next
```

```
        If Not vFlag = 1 Then
          arrRandomSeq(i) = vArrNum
        Else
          If i > 0 And i < 6 Then
            i = i - 1
          End If
          vFlag = 0
        End If
    Next
    vLottoNumbers = "Your numbers are"
    i = 0
    For i = 0 To 5
      vLottoNumbers = vLottoNumbers & " " & arrRandomSeq(i)
    Next
    MakeNumbers = vLottoNumbers
End Function
```

7

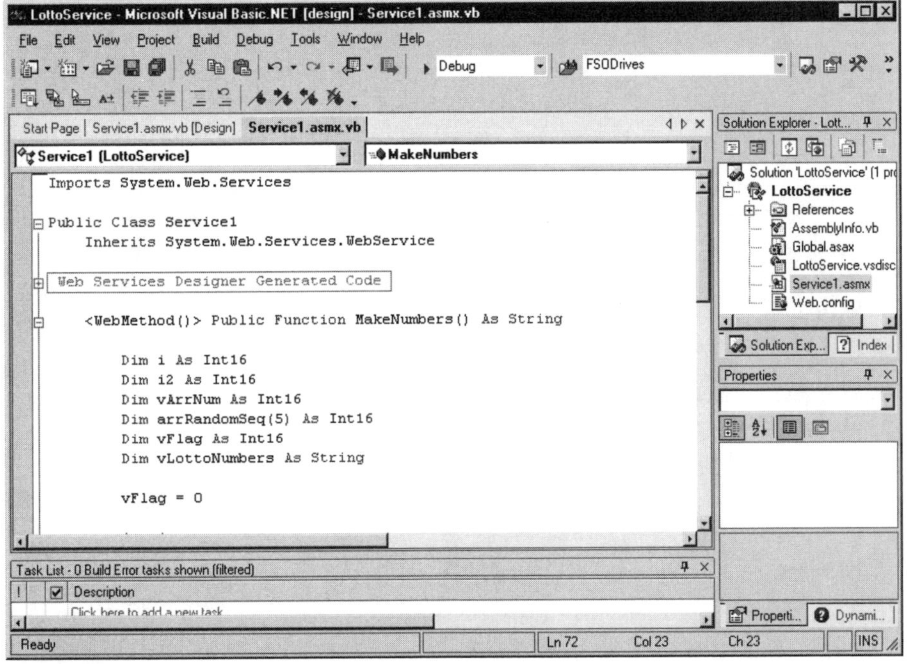

Figure 7-2 The code-behind file

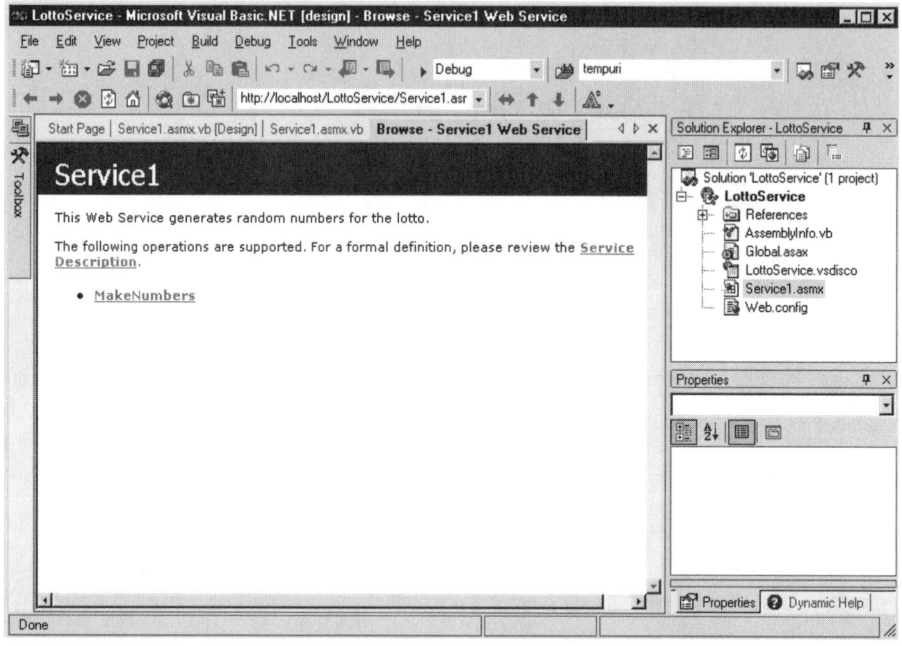

Figure 7-3 The service description page in HTML

9. To check your service, choose Build and Browse from the File menu, then click the link shown in Figure 7-3. To check that it produces the correct output, click the link shown in Figure 7-4. You should see XML output resembling Figure 7-5 in your browser (if you use IE to display the result, as we have in this example) or the IDE.

10. The XML output shown is the raw result of the Web Service being called. Naturally, you could create an XSL file to transform the results into proper XHTML output for the browser.

Project 7-3: Accessing a Web Service

In this project, you'll walk through the process of creating a web application (using Web Forms) that accesses the Web Service you just created. Web Services of many types will be created, and web application developers will often use prebuilt Web Services rather than create their own new Web Services each time. After all, the great achievement of Web Services is the reuse of code and not having to reinvent the wheel each time a particular service is required.

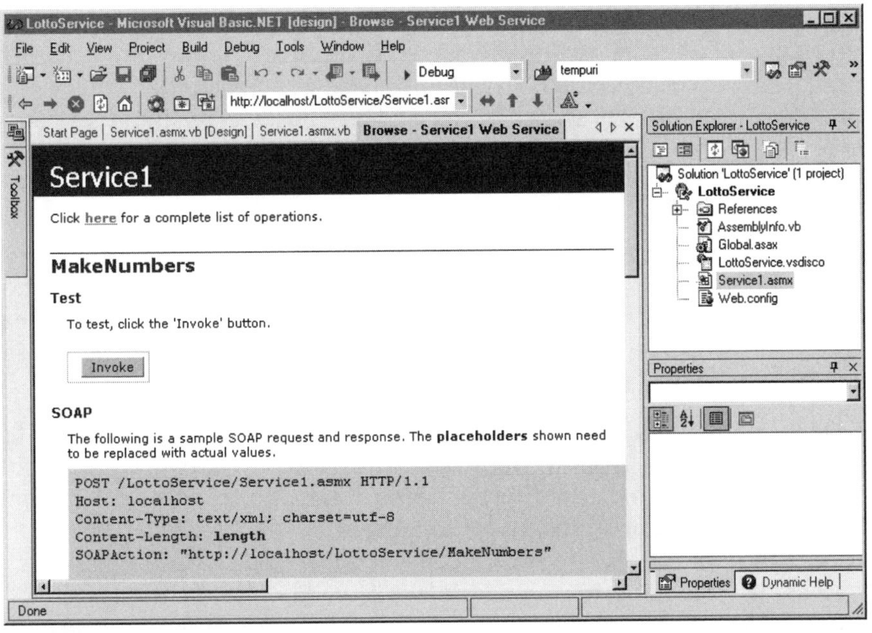

Figure 7-4 The MakeNumbers service

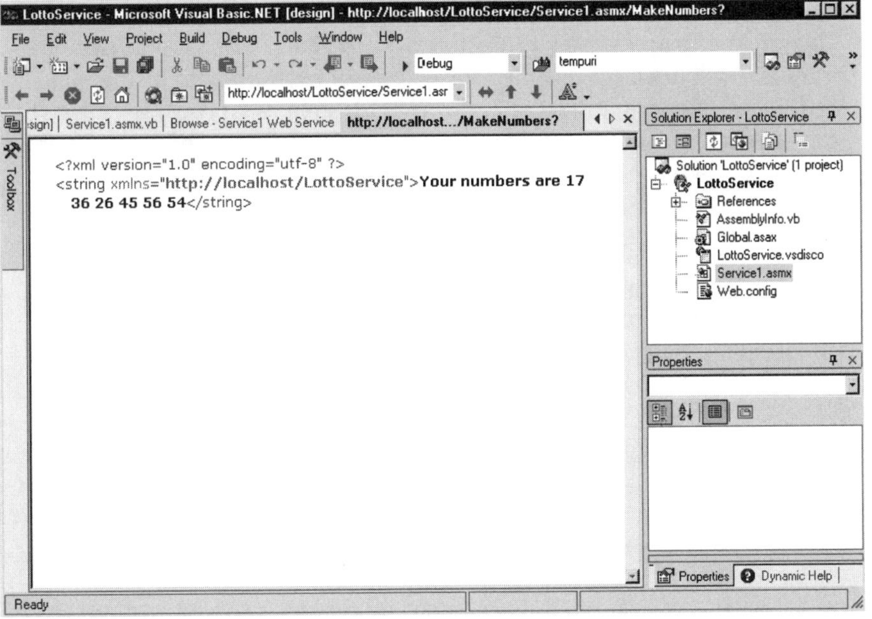

Figure 7-5 The result of the MakeNumbers text operation

Fortunately, VS.NET makes it easy to find Web Services and incorporate them into your web applications. This project will do just that for the Lotto Service Web Service you've already created. The Web Service you created generates random Lotto numbers when the service is accessed, so you'll be creating a web page (using Web Forms) that accesses the service when a user uses the page.

Step-by-Step

1. You'll need to create a web application project just like the others you've already built. In VS.NET, click File | New | Project to start a new project. When the dialog box opens, make sure ASP.NET Web Application is clicked (and that VB is the language), then name the project LottoServiceAccess and leave it in the localhost location. Click OK to start the project and create the files.

2. On your blank Web Form, add a label telling users what the purpose of the page is, such as "Hot Lotto Numbers". This form is informational only, so there is no need to give it a special name. Next, add another label (name this one LottoNumbers) and clear the text in its Text property. This will make the label blank, and you can fill it in with the user's Lotto numbers when they click a button. Of course, we'll need to give them a button to click, so add a button to the form and make it read "Click for Hot Lotto Numbers".

3. The next step is to add a connection (or reference) to the Web Service so it will produce Lotto numbers in response to your user clicking the button. To start this process, click Project | Add Web Reference. A browser-type interface will open up; in the address bar, enter the name of the local URL to the LottoService you've already created, such as **http://localhost/LottoService/Service1.asmx**. The browser interface is shown in Figures 7-6 and 7-7. The service available should show up, in this case the MakeNumbers service. Click Add Reference to complete the process. The resulting reference is added to solution Explorer, as shown in Figure 7-8.

4. Rename the web reference MakeNum, and then double-click the button you've added to your Web Form to create an event handling region and open the code-behind page to display it.

5. In the event-handling region, place the following code:

```
Dim ws As New MakeNum.Service1()
Dim vAnswer As String
vAnswer = ws.MakeNumbers
LottoNumbers.Text = vAnswer
```

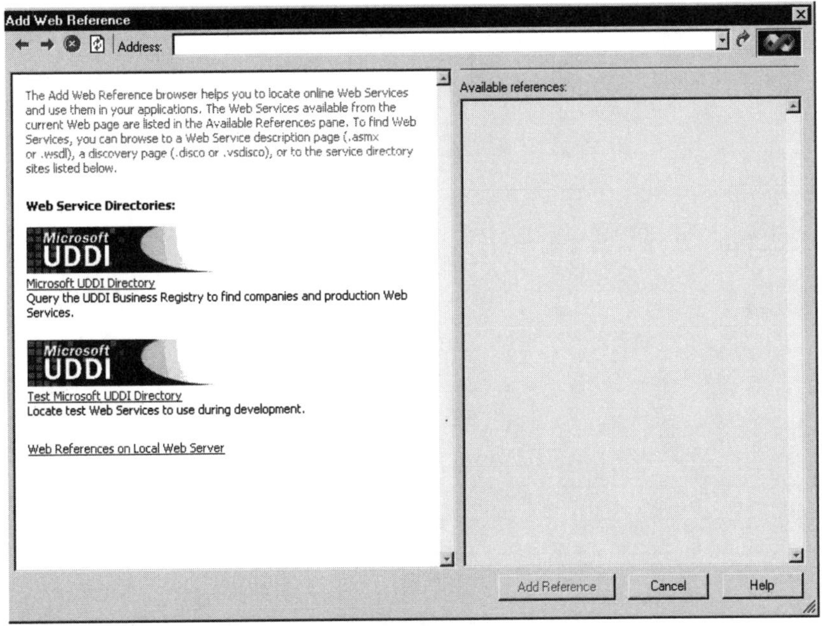

Figure 7-6 The browser interface for adding Web References

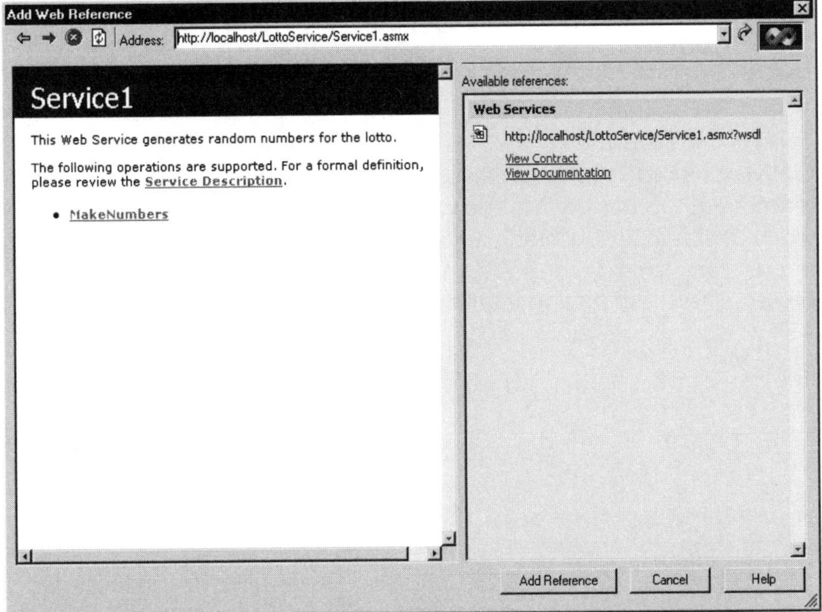

Figure 7-7 After entering the address for the Web Service Service1 page

7

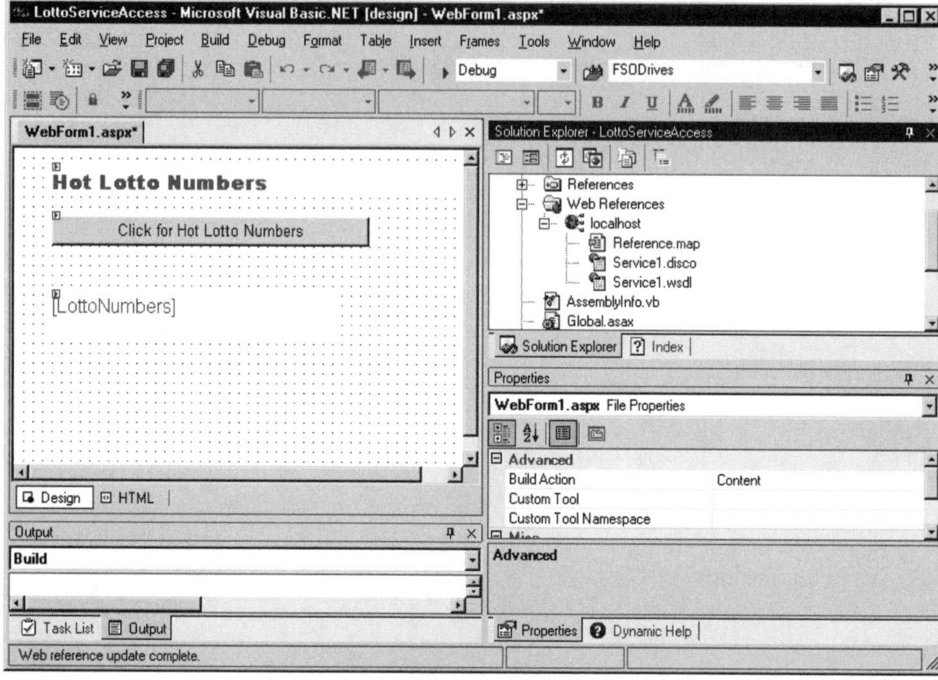

Figure 7-8 Solution Explorer files added with the Web Reference

6. This code creates the variable *ws* as the reference to the service and calls the MakeNumbers function of the service through it. When the information is received, it is placed into the vAnswer variable, and from there it can be worked with in any fashion you like, in this case becoming the text property of our blank label. Figures 7-9 and 7-10 show the finished form in the browser view, before and after the button is clicked.

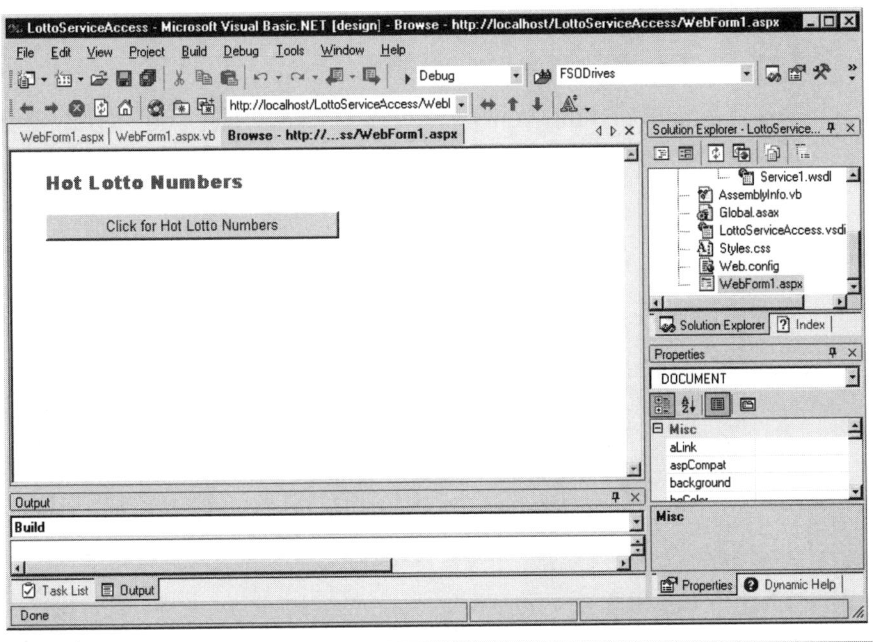

Figure 7-9 Web Form before clicking the button

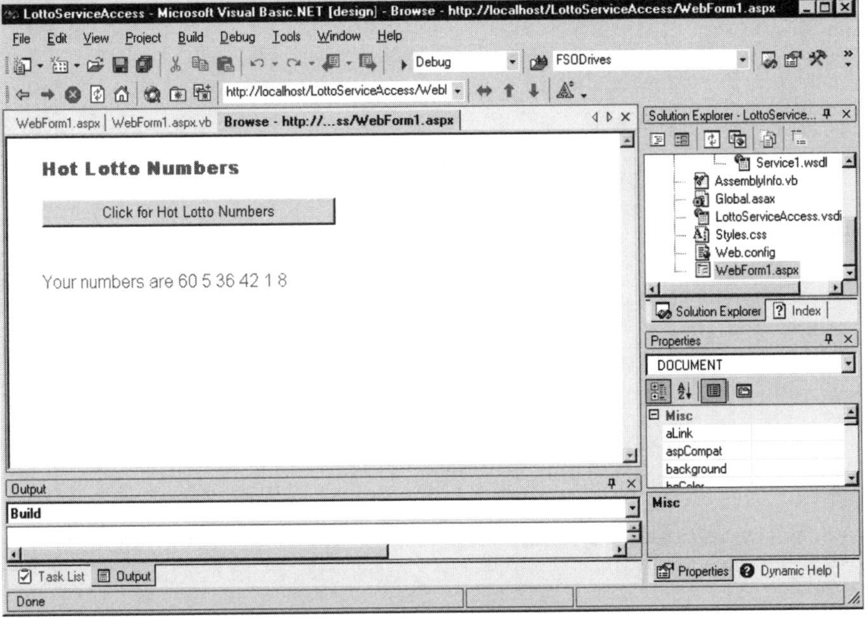

Figure 7-10 Web Form with Lotto Numbers returned

Mastery Check

1. What fundamental difference between Web Services and web applications made with Web Forms affects users?

   A. Web Services have no user interface.

   B. Web Services respond much more quickly.

   C. Web Services are written in XML.

   D. All of the above.

   E. None of the above.

2. eXtensible Markup Language (XML) is not a markup language per se, but instead a specification for writing markup languages. What XML-based languages are used in communications to and from Web Services?

   A. XHTML, XSLT

   B. WSDL, SOAP

   C. RPC, XML Query

   D. None of the above

3. XML documents should be ________, otherwise an XML processor will generate an error when trying to read them. If an XML document conforms to a DTD, the document is said to be ______ as well.

4. Describe the purpose of a DTD or an XML Schema and the primary structures they allow developers to build for XML languages.

   ____

   ____

5. What is a namespace, and what purpose does a namespace serve?

   A. A namespace represents a particular place on the Internet, like a URL, and serves to differentiate one place from another.

   B. A namespace represents a particular folder on a computer and serves to differentiate one set of XML attributes from another.

Mastery Check

C. A namespace represents a particular address containing definitions of elements, attributes, and other named structures, and serves to differentiate between structures with identical names.

D. None of the above.

6. What is the purpose of Web Services Discovery Language (WSDL)?

   A. To facilitate the discovery of Web Services

   B. To assist in automating the discovery of Web Services

   C. To help define available Web Services

   D. None of the above

   E. All of the above

7. What is the difference between WSDL and Universal Description, Discovery, and Integration (UDDI)?

   A. WSDL is for Web Services, and UDDI is for web applications.

   B. WSDL provides a language for describing Web Services, and UDDI provides a consistent set of statements that can be used to form the WSDL description so that the description will be complete.

   C. WSDL and UDDI are interchangeable standards, and there is no functional difference.

   D. None of the above.

8. Web Services created in ASP.NET have ____ for a file extension. They can be stand-alone services or part of a larger ________________.

9. Describe three ways in which you can use Web Services in your web applications.

   ____

   ____

Mastery Check

10. What data type is the output of a Web Service?

A. Any data type you choose.

B. Only numeric values

C. Text strings

D. None of the above

11. In what file do you enter your Web Service processing code when making a Web Service with VS.NET and the Web Services template?

A. The code-behind file of the service

B. The Visual Basic file

C. The interface file

D. Any of the above

E. None of the above

12. When developing a WebForms project in VS.NET, how are Web Services accessed?

13. To use a Web Service from within a WebForm, one way to access that service is by using a button with an ________ region. Inside that region you call the function, and from the results you may perform any additional ___________ required by your application.

14. Describe an advantage Web Services have over similar programmed services that have no Internet connection.

15. In what file is the WSDL description and discovery information kept when making a Web Service with VS.NET and the Web Services template?

A. The .uddi file

B. The .wsdl file

C. The .vsdisco file

D. None of the above

Module 8

ASP.NET and SQL Server

The Goals of This Module

- Discuss the capabilities of Microsoft enterprise servers
- Install SQL Server and build databases and tables
- Learn about database construction
- Discuss reverse-engineering and understand how it is performed
- Examine various database designs
- Review relational database design and what makes a database relational
- Learn about Structured Query Language (SQL) and write SQL statements
- Review the capabilities of ADO.NET

As you no doubt realize, most websites are constructed from a mixture of languages, including HTML/XHTML, JavaScript/JScript, VBScript/VB.NET, and so forth. Structured Query Language (SQL) is the language commonly used to communicate with databases. ActiveX Data Objects (ADO) are used to run SQL statements against a database or other data source and manipulate the records found. It's very important that you understand how SQL and ADO interact with ASP and ASP.NET to enable the process of working with databases required by your web application. The second portion of this module examines the relationships between these languages/technologies and their components and focuses on SQL statements as the key to opening up various databases.

Before we get too far into SQL and databases, we will examine some of the servers Microsoft produces for enterprise applications, in particular Microsoft's Content Management Server (CMS) and Microsoft's SQL Server. Both of these servers may be very useful in web applications you set up, especially for larger entities.

As you know, Microsoft produces software packages for a great range of applications, not just operating systems and programming environments. One of the markets Microsoft produces software for is the enterprise server market. Enterprise server software is designed to manage and coordinate the activities of other applications or services, or to serve high-volume requirements, or specialized enterprise-level applications.

Although we will devote a short discussion to many of the servers Microsoft makes for this market, our primary focus will be on using SQL Server (we will also discuss Microsoft Access a bit), as it is an excellent foundation for many Web Forms and Web Services application requirements.

Microsoft Enterprise Servers

Many of the Microsoft enterprise server packages we discuss provide important capabilities to assist in managing website applications. For example, the Application Center makes it easy to manage sites running multiple servers (computers), while BizTalk makes it easy to translate data formats into one integrated format (a common requirement in modern online applications). Some of the servers are designed to run standalone on their own machine, while others are commonly run concurrently on the same machine. All of them tend to be at the upper end of the scale in terms of price and performance and require specialized knowledge to install, configure, and maintain. There are often simple programmatic methods to reconfigure or manipulate these servers so that your applications can perform actions without the aid of a person when such actions are appropriate. In the following sections, we'll review the functions performed by some of Microsoft's most recent servers, discuss their capabilities and how they work together, and in the case of SQL Server, how to work with it both manually and programmatically.

Application Center 2000

Application Server 2000 is designed specifically to support high-volume web applications, especially when they operate on clusters of servers rather than on a single machine. Application Center 2000 makes it easy to set up clusters so that a group of servers can be managed as easily as a single server; it also makes it easy to add new servers to the group, thereby making it easier to scale your applications. Changes made to one server are propagated to other servers in the group, and if one server goes down (or must be taken down) it does not affect the availability of the overall application.

Application Center also makes it easy to deploy your applications, providing tools to assist in maintaining consistency between what you are developing and what you are deploying. As applications often consist of many resources, Application Center allows developers to construct logical resources groupings graphically, simplifying resource management.

Like many servers, Application Center includes performance monitoring tools, as well as logging facilities and analysis tools. It also has the capability to respond to preset events conditionally, so your application itself can manage many situations without the need for a person to intervene.

BizTalk Server

The purpose of BizTalk Server is to make it easy to integrate business processes (via applications) across businesses and the Internet. Essentially, this means it has tools that allow the visual development of business processes and uses standard language specifications (such as XML and EDI) and standard communications protocols (such as HTTP) as the interface between disparate applications, regardless of the native operating system, programming model, or programming language.

Commerce Server

Microsoft's Commerce Server is an application framework specifically designed for e-commerce applications. It includes tools for creating e-commerce solutions, managing products and services, conducting online transactions, and gathering and analyzing customer feedback. It also has an integrated personalization module, making it easy to customize the sales process.

Content Management Server

Microsoft's Content Management Server is designed to allow management of web content, something that is increasingly important to nontechnical users. Once the website has been designed and deployed, routine maintenance and updates are often difficult without a content management system. This server includes tools that allow content developers to create, maintain, and update content easily and provides an approval process to ensure only the proper content gets posted.

Exchange Server

Microsoft's Exchange Server is a messaging solution that does more than just deliver e-mail; it also provides instant messaging and other collaboration technologies.

Host Integration Server

Microsoft's Host Integration Server is designed for enterprise connections to mainframes and other hosts.

Internet Security and Acceleration Server

The purpose of Microsoft's Internet Security and Acceleration Server is to provide a means to connect multiple web servers (web farms) securely to the Internet, with a cache to speed responses.

Mobile Information Server

Microsoft's Mobile Information Server is designed to give user's the ability to conduct much of the business they ordinarily do on their desktop on their mobile devices, such as cell phones and PDAs.

Sharepoint Portal Server

Microsoft's Sharepoint Portal Server is designed to allow developers to quickly create portal solutions for their clients. The portal solution enables companies to provide critical internal information to employees and selected clients via a browser-based client. The portal solution may include search capabilities as well as document creation, routing, and approval processes.

SQL Server

Microsoft's SQL Server is an enterprise-scale, industrial-strength, relational database management solution. It contains all the features expected of high-end DBMS systems, as well as XML support.

Using SQL Server

Buying Microsoft enterprise server applications means doing just a bit of homework, as it's not always readily apparent what the purpose of the servers would be, what role they would fill, or how they might fit into your existing architecture. However, there is plenty of information on Microsoft's website to help. In addition, once you decide that a particular server would be helpful, it's a good idea to review the minimum system and platform requirements to determine if system upgrades are required. Once you've done this work, you'll be in a position to install and configure your new server.

Setting Up SQL Server

Microsoft's SQL Server is a good choice as an example of an enterprise server to use with ASP.NET and the .NET Framework, as there are special server controls already built-in to VS.NET that work with SQL Server, and databases in general are very commonly used with websites. In the next few sections, we'll discuss how SQL Server can be installed and configured for use with a web application. We'll also use Microsoft Access as an example for some of the ASP work we'll do.

Installing SQL Server

Installing SQL Server is simply a matter of putting the CD-ROM disks in and following the onscreen instructions. However, you'll have to choose between SQL Server authentication and Windows NT authentication. The choice will depend on what your system administrator recommends.

The finished installation will produce several SQL Server choices under the Start menu from the desktop, including Enterprise Manager. The version of SQL Server Enterprise Manager we're running is 8.00. Once installation is complete, open SQL Server Enterprise Manager and you'll see the screen shown in Figure 8-1.

- What server is used for managing large amounts of data?
- What server has built-in capabilities for managing web content?

- Microsoft's SQL Server is ideal for handling large amounts of data, especially data that is contained as rows and columns.
- Microsoft's Content Management Server is ideal for handling content that is web-based, such as text and images.

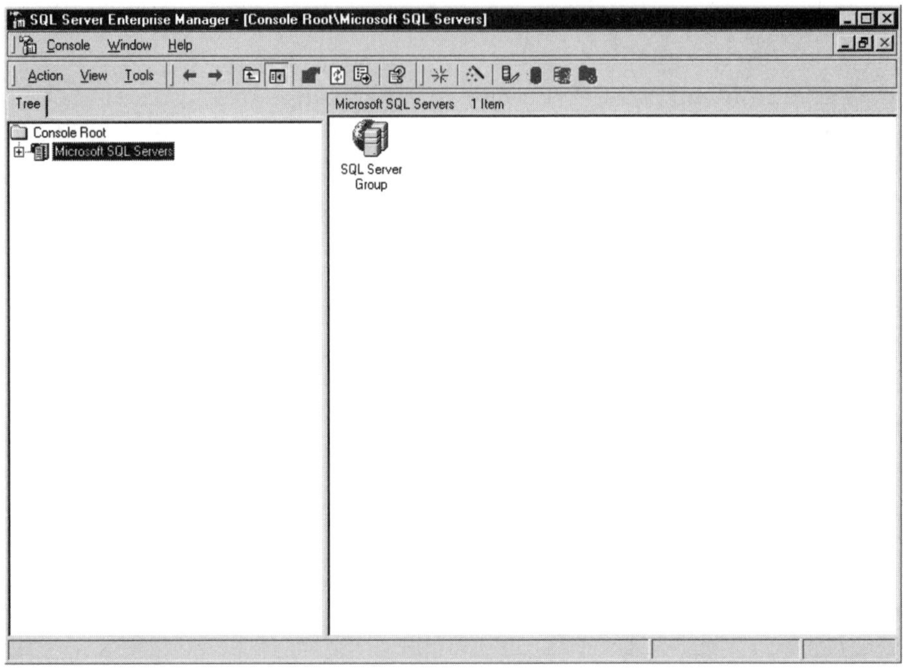

Figure 8-1 The main screen for SQL Server Enterprise Manager

Using Databases in ASP.NET Applications

In this and the next two modules, we'll be discussing how to create, install, and interact with databases behind the scenes of your ASP and ASP.NET applications. Databases play a special role in many applications because of their ability to store and manipulate data in very effective ways. While data can be stored in arrays for limited purposes, you'll often find that the ability to access a database makes building particular functions into your applications much easier.

In the next section, we briefly cover database design to lay the groundwork for some examples and to illustrate the connection between database structure and interactions with your web pages. Later in the module, we'll cover the mechanics of making a connection to a SQL Server database.

Database Design

If you've already worked with databases extensively, you may want to skip over this section, as it covers many of the basics of good database design. Or you might want to review design principles and learn more about how database design affects the performance of your ASP.NET applications. We'll also take a look at how the incorporation of a well-designed database can improve the functionality and decrease the maintenance requirements of your website.

Database Construction and Objects

A database is an information container, just like an e-mail or an XML document. It has a particular structure that makes it well suited to containing certain kinds of data. Usually it consists of the following objects and perhaps a few more, depending upon specific application requirements:

- **Tables** Data is stored in tables as records (each row is a record) of information related to a single subject. Records store pieces of information as fields, and each field may have a specific data type associated with it.
- **Queries** Queries are general purpose utility tools, not just for selectively retrieving data from tables but for a variety of other functions as well, such as updating or deleting specific records. Although queries are often used for retrieving or modifying many records at once, they are just as useful for working with individual records.
- **Forms** Forms are the user interface of database applications, generally being used either to directly access data residing in a table (adding, editing, deleting, or searching for individual records) or as a navigation device. In a web application, HTML-based Web Forms substitute for the forms you might use to work with a database application through the DBMS in which it was created.
- **Reports** Reports are primarily used for printing specific records or groups of records for specific purposes. In a web application, you will most likely not generate printable reports but will use data to display Web Forms instead.

Relational Databases

A database is said to be relational when it meets several criteria, notably when data for each entity of interest is allocated a table of its own, when the data in each field is discrete (not a mixture of first and last names, for example), and so forth. In fact, there are *normal forms* that categorize the level to which a database is properly relational. Normal forms begin at 1 (first normal form) and go to 5 and beyond. Each level of normal form means the database conforms more and more to relational database standards. In practice, most databases are third normal form.

So, in a relational database, how would data in the Customers table be related to data in the Orders table? Let's go over the construction of a table and the special fields inside it that can be linked to other tables.

Table Structure

The basic unit of storage in a database is a *table*. Data is stored in a table in the form of *records*, and inside the records individual items of data are stored in *fields*. The key to keep in mind is that tables are best constructed to contain data about one general class of thing (customers, for instance), with the exception of tables that mainly serve to link other tables.

Each record in a table will contain data about one of the classes of things (a single customer, for instance), while the fields store various important attributes of that one individual thing (a customer's name, address, and so forth). The attributes stored in a record depend on what you think is important or essential for fulfilling the purpose of the database. For example, if you want to be able to bill your customers, you would keep data about their addresses (so you can send them a bill), but you wouldn't need to know the names of their pets (although if you were a veterinarian, that might be useful data).

Primary Key Fields

A special field that is commonly included in a table is a *primary key* field. A primary key field always contains a unique value for each record, so that each individual record can be unambiguously distinguished from every other record in the table. Whenever a new record is added, it must always have a different primary key from every other record already existing in the table (the autonumber data type in Microsoft Access and the identity data type in SQL Server make sure primary key values are always one number higher than the last and therefore unique and different). These fields are used to link (or relate) tables to each other.

Why link the tables? Suppose you have a bunch of customers, and they each make hundreds of orders. You could keep all that data in one table, with fields for all the customer data plus fields for all the ordering data (items, quantity, price, description, and so on). But then you'd have to store massive quantities of repetitive data (each order repeats all the customer data), not to mention running a big risk of entering customer information incorrectly and making it extremely difficult to research old orders.

So instead of repeating customer data for each order, a link is created between the Customers table and the Orders table, based on the value of the Customers table's primary key field. For example, customer number 11 will have one entry in the Customers table. This entry will be a single record with a CustomerID number (the primary key) of 11, and other fields for important data such as name, address, phone number, and so on. In the Customers table, there will be only one record with a CustomerID number of 11, and no other CustomerID numbers can duplicate this.

In the Orders table, each record will contain an OrderID number (the primary key) to distinguish it from all the other orders, and each record will contain data such as order date, total due, and so forth. In addition, each order will contain a field called CustomerID. This field is of the same data type (see the next section for a discussion of data types) as the CustomerID field in the Customers table, but in the Orders table CustomerIDs may be duplicated. In the Orders table, CustomerID is referred to as the *foreign key*.

For each customer record in the Customers table, there may be many records in the Orders table that contain an identical CustomerID number. In practice, this means that a single customer (represented by their record in the Customers table) may have many orders (represented by their multiple records in the Orders table). For each order for the same customer, the only data that is duplicated is the CustomerID number, rather than the entire name, address, phone number, and so on. Today's DBMSs deal very effectively and automatically with tables in relational structures, making it easy to create primary and foreign keys, and link tables together. We'll demonstrate how to do so in coming sections.

Question: I understand how to create relational databases, but do I need to create a primary key for every table?

Answer: Primary keys need to be created only for those tables that link to other tables from the "1" or "parent" side, but it's still a good habit to create them for most of your tables anyway. It is not uncommon to find a need to perform this kind of linking later on in the game, and it is more convenient if you already have records with a primary key.

Question: How do I make a many-to-many relationship?

Answer: To make a many-to-many relationship, you'll have to create a junction table. This is a special table that serves as a link between two tables that are parents in their own right (both on the "1" side). Since you can't connect them directly to each other, you make a junction table containing both of their primary keys as foreign keys and connect them to the junction table. Try it, it works!

Building Database Tables

To create a Customers table in SQL Server, you must first create a database for the table to reside in. Open SQL Server Enterprise Manager and click the plus sign next to Microsoft SQL Servers, as shown in Figure 8-1. Keep opening nodes until you reach the Databases node, and then create a new database named ASPNETDB (just right-click the Databases node and you'll get a shortcut menu that gives you a New Database option). Your screen should now look like Figure 8-2.

Next, right-click Tables and start the process of creating a new table. You should get a screen like that shown in Figure 8-3. Enter the name of each field. Using SQL Server 2000 (and most other databases as well), you have the opportunity to specify data type when creating fields within tables. As you name each field, you will also be selecting the data type from a drop-down list, as shown in Figure 8-3.

When you get done with that table, name it Customers, and create another table named Orders with the fields shown in Figure 8-4.

Data Types

Data type refers to the kind of data stored in a field in a database or in a variable when you are programming. VBScript uses a variant as the primary data type,

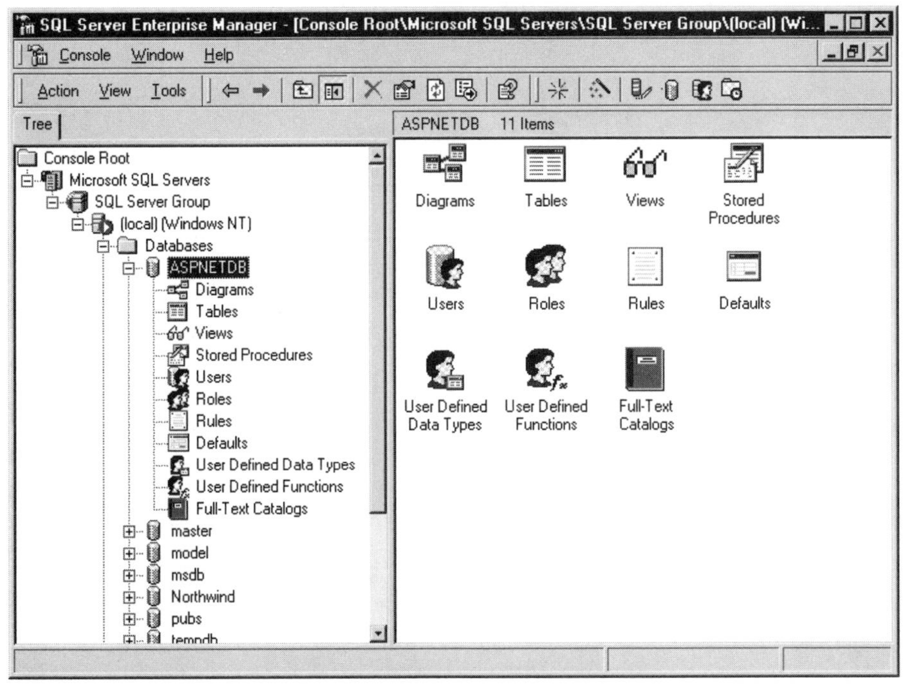

Figure 8-2 The main screen with the ASPNET database created

8

with subtypes that change to suit the needs of your programs. In a database, there are also a number of data types for columns of data kept in tables. The following types are found in Microsoft Access:

- **Text** Name, address, phone number, and so on
- **Number** Numbers that can be manipulated with arithmetic
- **Date/Time** Dates and times
- **Yes/No** Logical yes or no, on or off, and so forth
- **Hyperlink** Web addresses, URLs
- **Memo** Large, unstructured text data
- **BLOB** Binary large objects, such as image or application files

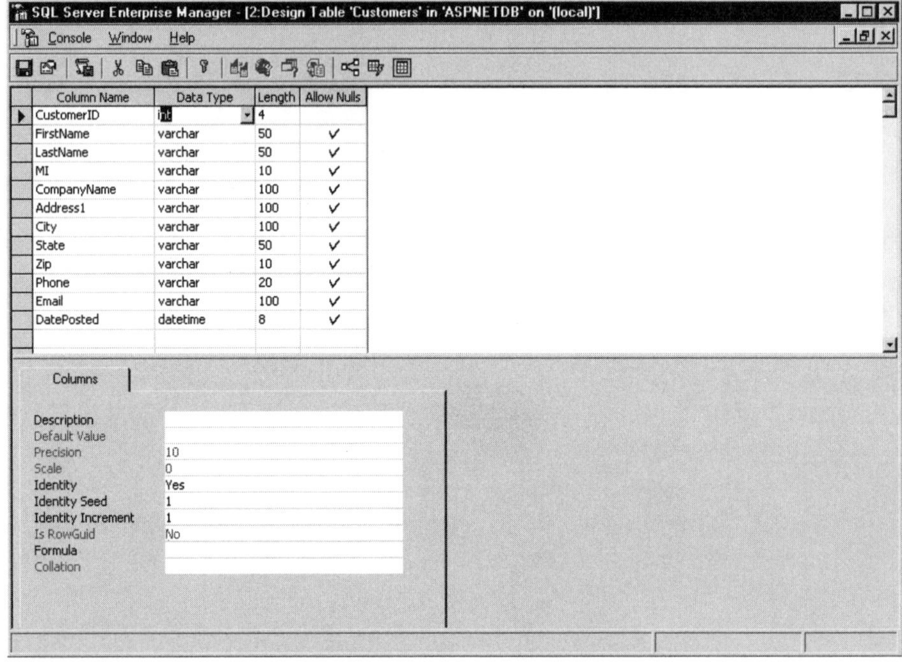

Figure 8-3 Creating fields for your database table

SQL Server provides many of the same data types, with slightly different names and some special types not present in Access:

- **Binary Data** Binary, varbinary, and image
- **Text Data** Char, varchar, and text
- **Unicode Data** Nchar, nvarchar, and ntext
- **Date and Time Data** Datetime and smalldatetime
- **Numeric Data** Bigint, int, smallint, and tinyint, decimal and numeric, and float and real
- **Monetary Data** Money and smallmoney
- **Special Data** Timestamp, bit, uniqueidentifier, sql-variant, table, and user-defined

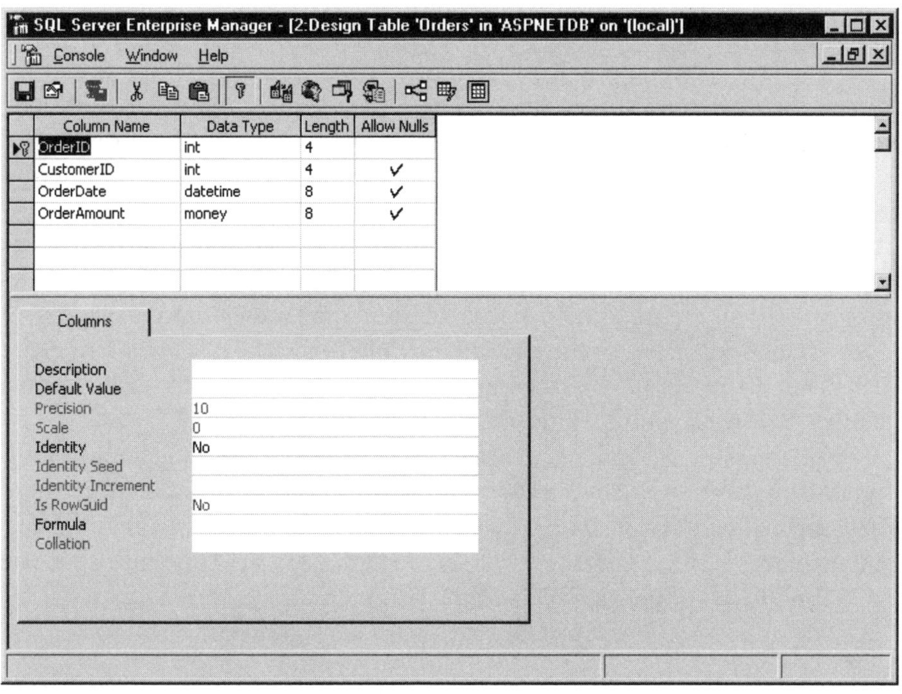

Figure 8-4 Creating the Orders table

It is important to choose the correct data type for each field when creating a Web database, as you need to make sure the right data is being input or queried to get the right answers. One thing to remember is that data received from an online form is sent as plain text, regardless of the data type you have assigned it. There may be some data type conversion necessary in your application to keep data types straight.

Another thing to keep in mind when creating fields is that you should strive to keep each field specific and unique for the data it contains. For example, you could put street address, city, state, and zip code all in one field. However, doing this makes it difficult to retrieve records by zip code later, because the field contains not only the zip code but also all that other data. For the same reason, it is usually best to split name fields into separate fields for first name and last name, because it is very common to retrieve records by last name only. Keeping this in mind makes your design cleaner from the beginning and easier to work with down the road.

Creating Relationships Between Tables

A relationship exists between tables when one table contains parent records and the other table contains child records. This is an example of a one-to-many relationship, and there are also one-to-one and many-to-many relationships. To create a one-to-many relationship between the Customers and Orders tables, you'll need to set primary key fields and create a database diagram.

In SQL Server, you can create relationships using the Database Diagram Wizard. In the Enterprise Manager, right-click Diagrams and choose New Database Diagram from the shortcut menu. You'll see a screen like that shown in Figure 8-5.

Go to the next screen of the Wizard and add the Customers and Orders tables as shown in Figure 8-6, then go to the next screen. You'll see both tables in a relationship, as yet unconnected, as shown in Figure 8-7.

The relationship from the Customers table to the Orders table will be made by connecting them by CustomerID (which is why both tables have a column for CustomerID numbers). Before you can connect the tables in a relationship, you'll need to make the CustomerIS field of the Customers table into a primary key. Right-click the CustomerID field in the Customers table, and a menu choice will appear to set the primary key field. Do so for the Customers table,

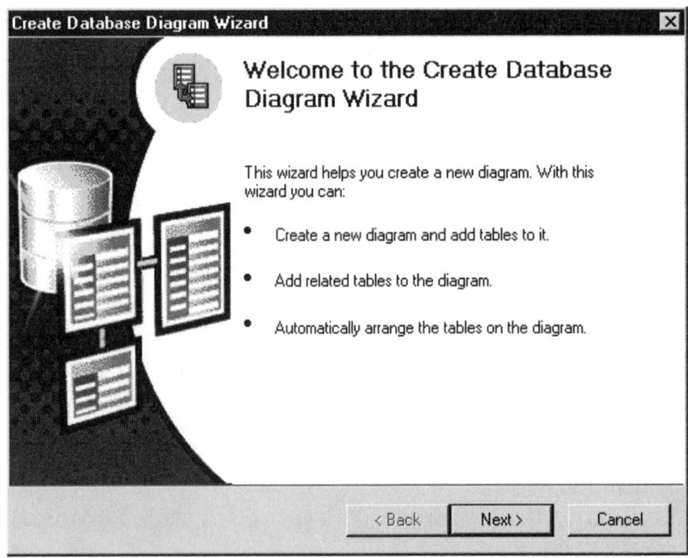

Figure 8-5 The Database Diagram Wizard

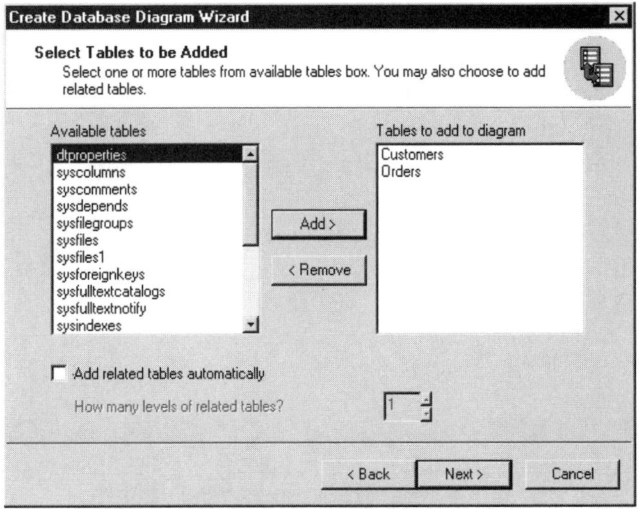

Figure 8-6 Adding the Customers and Orders tables

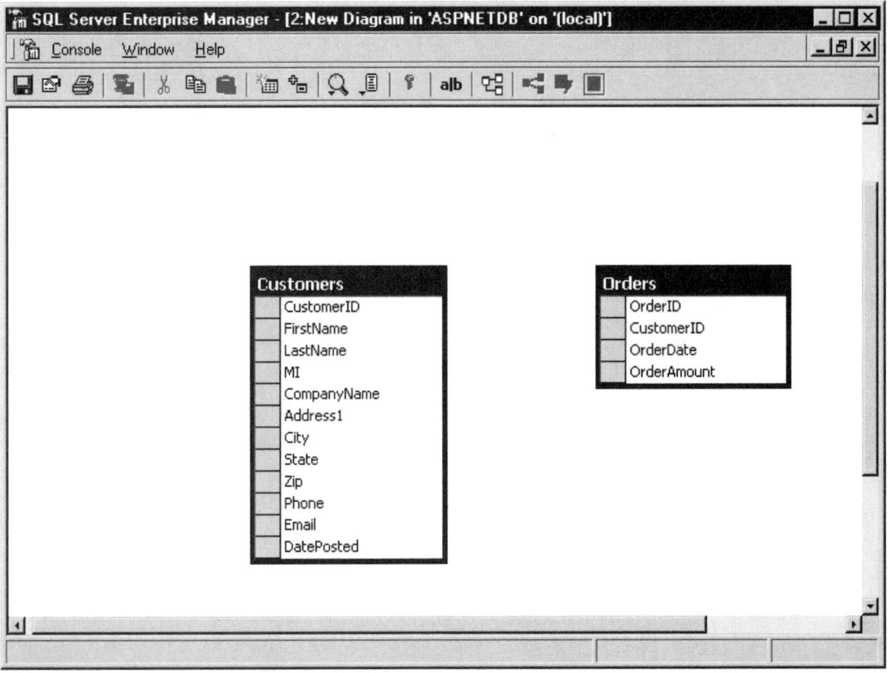

Figure 8-7 The Customers and Orders table, unconnected

and while you're at it, make the OrderID field a primary key for the Orders table. Doing so for the Orders table isn't necessary for this exercise, but it's good practice when making database tables.

To connect the tables in the relationship, drag the CustomerID field from the Customers table on top of the CustomerID field in the Orders table. You'll see the screen shown in Figure 8-8. It is essentially asking you to define the relationship as based on the fields in both tables. Click OK. The finished relationship should look like Figure 8-9. Save the diagram as DIAGRAM! (this is the default name assigned by SQL Server).

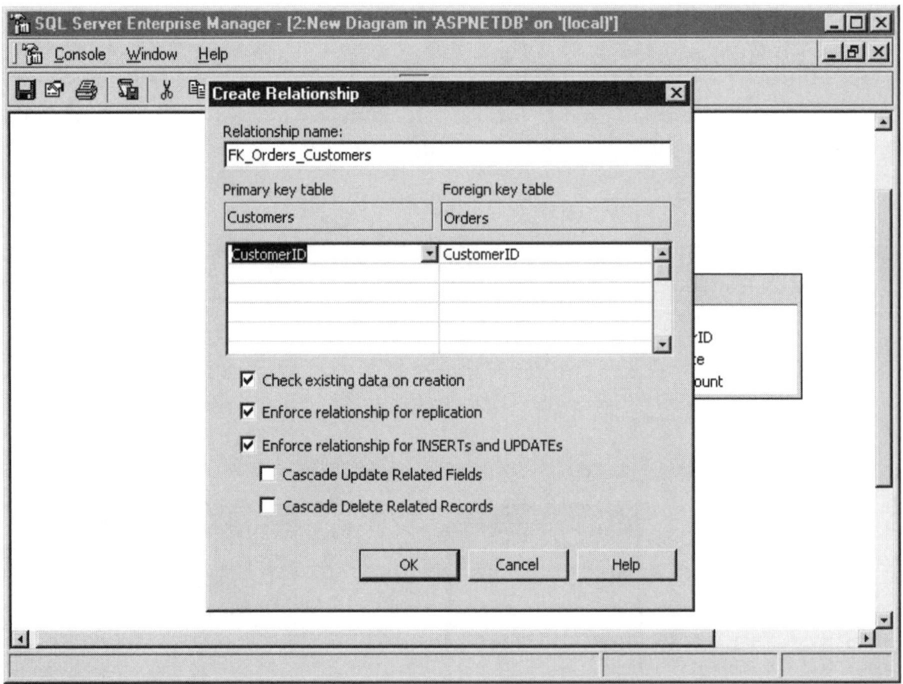

Figure 8-8 The relationship definition dialog box

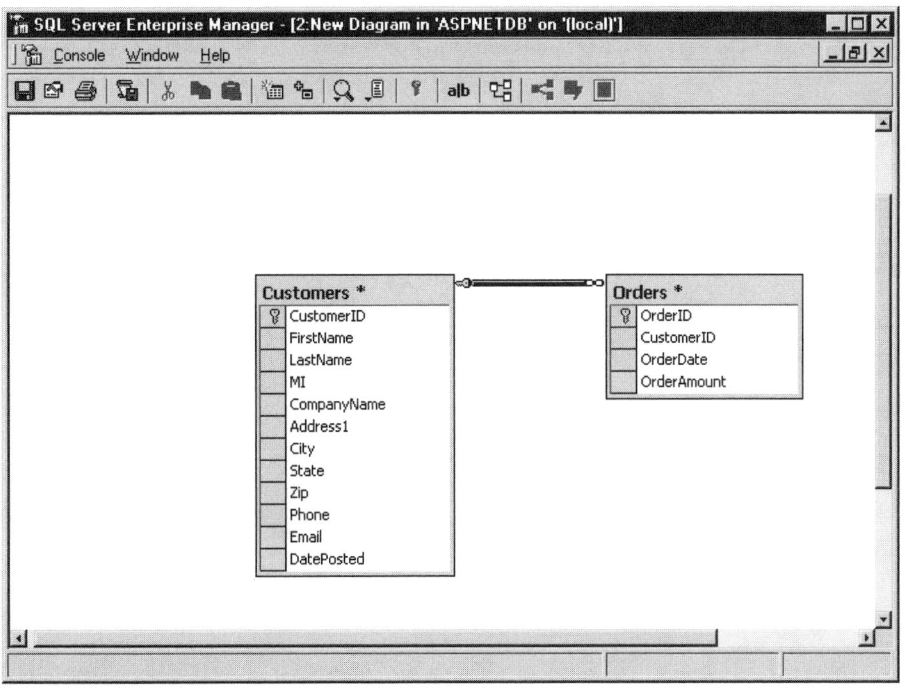

Figure 8-9 The Finished relationship in the Diagram

Queries and SQL

SQL Server comes with plenty of tools to make life easier when creating queries. For example, in Figure 8-10, the New View screen is shown. This view pulls all customers and has been named Allcustomers.

The view is shown in an interface called Query-By-Example (QBE). The QBE interface gives users a visual view of the columns or fields of data they are retrieving and makes it easy to specify the criteria used to select records. Figure 8-11 shows another simple query created in the QBE interface, using the example ASPNETDB database. To make this query, right-click Views and choose New View, then start adding tables to the QBE screen (click the Add tables

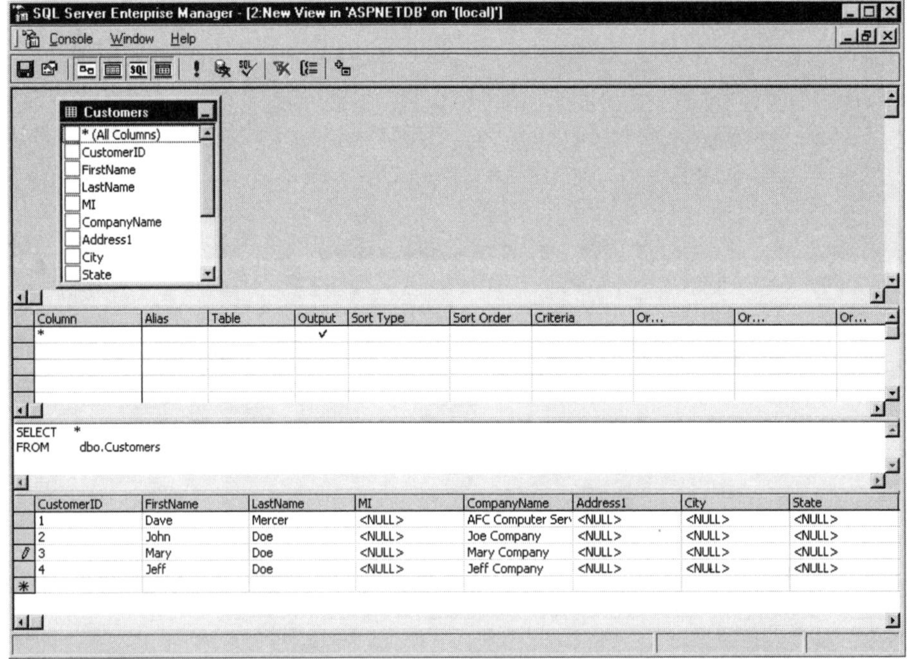

Figure 8-10 The Allcustomers view

button on the toolbar), as shown in Figure 8-11. Add the Customers and Orders tables, and then close the Add Tables dialog box. You'll see something resembling Figure 8-12. Notice that SQL Server is writing SQL statements for you as you go.

Notice both the Customers and Orders tables are included (with the join line), and the fields are arrayed in a row. Selecting fields by clicking in the box next to them will cause them to be retrieved as part of the query.

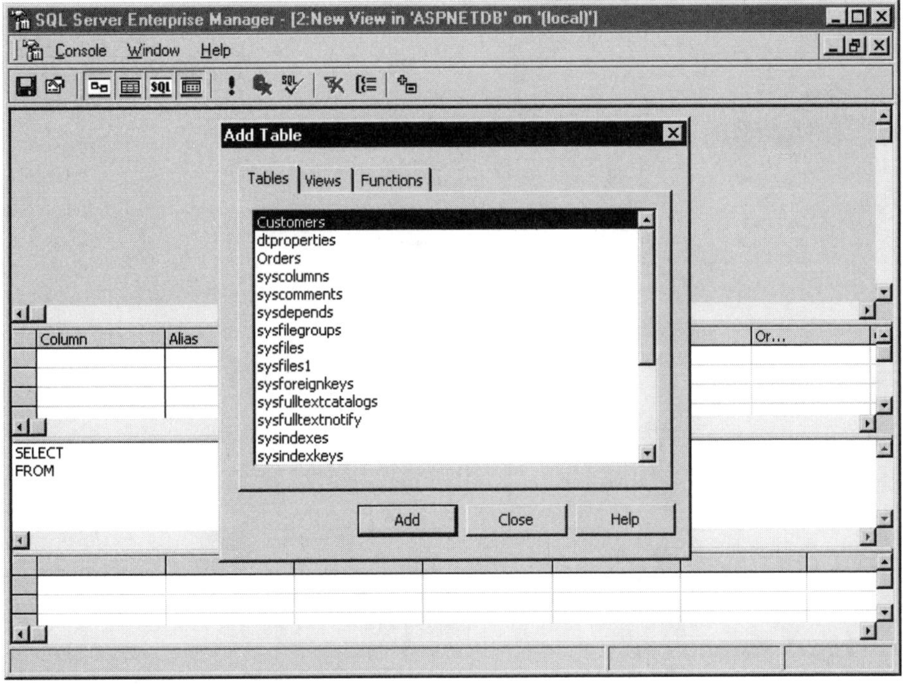

Figure 8-11 Adding tables for a view

In the next iteration of this view, notice that there are selection criteria present for the CompanyName and OrderDate fields (Figure 8-13). Only records having a company name of ShopHere.com and an order date of 6/6/01 will be retrieved.

It should be clear that CompanyName is a field of data type varchar, while OrderDate is a field of data type datetime. An important distinction between the two is the way they are entered in the query. Text data types are delimited by single quotes, while datetime data types are converted from a text type. You'll find this convention in use throughout scripting and programming languages.

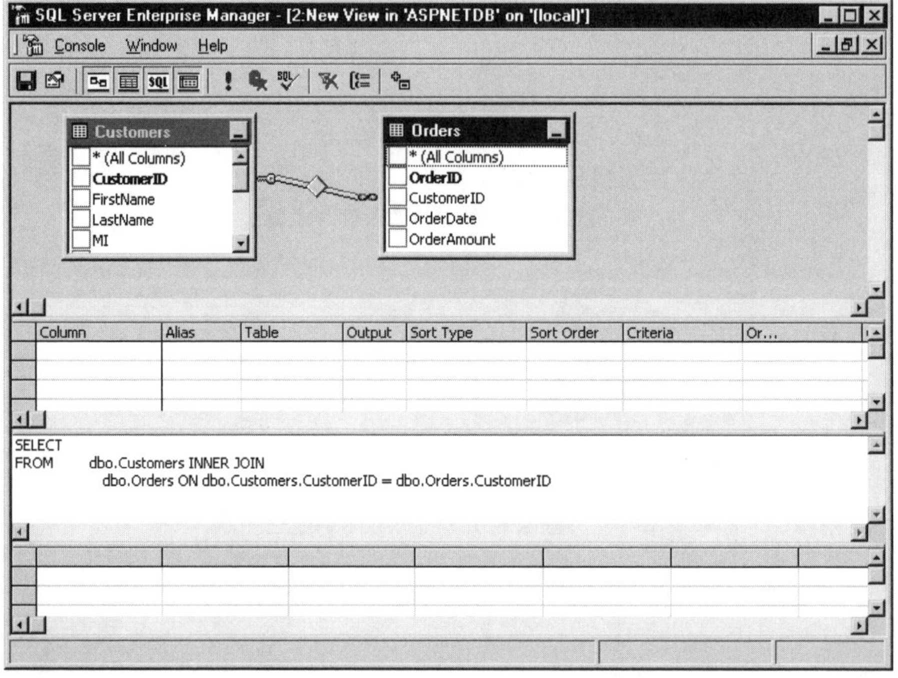

Figure 8-12 The finished CustomerOrders view

Setting up a query in SQL Server is simply a matter of choosing what tables play a role in the results, adding those tables to the query, and then choosing the fields from those tables. Clicking and dragging them into the query grid makes them part of the results.

After choosing the tables and fields, you have several options for query types:

- **Select Query** This query selects records based on the criteria you enter in the criteria row. The results contain every record matching those criteria with the fields you include.
- **Delete Query** This query deletes records matching the criteria you specify.
- **Append Query** This query appends records matching your criteria from the tables you include to another table.

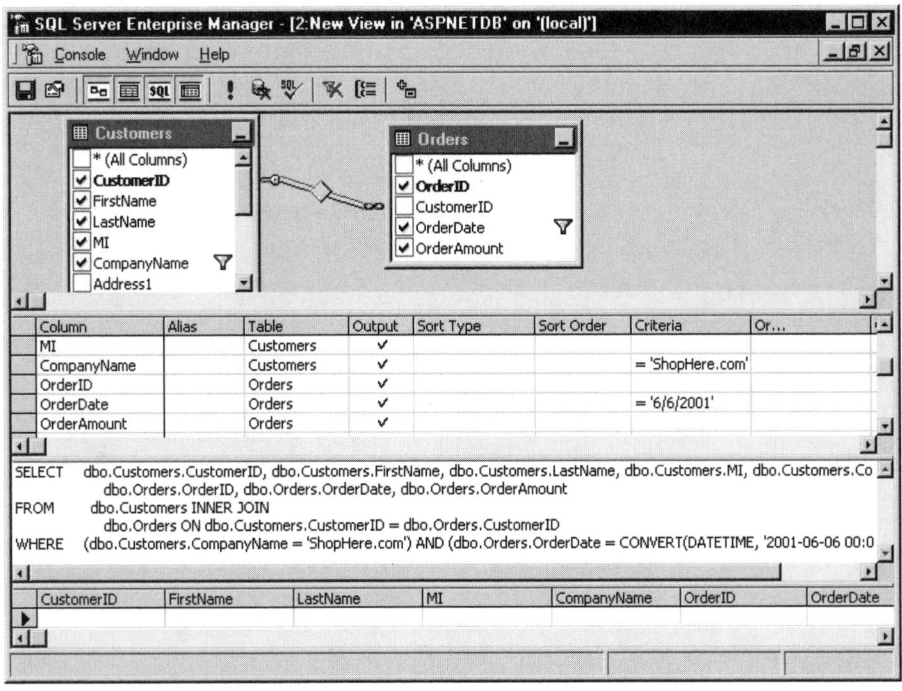

Figure 8-13 The CustomerOrders view with selection criteria

- **Update Query** This query updates all records matching your criteria from their existing value (for a given field) to a new value you enter.
- **Make-Table Query** This query makes a new table from all the records matching your criteria with the fields you include.

SQL Server and Structured Query Language (SQL)

SQL stands for Structured Query Language, and it is the industry-standard method for accessing databases. SQL is a set of English-language statements that specify the query to be performed. Although each DBMS seems to support its own particular version of SQL, the differences are slight and the commonalities are great, so knowing SQL is indispensable.

Fortunately, SQL Server 2000 actually writes SQL for you in the QBE interface, as you've seen. You can simply substitute in the appropriate SQL statements to change a SELECT query into a DELETE query, for example. As a matter of fact, you can write SQL statements and see them in QBE, or vice versa, quite easily.

The SQL is also shown here:

```
SELECT
 dbo.Customers.CustomerID, dbo.Customers.FirstName,
 dbo.Customers.LastName, dbo.Customers.MI,
 dbo.Customers.CompanyName, dbo.Orders.OrderID,
 dbo.Orders.OrderDate, dbo.Orders.OrderAmount
FROM
 dbo.Customers
 INNER JOIN dbo.Orders ON dbo.Customers.CustomerID
 = dbo.Orders.CustomerID
WHERE
 (dbo.Customers.CompanyName = 'ShopHere.com')
 AND (dbo.Orders.OrderDate =
 CONVERT(DATETIME, '2001-06-06 00:00:00', 102))
```

As you can see, SQL is made up of fairly easy-to-understand statements that are highly structured for initiating specific actions upon tables in a database. They can also perform many other actions in a database, and the SQL language has evolved far enough to allow complete control of databases.

The previous SQL code starts out with the SELECT statement, meaning the action to be performed in the selection of records. The next portion of the code specifies the names of the fields to be selected, combined with the table to select them from.

The FROM statement specifies which tables to select records from and how they are related (INNER JOIN specifies the relationship ON the CustomerID fields of both tables). The WHERE statement specifies the criteria by which to select records.

Forms as a User Interface

Forms are used primarily for two purposes: entering and editing data in tables and navigating your application. The most important thing to keep in mind when creating forms is to make them easy to understand and use for the specific task at hand. There's no need to include every field from a table in a form if only three of the fields will allow the user to do the job.

We won't be covering forms in great detail here, at least not the forms you can create in a DBMS, because you will most likely be developing those forms as Web Forms. HTML forms with links and command buttons contain many of the same capabilities as typical database forms, so you might want to develop a process flow for your applications first in the DBMS.

Online and Offline Processes and Forms

Ordinarily, you will be creating very different forms for each application (online versus offline) because each has very different business processes to support. Online, you might want to take orders. Offline, you might want to process orders. Online, users will be customers placing orders, while offline, users will be employees processing those orders.

You can use VS.NET Web Forms to create forms for your application. It can be helpful to use the same names for fields on your HTML forms as for the fields in the tables in your database—make sure to leave out spaces and special characters in field names and table names. Other than that, common sense will guide you in the construction of your forms. Make your forms easy to understand and use, and you will do fine.

1-Minute Drill

- What fields provide the data for linking tables in a relational format?
- QBE uses what format to build queries?

ActiveX Data Objects

ActiveX Data Objects (ADO) is a special class of ASP components specifically designed with database and data store support in mind. They work well with ASP by design because so many applications require database support. Behind the scenes you can use just about any database you like, whether it's Microsoft Access 2000, SQL Server, or any other ODBC-compliant database. There are also quite a few proprietary database and online database access technologies, if you care to investigate or have a special need.

- Key fields, primary, and foreign
- A visual format, with included tables or queries on top and a grid for columns and criteria on the bottom

While databases might be the most familiar data containers for most of us, there are many containers of data, from spreadsheets and word processing documents to e-mail clients and the newer directory services. In fact, just about any bits or bytes on- or offline can be thought of as a store of data. In addition, online applications are stateless, meaning ADO must work well with a lack of persistent connections to the data source.

Data Consumers and Data Providers

Any object that stores data can be thought of as a data provider, while any application that uses that data can be thought of as a data consumer. Microsoft has created a two-layer architecture for retrieving data, consisting of ADO and OLE DB. OLE DB is the mechanism for interacting directly with the data store, whatever it might be, and ADO interacts with OLE DB. This means you can program for ADO, and OLE DB will take care of all the technical stuff behind the scenes for you (well, almost).

OLE DB Providers

When you install Windows 2000, ADO is installed, and with it comes a set of OLE DB providers:

- **Jet OLE DB 4.0** Used to access Microsoft Access databases
- **DTS Packages** Used for SQL Server Data Transformation Services
- **Internet Publishing** Used to access web servers
- **Indexing Service** Used for index catalogs
- **Site Server Search** Used for the Site Server search catalog
- **ODBC drivers** Used for accessing ODBC data sources
- **OLAP services** Used for the Microsoft OLAP server
- **Oracle** Used to access Oracle databases
- **SQL Server** Used to access Microsoft SQL Server databases
- **Simple Provider** Used to access simple text files
- **MSDataShape** Used to access hierarchical data

- **Microsoft Directory Services** Used for the Windows 2000 Directory Services
- **DTS Flat File** Used for the SQL Server Data Transformation Services flat file manager

The ADO 2.5 Object Model

ADO 2.5 consists of a number of objects for connecting to and working with the data you retrieve. Like other components, there is a fairly simple syntax for using them, and once you've made your connection it's pretty straightforward to work with the data they gather.

The objects in ADO are the Connection and Command objects, the Recordset and Record objects, and the Stream object. The Connection object has an Errors collection, the Command object has a Parameters collection, and the Recordset and Record objects have a Fields collection. Each type of provider also exposes to the objects listed a unique Properties collection. The reason for a unique Properties collection for each provider is that providers can be just about anything, and some providers require properties that others don't need. For example, a database may have special security settings that a simple text file doesn't need.

The Connection Object

Let's discuss the workings of each of the objects in the ADO 2.5 object model. We'll start with the Connection object. The primary function of the Connection object is to allow you to connect to data stores via OLE DB. You can specify the provider to use, security parameters, and other parameters. Although it is common to create a Connection object in the course of accessing data, Connection objects are implicitly created whenever you use the other ADOs. Even though there is a separate Command object, you can use the Connection object to run commands against a data store.

The Command Object

The Command object is specifically designed to run commands against a data store, and it is more flexible and capable in this regard than the Connection object. In fact, when you run commands using the Connection object, a limited Command object is implicitly created to perform those commands. The Command object is more powerful than the Connection object in that it allows you to be very specific about how the commands you are running are formed and provides a more intuitive interface and programming structure for those commands.

The Recordset Object

If you've ever done any database programming with DBMSs such as Microsoft Access or Paradox for Windows, you've probably used recordsets. The Recordset object is kind of like a table in your hands. You can retrieve recordsets from a table and then manipulate those recordsets in a fashion similar to having a table open in front of you.

For example, you can navigate around a recordset, going to the first, last, previous, or next record. You can add, edit, and delete records, and you can filter or find and change records based on values in individual fields.

The Record Object

The Record object is new and was added to handle data not formatted in structured rows and columns. Data in databases and spreadsheets is nicely formatted, but other data sources may only be somewhat structured. For example, suppose your data is in an e-mail program within mailboxes and folders, and some messages contain attachments, hyperlinks, or embedded images. The structure of the mailboxes and folders may be uniform, but the properties of each e-mail message may differ significantly. The Record object is designed to cope with differences in structure between one record and the next. You won't be using the Record object for much of your work with this book, but as your applications begin to use more and varied data providers, your use of the Record object will also grow.

The Stream Object

If the contents of a field is a binary large object (BLOB) or some other type of data that does not fit well into the common data types, you can use the Stream object to retrieve and manipulate it.

1-Minute Drill

- What ADO is like a table in a database?
- What ADO is best for running commands against a database?

- The Recordset object, because it allows you to manipulate individual records as though the table were open in front of you
- The Command object, although you can also use the Connection object in a limited way

The ADO.NET Object Model

For ASP, Active Data Objects provides a set of objects that make it easy to work directly with data from databases. For ASP.NET, there is an updated version of ADO called ADO.NET. It uses the Connection and Command objects in the same way as ADO, but instead of using a Recordset object to retrieve a set of records and work with them using a cursor, ADO.NET uses the Dataset object, which is like a representation of the entire data store. You can make changes against the entire data store using the Dataset object, and those changes are eventually propagated back to the original data store with the DataAdapter object.

If you only need to display or scroll through data, you can use a DataReader object. Data is pulled once and held in memory for display without a connection being maintained.

Coding Structured Query Language (SQL)

In Module 2, we mentioned SQL and its role in working with databases and ASP scripting. The following section covers the major SQL commands and syntax with the objective of familiarizing you with SQL enough to build confidence when scripting SQL commands.

Although perhaps not the case for everyone, many find SQL easy to understand and use because the syntax is fairly simple and the commands so English-like. However, the structure of some of the commands is highly dependent upon the structure of whatever database you are accessing. You would be well advised to learn about relational database structure in general before trying to write complex table joins from scratch. That said, always remember that DBMS programs such as SQL Server have built-in SQL generators, and these can be a great help in properly formatting SQL commands quickly. Osborne/McGraw-Hill also publishes an excellent SQL reference book entitled (appropriately enough) *SQL: The Complete Reference* by James R. Groff and Paul N. Weinberg (ISBN 0-07-211845-8).

SQL Statements

Writing SQL code is a little bit different from writing scripting language code or using ASP, in that the code tends to have a query-like flavor. For example, a very common SQL statement is the SELECT statement (by convention, this book will list SQL commands as uppercase, although it is not required). The SELECT statement retrieves data from a database by specifying the columns (or fields) to retrieve, the table or tables from which to retrieve data, and any criteria limiting the records retrieved.

In SQL, you can use SELECT to retrieve data, INSERT to add records (or rows), DELETE to remove records, and UPDATE to edit or modify data in records. The SQL statement performing any of these actions would begin with one of these verbs and be followed by additional details about which tables and records are to be affected.

SQL also contains a variety of commands that affect the structure of the database or tables. These include CREATE TABLE, ALTER TABLE, and DROP TABLE, as well as similar commands affecting VIEWs, INDEXes, SCHEMAs, and DOMAINs. There are also a few statements for controlling access privileges, transactions, and for defining programmatic SQL functions such as using cursors and conducting dynamic operations.

SQL Keywords and Table/Field Names

There are quite a number of reserved keywords in SQL, and additional keywords may exist in the various flavors of SQL available. Naturally, you want to avoid using these keywords as table or field names. Fortunately, they are usually similar to reserved keywords in scripting languages, and it's not too hard to remember what words to avoid. For example, DATE, DAY, DELETE, DESC, ELSE, GET, GOTO, and IN are all SQL keywords. Many of these are also keywords in VBScript and VB.NET, and you may find client's with databases in which a field for descriptions (for a product record, for instance) has been shortened to DESC. SQL doesn't work well with this, so keep an eye out for this and other conflicting field names.

Project 8-1: Using SQL

For this module, we've devoted an entire project section to SQL queries. This will be a good reference for constructing your own SQL queries quickly as your applications become more and more database dependent.

Step-by-Step

Let's start with the simpler queries and build from there. We'll use SQL Server to construct the queries, then look at the SQL generated. After that, we'll construct the query in ordinary SQL to illustrate the differences.

1. Use the QBE interface to build a query. Start with a SELECT query using several variations.

2. We'll start by making a very simple SELECT query (Allcustomers) on the Customers table of the example database, using SQL Server's QBE interface. Following the figure is the SQL code generated by SQL Server.

```
SELECT *
FROM dbo.Customers
```

3. There are only two SQL commands, SELECT and FROM, in this code. The asterisk tells the query to pull all fields. The result of this query is a table consisting of all rows and columns in the original tables. In effect, this query creates a complete snapshot of the original table.

4. Figure 8-14 shows retrieving all fields by name, with the addition of a single criterion in the LastName column, making the query only return rows (records) in which the value of the LastName field is exactly equal to Johnson. The SQL code again follows the figure:

```
SELECT
 CustomerID, FirstName, LastName, MI, CompanyName,
 Address1, City, State, Zip, Phone, Email, DatePosted
FROM dbo.Customers
WHERE (LastName = 'Johnson')
```

Notice the way SQL Server has organized the WHERE clause. ANSI SQL doesn't require the parentheses.

5. Figure 8-15 shows sorting by the CompanyName field added to the returning results, in descending order so the DESC keyword would be included in the ORDER BY clause. If ascending order is desired, the sort order indicator is omitted.

```
SELECT
 CustomerID, FirstName, LastName, MI, CompanyName,
 Address1, City, State, Zip, Phone, Email, DatePosted
FROM dbo.Customers
WHERE (LastName = 'Johnson')
ORDER BY CompanyName DESC
```

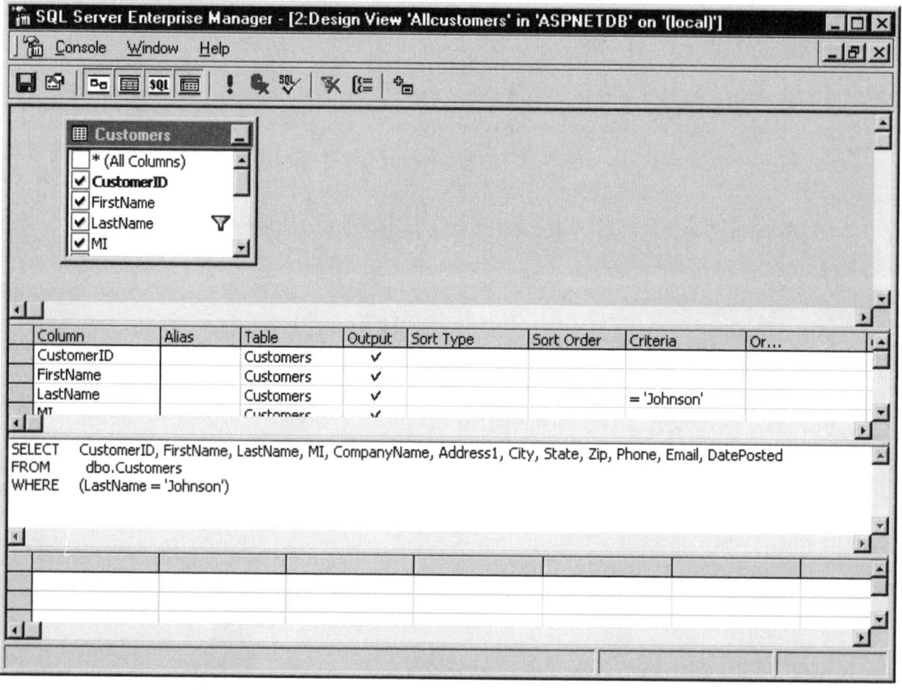

Figure 8-14 Selecting for records with LastName = "Johnson"

6. Figure 8-16 shows a modification to the query you've been building that allows the query to retrieve any record that starts with the first four characters "John" and then contains any number of characters after that as the value of the field named LastName. Pattern-matching expressions of this type use the Like keyword, and in SQL Server the percent sign (%) is used as the wildcard character, meaning any character any number of times.

   In SQL Server, the underscore (_) is used to match a single character.

```
SELECT
 CustomerID, FirstName, LastName, MI, CompanyName,
 Address1, City, State, Zip, Phone, Email, DatePosted
FROM dbo.Customers
WHERE (LastName LIKE 'John%')
ORDER BY CompanyName DESC
```

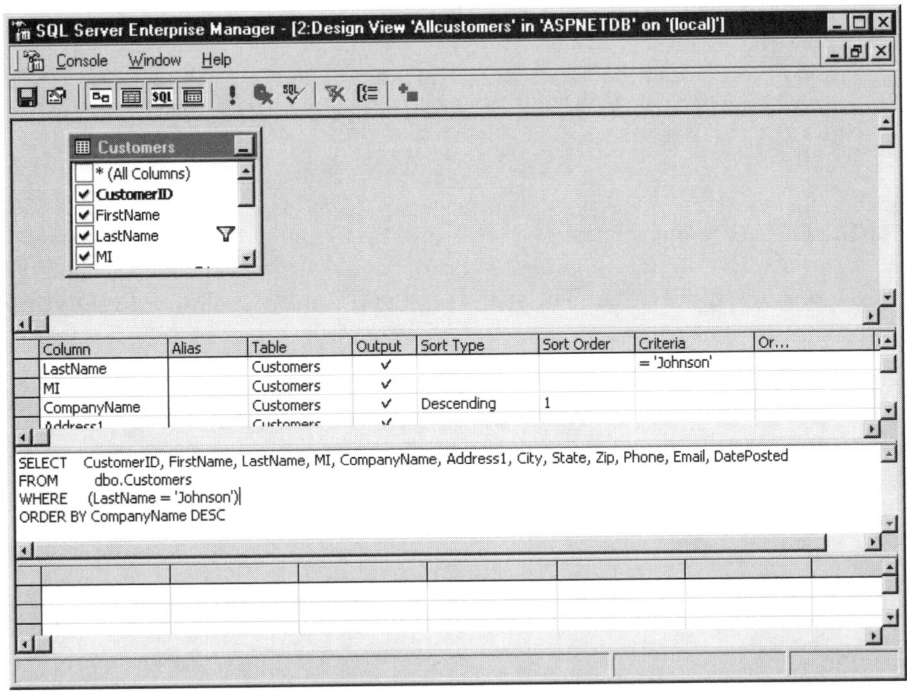

Figure 8-15 Query showing descending order in the CompanyName field

7. Like most languages, SQL can use comparison operators in expressions. Equals, not equal to, greater-than, less-than, and so forth can all be used in arithmetical operations, string comparisons, and date comparisons. If the comparison is true, the record is retrieved, but if the comparison is false or null, the record is not retrieved (we'll discuss null values shortly). The next figure (Figure 8-17) and code show how SQL Server queries compare date values in a field to the specified date, to find all records with a date later than 6/6/01. You have now closed the Allcustomers view and opened the CustomerOrders view to perform the retrieval

```
SELECT
 dbo.Customers.CustomerID, dbo.Customers.FirstName,
 dbo.Customers.LastName, dbo.Customers.MI,
 dbo.Customers.CompanyName, dbo.Orders.OrderID,
```

```
 dbo.Orders.OrderDate, dbo.Orders.OrderAmount
FROM dbo.Customers INNER JOIN
 dbo.Orders ON dbo.Customers.CustomerID =
 dbo.Orders.CustomerID
WHERE (dbo.Orders.OrderDate >
 CONVERT(DATETIME, '2001-06-06 00:00:00', 102))
```

8. The BETWEEN keyword (shown in Figure 8-18) can also be used to make a simpler version of two separate comparison tests to find values between a low and high value set. For example, if you wanted to find orders dated

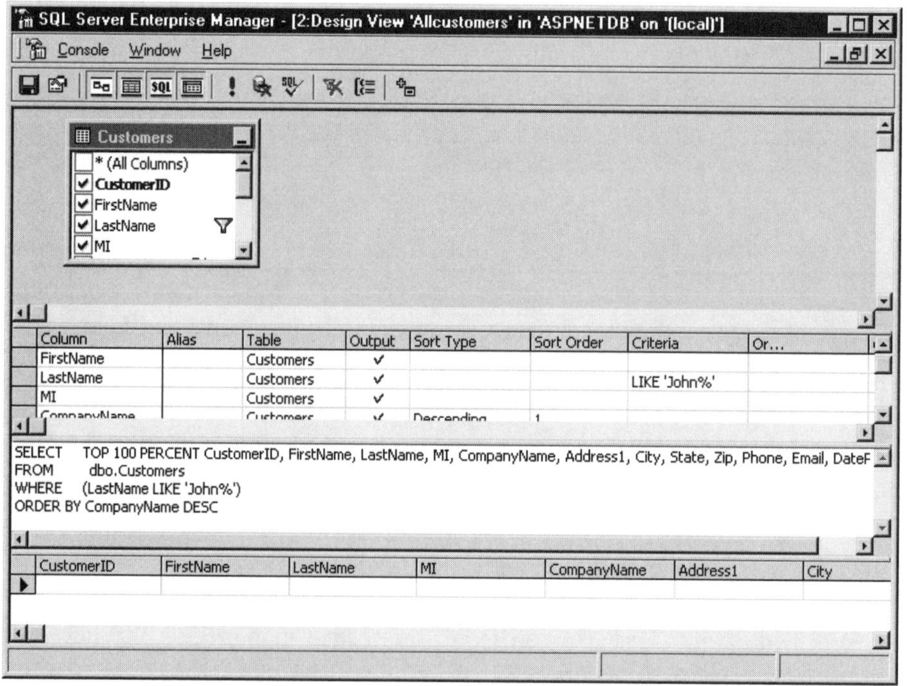

Figure 8-16 Query using wildcard characters for "John" and any characters

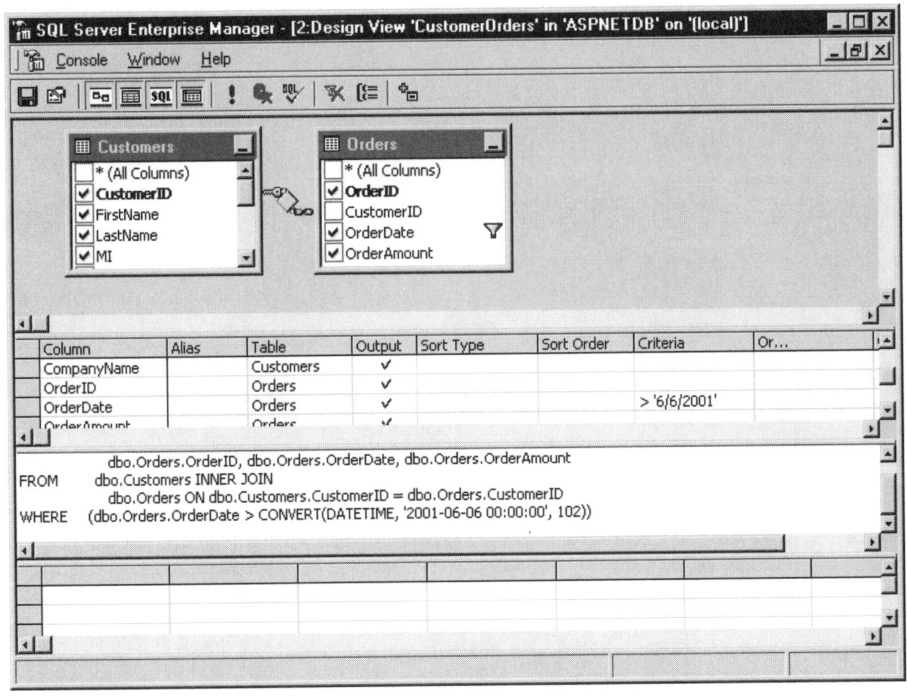

Figure 8-17 Query finding all records in the Orders table after 6/6/01

8

between 6/6/01 and 7/6/01, rather than forming two individual WHERE clauses you could use the following code:

```
SELECT
 dbo.Customers.CustomerID, dbo.Customers.FirstName,
 dbo.Customers.LastName, dbo.Customers.MI,
 dbo.Customers.CompanyName, dbo.Orders.OrderID,
 dbo.Orders.OrderDate, dbo.Orders.OrderAmount
FROM
 dbo.Customers INNER JOIN
 dbo.Orders ON dbo.Customers.CustomerID =
 dbo.Orders.CustomerID
WHERE
 (dbo.Orders.OrderDate BETWEEN
 CONVERT(DATETIME, '2001-06-06 00:00:00', 102) AND
 CONVERT(DATETIME, '2001-07-06 00:00:00', 102))
```

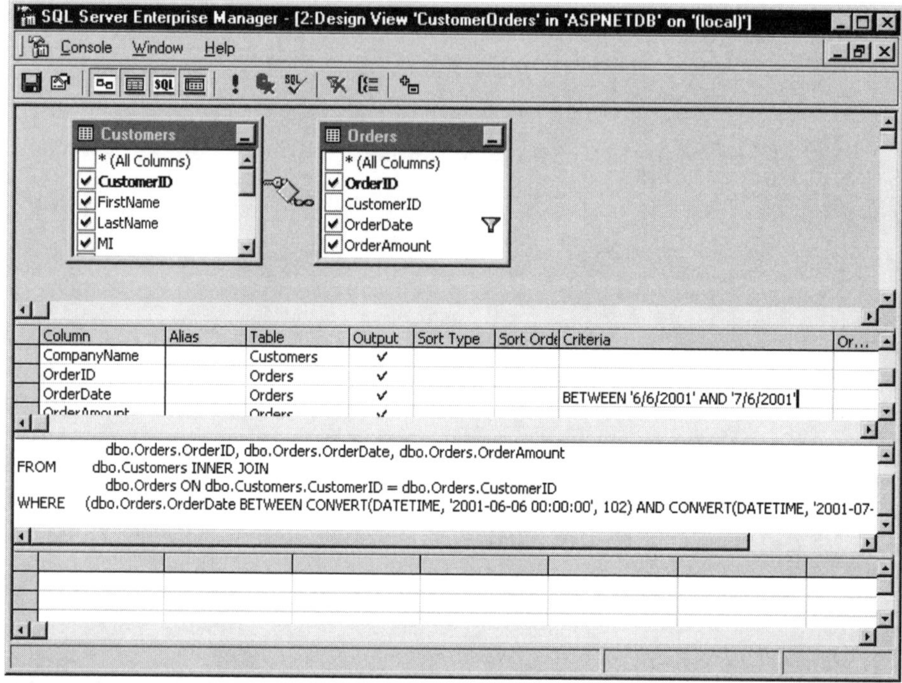

Figure 8-18 Showing the BETWEEN SQL statement

9. The term "null values" is actually a misnomer, as null means there is no value in a field. Technically, null means that the value is unknown, whereas a zero-length string means the value is "nothing." Finding null values in records becomes important under fairly common circumstances. For example, if you count all your customers in California by zip code, your count result may be 1,000, but suppose 15 of your customers in California have nothing entered for zip code? The real total of 1015 would not be the result you get. So to find null values, you would specify IS NULL in your query. Figure 8-19 and the code following it show the use of IS NULL in SQL Server in the Orders table, for finding all records where there is no Order Amount present.

```
SELECT
 dbo.Customers.CustomerID, dbo.Customers.FirstName,
 dbo.Customers.LastName, dbo.Customers.MI,
 dbo.Customers.CompanyName, dbo.Orders.OrderID,
```

```
 dbo.Orders.OrderDate, dbo.Orders.OrderAmount
FROM
 dbo.Customers INNER JOIN
 dbo.Orders ON dbo.Customers.CustomerID =
 dbo.Orders.CustomerID
WHERE
 (dbo.Orders.OrderDate BETWEEN
 CONVERT(DATETIME, '2001-06-06 00:00:00', 102) AND
 CONVERT(DATETIME, '2001-07-06 00:00:00', 102)) AND
 (dbo.Orders.OrderAmount IS NULL)
```

10. You will often require a query to select records based on criteria in two or more fields or based on two or more conditions for a single field. You can use the logical operators AND, OR, and NOT to find records in this fashion, as the previous figure and code illustrate.

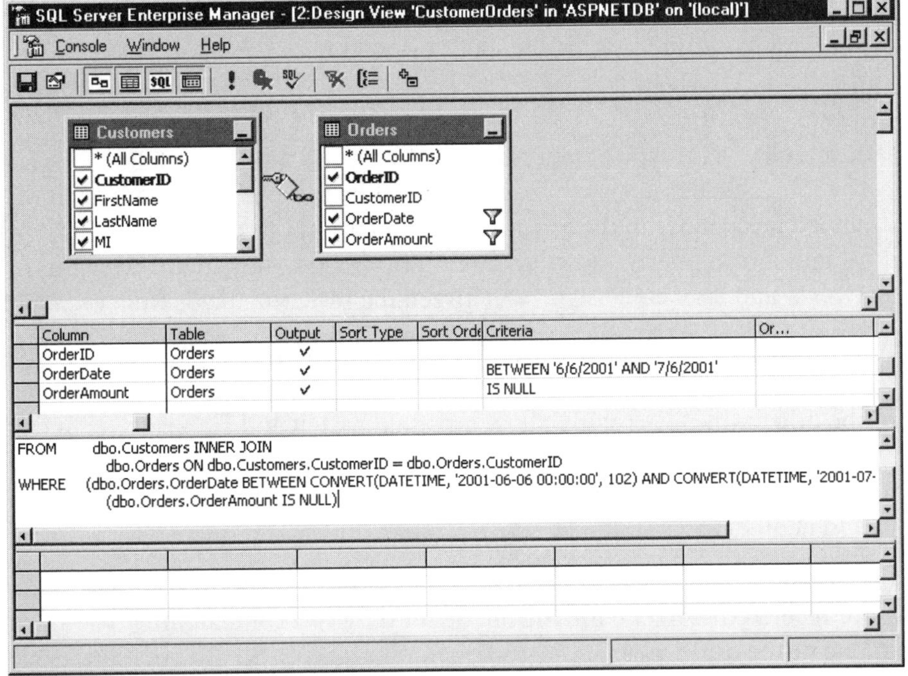

Figure 8-19 Query finding records without Order Amounts

11. When building your database, you will encounter field values that can be calculated based on other field values. Sales tax due, for example, is the result of a calculation multiplying the total cost of products ordered (individual product cost times the quantity ordered, added up) times the applicable sales tax rate.

12. The question is, do you add a field to your table for this amount, or do you just let the other fields hold the data and then calculate the total sales tax due whenever you need it? You will frequently perform the calculation whenever you need to view sales tax due or other calculated values. You can use SQL to calculate values during queries.

SQL Table Joins

In a relational database, data is kept in individual tables that keep track of a single subject, item, or thing. Customers, employees, orders, inventory items, and so on are all examples of things that might have their own tables. Relationships between tables can be defined using key fields (primary and foreign keys). To express a relationship between two or more tables in a SQL query, joins are used.

Joins come in several flavors:

- **Equi-join** This type of join results in recordsets where the values of the joined fields are exactly equal. All records in either table not matching joined field values in the other table do not appear in the results. This type of join is also referred to as an inner join. In SQL, the notation for this type of join is an equal sign (=) between the matching fields from each table.
- **Outer-join** This type of join results in recordsets where the values of the joined fields may be equal but also may *not* have a matching value in the other table. Therefore, all records that match and all records that don't match will be included, with null values where unmatched fields occur. In SQL, the notation for this type of join is an asterisk, an equal sign, and another asterisk (*=*).
- **Left and right outer joins** These types of joins result in recordsets where all records that match are included, but only the nonmatching records of one or the other table are included, not both. In SQL, the notation for this type of join is an asterisk on the side of the equal sign indicating the table from which nonmatching records are to be included (*= or =*).

The queries produced using the CustomerOrders view show the SQL code and QBE screen for INNER JOIN queries.

Summary Queries

SQL contains a number of functions that allow you to summarize field values. For example, you can compute the sum of all OrderAmount fields from the Orders table for each individual customer. You can also ascertain the average, minimum value, maximum value, total number of values, and total number of records. The keywords for these functions are: SUM, AVG, MIN, MAX, and COUNT. Figure 8-20 shows your SQL Server CustomerOrders query redesigned once again (this time saved as SumOfOrderAmounts), so it will produce the sum of all order amounts from the Orders table, using the summary function SUM.

The following code shows the way this is done in SQL:

```
SELECT SUM(dbo.Orders.OrderAmount) AS Expr1
FROM dbo.Customers INNER JOIN
 dbo.Orders ON dbo.Customers.CustomerID =
 dbo.Orders.CustomerID
```

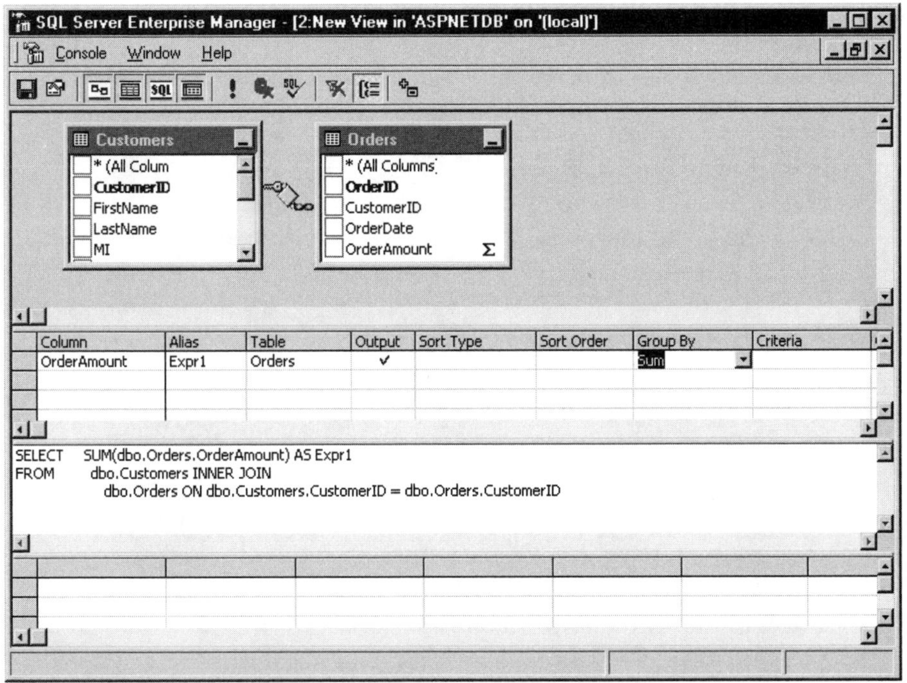

Figure 8-20 Query using aggregation or grouping to produce totals

Ask the Expert

Question: You've mentioned that SQL seems to be the standard language for working with databases. What relationship does SQL have with Microsoft products, other vendors' products, and websites in general?

Answer: Although there are many variations of SQL, they tend to be pretty slight variations, usually just subtle differences in the reserved words, special characters (such as wildcard characters), and delimiters. Each version of SQL is appropriate for the type of database it is accessing or the circumstances under which it is used. For example, if you insert a parameter in a SQL statement being used within Microsoft FrontPage, the delimiters will be different from those used with ASP to achieve the same result. Keep in mind that SQL is central to database access no matter what program or environment you are using, but be prepared to do some research (and a little trial and error) to get your SQL statements to work.

Question: I'm not quite sure I understand the concept of relational database design. How important is it, and can I get along without it?

Answer: You might want to do further research into relational database design, but I'm afraid it doesn't get much easier than this. There are actually several levels of relational structure (called the normal forms), and most designers use the third normal form for their designs. This means that no fields have more than one piece of data in them (no city-state-zip fields, for example), each trackable entity has its own table, and data is only stored once per entity. However, depending upon the use to which your database will be put, it may be expedient to break some of these rules. Good designers know when to break them.

Since there are basically three types of relationships between tables (one-to-one, one-to-many, and many-to-many), just ask yourself what the relationship is. For example, if you have employees in a company and you want to track them, that means one table for them. However, if an employee can be on several teams, while teams can have several employees on them, then the relationship between employees and teams can be stated as, "An employee may be on many teams, and a team may have many employees, therefore the relationship is many-to-many." Talking it out is helpful.

Mastery Check

1. What is the process of determining the end result and working backward to determine requirements called?

   A. From-the-ground-up engineering

   B. Backward-engineering

   C. Reverse-engineering

   D. None of the above

2. What is the SQL command for specifying criteria in a SELECT statement?

   A. WITHIN

   B. WHERE

   C. FROM

   D. None of the above

3. What are the SQL text field delimiters?

   A. Single-quote marks

   B. Double-quote marks

   C. The percent sign

   D. None of the above.

4. What takes the place of traditional DBMS navigational forms on a website?

   A. Queries

   B. Reports

   C. HTML forms

   D. Web forms

   E. C and D above

5. Why are databases commonly part of web applications?

   A. Web applications require databases to store their content.

Mastery Check

B. Content stored in databases is easier to manage than content stored as HTML pages.

C. Content stored in databases can be presented dynamically.

D. Content stored in databases can be searched with a simple user interface.

E. B, C, and D above.

F. All of the above.

6. To build a table in SQL Server, what steps should you take?

A. Decide what fields are required and enter them in the new table design view.

B. Make at least one field the primary key field and ensure that it will always have unique values.

C. Save your table with a descriptive name.

D. Decide what data types would be appropriate for each field.

E. All of the above.

F. None of the above.

7. Primary key fields are important because they uniquely _________ each record of data entered into the table. Therefore, a given table can be linked to another table in a _________, such as one-to-one, one-to-many, or many-to-many.

8. Describe three types of queries commonly found in databases.

____

____

9. What SQL query will retrieve all records from a table named "pets" in which the pet name is "Clyde", with the records including only the pet name field (pet_name) and the pet id field (pet_id)?

A. SELECT ALL FROM pets WHERE name='Clyde'

Mastery Check

B. SELECT * FROM pets WHERE pet_name='Clyde'

C. SELECT * FROM pets WHERE pet_name='Clyde' AND pet_id='*'

D. SELECT pet_name, pet_id FROM pets WHERE pet_name='Clyde'

E. None of the above

10. What is the difference between a null value and a zero-length string?

A. A null value means there is nothing in the field (it is unknown whether a value for this field exists), while a zero-length string means the value is known and it is "nothing" (it is known that there is no value for this field).

B. Null means the field is empty, while a zero-length string means the field is empty but has an unknown value.

C. There is no difference.

D. None of the above.

11. How are values inserted into SQL statements when the SQL query is part of your programming and the value to be inserted isn't known until the program is running and the user enters the value?

A. It is not possible to do this; all values must be written into the program in advance and then selected from a table of SQL statements.

B. This can be done using the SQL INSERT statement.

C. Using string concatenation operators appropriate for the language you are writing your program in.

D. B or C above.

E. None of the above.

12. If a table named "owners" has a one-to-many relationship with a table named "pets", this means that the table named "owners" is the ______ of the table named "pets", and that for every record in the "owners" table there may be _____ child records in the table named "pets".

Mastery Check

13. Describe the functions of the Connection, Command, and Recordset objects in ADO and how the Recordset object compares to the DataSet object in ADO.NET.

____

____

14. What table joins are available in SQL? What is the purpose of each?

A. Inner join, bottom join, and top join. The inner join connects tables, while the bottom and top joins connect queries.

B. Inner join, outer join, and prejoin. The inner and outer joins connect tables, while the prejoin is for previewing the results of a join before compiling your application.

C. Equi-join, outer-join, and left and right joins. The equi-join connects tables and allows all records from both tables to appear where the values in the joined fields are equal; the outer-join connects tables and allows all records to appear with null values for fields in records where the joining fields don't match; and the left and right joins connect tables but allow all records from one side while disallowing unmatched records from the other table.

D. None of the above.

15. What SQL aggregate function would you use if you wanted to add all values in a particular field, and what SQL aggregate function would you use if you wanted to figure out how many records were in a set of records?

A. ADD and COUNT

B. SUM and COUNT

C. SUM and ADD

D. Either B or C above

E. Any of the above

F. None of the above

Module 9

The ADO.NET Connection-Related Objects

The Goals of This Module

- Learn how to create DSNs and UDL files
- Connect to databases with the Connection object
- Examine the functions the Command object can perform
- Run action commands with the Command object
- Learn about cursors
- Set various cursor types
- Create stored procedures in SQL Server
- Run stored procedures with the Command object
- Insert parameters into Command objects

To retrieve and work with data in a database from a web application, you must establish a connection to it. The connection can only be established when the location of the data store is known, the appropriate driver is present on the server, and any required username or password is provided. In this module, you will learn how the basic connection and command methods work, as well as some things enabled by a connection. As we discussed in Module 8, ADO.NET is a flexible, XML-driven technology, and it offers several objects to work with databases and database records, including the Connection and Command objects as well as the DataSet, DataReader, and DataAdapter objects. In ASP and ADO, the Recordset object is used instead of the DataAdapter and Dataset objects.

Interactivity and Latency

ASP.NET is all about providing data to users, as well as gathering data from users or, more plainly, interactivity. *Latency* is the term for the waiting time users endure while they interact with your site. Latency is greatly affected by your ability to optimize the structure of your database and the connection methods you employ. How you make connections and what you can do with them are restricted by a range of factors, including server capability, bandwidth available, server and database software (and drivers), and the requirements of your application. This means making good connections and using them appropriately is important. A number of subjects are covered in this module to encourage you to develop good structural skills. Module10 contains further explanation of how to create and use connections effectively.

Optimizing Database Interactions

Working with a database behind the scenes makes your applications lively, but it can slow things down considerably if you don't take steps to optimize your application's database interactions. In this section, you learn a few ways to keep your applications speedy.

Opening and Closing Connections

You should know and practice a few things when you open a connection to keep your applications running efficiently. Opening a connection is a time-consuming operation, so you should do it as infrequently as possible. Fortunately,

OLE DB has connection pooling built-in, which means after you close a connection, it goes into a pool of inactive connections. If another connection of the same type is required by your application, the inactive connection is made active again, rather than reestablishing a whole new connection.

To optimize connection pooling, open your connections as late in your application as possible and close them as quickly as possible. This means fewer whole new connections will be opened, and your application then runs faster for more users. Remember to insert the connection close method after you finish using each connection. The connection is then available for the next user.

Using Stored Procedures

A stored procedure is a set of functions and queries that can be written and stored inside the DBMS itself. SQL Server has a wizard that helps write stored procedures, as you will see later in this module. Although you can code your processing to run within your scripts, you can often code some or all of a particular process to run as a stored procedure within the database itself. Wherever you can run stored procedures, you should, because they are precompiled and run much faster. Stored procedures are discussed more in just a bit.

Use Required Data Only

When you retrieve data, you don't always need to create a complete Recordset or Dataset and, if you do create one, you don't always need every field in a table or the capability to modify records. Limit what you retrieve to required data and functionality only. Less functionality translates to less processing overhead and less data transmitted back and forth.

The Connection Object

A connection to a database is made with an object, and the connection has properties and methods associated with it. For example, the Connection String property tells the object what driver to use and what database to connect to, and the Open and Close methods are responsible for opening and closing the connection. In ADO and ADO.NET, the Connection object can be used to make a connection to a database, and it can also be used to run SQL statements against a database. The SQL statements can be ordinary SELECT queries or they can insert, update, or delete records. Differences in functionality are offered by various data providers and, with some providers, some of the collections, methods, and properties discussed in the following section may not be available.

Hint

When making a connection, you can often apply constants (ADO Constants) that define the type of locking or cursor to be used. These constants take the form of various values. The constant names themselves—and the values to which they are equivalent—can be found in a file named adovbs.inc in the Program Files\Common Files\System\ado subfolder of the drive on which the operating system is installed. Copy that file into the folder in which your scripts are running, and then you can reference the file as an include file to make the constant names available within your connection strings, and so forth. We will follow this procedure when we create ASP scripts.

Storing and Accessing Connection Information

Connecting to a data source can be accomplished using a complete connection string, a separate file that contains the connection information, or via a *Data Source Name* (DSN). Many prefer to use DSNs, but sometimes you don't have that luxury.

A connection string typically contains the name and path of the database file, user ID and password, and a reference to the driver to be used with the data provider. The syntax isn't too difficult, but if you're using a connection string in several places or pages of your ASP application and some detail changes, it can make more work to change each instance. Better to store the connection details in an include file or as an Application variable, so you only have to change the details in one place.

Hint

If you store the connection details as an Application variable in your global.asa file, you must start and stop the Application each time you modify the connection details. As mentioned in earlier modules, this can be extra work.

Connection Strings

Following are two examples of acceptable connection strings, as well as a number of other methods for creating and holding connection string information.

Microsoft Access

```
Driver={Microsoft Access Driver (*.mdb)}; DBQ=the path and file name
Provider=Microsoft.Jet.OLEDB.4.0; Data Source=the path and file name
```

Microsoft SQL Server

```
Driver={SQL Server}; Server=the server name; Database=the database name;
UID=the user ID; PWD=the password
```

Data Link Files A *data link* file is another method you can use to connect to a database. It stores additional information about the connection, but you must have either a DSN or a connection string ready to use a data link file. Essentially, you create the DSN or connection sting, and then create a blank text file with a name of your choice. In Windows Explorer, rename the file extension to .udl, and then open the file's properties by right-clicking the file. You get several screens, as shown in the following figures, starting with Figure 9-1.

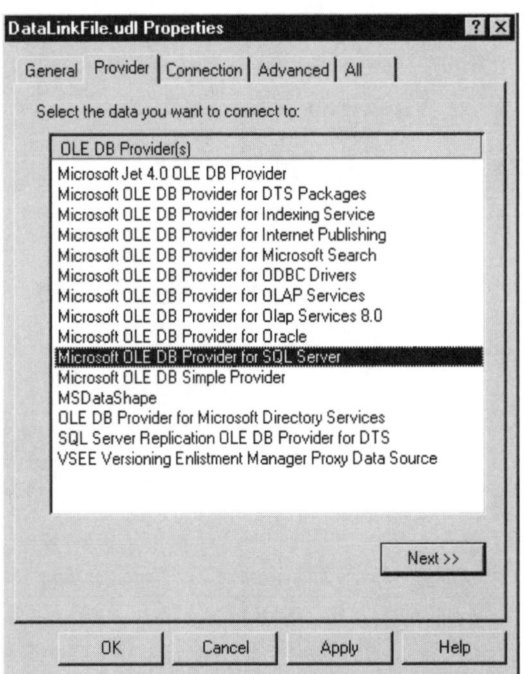

Figure 9-1 The Provider tab of a .udl file properties dialog box

9

The Microsoft OLE DB Provider for SQL Server is chosen here. Click Next to go to the next screen, or click the Connection tab. On the next screen (Figure 9-2), you see you can choose a server by name (in this case we've chosen one of the servers available on this machine). Next, we've chosen to use Windows Integrated Security, and finally, we've chosen the ASPNETDB database in SQL Server. Your screen should resemble Figure 9-2. You can also test the connection by using the Test Connection button.

Go straight to the All tab to see the results of your choices before you close the dialog box, as in Figure 9-3.

If you open the .udl file in Notepad, you can see it is storing the same information as a connection string. To reference it in your ASP scripts or ASP.NET programming, use the following syntax:

```
MyConn.Open("File Name=the path and file name")
```

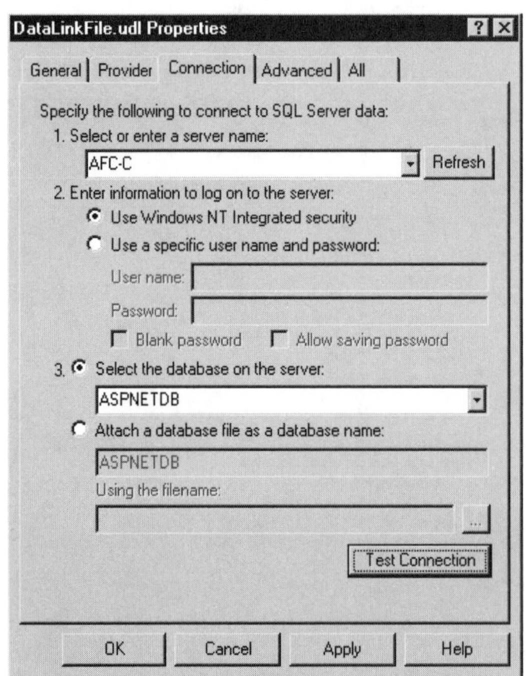

Figure 9-2 The Connection tab of a .udl file properties dialog box

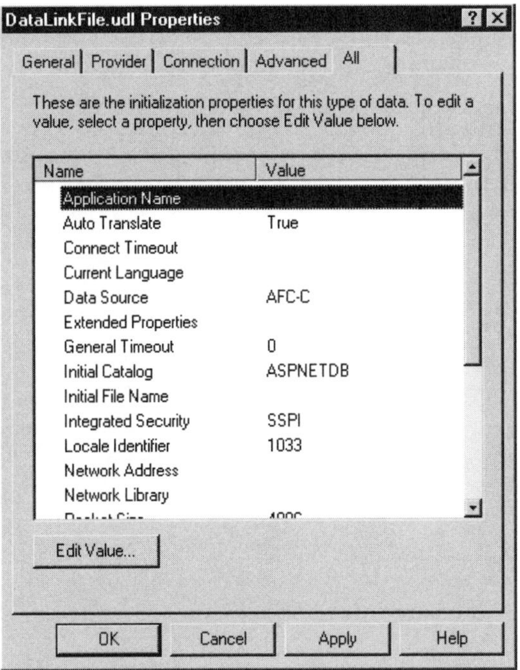

Figure 9-3 The All tab of a .udl file properties dialog box

DSNs To set up a DSN, go to the Administrative Tools section of the Programs menu (from the Start menu) and choose Data Sources (ODBC). This opens the ODBC Data Source Administrator, as shown in Figure 9-4.

Choose System DSN, and then choose Add to add a new one. You get a single additional screen listing the types of drivers available; you should choose the Access driver to go along with the Access database being used. Click Finish, and the wizard will walk you through the choices to finish creating your DSN, as shown in Figure 9-5. Name your new connection whatever you like (we chose ASPNET1), give it a description, choose the server to use, and on the next screen choose the database (we chose ASPNETDB). After you click through the screens you can test the connection.

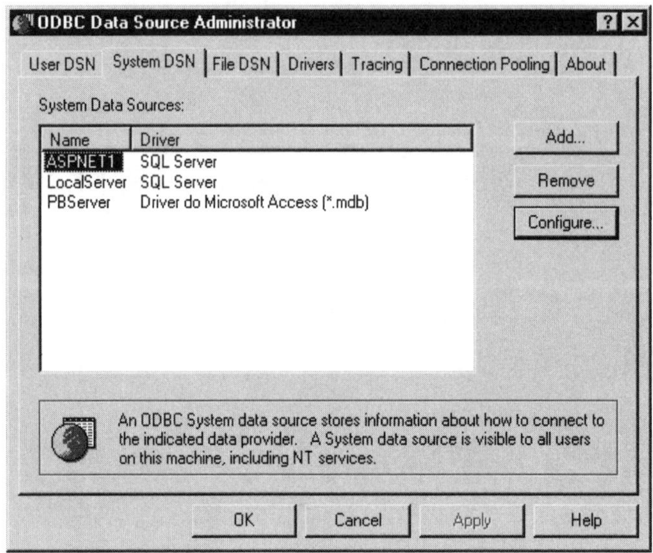

Figure 9-4 The ODBC Data Source Administrator

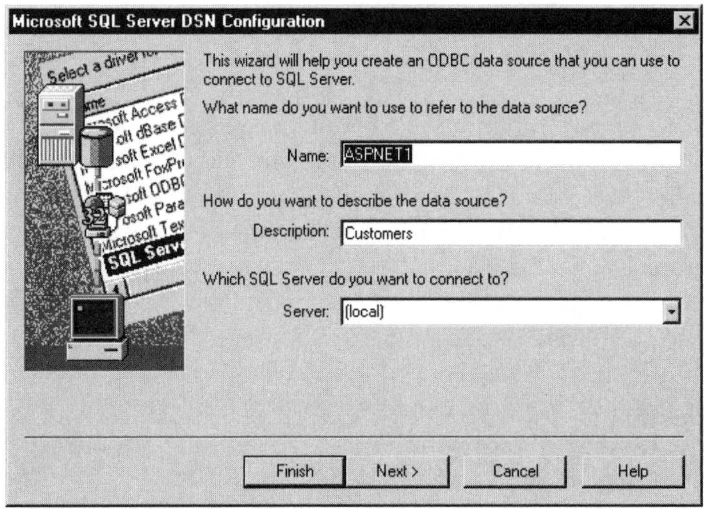

Figure 9-5 The DSN Configuration screen

After setting up a DSN, you can access it from your ASP scripts or ASP.NET programming with the following syntax when opening a connection:

```
MyConn.Open("theDSNname")
```

This follows the typical syntax for the Connection object, which is the name of the object (for this example, the name used is MyConn), the Open method, and either the DSN or the Connection string, followed by the UserID, the Password, and any options you want to set. The simpler syntax with a DSN is used for most of the following examples.

Connection Object Methods

The Connection object is associated with a number of useful properties. Some of them are primarily useful if you intend to manage transactions; others, you use in most of your database operations. In this module, the more common Connection methods are covered and, in Module 10, the transaction-related Connection methods are reviewed. To whet your appetite, transactions enable you to control the execution of changes to a data source so, if part of the changes fail, the entire set of changes is reversed, leaving your data intact—an important consideration in critical operations. In any case, here's a list of them all:

- **Open** This method opens a connection to a data source and accepts arguments such as a ConnectionString, a UserID, and a Password.
- **Execute** This method executes, via the CommandText argument, queries in the form of either SQL statements, stored procedures, or a call to a particular table. It also accepts options, such as the number of records affected and direction for evaluating the CommandText argument.
- **Close** This method closes the Connection object, but does not remove it from memory.
- **OpenSchema** This method enables you to gather schema information from the data provider and accepts arguments such as QueryType, Criteria, and SchemaID.
- **BeginTrans** This method is used to begin a new transaction.

- **CommitTrans** This method saves data changes permanently, in effect, completing the transaction.
- **RollbackTrans** This method cancels data changes made during the current transaction and ends the transaction.

Using Commands with the Connection Object

You probably noticed the Execute method in the previous listing. As with the Command object, you can run commands such as SQL statements, stored procedures, or direct references to database tables with the Connection object, but in a more limited way, just for convenience. You can speed processing of connections that have no requirement to return records by adding the ADO constant adExecuteNoRecords to the Options argument when you Execute your connection.

Connection Properties

The properties associated with the Connection object enable you to examine and configure the connection before and during the connection session. For example, the Provider property returns the name of the provider in use, and the Version property returns the version number of ADO running. Here are the properties of the Connection object:

- **Attributes** This property applies to other objects such as the Parameter object—for the Connection object the Attributes property is read/write. The Attributes property helps with transactions for supporting data providers.
- **CommandTimeout** This property specifies how long to wait while executing a command until ending processing and producing an error.
- **ConnectionString** This property contains the connection data, such as Provider, Data Source, UserID, Password, and so forth.
- **ConnectionTimeout** Similar to the CommandTimeout, this property specifies how long to wait while trying to make a connection before timing out and producing an error.
- **CursorLocation** This property specifies whether the cursor associated with a connection resides on the client or the server.

- **DefaultDatabase** This property specifies the default database for a connection.
- **IsolationLevel** This property specifies the isolation level of a connection and is useful for keeping your transactions straight.
- **Mode** This property tells you what permissions you have for making modifications to data in a connection, for example, read, write, or exclusive.
- **Provider** This property specifies the name of the data provider for a connection.
- **State** This property tells you whether the Connection object is open or closed.
- **Version** This property tells you the ADO version number.

1-Minute Drill

- What three techniques can be used to specify the information required to open a connection?
- What three connection methods actually make connections, and which one makes records available?

Many of the properties and methods previously listed have to do with transaction processing or with managing recordsets you've just made available with the Connection object. These are covered in more detail in Module 10. For now, let's examine the Errors collection, a child of the Connection object within the ADO 2.5 data model.

Advanced Error-Handling Techniques

The Errors collection is contained in the Connection object. This collection consists of an Error object for each error occurring in any given connection to the database via ADO, whether using an explicit Connection object or making an implicit connection with a Command or Recordset object. If an error occurs

---

- A connection string, a .udl file, and a DSN
- The Open, Close, and Execute methods, and the Execute method make records available.

when a connection is made, a command is run, or a recordset is retrieved, any existing errors in the Errors collection are removed and the new one(s) is inserted. If no error occurs, however, any existing errors *will remain in the collection*. The Errors collection always contains the most recent errors.

Handling Errors

Retrieving error values can be done by accessing the Error objects within the Errors collection from the Connection object (MyConn.Errors, for example) or by going through the ActiveConnection property of the Recordset object (myRs.ActiveConnection.Errors, for example). Either way, you find the values you need in each individual Error object. These values include the following properties:

- **Number** The ADO error number
- **HelpContext, HelpFile** The filename or topic associated with an Error object
- **NativeError** The error number assigned by the data provider
- **SQLState** The SQL state code
- **Source** The object from which the error came
- **Description** A description of the error

To retrieve these values, you can use ASP code like the following to iterate through all the errors present:

```
For Each erroritem in MyConn.Errors
    Response.Write "The Error number =
"  & erroritem.Number & "<BR>"
    Response.Write "The Native Error number is =
"  & erroritem.NativeError & "<BR>"
    Response.Write "The SQL state code is =
"  & erroritem.SQLState & "<BR>"
    Response.Write "The Source object of the error is =
"  & erroritem.Source & "<BR>"
    Response.Write "The Description of the error is =
"  & erroritem.Description & "<BR>"
Next
```

Ask the Expert

Question: What's the difference between the Errors collection and Error objects?

Answer: The Errors collection is a child collection of the Connection object, while Error objects represent individual errors that occurred during an ADO operation. They are generated by the data provider and are not cleared out unless a new error occurs.

Question: How are errors generated, and how can they be trapped and worked with?

Answer: When the data provider detects an error, it places an Error object in the Errors collection. Because several errors may occur, several errors may be present in the collection. Examining the Errors collection with the code we presented earlier enables you to determine error values and work with them. ADO can also produce errors, and you can trap them just like any other runtime error.

Project 9-1: Using the Connection Object

Although the Connection object will be used often when datasets are discussed in Module 10, let's do a small project now to make and work with connections with the example SQL Server database. You can see what SQL Server can do for you as the properties of the connections that can be made are examined.

Step-by-Step

You'll start by making a new VS.NET project named DataMakeConnection using the WebApplication template. You'll create a DSN and then use a Web Form in the project to list connection properties.

1. The first step in this project is to create the DSN using the method shown earlier in the chapter. If you've been following along with the book, you

should already have a DSN named ASPNET1 connected to the SQL Server database named ASPNETDB. If not, make one following the instructions in the section titled "DSNs."

2. In the blank Web Form, open the toolbox and drag an OleDbConnection object onto the grid from the Data section of the toolbox. It will appear as a small box at the bottom of the Web Form named OleDbConnection1. Rename it MyConn. Click in its ConnectionString property and choose the first connection in there. That will place an appropriate connection string into the object. At this point, your screen should resemble Figure 9-6.

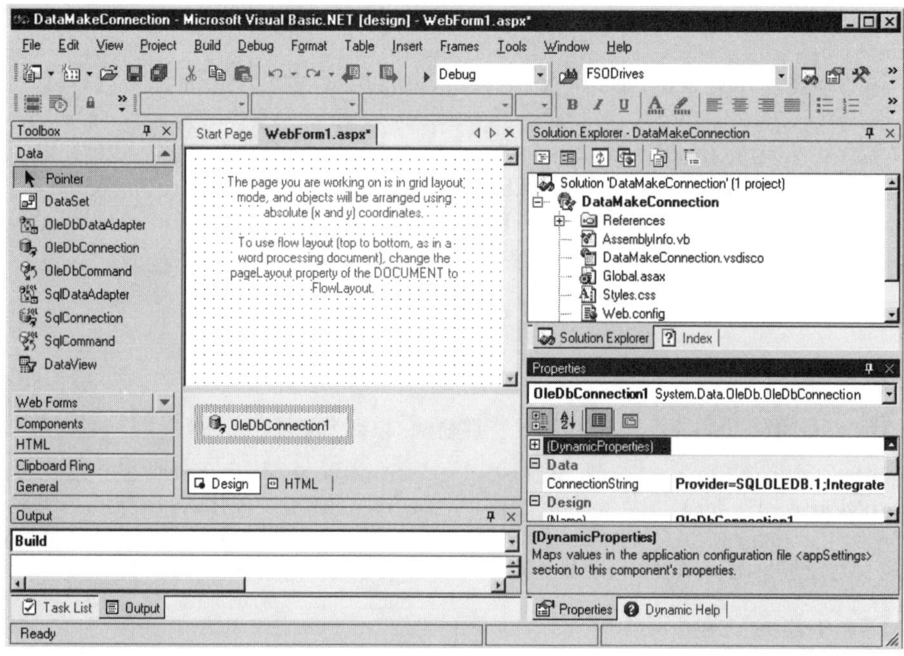

Figure 9-6 The Web Form in Design view

3. Next, add the following code to the code-behind page in the page load event:

```
MyConn.Open()
 Response.Write("The value for Connection String
 is <B>" & MyConn.ConnectionString & "</B><BR>")
 Response.Write("The value for Connection Timeout
 is <B>" & MyConn.ConnectionTimeout & "</B><BR>")
 Response.Write("The value for Database
 is <B>" & MyConn.Database & "</B><BR>")
 Response.Write("The value for DataSource
 is <B>" & MyConn.DataSource & "</B><BR>")
 Response.Write("The value for Provider
 is <B>" & MyConn.Provider & "</B><BR>")
 Response.Write("The value for ServerVersion
 is <B>" & MyConn.ServerVersion & "</B><BR>")
 Response.Write("The value for State
 is <B>" & MyConn.State & "</B><BR>")
MyConn.Close()
```

4. This code will run when the page loads. It opens the Connection object and uses the Response object to write values for connection properties into the form and thus back to the user. The purpose of this code is to demonstrate that the values can be captured and worked with, but in practice it's unlikely you would tell the user any of these properties.

5. The displayed connection properties are shown in Figure 9-7.

The Command Object

The Connection object can open connections and run some commands, but for added flexibility there is a Command object. When using the Command object, you can use the Connection object to open an active connection and the Command object for specialized functions, as you will do in subsequent projects.

The Command object can open connections (implicitly) and has the added advantage of being able to pass parameters to the stored procedures it runs. This gives you the flexibility you need for working with stored procedures, rather than doing all your processing in the scripting code. As previously mentioned, stored procedures usually run much more quickly than scripts.

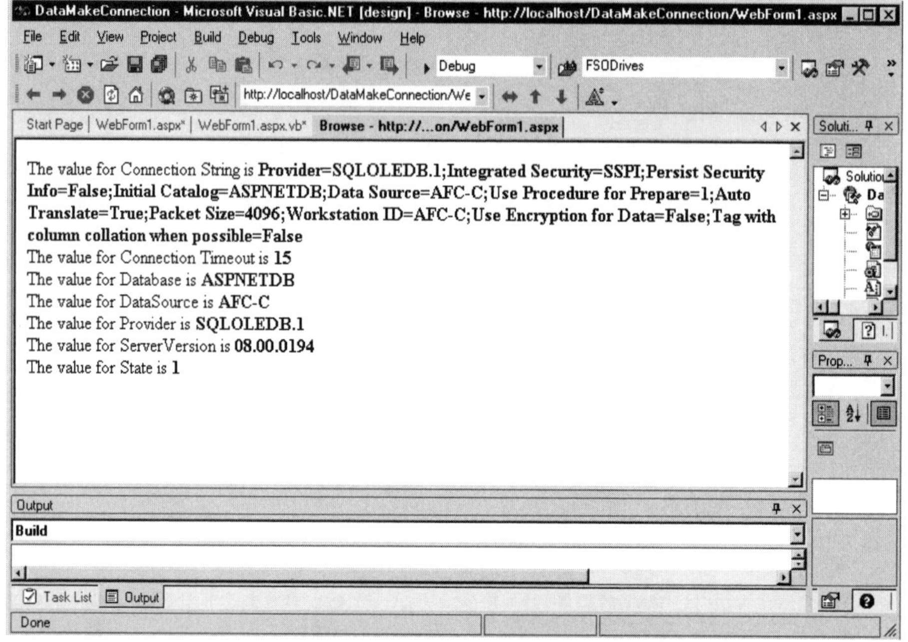

Figure 9-7 The Web Form with connection properties displayed

The Command object can accept several arguments:

- **RecordsAffected** This is a variable specifying how many records are affected by the command.
- **Parameters** This is an array of parameter values. Parameters are discussed in more detail shortly.
- **Options** This value specifies how to process the commands given (as a table, stored procedure, and so forth).

The basic ASP code for opening a connection and running a command is as follows:

```
Set myCmd = Server.CreateObject("ADODB.Command")
myCmd.CommandText = "Products"
Set myRs = myCmd.CommandText
```

Notice that in ASP code you must set the CommandText property to the name of the table you want to open (or the SQL statement, and so forth) to produce the read-only recordset that is the default. You can use the CommandType property to set the type of command you are using. This is a good idea when you know the type because it reduces calls to the provider to determine the CommandType value before completing execution. Insert a line of ASP code like the following (for retrieving a table as a recordset) after the line setting the CommandText argument:

```
MyCmd.CommandType = adCommandTable
```

Another way to set the arguments for the Command object with ASP code is simply to put them right in the line of the Execute method, where the first space represents the RecordsAffected argument, the second space represents the Parameters argument, and the third space represents the Options argument. Your ASP code may look something like the following:

```
Set myCmd = Server.CreateObject("ADODB.Command")
myCmd.CommandText = "Products"
Set myRs = myCmd.Execute(, , adCmdTable)
```

Although Module 10 covers recordsets and datasets in greater detail, some discussion about creating recordsets is necessary here because some of the arguments you can use with the Command object directly affect the functionality you get when your recordset is retrieved. The next two sections discuss cursors and locking and how to use the Command object to set them for a given recordset. Note that when using ADO.NET, you do not receive cursors in the same fashion as when using ADO.

Recordset Cursors

If you open a SQL Server database table with records in it, you see a pointer showing which record you are currently on, similar to what is displayed in Figure 9-8 (you're going to create this table in just a bit). This pointer defines the current record and is handled by what is known as a cursor. The purpose of the *cursor* is to manage navigation through a table via the pointer. A cursor is also essential for navigating through a recordset. In ADO, without the cursor you could neither tell what record you are working with nor get to other records.

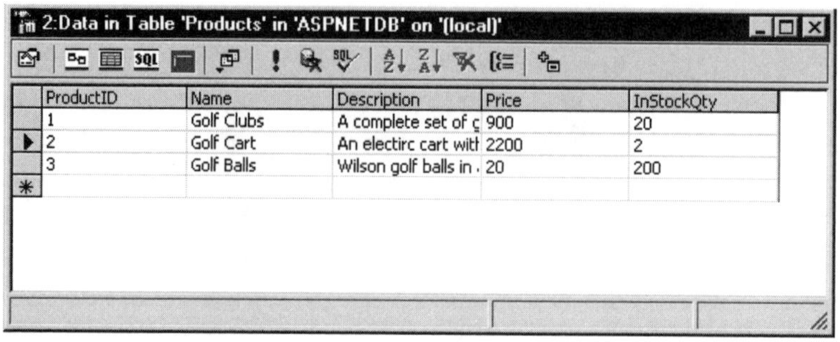

2:Data in Table 'Products' in 'ASPNETDB' on '(local)'

ProductID	Name	Description	Price	InStockQty
1	Golf Clubs	A complete set of c	900	20
2	Golf Cart	An electirc cart witl	2200	2
3	Golf Balls	Wilson golf balls in .	20	200

Figure 9-8 The Products table with the cursor on record 2

Cursor Types

When you retrieve a recordset, several types of cursors can be used with it. You must specify the type of cursor you want to use with the recordset, or the recordset will be assigned the default cursor. The cursor types are

- **Forward Only** This is the default cursor type, which enables you to move only forward through the recordset. The ADO Constant for this cursor type is adOpenForwardOnly.
- **Static** This cursor type enables movement forward and backward through the recordset, but it does not reflect any changes made by other users. The ADO Constant for this cursor type is adOpenStatic.
- **Dynamic** This cursor type enables movement in both directions and reflects changes made by other users. The ADO Constant for this cursor type is adOpenDynamic.
- **Keyset** This cursor type enables movement in both directions and reflects changes made by other users, except added records are not visible and deleted records remain in the set. The ADO Constant for this cursor type is adOpenKeyset.

Note

Cursors are not used with the ADO.NET data model. ADO.NET assumes that you will be retrieving a dataset or DataReader in most cases, and these behave in a manner similar to recordsets with cursors but are more efficient.

Coding the Cursor Type To set the cursor type of a recordset when using a Command object, you need to use the Open method for the recordset. There are several arguments for the Open method of the Recordset object, including the Source (myCmd, in the following example) and the Cursor Type (adOpenDynamic, in the following example). The code for setting the cursor type could be something similar to:

```
myRs.Open = myCmd, , adOpenDynamic
```

Recordset Locking

Like any data being used by more than one person at a time, some mechanism must exist to prevent records from being overwritten by someone else at the same time. ADO has several constants available that enable the developer to specify a lock type when retrieving a recordset. The lock types you can choose from are

- **Read Only** This lock type enables you to read records but not to change them. It is the default type and places the lightest load on the server because no special processing is required. The ADO Constant for this lock type is adLockReadOnly.
- **Pessimistic** This lock type locks the record you are changing as soon as you begin to edit it. This is the best type to ensure data integrity because no other users can work with that record once you start to change it, but this restriction also makes less records available to other users during that time. The ADO Constant for this is adLockPessimistic.
- **Optimistic** This lock type doesn't lock the record until the change is committed. Other users can still see the record and make changes to it

until it is committed. The ADO Constant for this lock type is adLockOptimistic.

- **Batch Optimistic** This lock type enables you to change more than one record in a batch. Lock types are only locked when they are committed.

Coding the Lock Type To set the lock type of a recordset when using the Command object, the Open method for the recordset is used again. Using the previous example from the Cursor Type section, the code for setting the cursor type could be something similar to:

```
myRs.Open = myCmd, , adOpenDynamic, adLockOptimistic
```

1-Minute Drill

- What default cursor type do you get when you connect to a database using ADO?
- What cursor type is the most flexible?

Stored Procedures

As discussed earlier, stored procedures are quite useful for performing interactions with your databases because they are compiled and run from within the database, and they are almost always much faster. In this section, a few stored procedures are built, first as ordinary update queries, and then with the capability to pass parameters back and forth.

Stored Procedures with SQL Server

Before you create a stored procedure in SQL Server, you need to make a new table to contain the data you'll work with. Since the ASPNETDB database could be an e-commerce database, you'll create a table named Products to hold all the products your site sells. You'll create the table and our first stored procedure as Project 9-2.

- A Forward-only cursor
- The Dynamic cursor

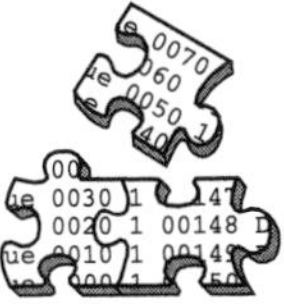

Project 9-2: Creating a Stored Procedure

In SQL Server, stored procedures are actually stored as code written in Transaction-SQL, a SQL-like programming language with some additional features to make it easier to work with and more capable. Before you create the new procedure, you'll need to create a table named Products.

Step-by-Step

To get started, open the SQL Server Enterprise Manager and find the ASPNETDB database. Click the plus sign (+) next to the ASPNETDB node to see all the objects in the database.

1. Right-click the Tables node in the ASPNETDB and choose New Table to begin creating a new table named Products. Enter the field names ProductID, Name, Description, Price, and InStockQty, and use the data types shown in Figure 9-9. Make sure to make the ProductID field an Identity field, so that it will increment itself by one each time a new record is added.

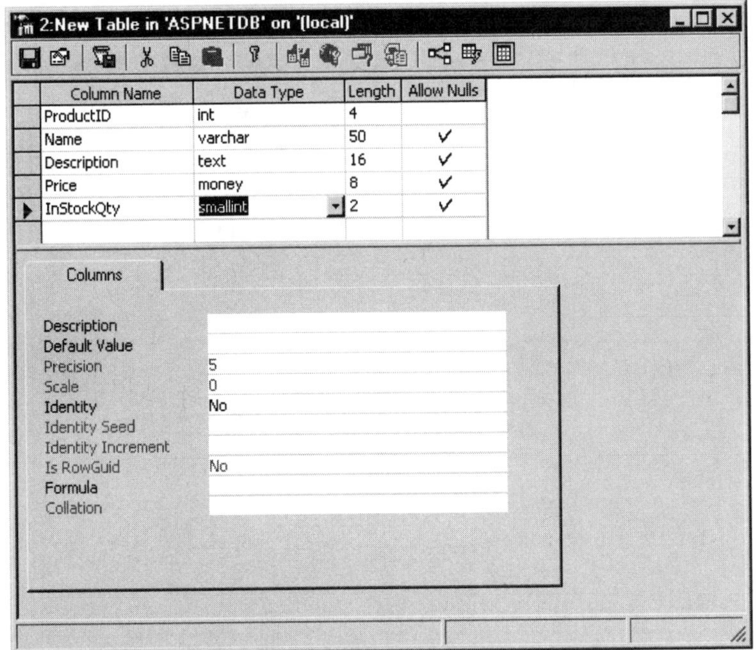

Figure 9-9 The Products table under construction

2. When you're finished with the table, save it as Products. Next, right-click the table itself (in the Enterprise Manager) and choose Open from the shortcut menu. Open the table with all rows showing, and enter three records. Use any names, prices, and in stock quantities you like. This gives your table some records to update when you run the stored procedure.
3. Now you can create a stored procedure in SQL Server by building a SQL statement that performs an action, such as updating records. Our stored procedure will update prices in the Products table by 10 percent.
4. One way to create a stored procedure in SQL Server is to right-click the Stored Procedures node (inside the appropriate database, of course) and choose New Stored Procedure. In this dialog box, you can then enter the code for the stored procedure of your choice.
5. An easier way to make a stored procedure is to click the Tools menu, then choose Wizards. When the Select Wizard dialog box opens, go into the Database node and select Create Stored Procedure Wizard. You'll get a screen that resembles Figure 9-10.

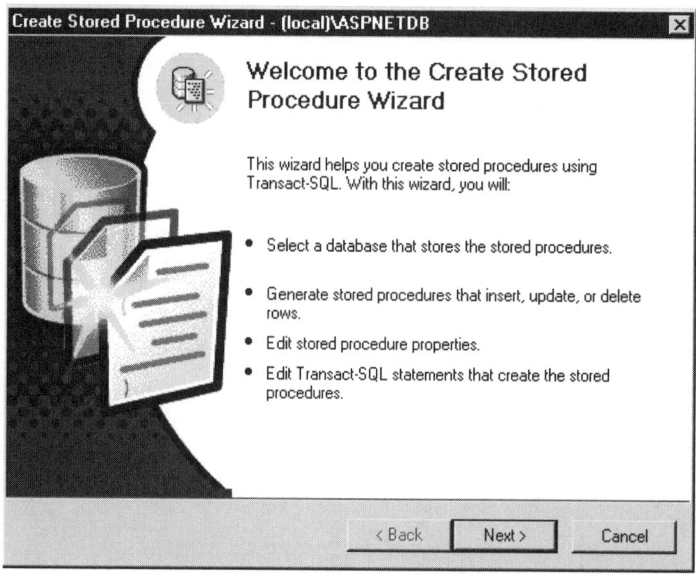

Figure 9-10 The Create Stored Procedure Wizard

6. Click to the second screen and you'll see the choice of database shown in Figure 9-11. Click past to the third screen, and click the Update check box to update rows in the Products table (Figure 9-12).

7. Click Next. Click the Edit SQL button and then change the name of the procedure to UpdateProductPrices. Also, remove all but the Price field from the stored procedure, as you only want to update Prices (as shown in Figure 9-13). To get the procedure to modify prices (you're going to increase prices 10 percent when this procedure runs), rewrite the SQL as shown in this code and in Figure 9-14 (click Edit SQL to get to a screen where you can change the SQL):

```
CREATE PROCEDURE [UpdateProductPrices]
AS UPDATE [ASPNETDB].[dbo].[Products]
SET [Price] = [Price]*1.1
GO
```

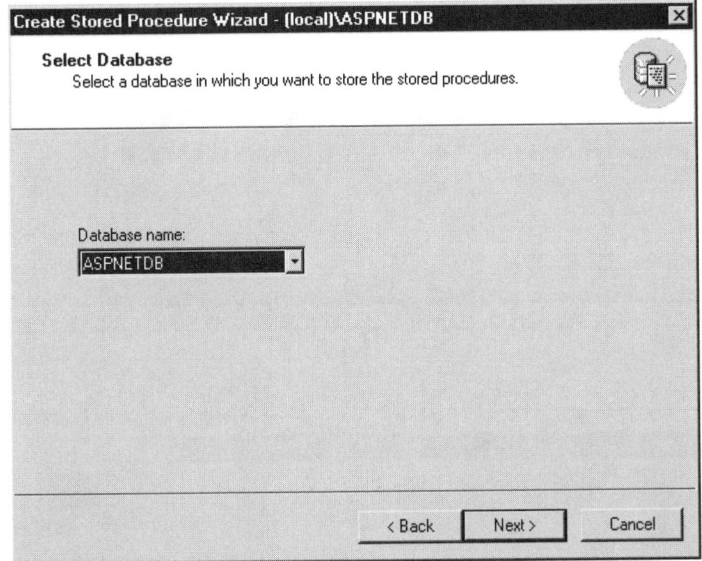

Figure 9-11 Choosing the database in the Create Stored Procedures Wizard

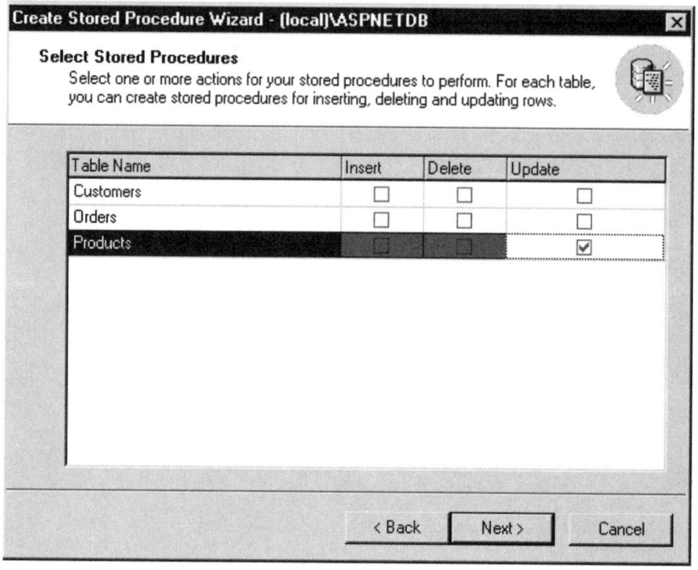

Figure 9-12 Setting the procedure to update rows in the Products table

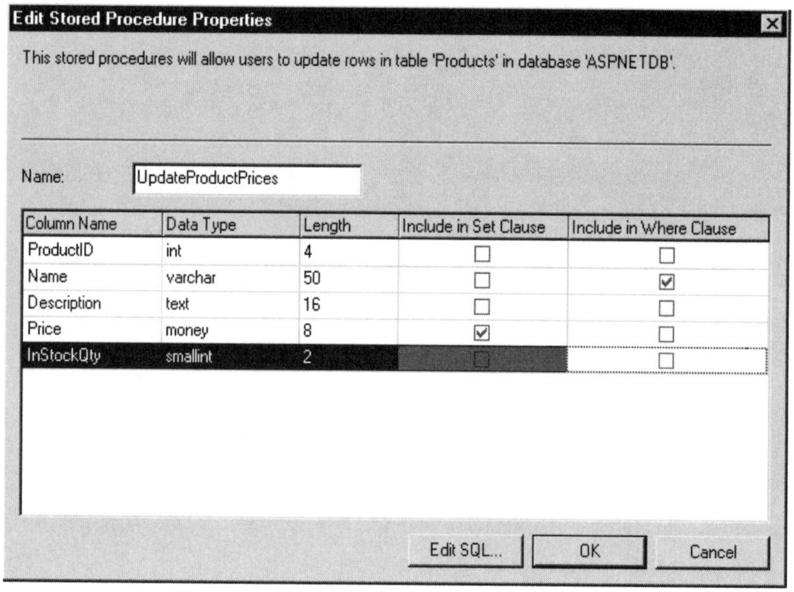

Figure 9-13 Changing the fields that are updated

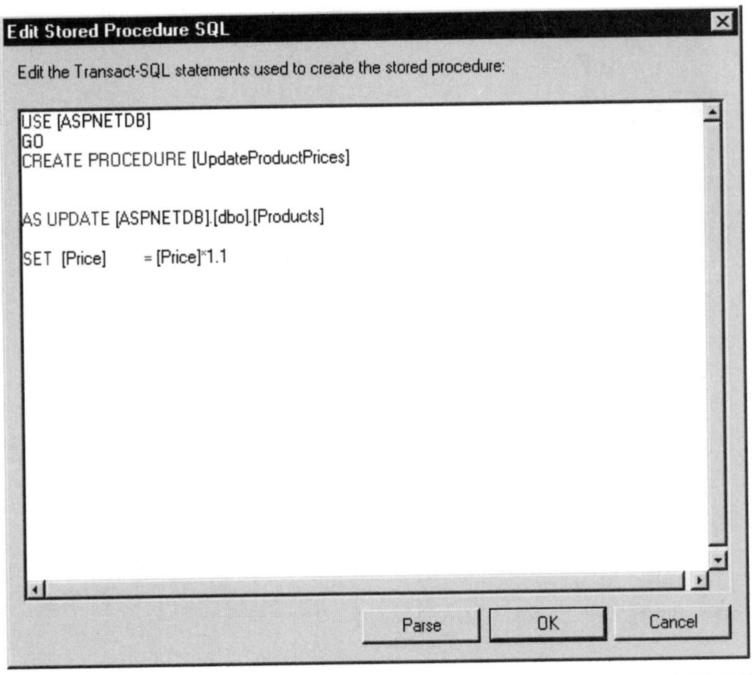
Edit Stored Procedure SQL
Edit the Transact-SQL statements used to create the stored procedure:
USE [ASPNETDB]
GO
CREATE PROCEDURE [UpdateProductPrices]
AS UPDATE [ASPNETDB].[dbo].[Products]
SET [Price] = [Price]*1.1
Parse
OK
Cancel

Figure 9-14 Modifying the SQL Code

Then click Finish (as shown in Figure 9-15), and the stored procedure will be created.

8. Now that you've got your new table and stored procedure set up in SQL Server, you can build an application that activates the stored procedure. To begin the process, in VS.NET, create a new project using the WebApplication template and name it DataStoredProcedures.

9. On the blank Web Form, add a label and a button from the Web Forms controls Toolbox. Name the label ResponseLabel and set its Text property to Update Prices 10%.

10. Add an OleDbConnection object and an OleDbCommand object to the Web Form. Name them MyConn and MyComm, respectively. Set the connection string property of MyConn to the SQL Server database connection, and set the Connection property of MyComm to MyConn. Set the CommandText property of MyComm to UpdateProductPrices and the CommandType property to StoredProcedure.

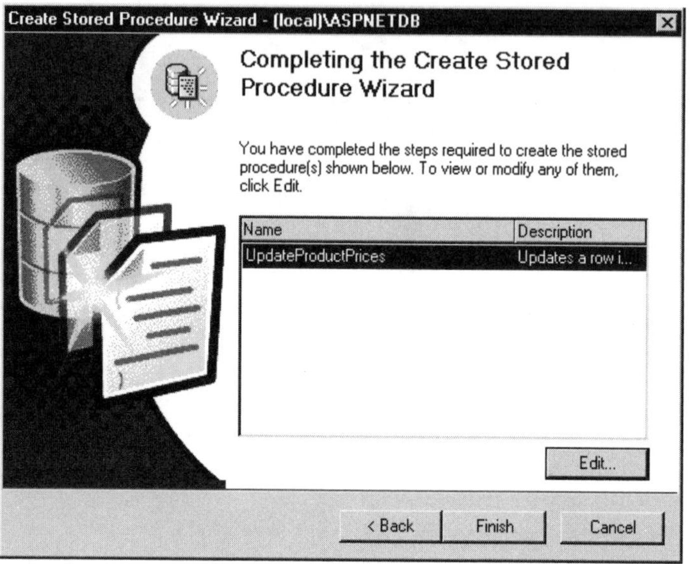

Figure 9-15 The final screen of the wizard

11. Set the Text property for the button to Update and double-click it to go into an event handler for the Click event of the button in the code-behind page. In the code-behind page enter the following code:

```
MyConn.Open()
MyComm.ExecuteNonQuery()
MyConn.Close()
ResponseLabel.Text = "Prices Updated"
```

12. To run the UpdateProductPrices stored procedure, choose Browse and Build from the File menu, and then click the button on the form. Each time you do so, prices in the Products table will be increased by 10 percent. You can check prices directly in SQL Server by opening the Enterprise Manager and opening the Products table.

Stored Procedures with Parameters

Parameters are like variables. They can be used to store values that can then be inserted into or returned from queries and used with any calculations or functions you wish. For example, you can make a Web Form that receives a value from a user (entered into a text box, most likely) and turn this value into a parameter that is inserted into a query back on the server. The query can then be run with the parameter. Once a result is returned, it can then be fed back to the user.

By using the capability of SQL Server or other DBMSs to accept and return parameters with their stored procedures, you can dramatically increase the usefulness of stored procedures running from your scripts. Following the same process you used previously, you can create stored procedures in SQL Server that use parameters.

The Parameters Collection

The *Parameters collection* is a collection of the Command object and contains a Parameter object whenever you use the Append method to add one to the collection (one for each parameter you want to pass to the stored procedure). To create Parameter objects, you need to give them a name, a data type, a direction, and, perhaps, a size and a value. While you can create the parameters and their values directly in your scripting code, usually you leave off the value and allow the user to pass the value in by a variable from a form. When you create Parameter objects with ASP.NET, you can simply use the tools in VS.NET to create them and set their properties.

Creating Parameter Objects with ASP

You can use code like the following to create Parameter objects:

```
Set myParam = myComm.CreateParameter
("UpdatePercentage", adSingle, adParamInput)
myComm.Parameters.Append myParam
```

Make up a variable name, such as myParam, and use the Set command to set it equal to the contents of a CreateParameter method. Inside the CreateParameter method, the first thing you find is the name of the Parameter you're creating.

Hint

You can use whatever name you like for the Parameter object, but remembering what you're working with is easier if you use the same name as the parameter you created inside the stored procedure in SQL Server.

The next thing you find is the ADO Constant for the data type. Look in the DataTypeEnum section of your adovbs.inc file to find the allowable data types. In this case, use the Single data type because you want to specify the percentage by which to increase prices of the products.

The last attribute set in the CreateParameter method is the type of Parameter it is, namely, an Input parameter. Parameters can be

- **adParamInput** Meaning they pass values to the stored procedure.
- **adParamOutput** Meaning they accept values being passed from the stored procedure.
- **adParamInputOutput** Meaning they can do either of the previous.
- **adParamReturnValue** Meaning they hold the return status of the stored procedure.

You could also set the size of the parameter, but you needn't do this because the size is fixed by the data type Single at 4. If you were using a text data type, you might want to set the size. And you could set the value but, because you're going to retrieve the value from the user, there's no need to do that either.

Using Parameters with ASP.NET and ADO.NET

VS.NET has built-in properties and collections that make it easier to work with parameters in stored procedures in SQL Server. In your next project, you'll create another stored procedure with parameters, and then connect to those parameters in a web application.

Project 9-3: Creating a Stored Procedure with Parameters

In SQL Server, the default stored procedure created with the wizard has parameters in it. They follow the naming guidelines for SQL Server and are preceded with the @ sign. The wizard makes it easy to create a stored procedure with parameters, but you still need to do some thinking. If you want the user to be able to enter a value to search by, you'll need to leave checked in the Where clause the field they will be searching by. If you want the user to be able to set the value of a field, you'll need to leave that field checked in the Set clause. This will all be a little clearer as you go through the process in this project.

Step-by-Step

To get started, open the SQL Server Enterprise Manager and find the ASPNETDB database. Click the plus (+) sign next to the ASPNETDB node to see all the objects in the database. The Products table is already built and populated, so you can start making your stored procedure immediately. It would be a good idea now to open the Products table and examine the values for Prices, so later when you're checking to see whether prices have been updated you'll remember what the current values are.

1. Use the same procedure you used in Project 9-2 (going to the Tools menu and so forth) to create a new stored procedure named UpdateProducts. Leave ProductID as the Where criteria, and leave the Price and InStockQty fields as the Set clauses, as shown in the following code:

```
CREATE PROCEDURE [UpdateProducts]
(@ProductID_1      [int],
@Price_2 [money],
@InStockQty_3 [smallint])
AS UPDATE [ASPNETDB].[dbo].[Products]
SET [Price] = @Price_2,
[InStockQty] = @InStockQty_3
WHERE
([ProductID] = @ProductID_1)
GO
```

2. Notice the three parameters that were automatically created in SQL Server by leaving the three fields as Where and Set clauses. These fields will have parameters associated with them in your web application.

3. Now that the stored procedure is ready in SQL Server, you can create a web application to activate it, this time giving the user the capability to insert their own update values. To start the process, create a new project in VS.NET based on the web application template and name it DataUseParameters.

4. To the blank Web Form, add OleDbConnection and OleDbCommand objects, name them MyConn and MyComm respectively, and make the connections and set the properties the same as in Project 9-2. What you're

9

going to do differently this time is create parameters for the Parameters collection of the MyComm object and use them to send values to your stored procedure in SQL Server. Then, you're going to place controls on the Web Form to accept values from the user and run the stored procedure based on those values.

5. Notice in the code for the UpdateProducts stored procedure you have created parameters in SQL Server named ProductID_1, Price_2 and InStockQty_3. You must pass to the stored procedure a value to go into the ProductID parameter so the query will know which record to change, and you must pass into the stored procedure values for Price and InStockQty so the query will know what value to set these fields to. To handle these values in your programming, create parameters for the Parameters collection in your VS.NET web application.

6. Click the MyComm object to select it, and then click in the Parameters property of the MyComm object. Click the ellipsis button to open the OleDbParameter Collection Editor dialog box (as shown in Figure 9-16).

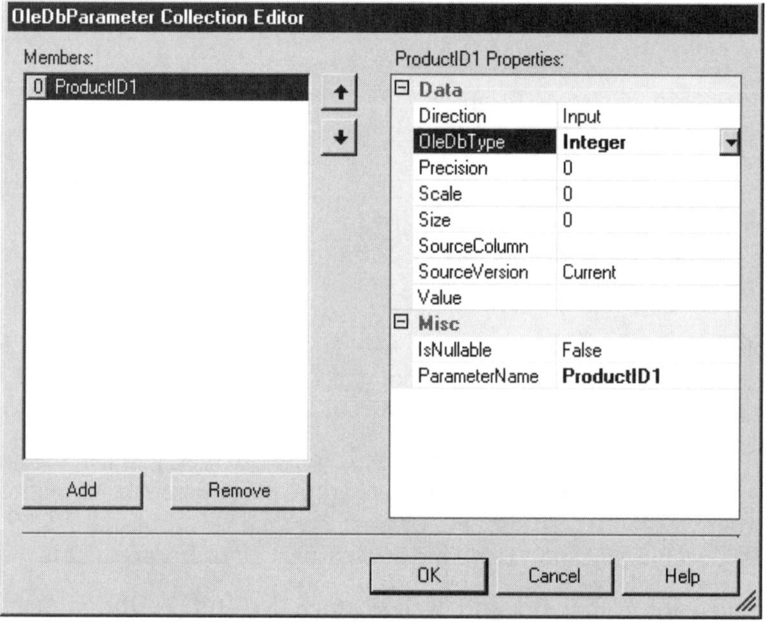

Figure 9-16 The OleDbParameter Collection Editor dialog box.

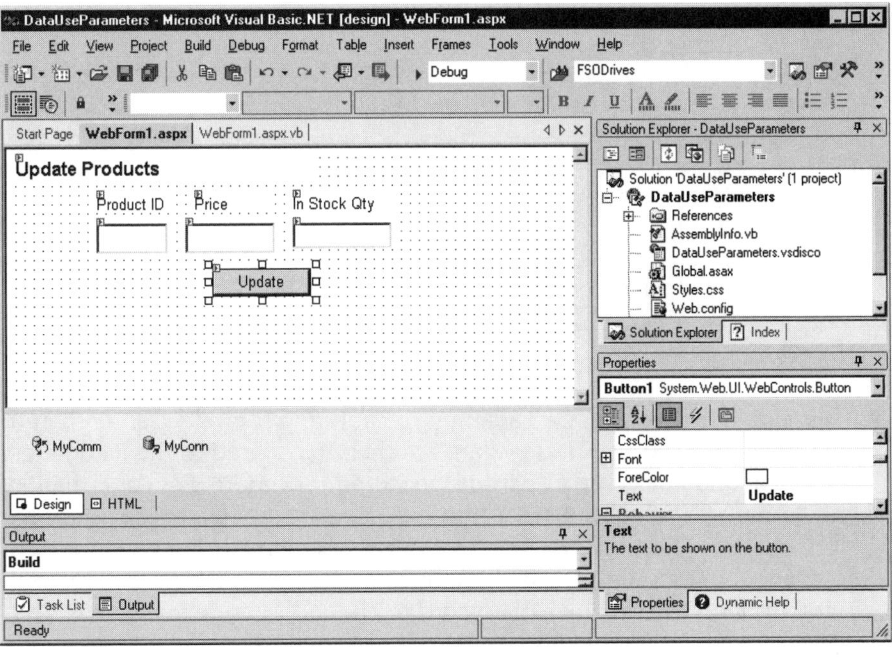

Figure 9-17 The Web Form under construction

7. Create parameters as follows:

Name	**Data Type**
ProductID1	Integer
Price2	Currency
InStockQty3	SmallInt

8. On the Web Form, place a label, three text boxes, and a button from the Web Forms menu. Name the label ResponseLabel and change its Text property to read Update Products. Name the text boxes ProductID, Price, and InStockQty. Change the Text property of the button to read Update. Arrange these objects as shown in Figure 9-17.

Double-click the button to open an event handler in the code-behind page. Place the following code in the event handler:

```
Dim vProductID1 As Integer
Dim vPrice2 As Decimal
```

```
Dim vInStockQty3 As Integer

vProductID1 = ProductID.Text
vPrice2 = Price.Text
vInStockQty3 = InStockQty.Text
MyConn.Open()
MyComm.Parameters("ProductID1").Value = vProductID1
MyComm.Parameters("Price2").Value = vPrice2
MyComm.Parameters("InStockQty3").Value = vInStockQty3
MyComm.ExecuteNonQuery()
MyConn.Close()
ResponseLabel.Text = "Products Updated"
```

9. This code dimensions a few variables for capturing the values entered in the text boxes by the user. These values are then transferred to the Parameters collection and finally run as part of the stored procedure. For confirmation, the ResponseLabel tells the user that the values in the database have been updated. Note that this will only work if the user already knows what record to change. In Module 10, we'll examine how to retrieve individual records, scroll through them to pick the record to change, change the record, and then show the user what updates have been done.

Ask the Expert

Question: Stored procedures seem to be the way to go. Instead of writing all my code in ASP to get processing done, I can simply call a query I've made in the database and run that. Besides running faster, what other advantages are there?

Answer: When a database runs a query, it relies on an execution plan to perform the query. *Execution plans* are required because there are often many ways to get the query action accomplished, and some are more efficient than others. The DBMS has a query optimization mechanism in it, and this mechanism attempts to apply the most efficient execution plan to any given query. It then compiles the execution plan ahead of time.

Another advantage is your SQL code is kept inside the database and may, therefore, be more secure, and it certainly keeps your ASP code easier to maintain. If you've ever used a long set of SQL statements to process a query from ASP, you know what we mean.

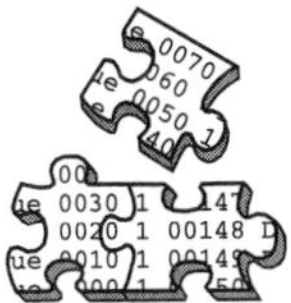

Project 9-4: Using the Command Object

We've shown how to use ASP.NET, ADO.NET, VS.NET, and SQL Server to create and run stored procedures using parameters, and now we'll do essentially the same thing with ASP and ADO. We'll put together an HTML form and ASP script to enable running commands with stored procedures and parameters. The format to use is similar to the one used for the Connection object, but some of the coding is specific to the Command object.

Step-by-Step

To create the components of this project, you'll build the form and then add the code to run the stored procedures with parameters. Use the existing ASPNETDB database and the UpdateProducts and UpdateProductPrices procedures you created.

1. Enter the following code in a blank HTML page (you can use any HTML editor you like, such as Dreamweaver). Name the resulting file ADOCommands.asp.

```
<%
Option Explicit
Dim myComm
Dim vParameter
Dim myParam
%>
<!-- #include file="adovbs.inc" -->
<%
%>
<html><head><title>Running Commands against
 a Database with ADO</title>
<meta http-equiv="Content-Type"
 content="text/html; charset=iso-8859-1">
</head>
<body bgcolor="#77FF77">
<H2><font size="6">Running ADO Commands</font></H2>
<TABLE border=1>
<TR><TD>
</TD></TR><TR><TD bgcolor="white">
<%
vParameter = Request.Form.GetValue("Parameter")
Set myComm = Server.CreateObject("ADODB.Command")
myComm.ActiveConnection = "ASPNET1"
myComm.CommandText = "UpdateProducts"
myComm.CommandType = adCmdStoredProc
Set myParam = myComm.CreateParameter
("UpdatePercentage", adSingle, adParamInput)
```

9

```
myComm.Parameters.Append myParam
myComm.Parameters("UpdatePercentage") = vParameter
myComm.Execute , , adExecuteNoRecords
Set myComm = Nothing
%>
</TD></TR></TABLE>
<P>
<TABLE border=1 width="50%">
<TR>
<TD bgcolor="#00CC99" COLSPAN=3>
<H3><font size="6">Values</font></H3>
</TD>
</TR>
<TR>
<TD colspan="3">
<form method=POST action="ADOCommands.asp">
<table width="50%" border="1">
<tr>
<td><b>Enter your Parameter for the Price Update</b>
<input type="submit" name="btnval" value="Parameter">
</td>
</tr>
<tr>
<td> <b>Price Update Percentage: </b>
<input type="text" name="Parameter" size="20">
</td>
</tr>
</table>
</form>
</TD>
</TR>
</TABLE>
</BODY></HTML>
```

2. In SQL Server, open the UpdateProductPrices stored procedure and modify the code so that a parameter is created named @UpdatePercentage. This parameter will be used as the update percentage multiplier, rather than the hard-coded value 1.1. Once you have inserted the code to make the new parameter in the stored procedure, change the line that contains the hard-coded value so that instead of multiplying by 1.1 the field value is multiplied by @UpdatePercentage.

3. Open the file in your browser, and you should be able to set the appropriate values and use them to modify the database via the stored procedures you've already created.

Mastery Check

1. What can you do to optimize your database interactions?

A. Limit user searches.

B. Compact your database every time it is accessed.

C. Close connections, use stored procedures, and use only required data.

D. None of the above.

2. What is the SQL command for specifying a parameter in Access?

A. PARAMETERS [parametername] data type

B. INSERT PARAMETER

C. CREATE VARIABLE

D. None of the above

3. What does the Direction attribute mean for Parameter objects?

A. Whether or not the numeric value is positive or negative

B. Whether the returned sort order is ascending or descending

C. Whether or not data is going to or coming from the stored procedure

D. None of the above

4. What lock type is the default?

A. Lock All

B. Optimistic

C. Read-Only

D. Batch Optimistic

5. You can establish a connection to a database provided you have the right information, such as a driver, database name, and so forth. This information can be used directly in your program as a ________________, or it can be stored in a _______ or in a ______ file.

Mastery Check

6. Describe stored procedures and why they are often better to use than the same procedures written into your application.

____

____

7. What property of the Connection object may contain information such as UserID and Password?

A. The ConnectionString property

B. The AuthorizedBy property

C. The Command property

D. Any of the above

E. None of the above

8. What properties of the Connection object open and close the connection, and what property tells you whether the connection is open or closed?

A. ConnOpen, ConnClose, and ConnStatus

B. Open, Close, and Status

C. Open, Close, and State

D. None of the above

E. All of the above

9. What is a cursor, and what difference does it make what type of cursor you get with a recordset?

A. A cursor is a special data type that allows nonlinear operations on records in a recordset. There are a multitude of cursor types, each representing a particular database operation.

B. A cursor is a mechanism for navigating through records in a recordset. Some cursors are more flexible than others, allowing more operations but requiring more processing power and memory to perform their functions.

Mastery Check

C. A cursor is a mouse pointer that moves as you move the mouse in a word-processing document and has nothing to do with databases.

D. None of the above.

10. When setting up a Command object, the records retrieved depend on what is entered in the _______ property, which may be the name of a _______ or a _____ statement.

11. Describe how parameters work, in what object they may be set and found, and why they are useful.

____

____

12. What is the relationship between the Errors collection and the Error object? When errors are generated where do they go?

A. The Errors collection and the Error object are identical; they are just addressed differently in different situations. Errors all go into the general Error module.

B. The Errors collection applies to recordsets having multiple records, while the Error object applies to a single Connection object. Errors go into the Errors collection.

C. The Errors collection is a collection of Error objects that is attached to the Command object. Errors become individual Error objects in the Errors collection.

D. None of the above.

13. When using ADO, why would you include the adovbs.inc file in your program?

A. This file contains settings that equate ADO constant names with particular ADO values. Using the constant names is easier to correctly remember (and to debug) than using the actual constant values themselves.

Mastery Check

B. No database access can take place without including this file.

C. Including this file is not necessary, but is a common coding practice for compatibility.

D. None of the above.

14. What features does a Dynamic cursor have?

____

____

15. In a stored procedure in SQL Server, the _______ symbol is used to signify the beginning of a parameter name.

Module 10

The ADO/ADO.NET Recordset and DataSet-Related Objects

The Goals of This Module

- Retrieve records with DataSet-related and Recordset objects
- Learn about the DataAdapter object
- Learn about the DataSet and Recordset objects
- Learn about the DataReader object
- Work with the DataGrid control
- Navigate records in a DataSet and Recordset
- Filter records in a DataSet and Recordset
- Modify records in a DataSet and Recordset

It's pretty easy to use SQL queries to pull sets of records from a table using the DataSet and DataAdapter objects, a DataReader object, or, for ASP and ADO, a Recordset object. Just think of Recordsets as tables in a kind of spreadsheet view. The DataSet and DataAdapter objects represent a kind of enhanced Recordset.

Depending upon the cursor you set in your ASP code, when using ASP and ADO, you can navigate through Recordsets, edit, update, add new records or delete records, even filter, sort, and sum them, all with the methods available to the Recordset object. And in ADO 2.5, there are a few new objects: the Record object and the Stream object.

In this module, we'll focus on all the things you can actually do to data in common databases once you've established a connection (and perhaps added a Command object as well). For ASP and ADO, the main tool is the Recordset object, while for ASPS.NET and ADO.NET, the Recordset's functionality has been divided among several objects, including the DataSet, DataAdapter, and DataReader objects. There are quite a few other new Data objects as well, and we'll discuss their capabilities throughout this module following our discussion of the Recordset object.

The Recordset Object

If you've ever built a spreadsheet, you are intimately familiar with the columns and rows format for data. In fact, before computers came along, accountants were very busy adding up columns of figures and working out by hand various results based on columns and rows. It's not surprising that a computerized method for doing the same thing was developed long ago.

The Recordset object is just another iteration in a long line of information-processing formats people seem to work with easily. Each column represents a field, and each row contains values related to a single instance of the entity type being tracked in the record. The Recordset object includes methods for moving from one record to the next (either to a particular record number, or to the next, previous, first, or last record). The fields in a recordset are represented by the Fields collection, and you can work with the values in a field in a particular record with the following syntax:

```
vMyVariable = MyRecordset.Fields("fieldname")
```

To recap, you use the Connection and/or Command objects to make the connection to a data source (such as a table in a database) and, perhaps, set some parameters for retrieving the records with a particular cursor type. You use SQL statements or even calls to entire tables to specify the records retrieved (or commands to run against those data sources when no recordset is retrieved). Once you have created a Recordset, you can use the Recordset object and its methods to manipulate the records for your own purposes. In addition to being able to navigate through records, you can edit and update them and add new records or delete them.

Recordset Methods and Properties

Like the other objects we've encountered, the Recordset object supports a variety of methods and properties. The Recordset methods give you many of the same capabilities you have when there is a database table open in front of you, such as enabling you to move around the records, add, edit, and delete them, and so on. Once you get used to these methods, working with records in Recordsets will become second nature.

Recordset Methods

Here are the supported methods:

- **Open** Opens a Recordset and has optional arguments that can set the cursor type and so forth.
- **Close** Closes a Recordset.
- **AddNew** Enables you to place a new record in a Recordset and specify the values to be entered in each field.
- **Move** Moves the cursor forward or backward a specified number of records through the Recordset a specified number of records.
- **MoveFirst** Moves the cursor to the first record in a Recordset.
- **MoveLast** Moves the cursor to the last record in a Recordset.
- **MoveNext** Moves the cursor to the next record in a Recordset.
- **MovePrevious** Moves the cursor to the previous record in a Recordset.

- **Delete** Deletes the specified record from the Recordset.
- **Update** Saves changes you've made to the current record in a Recordset.
- **UpdateBatch** Updates the records affected (specified by an ADO constant for current, filtered, or all records) for changes you've made to these records.
- **NextRecordset** Returns the next Recordset when you've placed commands returning more than one Recordset in your command or stored procedure.
- **Requery** Updates the data in your Recordset, based on reexecuting the original query statement.
- **Resync** Refreshes the data in the Recordset object from the underlying database.
- **Clone** Creates a duplicate of the current Recordset object.
- **GetRows** Puts records from a Recordset into an array.
- **Supports** Returns a value indicating what functions the data provider supports.
- **CancelUpdate** Cancels changes you've made to records, as long as you use it before the final Update method call.
- **CancelBatch** Cancels batch updates to records in a Recordset.

Recordset Properties

The properties available with a Recordset tell you quite a bit about where you are in a Recordset, the size and composition of the Recordset, and such things as the source and status of a Recordset. Here are the supported properties:

- **BOF** Indicates that the record pointer for the cursor is located at the beginning of the Recordset, before the first record.
- **EOF** Indicates that the record pointer for the cursor is located at the end of the Recordset, after the last record.
- **RecordCount** Indicates the number of records in the current Recordset.

- **MaxRecords** Used to set the number of records to return with a Recordset.
- **PageSize** Sets or returns the number of records that make up a page of records for the current Recordset.
- **PageCount** Indicates the number of pages of records in the current Recordset, based on the PageSize setting.
- **Bookmark** Returns or sets a bookmark, which uniquely identifies a specific record in the current Recordset.
- **AbsolutePosition** Specifies the ordinal or numeric position of a record within the current Recordset, or returns an ADO constant indicating that the position is unknown, or BOF, or EOF.
- **AbsolutePage** Specifies the page for the current record.
- **ActiveConnection** Indicates the Connection object to which the Recordset belongs.
- **CacheSize** Indicates the number of records in the Recordset that are cached locally in memory.
- **CursorType** Tells you what kind of cursor the Recordset has.
- **EditMode** Indicates the editing status of the current record and can be none, in-progress, or addnew.
- **Filter** Enables you to filter records based on criteria, changing the viewable contents of the current Recordset.
- **LockType** Reflects the lock type in force when the Recordset was retrieved.
- **MarshallOptions** Is only available for client-side Recordsets and is used to optimize performance when sending records back to the server.
- **Source** Indicates the source of the records in the Recordset.
- **State** Indicates whether the Recordset is open or closed.
- **Status** Indicates the status of the current record regarding batch update operations.

1-Minute Drill

- What method of the Recordset object tells you the functions the data provider provides?
- If the Recordset BOF property is True, what does this mean?

Recordset Navigation and Manipulation Operations

In this section, Recordset object methods and properties are used to maneuver around a Recordset and to make some updates and changes. Being familiar with the various connection and command parameters affecting the kind of Recordsets retrieved is important because some of the Recordset methods and properties may be unavailable unless they're supported by the provider and specified in the commands used.

Creating and Using Recordsets

To start manipulating records programmatically with Recordsets, you'll need to make a connection, run some commands, and retrieve some records. Therefore, the first thing to do is to make sure you have plenty of records to play with in the ASPNETDB database. Open the Enterprise Manager and find the database you've been using. Enter some additional records for products, customers, and orders.

Next, write some ASP code that makes the connection and returns a Recordset that can be worked with, meaning a dynamic cursor type. Just build a plain HTML file named GetRecordset.asp and save it on your server. The ASP part of the code might resemble this:

```
set myConn = Server.CreateObject("ADODB.Connection")
Set myrs = Server.CreateObject("ADODB.RecordSet")
myConn.Open "Driver=SQLOLEDB.1;User ID=sa;
Password=;Initial Catalog=ASPNETDB;Data Source=ASPNET1"
sql = "SELECT * FROM Products"
myrs.Open sql, myConn, adOpenDynamic, adLockOptimistic
```

- The Supports method.
- You have reached a record position before the first record.

As you can see from the code, the Connection object was used to open a connection via ASPNET1 DSN. Then the Recordset object was used to set the Source (using a variable named sql to hold the SQL statement), ActiveConnection, CursorType, and LockType for the Recordset.

If you want to view the properties of the Recordset, you can use code like the following in your ASP page:

```
Response.Write "The AbsolutePage Property of the
 Recordset is <B>" & myRs.AbsolutePage & "</B><BR>"
```

Navigating Through the Recordset

To navigate the open Recordset, the first thing you want to do is check to see whether any records were returned. Following this check, you can use the Move methods of the Recordset to navigate around. Use code like this to get started:

```
If myRs.EOF Then
 Response.Write "There are no records in this table"
Else
 myRs.MoveFirst
 Response.Write "The Product Name is
 " & myRs.Fields("Name") & " and the Price is
 " & myRs.Fields("Price")
End If
```

The code to go to the next, previous, and last records is essentially the same, substituting in the MoveNext, MovePrevious, and MoveLast methods for the MoveFirst method. Because you might end up before the first record or after the last record (at BOF or EOF), use some additional code (after the rst.MovePrevious, for instance) for the next and previous records that checks for this condition, such as:

```
If myRs.BOF OR myRs.EOF Then
 Response.Write "You are not on a record"
Else
 Response.Write "The Product Name is
 " & myRs.Fields("Name") & "
 and the Price is " & myRs.Fields("Price")
End If
```

To move to a specific record in the Recordset, use code like this:

```
MyRs.Move vMoveNumber
```

In this case, vMoveNumber is a number contained in a variable representing the record number to which to move. If you like, you can collect this number from the user via an HTML form. This can become the basis for a system enabling the user to navigate records in a Recordset.

- What common programming structure checks whether or not any records have been retrieved?
- What common programming structure enables you to travel through records one at a time until you've traversed the entire Recordset?

Editing Records in a Recordset

Now that you can move through the records and, perhaps, find a specific record, it would be nice to being able to change the contents of a record. To do this, you'll need to display the contents of the record in such a way that changes are possible. An easy way to do this is to make the field values show up inside HTML form elements. The user can then make changes to the form elements, and the changed values can be used to update the record they came from. It's as simple as the following code:

```
%>
<Form Method=Post Action="GetRecordset.asp">
<Table><TR><TD><B>Product ID</B></TD>
<TD><B>Name</B></TD>
<TD><B>Price</B></TD>
<TD><B>Delete?</B></TD></TR>
<%
Do While not myRs.EOF
%>
<TR><TD><INPUT TYPE="text"
```

- The If Recordset.EOF Then structure checks for no records returned.
- The Do While Not Recordset.EOF structure visits all the records.

```
 name="ProductID<% Response.Write
 myRs.Fields("ProductID") %>"
 value="<% Response.Write
 myRs.Fields("ProductID") %>"></TD>
<TD><INPUT TYPE="text"
 name="Name<% Response.Write
 myRs.Fields("ProductID") %>"
 value ="<% Response.Write
 myRs.Fields("Name") %>"></TD>
<TD><INPUT TYPE="text"
 name="Price<% Response.Write
 myRs.Fields("ProductID") %>"
 value = "<% Response.Write
 myRs.Fields("Price") %>"></B></TD>
<TD><INPUT TYPE="checkbox"
 name="chkbx<% Response.Write
 myRs.Fields("ProductID") %>"></TD></TR>
<%
 myRs.MoveNext
Loop
%>
<TR><TD COLSPAN=3><INPUT TYPE="submit"
 name="btnval" value="Change Records">
<INPUT TYPE="submit" name="btnval"
 value="Delete Records"></TD></TR>
</Form>
</Table>
```

Ask the Expert

Question: Recordsets seem to be pretty powerful objects. What are the primary limitations, and how can I cope with them?

Answer: Like most data structures related to a database, Recordsets are just a snapshot of data and must be locked appropriately in order to accurately update the values your users change accurately. If you are running a multiuser environment, you'll have the same types of concurrency problems you would with an ordinary application. Fortunately, you can use a variety of lock types, and there is the Requery method to update the contents of the Recordset as often as necessary.

Question: How do I know what methods a given provider supports? I know the Supports method is available, but it seems like a lot of work to examine all the available properties every time I want to connect to a data source. Is there some easy way around this?

Answer: Chances are, you'll be using a data provider whose properties are very familiar to you, so you'll know what functions the provider supports without having to check every time you connect. If you are connecting to multiple unfamiliar data sources, you can program a tool that will immediately check all functions supported as soon as a connection is made. The programming logic would be a bit complex, similar to using the browser capabilities component to check the functions the user's platform supports, but it's worth it as you attempt to provide your users with the functionality they need to work with your application.

Project 10-1: Building a Data Management Page

One of the things you'll run into often is the need for a data management page. Users will want you to make their data and records available for additions, updates, deletions, and so forth. You can use the functions we've coded for the Recordset object to do just that in a fairly straightforward way.

For Access databases, the provider does not support bookmarks. In the code in this project, you can see that the Bookmark property statement is commented out because of this. You can determine what the data provider supports using the Supports method. For example, you can code a conditional statement, such as the following, to determine whether a particular data provider supports bookmarks:

```
If myRs.Supports(adBookmark) Then
 Response.Write "The bookmark is " & myRs.Bookmark
End If
```

Step-by-Step

You'll start by building a single page that enables the user to reveal all the properties of a connection, navigate the records, and make changes to them as desired. You'll use the typical Select Case structure to capture which button they pressed combined with an HTML form to let the user give input to the processing. Figure 10-1 shows how the web page looks before activating any of the Recordset functions.

1. First, set up the variables and include the adovbs.inc file, like so:

```
<%
Option Explicit
Dim btnClicked
Dim myConn
Dim myRs
Dim collitem
Dim vParameter
Dim myParam
Dim vMoveNumber
Dim vName
Dim vNamen
Dim vPricen
Dim vPrice
Dim intI
Dim vRecordToDelete
%>
<!-- #include file="adovbs.inc" -->
<%
```


2. Next, layout the HTML for the top of the resulting page, as follows:

```
%>
<html><head><title>Working with ADO Recordsets</title>
<meta http-equiv="Content-Type"
 content="text/html; charset=iso-8859-1">
</head>
<body bgcolor="#77FF77">
<H2><font size="6">Working with ADO
 Recordsets</font></H2>
<TABLE border=1><TR><TD>
 <H3>Recordset Properties and Data</H3>
 </TD></TR><TR><TD bgcolor="white">
<%
```

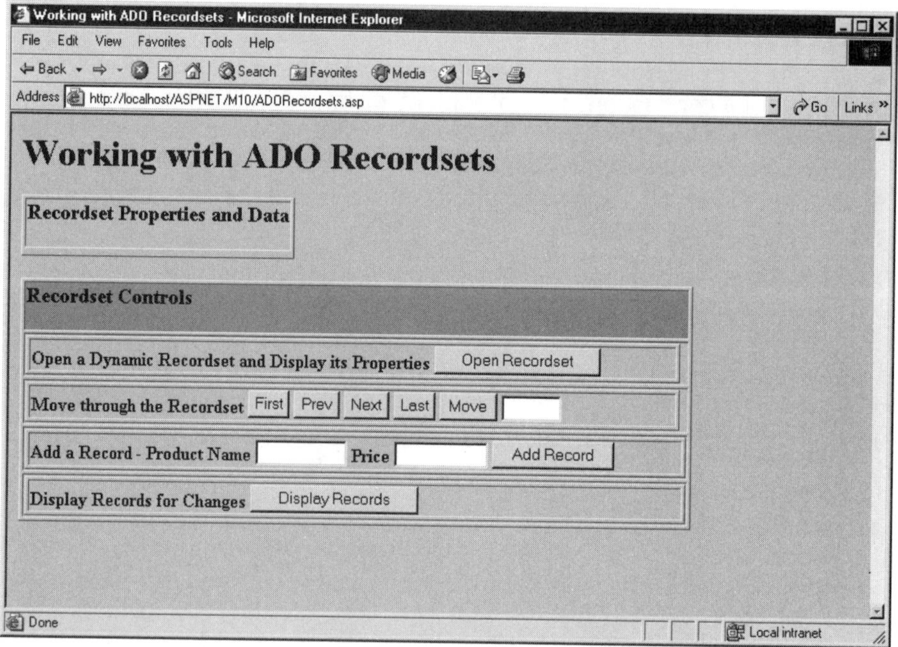

Figure 10-1 The initial Recordset web page

3. Next, set up the capture of the value of the button clicked using the name of the button (they're all named btnval) and the variable btnClicked, and then begin the first case for the Select Case structure. This case shows the properties available for this data provider, and is shown in Figure 10-2 following the code.

```
btnClicked = Request.Form("btnval")
Select Case btnClicked
 Case "Open Recordset"
set myConn = Server.CreateObject("ADODB.Connection")
Set myrs = Server.CreateObject("ADODB.RecordSet")
myConn.Open "Driver=SQLOLEDB.1;User ID=sa;
Password=;Initial Catalog=ASPNETDB;Data Source=ASPNET1"
sql = "SELECT * FROM Products"
```

```
myrs.Open sql, myConn, adOpenDynamic, adLockOptimistic
  Response.Write "The AbsolutePage Property of the
Recordset is <B>" & myRs.AbsolutePage & "</B><BR>"
  Response.Write "The AbsolutePosition Property of the
Recordset is <B>" & myRs.AbsolutePosition & "</B><BR>"
  Response.Write "The ActiveConnection Property of the
Recordset is <B>" & myRs.ActiveConnection & "</B><BR>"
  Response.Write "The BOF Property of the
Recordset is <B>" & myRs.BOF & "</B><BR>"
  'Response.Write "The Bookmark Property of the
Recordset is <B>" & myRs.Bookmark & "</B><BR>"
  Response.Write "The CacheSize Property of the
Recordset is <B>" & myRs.CacheSize & "</B><BR>"
  Response.Write "The CursorLocation Property of the
Recordset is <B>" & myRs.CursorLocation & "</B><BR>"
  Response.Write "The CursorType Property of the
Recordset is <B>" & myRs.CursorType & "</B><BR>"
  Response.Write "The EditMode Property of the
Recordset is <B>" & myRs.EditMode & "</B><BR>"
  Response.Write "The EOF Property of the
Recordset is <B>" & myRs.EOF & "</B><BR>"
  Response.Write "The Filter Property of the
Recordset is <B>" & myRs.Filter & "</B><BR>"
  Response.Write "The LockType Property of the
Recordset is <B>" & myRs.LockType & "</B><BR>"
  Response.Write "The MarshalOptions Property of the
Recordset is <B>" & myRs.MarshalOptions & "</B><BR>"
  Response.Write "The MaxRecords Property of the
Recordset is <B>" & myRs.MaxRecords & "</B><BR>"
  Response.Write "The PageCount Property of the
Recordset is <B>" & myRs.PageCount & "</B><BR>"
  Response.Write "The PageSize Property of the
Recordset is <B>" & myRs.PageSize & "</B><BR>"
  Response.Write "The RecordCount Property of the
Recordset is <B>" & myRs.RecordCount & "</B><BR>"
  Response.Write "The Source Property of the
Recordset is <B>" & myRs.Source & "</B><BR>"
  Response.Write "The State Property of the
Recordset is <B>" & myRs.State & "</B><BR>"
  Response.Write "The Status Property of the
Recordset is <B>" & myRs.Status & "</B><BR>"
Set myRs = Nothing
Set myConn = Nothing
```

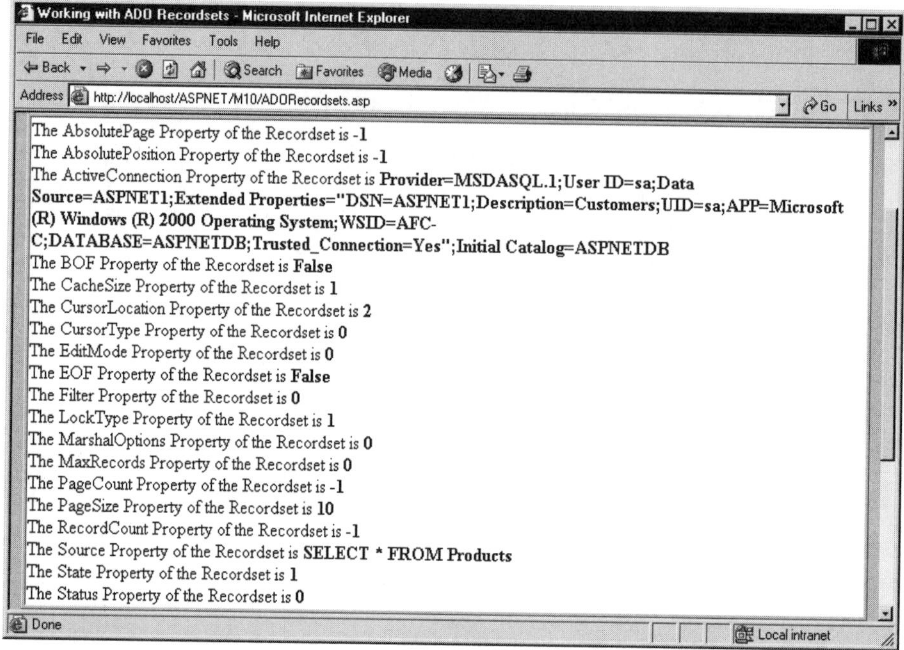

Figure 10-2 The properties returned for the Recordset

4. The next five cases all use similar structures to navigate the Recordset. They open the Recordset, use the If rst.EOF Then structure to check if any records were actually returned, and then call the appropriate method to move through the Recordset. The last case (the Move method) accepts input from the user to determine what record to move to. Figure 10-3 shows the results returned for one of the records after navigating to it.

```
Case "First"
set myConn = Server.CreateObject("ADODB.Connection")
Set myRs = Server.CreateObject("ADODB.RecordSet")
myConn.Open "Driver=SQLOLEDB.1;User ID=sa;
Password=;Initial Catalog=ASPNETDB;Data Source=ASPNET1"
sql = "SELECT * FROM Products"
myRs.Open sql, myConn, adOpenDynamic, adLockOptimistic
 If myRs.EOF Then
  Response.Write "There are no records in this table"
 Else
  myRs.MoveFirst
```

```
Response.Write "The Product Name is
" & myRs.Fields("Name") & "
and the Price is " & myRs.Fields("Price")
End If
Set myRs = Nothing
Set myConn = Nothing
Case "Prev"
set myConn = Server.CreateObject("ADODB.Connection")
Set myRs = Server.CreateObject("ADODB.RecordSet")
myConn.Open "Driver=SQLOLEDB.1;User ID=sa;
Password=;Initial Catalog=ASPNETDB;Data Source=ASPNET1"
sql = "SELECT * FROM Products"
myRs.Open sql, myConn, adOpenDynamic, adLockOptimistic
 If myRs.EOF Then
  Response.Write "There are no records in this table"
 Else
  myRs.MovePrevious
  If myRs.BOF OR myRs.EOF Then
   Response.Write "You are not on a record"
  Else
   Response.Write "The Product Name is
 " & myRs.Fields("Name") & "
 and the Price is " & myRs.Fields("Price")
  End If
 End If
 Set myRs = Nothing
 Set myConn = Nothing
Case "Next"
set myConn = Server.CreateObject("ADODB.Connection")
Set myRs = Server.CreateObject("ADODB.RecordSet")
myConn.Open "Driver=SQLOLEDB.1;User ID=sa;
Password=;Initial Catalog=ASPNETDB;Data Source=ASPNET1"
sql = "SELECT * FROM Products"
myRs.Open sql, myConn, adOpenDynamic, adLockOptimistic
 If myRs.EOF Then
  Response.Write "There are no records in this table"
 Else
 myRs.MoveNext
 If myRs.BOF OR myRs.EOF Then
  Response.Write "You are not on a record"
 Else
  Response.Write "The Product Name is
 " & myRs.Fields("Name") & "
 and the Price is " & myRs.Fields("Price")
 End If
```

```
End If
 Set myRs = Nothing
 Set myConn = Nothing
Case "Last"
set myConn = Server.CreateObject("ADODB.Connection")
Set myRs = Server.CreateObject("ADODB.RecordSet")
myConn.Open "Driver=SQLOLEDB.1;User ID=sa;
Password=;Initial Catalog=ASPNETDB;Data Source=ASPNET1"
sql = "SELECT * FROM Products"
myRs.Open sql, myConn, adOpenDynamic, adLockOptimistic
 If myRs.EOF Then
  Response.Write "There are no records in this table"
 Else
  myRs.MoveLast
 If myRs.BOF OR myRs.EOF Then
  Response.Write "You are not on a record"
 Else
  Response.Write "The Product Name is
 " & myRs.Fields("Name") & "
 and the Price is " & myRs.Fields("Price")
 End If
End If
 Set myRs = Nothing
 Set myConn = Nothing
Case "Move"
 vMoveNumber = request.form("MoveNumber")
set myConn = Server.CreateObject("ADODB.Connection")
Set myRs = Server.CreateObject("ADODB.RecordSet")
myConn.Open "Driver=SQLOLEDB.1;User ID=sa;
Password=;Initial Catalog=ASPNETDB;Data Source=ASPNET1"
sql = "SELECT * FROM Products"
myRs.Open sql, myConn, adOpenDynamic, adLockOptimistic
 If myRs.EOF Then
  Response.Write "There are no records in this table"
 Else
  myRs.Move vMoveNumber
  If myRs.BOF OR myRs.EOF Then
   Response.Write "You are not on a record"
  Else
   Response.Write "The Product Name is
 <B>" & myRs.Fields("Name") & "</B>
 and the Price is <B>" & myRs.Fields("Price") & "</B>"
  End If
 End If
 Set myRs = Nothing
 Set myConn = Nothing
```

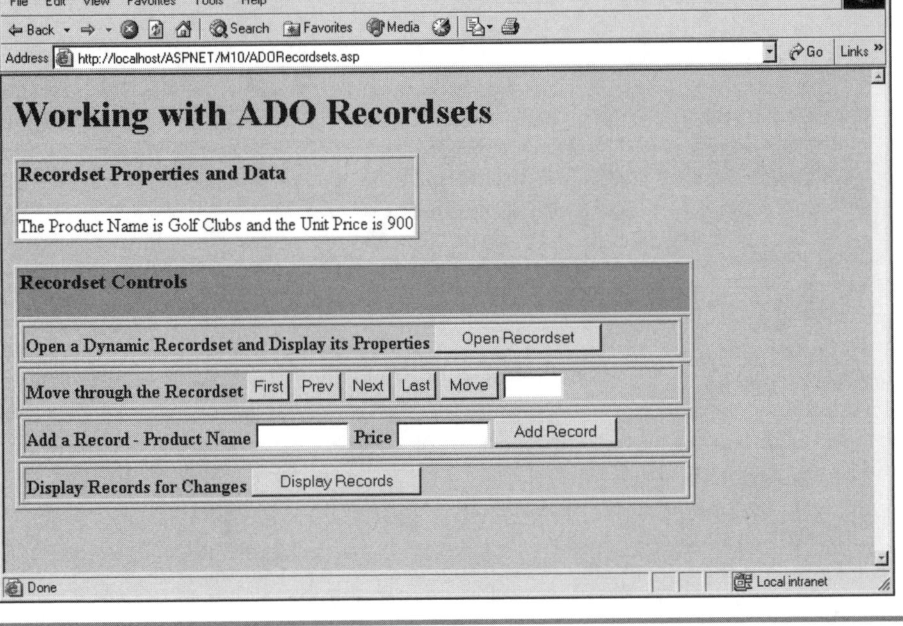

Figure 10-3 Navigating to the first record with the First button

10

5. The next cases enable the user to add, change, and delete records. This is done using the AddNew method, the Update method, and the Delete method. Of course, you need to collect the additions, changes, and deletions from the user, so you use HTML form elements to capture this data and insert it into the appropriate places. The resulting records are displayed, as shown in Figure 10-4 after adding a record, Figure 10-5 after changing a record, and Figure 10-6 ready to delete a record.

```
Case "Add Record"
 vProductName = request.form("ProductName")
 vUnitPrice = request.form("UnitPrice")
set myConn = Server.CreateObject("ADODB.Connection")
Set myRs = Server.CreateObject("ADODB.RecordSet")
myConn.Open "Driver=SQLOLEDB.1;User ID=sa;
Password=;Initial Catalog=ASPNETDB;Data Source=ASPNET1"
sql = "SELECT * FROM Products"
myRs.Open sql, myConn, adOpenDynamic, adLockOptimistic
 With myRs
```

```
  .AddNew
  .Fields("Name") = vName
  .Fields("Price") = vPrice
  .Update
 End With
 myRs.Requery
 Response.Write "<TABLE border=1>"
 Do While not myRs.EOF
  Response.Write "<TR><TD>ProductID is
 <B>" & myRs.Fields("ProductID") &
 "</B></TD><TD> Product Name is
 <B>" & myRs.Fields("Name") &
 "</B></TD><TD> Price is
 <B>" & myRs.Fields("Price") & "</B></TD></TR>"
  myRs.MoveNext
 Loop
 Response.Write "</table>"
 Set myRs = Nothing
 Set myConn = Nothing
Case "Display Records"
set myConn = Server.CreateObject("ADODB.Connection")
Set myRs = Server.CreateObject("ADODB.RecordSet")
myConn.Open "Driver=SQLOLEDB.1;User ID=sa;
Password=;Initial Catalog=ASPNETDB;Data Source=ASPNET1"
sql = "SELECT * FROM Products"
myRs.Open sql, myConn, adOpenDynamic, adLockOptimistic
%>
<Form Method=Post Action="GetRecordset.asp"><Table>
<%
Do While not myRs.EOF
%>
<TR><TD>ProductID is <B><INPUT TYPE="text"
 name="ProductID<% Response.Write
 myRs.Fields("ProductID") %>"
 value="<% Response.Write
 myRs.Fields("ProductID") %>"></B></TD>
<TD> Product Name is <B><INPUT TYPE="text"
 name="Name<% Response.Write
 myRs.Fields("ProductID") %>"
 value ="<% Response.Write
 myRs.Fields("Name") %>"></B></TD>
<TD> Price is <B><INPUT TYPE="text"
```

```
 name="Price<% Response.Write
 myRs.Fields("ProductID") %>"
 value = "<% Response.Write
 myRs.Fields("Price") %>"></B></TD></TR>
<%
 myRs.MoveNext
Loop
%>
<TR><TD COLSPAN=3><INPUT TYPE="submit"
 name="btnval" value="Change Records"></TD></TR>
</Form>
</Table>
<%
Set myRs = Nothing
Set myConn = Nothing
```

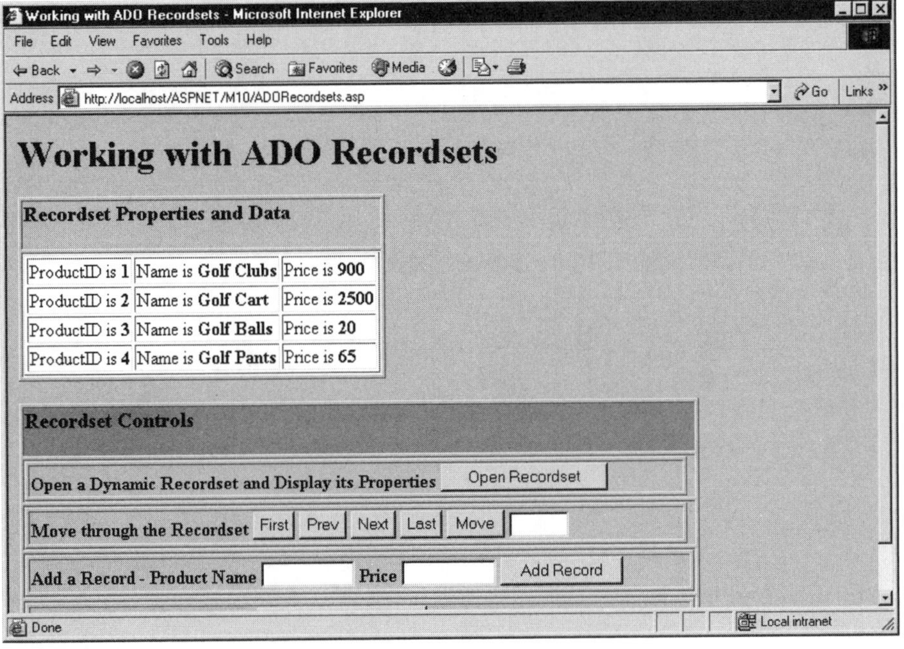

Figure 10-4 The displayed records after adding a record

10

```
Case "Change Records"
 Set myConn = Server.CreateObject("ADODB.Connection")
 myConn.Open "ASPNET1"
 Set myRs = Server.CreateObject("ADODB.Recordset")
 With myRs
  .Source = "Products"
  .ActiveConnection = myConn
  .CursorType = adOpenDynamic
  .LockType = adLockOptimistic
  .Open
 End With
 Do While not myRs.EOF
  vNamen = "Name"
 & myRs.Fields("ProductID")
  vName = request.form(vNamen)
  vPricen = "Price" & myRs.Fields("ProductID")
  vPrice = request.form(vPricen)
  With myRs
   .Fields("Name") = vName
   .Fields("Price") = vPrice
   .Update
  End With
  myRs.MoveNext
 Loop
 myRs.Requery
%>
<Form Method=Post Action="GetRecordset.asp">
<Table><TR><TD><B>Product ID</B></TD>
<TD><B>Product Name</B></TD>
<TD><B>Unit Price</B></TD>
<TD><B>Delete?</B></TD></TR>
<%
Do While not myRs.EOF
%>
<TR><TD><INPUT TYPE="text"
 name="ProductID<% Response.Write
 myRs.Fields("ProductID") %>"
 value="<% Response.Write
 myRs.Fields("ProductID") %>"></TD>
<TD><INPUT TYPE="text"
 name="Name<% Response.Write
 myRs.Fields("ProductID") %>"
 value ="<% Response.Write
 myRs.Fields("Name") %>"></TD>
<TD><INPUT TYPE="text"
 name="Price<% Response.Write
```

```
 myRs.Fields("ProductID") %>"
 value = "<% Response.Write
 myRs.Fields("Price") %>"></B></TD>
<TD><INPUT TYPE="checkbox"
 name="chkbx<% Response.Write
 myRs.Fields("ProductID") %>"></TD></TR>
<%
 myRs.MoveNext
Loop
%>
<TR><TD COLSPAN=3><INPUT TYPE="submit"
 name="btnval" value="Change Records">
<INPUT TYPE="submit" name="btnval"
 value="Delete Records"></TD></TR>
</Form>
</Table>
<%
Set myRs = Nothing
Set myConn = Nothing
```

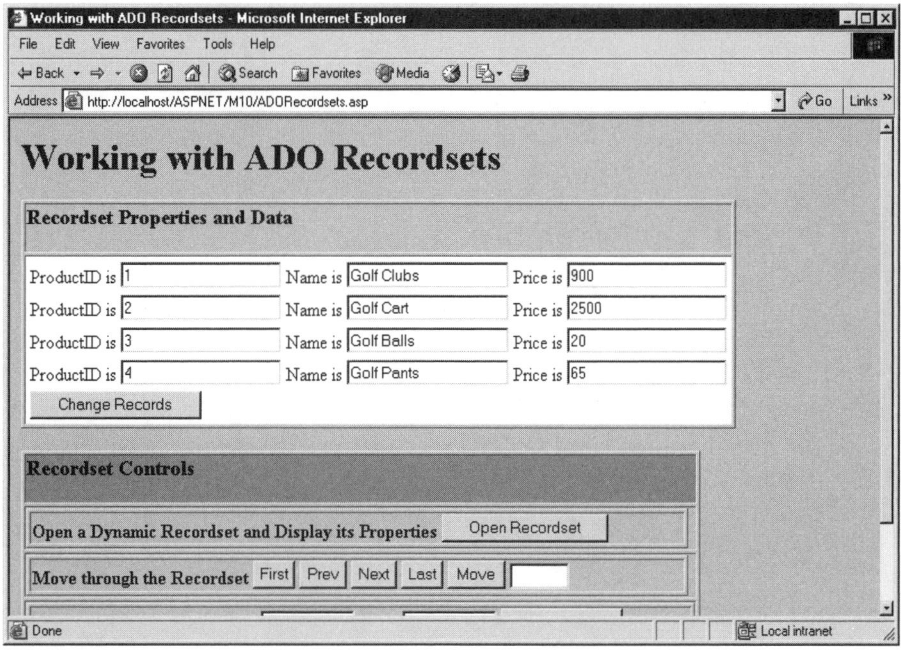

Figure 10-5 The displayed records ready for changes

```
Case "Delete Records"
set myConn = Server.CreateObject("ADODB.Connection")
Set myRs = Server.CreateObject("ADODB.RecordSet")
myConn.Open "Driver=SQLOLEDB.1;User ID=sa;
Password=;Initial Catalog=ASPNETDB;Data Source=ASPNET1"
sql = "SELECT * FROM Products"
myRs.Open sql, myConn, adOpenDynamic, adLockOptimistic
  For Each collitem in Request.Form
   If Left(collitem, 5) = "chkbx" Then
    vRecordToDelete = Mid(collitem, 6, 10)
    myRs.Find "ProductID = " & vRecordToDelete & ""
    If myRs.BOF Then
     Response.Write "Record " & vRecordToDelete & "
 was not found.<BR>"
    Else
     If myRs.EOF Then
      Response.Write "Record " & vRecordToDelete & "
 was not found.<BR>"
     Else
      myRs.Delete
      Response.Write "Record " & vRecordToDelete & "
 was deleted.<BR>"
     End If
    End If
   End If
  Next
  myRs.Requery
%>
<Form Method=Post Action="GetRecordset.asp">
<Table><TR><TD><B>Product ID</B></TD>
<TD><B>Product Name</B></TD>
<TD><B>Unit Price</B></TD>
<TD><B>Delete?</B></TD></TR>
<%
Do While not myRs.EOF
%>
<TR><TD><INPUT TYPE="text"
 name="ProductID<% Response.Write
 myRs.Fields("ProductID") %>"
 value="<% Response.Write
 myRs.Fields("ProductID") %>"></TD>
<TD><INPUT TYPE="text"
 name="Name<% Response.Write
 myRs.Fields("ProductID") %>"
 value ="<% Response.Write
 myRs.Fields("Name") %>"></TD>
```

```
<TD><INPUT TYPE="text"
 name="Price<% Response.Write
 myRs.Fields("ProductID") %>"
 value = "<% Response.Write
 myRs.Fields("Price") %>"></B></TD>
<TD><INPUT TYPE="checkbox"
 name="chkbx<% Response.Write
 myRs.Fields("ProductID") %>"></TD></TR>
<%
 myRs.MoveNext
Loop
%>
<TR><TD COLSPAN=3><INPUT TYPE="submit"
 name="btnval" value="Change Records">
<INPUT TYPE="submit" name="btnval"
 value="Delete Records"></TD></TR>
</Form>
</Table>
<%
 Set myRs = Nothing
 Set myConn = Nothing
End Select
```

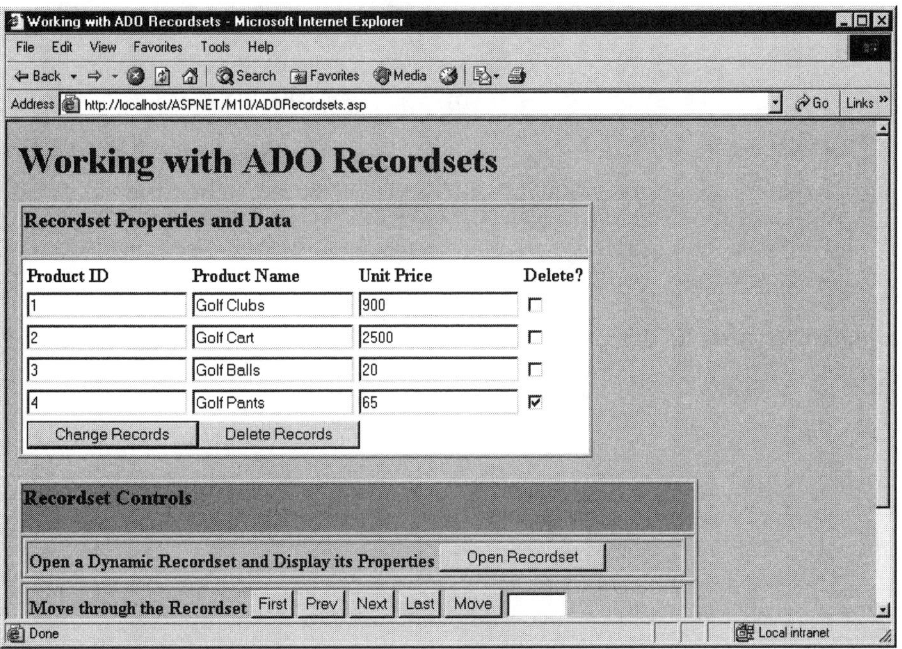

Figure 10-6 The displayed records ready to be deleted

6. The last job with this management page is to set up the rest of the part that the user sees, essentially a series of tables and form elements, mainly buttons, for controlling the page.

```
%>
</TD></TR></TABLE>
<P>
<TABLE border=1 width="80%"><TR>
<TD bgcolor="#00CC99" COLSPAN=3>
<H3>Recordset Controls</H3>
</TD></TR><TR>
<TD colspan="3">
<form method=POST action="GetRecordset.asp">
<table width="99%" border="1">
<tr>
<td><b>Open a Dynamic Recordset
 and Display its Properties</b>
<input type="submit" name="btnval"
 value="Open Recordset">
</td></tr></table>
</TD></TR><TR>
<TD colspan="3">
<table width="99%" border="1"><tr>
<td><b>Move through the Recordset</b>
<input type="submit" name="btnval" value="First">
<input type="submit" name="btnval" value="Prev">
<input type="submit" name="btnval" value="Next">
<input type="submit" name="btnval" value="Last">
<input type="submit" name="btnval" value="Move">
<input type="text" name="MoveNumber" size="5">
</td></tr></table>
</TD></TR><TR>
<TD colspan="3">
<table width="100%" border="1">
<tr>
<td><B>Add a Record - Product Name</B>
<input type="text" name="Name" size="10">
<B>Unit Price</B>
<input type="text" name="Price" size="10">
<input type="submit" name="btnval" value="Add Record">
</td></tr></table>
</TD></TR><TR>
<TD colspan="3">
<table width="100%" border="1">
<tr><td><B>Display Records for Changes</B>
```

```
<input type="submit" name="btnval"
 value="Display Records">
</td></tr>
</table></TD></TR>
</form>
</TR></TABLE>
</BODY></HTML>
```

The Stream and Record Objects

The Stream and Record objects represent important capabilities for ADO. Previous versions of ADO allowed access to simple Recordset and field data, but many data sources are not structured as database tables, so the need for additional objects to support other data structures became apparent. The Stream and Record objects provide this capability.

The Record object can be used to work with folders and files in a file system, e-mails and folders in an e-mail system, and rows in a Recordset. It has somewhat different methods and properties from a Recordset object, because the Record object has unique properties dependent upon the data source being represented.

Record Object Properties and Methods

The Record object, like the Recordset object, enables you to work with fields via the Fields collection, and, if a Record object happens to represent a row in a Recordset, you can get back to the Recordset from the record. In addition, the Record object can also represent hierarchical data structures such as file systems and allows another method for manipulating and navigating around these data structures.

When you open a Record object, a connection is created implicitly and, if you choose, you can also set the connection explicitly. Like other ADO objects, records have their own methods and properties.

Record Object Methods

The Record object has the following methods:

- **Open and Close** Open or close the Record object.
- **CopyRecord, MoveRecord, and DeleteRecord** Copy, move, or delete files, folders, and subfolders represented by a Record object.

- **GetChildren** Opens a Recordset with rows representing each subfolder or file of the current Record object.
- **Cancel** Cancels an asynchronous operation of the Record object.

Record Object Properties

The Record object has the following properties:

- **ActiveConnection** Sets or retrieves the connection for the Record object.
- **Mode** Tells what permissions are available for the Record object.
- **ParentURL** Tells the name of the folder that contains the file or folder represented by the Record object.
- **Source** Tells the absolute URL, relative URL, or Recordset associated with the Record object.
- **RecordType** Tells whether the Record type is simple, collection, or structured document.
- **State** Tells whether the Record object is open or closed.

Stream Object Properties and Methods

The Stream object can be used with the Recordset and Record objects to provide access to the actual contents of files, including binary data. It is very useful for working not only with typical text files, but also all kinds of other file types, including images. The Stream object, like other ADO objects, has properties and methods associated with it.

In a hierarchical data structure such as a file system or an e-mail system, the Record object can also deliver a stream of bits representing the file or resource. This stream consists of the contents of the file or resource and is a Stream object. The Stream object can be used to manipulate fields or records containing binary data. A Stream object can be generated using a variety of methods. For example, you could retrieve a Stream object from a URL, you could open the default Stream object of a Record object, or you could actually instantiate a Stream object using the OBJECT tag.

Stream Object Methods

The Stream object has the following methods:

- **Open** Opens a stream from a Record object or a particular URL.
- **Close** Closes an open Stream object.
- **Write and WriteText** Write bytes or plain text to a stream, effectively inserting them into the stream.
- **Read and ReadText** Read bytes or text from a stream.
- **Flush** Sends any data remaining in the buffer to the underlying object associated with the stream.
- **CopyTo** Allows you to specify a certain number of characters from one open stream to another stream.
- **SetEOS** Sets the position that is considered as the end of a stream.
- **SkipLine** Skips an entire line when reading text from a stream.
- **SaveToFile** Saves the contents of a stream to a file, the name of which you can specify.
- **LoadFromFile** Loads the contents of a file you can specify into a stream.
- **Cancel** Terminates an asynchronous call to the Open method.

Stream Object Properties

The Stream object also has the following properties:

- **LineSeparator** Sets or retrieves the character to be used as a line separator in a stream.
- **EOS** Tells whether the current position is at the end of the stream.
- **Charset** Tells what character set the stream should be translated into.
- **Size** Tells the size of the stream in bytes.
- **Position** Tells the position, as a Long value, the number of bytes from the beginning of the stream.
- **Type** Tells whether the type of data is text or binary.
- **State** Tells whether the stream is open or closed.
- **Mode** Tells, via an ADO constant, what permissions are available for working with the stream.

Question: For what kinds of applications can I use the Record and Stream objects? Why wouldn't I use the FileSystemObject object and other related objects to perform these kinds of functions?

Answer: Good question. For the time being, you'll end up using the FileSystemObject and its related objects because the Record and Stream objects are not currently as well supported. However, you'll find the Record and Stream objects useful for XML applications. XML documents are hierarchical in nature, so the Record and Stream objects are a natural fit.

Record and Stream Object Overview

Record and Stream objects are relatively new, and there are not too many applications that we can cover in this book. However, it should be apparent from the methods and properties associated with the Record and Stream object that they will come to play a very important role in your applications in the future.

1-Minute Drill

- How does the Record object differ primarily from the Recordset object?
- What special type of data does the Stream object handle?

Retrieving Records with ADO.NET Objects

For the .NET Framework, ASP.NET, and ADO.NET, Microsoft has chosen to upgrade the entire ADO object model. While the Recordset object is very useful, it is quite large and can only represent a single table (although that

---

- The Record object has special properties depending upon the type of data source it represents.
- Binary data.

table may actually be a view generated with a JOIN). The upgraded data model includes objects that allow data from a database to be represented and worked with more realistically.

Data Objects in ADO.NET

One of the primary Data objects in ADO.NET (there is no similar object in ADO) is the DataSet object. It acts as a container for other Data objects. For example, a DataSet can contain several DataTable objects. Each DataTable object can represent the rows and columns of a single table from the database and allows navigation, filtering, adds, edits, and deletes, and so forth. The DataSet object can also contain DataRelation objects, and DataRelation objects can represent relationships between DataTable objects, thereby providing functionality similar to a relational database.

The DataView object can be used to retrieve a subset of records and bind them to Web Forms controls, and the DataTableMapping object maintains the links between data columns in a DataSet and the real columns of data in the data source (such as a table in the database). The DataReader object provides a mechanism for quickly iterating through records, allowing only forward movement and read-only access.

Project 10-2: Reading Data with a DataReader Object

A DataReader object is similar to a Recordset object with a read-only, forward-only cursor. It simply pulls data from a database with a SQL statement and makes it available for display. For this project, you'll retrieve data from the Customers table you built and populated in SQL Server and bind it to a data grid control on a Web Form.

Step-by-Step

For this project, you'll use an existing table (Customers). Since you've already entered some data in it, there's nothing more to do in SQL Server. Also, you've already created a DSN so you're ready to go.

1. To start the project, open VS.NET and create a new project from the web applications template. Name the project DataReadOnly.

2. Open the toolbox and add an OleDbConnection object and an OleDbCommand object to the Web Form. Name them MyConn and MyComm, respectively, and set the Connection String property of the Connection object to the appropriate SQL Server database. Set the Connection property of the Command object to MyConn.

3. To set the data to retrieve, click in the CommandText property of the Command object. An ellipsis button will appear. Click the button and the Query Builder dialog box will open. It closely resembles the query builder dialog box in SQL Server. Inside the dialog box, a smaller dialog box appears (see Figure 10-7). Use it to select the Customers table, and then close it. Click the All Columns field in the Customers table, and the query builder will write a SQL statement, as shown in Figure 10-8.

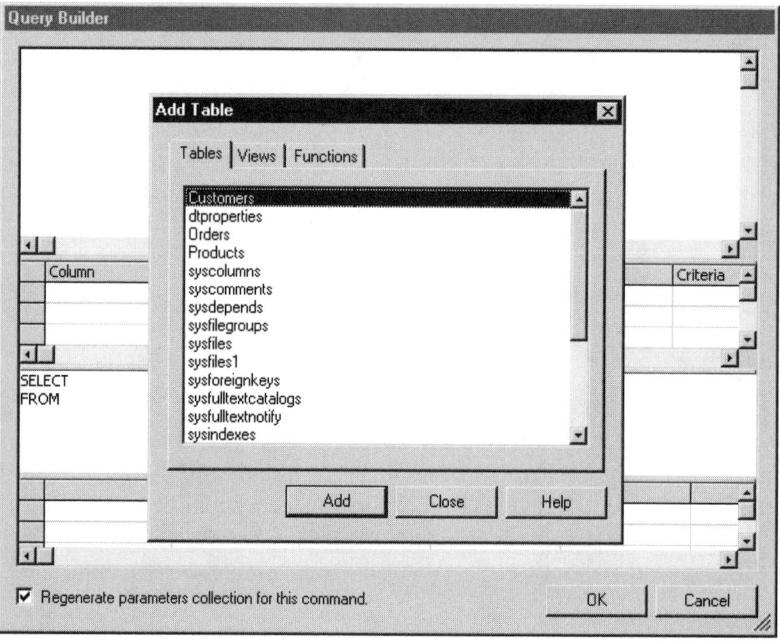

Figure 10-7 The Query Builder with the Add Table box inside

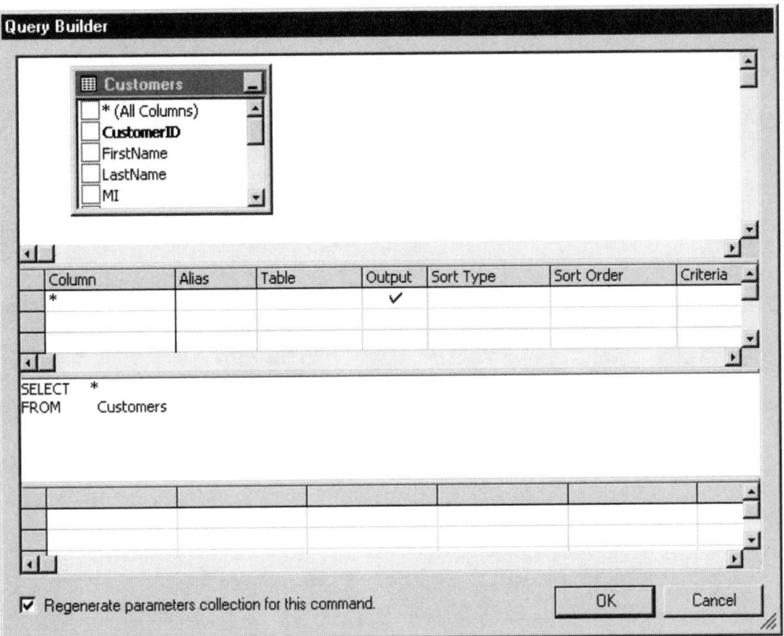

Figure 10-8 The finished SQL query

4. Add a datagrid control to the blank Web Form from the Web Forms portion of the toolbox. Name the datagrid MyDG. This control will display the data retrieved from the Customers table.

5. To create a DataReader object and connect it to the datagrid control, insert the following code into the code-behind page in the Page Load event:

```
MyConn.Open()
Dim dReader As System.Data.OleDb.OleDbDataReader
dReader = MyComm.ExecuteReader()
MyDG.DataSource = dReader
MyDG.DataBind()
```

```
dReader.Close()
MyConn.Close()
```

6. Choose Build and Browse from the file menu to check that the records are being pulled into the datagrid control. They should be displayed as shown in Figure 10-9.

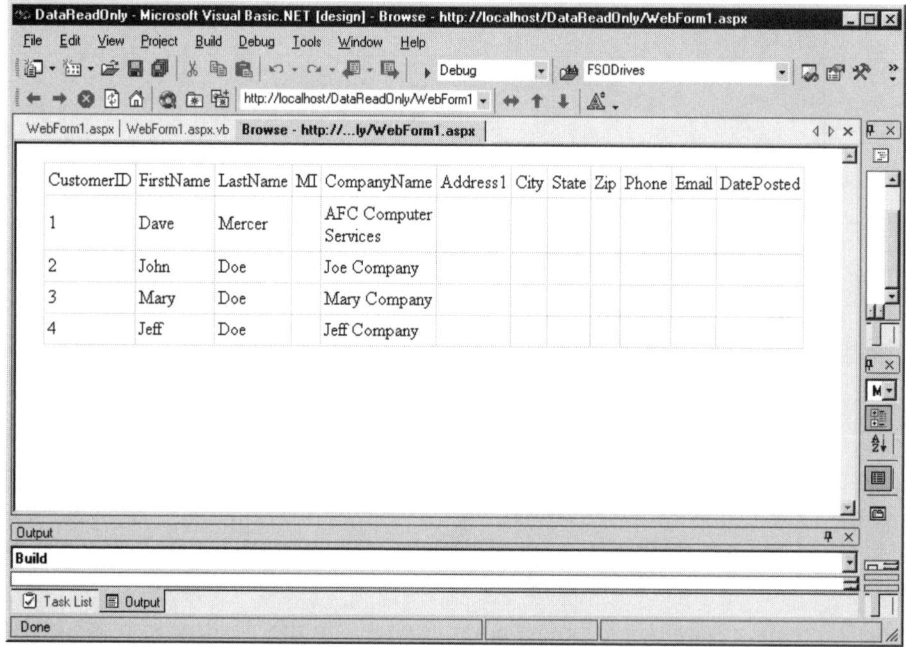

Figure 10-9 The Web Form with customer records in the datagrid

Mastery Check

1. What is the difference between the Requery and Resync methods of the Recordset object?

   A. Requery and Resync both perform the same function, but Requery is faster.

   B. Requery reperforms the original query, while Resync just refreshes the existing data in the Recordset.

   C. Requery works for the Recordset object and Resync doesn't.

   D. None of the above.

2. What property would you set to limit the number of records returned in a Recordset?

   A. PageSize

   B. PageCount

   C. MaxRecords

   D. RecordCount

   E. None of the above

3. What mechanism could you use to gather user data for record updates?

   A. Hard-coded HTML Form elements

   B. HTML Form elements named after unique records

   C. HTML Form elements with cookies attached

   D. All of the above

4. What property of a Stream object is similar to the Recordset's BOF and EOF properties?

   A. Position

   B. SetEOS

Mastery Check

C. EOS

D. None of the above

5. What information does the State property convey for many ADO objects?

   A. What state the user is in, for tax purposes

   B. What state the object is in, receiving or sending

   C. Whether the object is open or closed

   D. Whether the object is positive or negative

6. ADO makes use of the ______, ________, and ________ objects to retrieve and manipulate records and data in databases, while ADO.NET uses the _______, _______, and __________ objects for a similar purpose. The _______ object represents an entire data store, and when changes are made to records or data, the changes are propagated back to the data store with the ______ object.

7. Describe how (in ASP) you would address a field named Quantity from a table named Products in a Recordset named rcdst.

   ____

   ____

8. To navigate among records in a Recordset, there are several methods available. Name the methods allowing movement forward, backward, and to a specific record.

   A. MoveForward, MoveBackward, MoveNumber

   B. MoveNext, MovePrevious, MoveNumber

   C. MoveFirst, MovePrevious, MoveNext, MoveLast, and Move

   D. All of the above

   E. None of the above

Mastery Check

9. What properties allow you to determine if you have moved past the first or last records in a Recordset?

   A. FirstRecord, LastRecord

   B. FR, LR

   C. BOF, EOF

   D. BOR, EOR

   E. None of the above

10. What methods allow you to update or delete records in a Recordset?

    A. The Update method will update a particular record, and the Delete method will delete a particular record.

    B. The UpdateRecord method will update a particular record, and the DeleteRecord method will delete a particular record.

    C. The UR method will update a particular record, and the DR method will delete a particular record.

    D. B and C.

    E. None of the above.

11. To open a Recordset, you must use at least a __________ object, and to retrieve records you must use a __________ or _____ statement. You can create your own name for the Recordset, and you can also set the _______ type, and _____ type.

12. Describe a workable strategy (based on primary key values) for updating records in a database when the user edits the data in one of a series of records written into a web page and then submits that edited data as a posted HTML form.

    ____

    ____

Mastery Check

13. Why might it be useful to have the Record and Stream objects available in ADO?

A. Not all data sources are formatted as databases, and the Record and Stream objects assist with collecting and manipulating data in nondatabase formats.

B. Some databases provide a binary stream of data rather than a structured set of records, and the Stream object turns the data into individual records that can be captured in Record objects.

C. The Record and Stream objects are simply extensions of the Recordset object, and provide no significant additional functionality.

D. All of the above.

E. None of the above.

14. The DataReader object is best used when:

A. Speed is not an issue, but you require the most flexibility and functionality for manipulating data.

B. Speed is an issue, and you don't need much flexibility or functionality for manipulating data.

C. The developer wishes to read the contents of a database during the development process to ensure the appropriate data is being displayed to the user .

D. More than one user will use an application at a given time.

E. All of the above.

F. None of the above.

15. What methods are used when a DataReader object is required on a Web Form?

____

____

Module 11

ASP Transactions and Mail

The Goals of This Module

- Learn what transaction processing means
- Create an ASP transaction script
- Delete and insert records within the transaction
- Learn about mail servers (POP and SMTP)
- Create a simple e-mail-generating application
- Understand security weaknesses in website applications
- Learn how to assess security and recommend improvements

To introduce you to transactions and show how they are important to ASP applications, let's create a little scenario. Suppose you have a user registration form on your website. While users are being registered, they can also order a copy of the weekly e-mail newsletter you publish. Your business rules state no unregistered users can receive the newsletter. On the back end, you maintain user registration data in one table and subscriptions to the newsletter in another.

When users register, their personal or contact data is recorded in the users table and their subscription data is recorded in the subscriptions table. This means two records are created, one in each table. Now suppose the process you are using to create these records fails in one instance but not in the other. You could potentially have a subscription record in the subscriptions table without an associated user record in the users table.

Now imagine the previous scenario multiplied many thousands of times, using highly complex sets of business rules. It's easy to see that some mechanism must exist to ensure that whenever a set of record modifications (adds, edits, deletes, and so forth) must be completed together, either they are all completed or they all fail. And, if they do fail, a means of reverting everything back to how it was before any of the modifications started must exist.

Linking separate processing steps together so they succeed or fail as a whole makes them a *transaction*. When formed into a transaction, they are no longer considered separate steps; they are now considered one atomic step, *atomic* meaning you can't break them apart into smaller pieces.

Consistency and the ACID Test

If you have done your database design properly, when you first start using it, the database is said to be in a *consistent* state, which means no exceptions exist to the business rules you have programmed in. No values are out of range, no child records exist without the appropriate parent records, and so on. Each time a modification of records occurs, the end result of the modification still leaves the database in a consistent state.

In this scenario, if the creation of a user record failed, then the creation of a subscription record wouldn't occur, thereby leaving the database still in a consistent state. Typically, in the scenario described, the database itself wouldn't let you add a record to the subscribers table without a corresponding record in the user table because you would have set referential integrity. Many instances may occur, however, in which the database itself wouldn't automatically enforce your business rules and, in these cases, you would undoubtedly build in a means to capture the error or try the modifications again until they succeed. The point is, you may need to set up transactions for your applications explicitly and, to make your transactions function properly, you may need to build additional support into your application to cope with potential failure points. Fortunately, there are tools you can use to make it easier to create and properly complete application transactions, and these tools are discussed in just a moment. First, let's talk about the ACID test.

ACID (Atomicity, Consistency, Isolation, and Durability)

When a system meets the ACID test, it is said to embody the ACID properties. The ACID properties are

- **Atomicity** Either all or none of the changes are effected. Typically, before any change is committed to permanent storage, they are all written to temporary storage of some kind and then written as a group to permanent storage.
- **Consistency** The application remains in a consistent state after the entire set of modifications is made. The assumption here, of course, is that the system was in a consistent state before the transaction started.
- **Isolation** Any data or records taking part in a transaction are isolated from all other uses or transactions, until the entire transaction is either committed or aborted. Locking the data being used by a transaction ensures that other users or transactions won't be able to view inconsistent or partially modified records.
- **Durability** Once a transaction is committed, the changes to data are permanent and can be recovered, even if a system crashes or hardware failure occurs.

The ACID properties are good guidelines for creating industrial-strength applications, but the actual implementation is somewhat more complicated because many of today's applications function in a distributed fashion. *Distributed* means many components, databases, and other players at many different locations may be involved when a transaction is performed, and all must either complete the transaction or abort the transaction as a group.

Two-Phase Commit and Microsoft-Distributed Transaction Coordinator

To enable distributed transactions to be performed correctly, a protocol called the "two-phase commit" breaks the commit process into two steps. The first step is to notify all players in the transaction to write the transaction to disk in a buffer, waiting for the final go-ahead. Once all players have done this and returned a signal that they are ready to commit, the second phase is to write the change to disk permanently, provided the *Distributed Transaction Coordinator* (DTC) receives no failure signals from any player. If a failure signal is received, the transaction is rolled back across all players.

ASP Transactions

Because ASP is a widely used tool for creating online applications, Microsoft has incorporated support for transactions into ASP. If you need to call several components or databases to get a particular job done in its entirety, you can do so from an ASP script. You should do two things to ensure consistent transactions, however:

- Put all your transaction-related actions on one script page. While you may have a single business process that spans several ASP files, you should break the business process into physical transactions so that each fits on a single script. In ASP 3.0, the Server.Execute and Server.Transfer methods enable you to write transacted scripts that span several ASP files, but it isn't recommended.
- Manually code rollback procedures into your scripts. You should do this because, while your script can receive notification of the success or failure of a particular transaction, the transaction coordinator cannot roll back variables and values set within the context of the script itself, such as Application and Session variables or other nontransactional resources. Upon notification, your script must reset these values on its own.

Component Services

Component Services must be running to make use of the transaction management capabilities built into the web server. You have probably installed it during the installation of Windows 2000, and if you open it up you will see the transaction-processing parts (as shown in Figure 11-1).

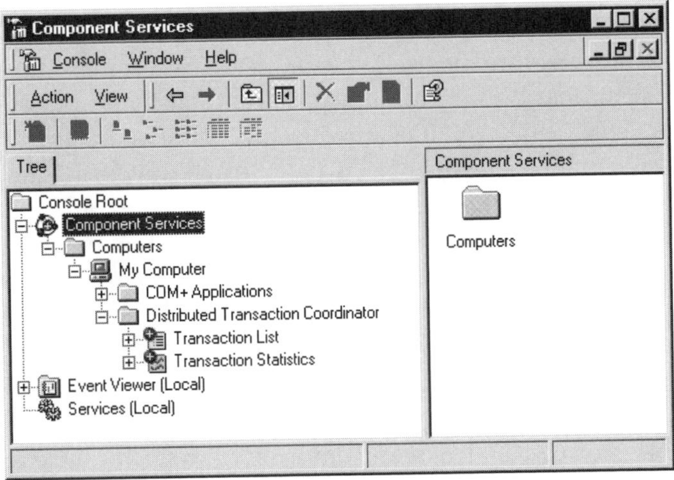

Figure 11-1 The Component Services Manager

To declare your ASP script as a transaction, use the following statement as the *first* statement in the file:

```
<%@ TRANSACTION=Required %>
```

You could also include the LANGUAGE attribute in this statement, if you like. The Required value is one of several settings the TRANSACTION directive can take. These settings give you some degree of control over how your script behaves. The settings are

- **Required** Starts a new transaction or joins one that already exists
- **Supported** Joins a transaction that already exists, but does not start a new one
- **Not_Supported** Neither starts nor joins a transaction
- **Requires_New** Starts a new transaction every time

Using Components in Transacted ASP Scripts

If your transactions require the use of components, you can use the properties of the components and the ObjectContext object to perform transactions within an ASP script. The TRANSACTION directive must still be the first line of your script, and you simply create the objects in the usual way, using the Set myObj = Server.CreateObject("componentname") statement.

Your script should then evaluate whether the transaction processing for each individual component succeeded or failed and, unless all components return the appropriate value to show they succeeded, should change the ObjectContext of the objects to SetAbort, aborting or rolling back the transaction.

Transaction Events

In the example project, a SQL Server database for processing a transaction is used. SQL Server is one of a number of databases supported for transactions by Component Services. When a change is made to the database within the ASP script (started by the TRANSACTION directive), Component Services processes the transaction. Inside the ASP script, you can tell whether the transaction succeeded or aborted by listening for either of two events: OnTransactionCommit and OnTransactionAbort.

To code the workings of these two objects into your script, you use something like the following (this is pseudocode):

```
<%@ TRANSACTION=Required %>
Make a change to the database
Sub OnTransactionCommit
Do something if the transaction committed
End Sub
Sub OnTransactionAbort
Do something if the transaction aborted
End Sub
```

1-Minute Drill

- What makes a transaction different from ordinary database updates?
- How can ASP scripts tell whether a change has been made?

- A transaction usually has more than one change to make, and all changes must be complete, or none of them will be committed to permanent memory.
- The OnTransactionCommit and OnTransactionAbort events tell ASP whether a change has been made.

The Transaction Database Design

To build an ASP or ASP.NET application that uses transactions, you need a database that supports the transaction environment. For the next project (Project 11-1), you can use the SQL Server database you've already created (ASPNETDB). You can also use the DSN you've already created to connect to the database.

To support Project 11-1 you'll need one table for the beginning checking balance and all existing deposits and withdrawals and another table for all forecasted deposits and withdrawals. Your HTML pages and forms enable you to view the checking records and the forecasted records and add, delete, or modify any records in either table. You can also see what the balance is at every record.

The Application's SQL Server Tables

For your transaction application, you need two tables:

- **CurTransRec** Contains all the current transaction records
- **ForTransRec** Contains all the forecasted transaction records

The first table is where you enter all transactions that have actually occurred. The second table is where you enter transactions that haven't occurred, but probably will. This allows you to forecast what your balance might be in the future, and identify shortfalls. The tables are very similar in design; each table requires the following fields:

- **TransactionID** A primary key field (that is an identity field) for tracking each individual record
- **TType** The type of the transaction
- **TDate** The date of the transaction
- **TAmount** The amount of the transaction
- **AuthorizedBy** The name of the person authorizing the transaction (and, in this case, physically making the transaction)
- **ForWhat** A general description of the purpose of the deposit or withdrawal

- **CheckNumber** If the transaction had a check written for it, the check number
- **MadeOutTo** The name the check was made out to, if applicable
- **ToAccountNumber** The account number the payment was made for, if applicable

Project 11-1: ASP Transactions on SQL Server

The objective of Project 11-1 is to demonstrate transactions, so you need to have several things to update at once. This project allows entry of simple financial data, such as you might keep to balance a checkbook and forecast your next month's expenses.

The current balance is calculated by the application and displayed next to each record, and the starting balance for forecasted deposits and withdrawals is always the existing balance in the CurTransRec table. At the top of each table, the beginning date, beginning balance, ending date, and ending balance are displayed, and on the last row is a space for entering new records. Each record has a Delete button so it can be deleted, but there is no capability to modify existing records after adding them (they can be deleted and reentered, if necessary).

Step-by-Step

Using the design just discussed, you're going to make a set of tables in your SQL Server database to support an online management system that tracks simple financial records for a small company you can call Online Systems Services. Your first step is to make a script to create the tables (although you could do this function with the visual interface SQL Server provides, better practice is to use pure SQL statements in a script). Note, if you do it correctly, you only have to use this script once.

1. The code for the script should look something like this:

```
<%
set Conn = Server.CreateObject("ADODB.Connection")
Set rst = Server.CreateObject("ADODB.RecordSet")
Conn.Open "Driver=SQLOLEDB.1;User ID=sa;
Password=;Initial Catalog=ASPNETDB;Data Source=ASPNET1"
sql = "CREATE TABLE CurTransRec (TransactionID INTEGER
IDENTITY NOT NULL PRIMARY KEY, "
sql = sql & "TType VARCHAR(20), TDate DATETIME, "
sql = sql & "TAmount MONEY DEFAULT 0, AuthorizedBy
```

```
VARCHAR(10), "
sql = sql & "ForWhat VARCHAR(50), CheckNumber VARCHAR(6),
MadeOutTo VARCHAR(50), "
sql = sql & "ToAccountNumber VARCHAR(20))"
rst.Open sql, Conn
Response.Write "Table Created"
%>
```

Notice the connection string contains the DSN your administrator setup, the database in SQL Server the administrator has created for your use, and the simple username and password we chose for you. The rest of the code simply constructs a CREATE TABLE statement in SQL and loads it into the variable sql. The data type assigned to the first field (INTEGER IDENTITY) is specific to SQL Server, results in an autonumbering unique value for this field, and is ideal for a primary key field. The rest of the data types are standard SQL data types, such as VARCHAR, MONEY, and DATETIME. To make calculations easier, the value for the Amount field is set to default to zero if an amount has not been entered. The final Response.Write statement tells you the table was created. You can then substitute in the table name ForTransRec and create another table just like the first one, with the second table being for forecasted records.

2. Your next step is to build an ASP script to process data in and out of the database and an include file to display the results of our processing. First, you build the interface screen. You can use an ordinary HTML editor, such as Dreamweaver, to construct the interface screen and a simple text editor, such as Notepad, to make the script file.

3. The purpose of the interface screen is to show the current financial records as rows in a table, with the balance showing on each row and all the necessary fields also showing. On the same page, you also show the forecasted deposits and withdrawals as a table, with basically the same information displayed. The interface screen could be made up of HTML, such as the following (see Figure 11-2 for an example):

```
<html><head><title>Online Services Systems</title>
<meta http-equiv="Content-Type" content="text/html;
 charset=iso-8859-1">
</head>
<body bgcolor="#77FF77">
<H2><font size="6">Online Services Systems - Financial
 Transactions</font></H2>
<%
set Conn = Server.CreateObject("ADODB.Connection")
```

```
Set rst = Server.CreateObject("ADODB.RecordSet")
Conn.Open "Driver=SQLOLEDB.1;
User ID=sa;Password=;
Initial Catalog=ASPNETDB;Data Source=ASPNET1"
sql = "SELECT SUM(TAmount) As SumTAmount
 FROM CurTransRec"
rst.Open sql, Conn
If Not rst.EOF Then
      vCurBal = rst.Fields("SumTAmount")
Else
      vCurBal = 0
End If
Set rst = Nothing
```

The section of code above starts an ordinary web page with HTML, then opens a Recordset that shows the sum total of current transactions from the table CurTransRec, and if there are no records sets that amount to zero.

```
set Conn = Server.CreateObject("ADODB.Connection")
Set rst = Server.CreateObject("ADODB.RecordSet")
Conn.Open "Driver=SQLOLEDB.1;
User ID=sa;Password=;
Initial Catalog=ASPNETDB;Data Source=ASPNET1"
sql = "SELECT SUM(TAmount) As
 SumTAmount FROM ForTransRec"
rst.Open sql, Conn
If Not  rst.EOF Then
      vCurBFor = rst.Fields("SumTAmount")
Else
      vCurBFor = 0
End If
Set rst = Nothing
```

The section of code above opens a connection and retrieves a Recordset that shows the sum of transactions from the table ForTransRec (forecasted transactions), and if there are no records sets that amount to zero.

```
set Conn = Server.CreateObject("ADODB.Connection")
Set rst = Server.CreateObject("ADODB.RecordSet")
Conn.Open "Driver=SQLOLEDB.1;
User ID=sa;Password=;
Initial Catalog=ASPNETDB;Data Source=ASPNET1"
sql = "SELECT TAmount, TDate FROM
```

```
 CurTransRec WHERE TType = 'Start'"
rst.Open sql, Conn
If Not rst.EOF Then
      vStartAmount = rst.Fields("TAmount")
      vStartDate = rst.Fields("TDate")
Else
      vStartAmount = 0
      vStartDate = 0
End If
Set rst = Nothing
```

The section of code above sets values for the starting record in the displayed Current Transactions.

```
set Conn = Server.CreateObject("ADODB.Connection")
Set rst = Server.CreateObject("ADODB.RecordSet")
Conn.Open "Driver=SQLOLEDB.1;
User ID=sa;Password=;
Initial Catalog=ASPNETDB;Data Source=ASPNET1"
sql = "SELECT TAmount, TDate FROM
 ForTransRec WHERE TType = 'Start'"
rst.Open sql, Conn
If Not rst.EOF Then
      vStartAFor = rst.Fields("TAmount")
      vStartDFor = rst.Fields("TDate")
Else
      vStartAFor = 0
      vStartDFor = 0
End If
Set rst = Nothing
```

The section of code above sets the values for the start record in the displayed Forecasted Transactions.


```
set Conn = Server.CreateObject("ADODB.Connection")
Set rst = Server.CreateObject("ADODB.RecordSet")
Conn.Open "Driver=SQLOLEDB.1;
User ID=sa;Password=;
Initial Catalog=ASPNETDB;Data Source=ASPNET1"
sql = "SELECT * FROM CurTransRec ORDER BY TDate"
rst.Open sql, Conn
%>
<form method="post" action="FinancialTransactions.asp">
```

```
  <table border=1 width="885">
    <tr>
      <td bgcolor="#00CC99" colspan=4>
        <h3>Current Transactions</h3>
      </td></tr><tr>
      <td bgcolor="#00CC99" width="196">
        <div align="left"><b>Beginning Date:
 <% Response.Write vStartDate %></b></div>
      </td><td bgcolor="#00CC99" width="216">
        <div align="left"><b>Beginning Balance:
 <% Response.Write vStartAmount %></b></div>
      </td><td bgcolor="#00CC99" width="256">
        <div align="left"><b>Ending Balance:
 <% Response.Write vCurBal %></b></div>
      </td></tr><tr><td colspan="4">
        <table width="100%" border="1">
          <tr valign="top">
            <td width="4%" height="7">
              <div align="center"><font size="-1">
</font></div>
            </td><td width="4%" height="7">
              <div align="center"><font size="-1">
<b>ID</b></font></div>
            </td><td width="4%" height="7">
              <div align="center"><font size="-1">
<b>Balance</b></font></div>
            </td><td width="10%" height="7">
              <div align="center"><font size="-1">
<b>Type</b></font></div>
            </td><td width="8%" height="7">
              <div align="center"><font size="-1">
<b>Date</b></font></div>
            </td><td width="8%" height="7">
              <div align="center">
                <p><font size="-1"><b>Amount</b>
</font></p>
              </div></td><td width="8%" height="7">
              <div align="center"><font size="-1">
<b>Authorized<br>
                By</b></font></div>
            </td><td width="16%" height="7">
              <div align="center"><font size="-1">
<b>For What</b></font></div>
            </td><td width="5%" height="7">
```

```
            <div align="center"><font size="-1">
<b>Check #</b></font></div>
          </td><td width="16%" height="7">
            <div align="center"><font size="-1">
<b>Made Out To</b></font></div>
          </td><td width="17%" height="7">
            <div align="center"><font size="-1">
<b>To Account #</b></font></div>
          </td></tr>
```

The section of code above displays the contents of the start record.

```
     <% If Not rst.EOF Then
           vRecordBal = rst.Fields("TAmount")
        Else
           vRecordBal = 0
        End If
      Do While Not rst.EOF
     %>
      <tr><td width="4%">
             <input type="submit" name="cmdButton"
 value="DeleteCur<%
 Response.Write rst.Fields("TransactionID") %>">
           </td><td width="4%"><font size="-1">
<% Response.Write rst.Fields("TransactionID") %>
</font></td>
           <td width="4%"><font size="-1">
<% Response.Write vRecordBal %></font></td>
           <td width="10%"><font size="-1">
<% Response.Write rst.Fields("TType") %></font></td>
           <td width="8%"><font size="-1">
<% Response.Write rst.Fields("TDate") %></font></td>
           <td width="8%"><font size="-1">
<% Response.Write rst.Fields("TAmount") %></font></td>
           <td width="8%"><font size="-1">
<% Response.Write rst.Fields("AuthorizedBy") %>
</font></td>
           <td width="16%"><font size="-1">
<% Response.Write rst.Fields("ForWhat") %></font></td>
           <td width="5%"><font size="-1">
<% Response.Write rst.Fields("CheckNumber") %>
</font></td>
           <td width="16%"><font size="-1">
<% Response.Write rst.Fields("MadeOutTo") %>
```

```
</font></td>
            <td width="17%"><font size="-1">
<% Response.Write rst.Fields("ToAccountNumber") %>
</font></td>
          </tr>
      <%
      If Not rst.Fields("TType") = "Start" Then
            vRecordBal = vRecordBal +
 rst.Fields("TAmount")
      End If
      rst.MoveNext
      Loop
      Set rst = Nothing
      %>
```

The section of code above runs a Do…While loop to display each record in the Recordset (from the table of current transactions) in a table formatted in HTML.

```
          <tr><td width="4%">
              <input type="submit" name="cmdButton"
value="AddCur">
            </td><td width="4%"> </td>
            <td width="4%">  </td>
            <td width="10%">
              <select name="TType">
                <option value="Start">
Start</option>
                <option value="Deposit">
Deposit</option>
                <option value="Withdrawal">
Withdrawal</option>
              </select>
            </td><td width="8%">
              <input type="text" name="TDate"
 size="10" maxlength="10">
            </td><td width="8%">
              <input type="text" name="TAmount"
 size="10" maxlength="10">
            </td><td width="8%">
              <select name="AuthorizedBy">
                <option value="John">John</option>
                <option value="Jimmy">Jimmy</option>
                <option value="Roger">Roger</option>
                <option value="Steve">Steve</option>
```

```
            </select>
          </td><td width="16%">
            <input type="text" name="ForWhat">
          </td><td width="5%">
            <input type="text" name="CheckNumber"
size="6" maxlength="6">
          </td><td width="16%">
            <input type="text" name="MadeOutTo">
          </td><td width="17%">
            <input type="text"
name="ToAccountNumber">
          </td></tr></table>
      </td></tr></table>
  <p></p><p>
```

The section of code above provides a means for the user to add new transaction records.

```
  <table border=1 width="885">
    <tr><td bgcolor="#00CC99" colspan=4>
        <h3>Forecasted Transactions</h3>
      </td></tr><tr><td bgcolor="#00CC99" width="196">
        <div align="left"><b>Beginning Date:
<% Response.Write vStartDFor %></b></div>
      </td><td bgcolor="#00CC99" width="216">
        <div align="left"><b>Beginning Balance:
<% Response.Write vStartAFor %></b></div>
      </td><td bgcolor="#00CC99" width="256">
        <div align="left"><b>Ending Balance:
<% Response.Write vCurBFor %></b></div>
      </td></tr><tr><td colspan="4">
        <table width="100%" border="1">
          <tr valign="top">
            <td width="4%" height="7">
              <div align="center"><font size="-1">
</font></div>
            </td><td width="4%" height="7">
              <div align="center"><font size="-1">
<b>ID</b></font></div>
            </td><td width="4%" height="7">
              <div align="center"><font size="-1">
<b>Balance</b></font></div>
            </td><td width="10%" height="7">
              <div align="center"><font size="-1">
```

```
<b>Type</b></font></div>
            </td><td width="8%" height="7">
              <div align="center"><font size="-1">
<b>Date</b></font></div>
            </td><td width="8%" height="7">
              <div align="center">
                <p><font size="-1"><b>Amount</b>
</font></p>
              </div></td><td width="8%" height="7">
              <div align="center"><font size="-1">
<b>Authorized<br>
                By</b></font></div>
            </td><td width="16%" height="7">
              <div align="center"><font size="-1">
<b>For What</b></font></div>
            </td><td width="5%" height="7">
              <div align="center"><font size="-1">
<b>Check #</b></font></div>
            </td><td width="16%" height="7">
              <div align="center"><font size="-1">
<b>Made Out To</b></font></div>
            </td><td width="17%" height="7">
              <div align="center"><font size="-1">
<b>To Account #</b></font></div>
            </td></tr>
```

The section of code above begins the display for the forecasted transaction records, and the section below performs functions similar to those that display the current transaction records.

```
        <%
set Conn = Server.CreateObject("ADODB.Connection")
Set rst = Server.CreateObject("ADODB.RecordSet")
Conn.Open "Driver=SQLOLEDB.1;
User ID=sa;Password=;
Initial Catalog=ASPNETDB;Data Source=ASPNET1"
sql = "SELECT * FROM ForTransRec ORDER BY TDate"
rst.Open sql, Conn
If Not rst.EOf Then
      vRecordBal = rst.Fields("TAmount")
Else
      vRecordBal = 0
End If
Do While Not rst.EOF
```

```
    %>
     <tr><td width="4%">
            <input type="submit"
 name="cmdButton" value="DeleteFor
<% Response.Write rst.Fields("TransactionID") %>">
          </td>
          <td width="4%"><font size="-1">
<% Response.Write rst.Fields("TransactionID") %>
</font></td>
          <td width="4%"><font size="-1">
<% Response.Write vRecordBal %></font></td>
          <td width="10%"><font size="-1">
<% Response.Write rst.Fields("TType") %></font></td>
          <td width="8%"><font size="-1">
<% Response.Write rst.Fields("TDate") %></font></td>
          <td width="8%"><font size="-1">
<% Response.Write rst.Fields("TAmount") %></font></td>
          <td width="8%"><font size="-1">
<% Response.Write rst.Fields("AuthorizedBy") %>
</font></td>
          <td width="16%"><font size="-1">
<% Response.Write rst.Fields("ForWhat") %></font></td>
          <td width="5%"><font size="-1">
<% Response.Write rst.Fields("CheckNumber") %>
</font></td>
          <td width="16%"><font size="-1">
<% Response.Write rst.Fields("MadeOutTo") %>
</font></td>
          <td width="17%"><font size="-1">
<% Response.Write rst.Fields("ToAccountNumber") %>
</font></td>
        </tr>
<%
    If Not rst.Fields("TType") = "Start" Then
          vRecordBal = vRecordBal +
 rst.Fields("TAmount")
    End If
    rst.MoveNext
    Loop
    Set rst = Nothing
    %>
        <tr><td width="4%">
            <input type="submit"
 name="cmdButton" value="AddFor">
```

11

```
            </td>
            <td width="4%"> </td>
            <td width="4%">  </td>
            <td width="10%">
              <select name="TType2">
                <option value="Start">
Start</option>
                <option value="Deposit">
Deposit</option>
                <option value="Withdrawal">
Withdrawal</option>
              </select>
            </td><td width="8%">
              <input type="text" name="TDate2"
 size="10" maxlength="10">
            </td><td width="8%">
              <input type="text" name="TAmount2"
 size="10" maxlength="10">
            </td>
            <td width="8%">
              <select name="AuthorizedBy2">
                <option value="John">John</option>
                <option value="Jimmy">Jimmy</option>
                <option value="Roger">Roger</option>
                <option value="Steve">Steve</option>
              </select>
            </td><td width="16%">
              <input type="text" name="ForWhat2">
            </td><td width="5%">
              <input type="text" name="CheckNumber2"
 size="6" maxlength="6">
            </td><td width="16%">
              <input type="text" name="MadeOutTo2">
            </td><td width="17%">
              <input type="text"
 name="ToAccountNumber2">
            </td></tr></table>
      </td></tr></table>
</form>
<p> </p>
</BODY></HTML>
```

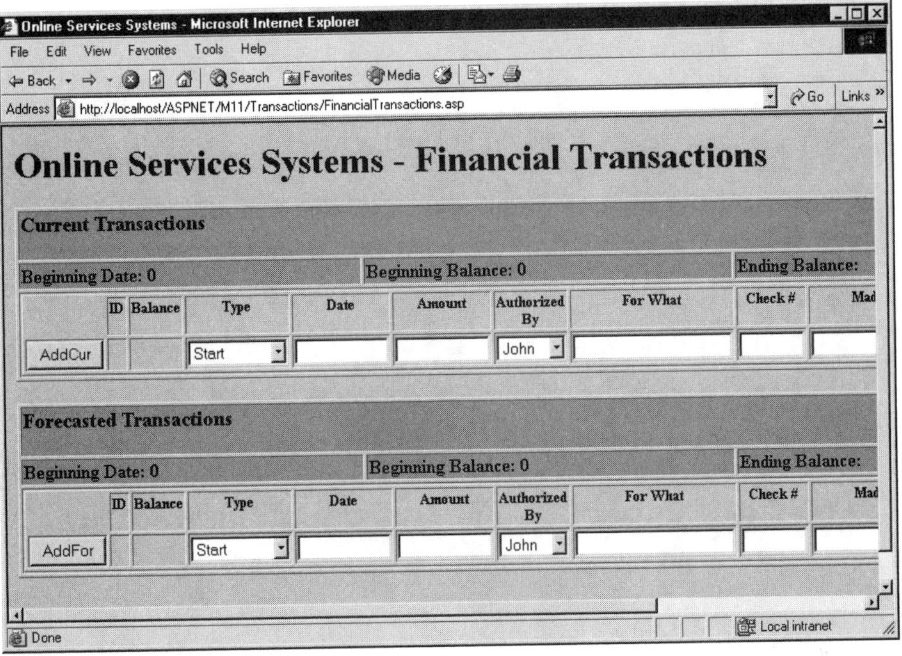

Figure 11-2 The table display interface screen

4. The next step in the construction of your application is the creation of the script to process the transaction; it has only four functions. This step adds a record to either the current or the forecasted records tables, or it deletes a record form either table. There is no update or edit, because it's easy enough to delete a record and reenter the data. The code looks like this:

```
<% TRANSACTION=required Option Explicit
Dim Conn
Dim rst
Dim sql
Dim btnClicked
Dim vDeleteRec
Dim vCurBal
Dim vCurBFor
```

```
Dim vStartAmount
Dim vStartAFor
Dim vStartDate
Dim vStartDFor
Dim vRecordBal
Dim collitem
If Left(Request.Form("cmdButton"), 9) =
 "DeleteCur" Then
      btnClicked = "DeleteCur"
End If
If Left(Request.Form("cmdButton"), 9) =
 "DeleteFor" Then
      btnClicked = "DeleteFor"
End If
If Request.Form("cmdButton") = "AddCur" Then
      btnClicked = "AddCur"
End If
If Request.Form("cmdButton") = "AddFor" Then
      btnClicked = "AddFor"
End If
Select Case btnClicked
  Case "DeleteCur"
    vDeleteRec = Mid(Request.Form("cmdButton"), 10, 10)
    set Conn = Server.CreateObject("ADODB.Connection")
    Set rst = Server.CreateObject("ADODB.RecordSet")
    Conn.Open "Driver=SQLOLEDB.1;
User ID=sa;Password=;
Initial Catalog=ASPNETDB;Data Source=ASPNET1"
    sql = "DELETE FROM CurTransRec WHERE
 TransactionID = " & vDeleteRec & ""
    rst.Open sql, Conn
    Sub OnTransactionCommit()
    %>
    <!-- #include file=
"IncludeDisplayTransactions.txt" -->
    <%
    End Sub
    Sub OnTransactionAbort()
    Response.Write "Unable to delete this record
 at this time. Please try again later."
    End Sub
 Case "DeleteFor"
    vDeleteRec = Mid(Request.Form("cmdButton"), 10, 10)
```

```
    set Conn = Server.CreateObject("ADODB.Connection")
    Set rst = Server.CreateObject("ADODB.RecordSet")
    Conn.Open "Driver=SQLOLEDB.1;
User ID=sa;Password=;
Initial Catalog=ASPNETDB;Data Source=ASPNET1"
    sql = "DELETE FROM ForTransRec WHERE
 TransactionID = " & vDeleteRec & ""
    rst.Open sql, Conn
    Sub OnTransactionCommit()
    %>
    <!-- #include file=
"IncludeDisplayTransactions.txt" -->
    <%
    End Sub
    Sub OnTransactionAbort()
    Response.Write "Unable to delete this record
 at this time. Please try again later."
    End Sub
 Case "AddCur"
    set Conn = Server.CreateObject("ADODB.Connection")
    Set rst = Server.CreateObject("ADODB.RecordSet")
    Conn.Open "Driver=SQLOLEDB.1;
User ID=sa;Password=;
Initial Catalog=ASPNETDB;Data Source=ASPNET1"
    sql = "INSERT INTO CurTransRec (TType, TDate, "
    sql = sql & "TAmount, AuthorizedBy, ForWhat,
CheckNumber, "
    sql = sql & "MadeOutTo, ToAccountNumber) VALUES "
    sql = sql & "('" & Request.Form("TType") & "', "
    sql = sql & "'" & Request.Form("TDate") & "', " &
Request.Form("TAmount") & ", "
    sql = sql & "'" & Request.Form("AuthorizedBy")
 & "', '" & Request.Form("ForWhat") & "', "
    sql = sql & "'" & Request.Form("CheckNumber")
 & "', '" & Request.Form("MadeOutTo") & "', "
    sql = sql & "'" & Request.Form("ToAccountNumber")
 & "')"
    rst.Open sql, Conn
    Sub OnTransactionCommit()
    %>
    <!-- #include file="
IncludeDisplayTransactions.txt" -->
    <%
```

```
    End Sub
    Sub OnTransactionAbort()
    Response.Write "Unable to add this record
 at this time. Please try again later."
    End Sub
 Case "AddFor"
    set Conn = Server.CreateObject("ADODB.Connection")
    Set rst = Server.CreateObject("ADODB.RecordSet")
    Conn.Open "Driver=SQLOLEDB.1;
User ID=sa;Password=;
Initial Catalog=ASPNETDB;Data Source=ASPNET1"
    sql = "INSERT INTO ForTransRec (TType, TDate, "
    sql = sql & "TAmount, AuthorizedBy, ForWhat,
 CheckNumber, "
    sql = sql & "MadeOutTo, ToAccountNumber) VALUES "
    sql = sql & "('" & Request.Form("TType2") & "', "
    sql = sql & "'" & Request.Form("TDate2") & "', " &
Request.Form("TAmount2") & ", "
    sql = sql & "'" & Request.Form("AuthorizedBy2")
 & "', '" & Request.Form("ForWhat2") & "', "
    sql = sql & "'" & Request.Form("CheckNumber2")
 & "', '" & Request.Form("MadeOutTo2") & "', "
    sql = sql & "'" & Request.Form("ToAccountNumber2")
 & "')"
    rst.Open sql, Conn
    Sub OnTransactionCommit()
    %>
    <!-- #include file=
"IncludeDisplayTransactions.txt" -->
    <%
    End Sub
    Sub OnTransactionAbort()
    Response.Write "Unable to add this record
 at this time. Please try again later."
    End Sub
End Select
  If LEN(Request.Form("cmdButton")) = 0 Then
    %>
    <!-- #include file=
"IncludeDisplayTransactions.txt" -->
    <%
  End If
%>
```

Collaborative Technologies and CDONTS

One of the most common CGI scripts available with traditional web hosting accounts is one that takes the name/value pairs submitted with a web page form, turns them into an e-mail, and sends them to the website owner. The capability to send e-mails from an application opens up a whole new world of possibilities and, naturally, you can do the same thing with ASP. The enabling technology is called *Collaboration Data Objects* (CDO).

CDO works with Microsoft Exchange Server to provide e-mail, calendaring, collaboration, and workflow services that are accessible to your ASP applications. A subset of these capabilities, called *CDO for Windows NT Server* (CDONTS), provides only the e-mail service when your Windows 2000 SMTP Service is installed. Using CDONTS for sending e-mail makes it easy to whip up an application quickly with e-mail capability. Unfortunately, at press time, CDONTS doesn't seem to offer direct support for such collaborative capabilities as whiteboarding, remote client control, and video conferencing. These collaborative capabilities can be generated using Microsoft NetMeeting and its associated server. As yet, however, no direct way exists to manipulate NetMeeting or the server from ASP, although a simple scripting interface has been added in the latest version that enables developers to embed NetMeeting in web pages.

The CDONTS Object Model

The object model for CDONTS has two primary objects at the top level: the Session object and the NewMail object. First, you'll learn about how the NewMail object works, and then you'll learn about the Session object.

The NewMail Object

The *NewMail* object is essentially an e-mail message in programmatic form, and it has properties containing the appropriate values for things such as who the message is from, who it is addressed to, and so on. If you were to imagine the screen of a common e-mail client in which you are sending a new e-mail message, the NewMail object has a property for each text field on the screen. It also has a property for Importance, which is not yet common in e-mail clients but seems pretty handy from a programming perspective.

The From, To, CC, BCC, and Subject properties are self-explanatory; just make sure the values they take on are equivalent to what you would enter if you were in the new message screen of a typical e-mail client. As you'll see shortly, you can retrieve these values from an HTML form in a web page and then assign them to the appropriate properties of a NewMail object before you send it.

The *Importance* property is a little different. The values it can take on are 2, 1, and 0, representing High, Normal, and Low importance. If you use an HTML form to capture the Importance value a user assigns to her message, make sure to use the numerical values rather than the text equivalents. And remember, support for Importance values is not solid across the Internet, so it may not provide any additional functionality.

The *Body* property contains the contents of the message and, by default, it is formatted as plain text. You can change the BodyFormat property to HTML using the CdoBodyFormatHTML constant, in which case you could send a message formatted as HTML to a user and it would be properly rendered (assuming his e-mail client supports HTML). The MailFormat property is, by default, plain text, but you can change that to *Multipurpose Internet Mail Extension* (MIME) if you need to send a message in a rich content format. Setting the MailFormat property equal to CdoMailFormatMIME does the trick. The Version property of the NewMail object returns the version of CDONTS being used.

Hint

To use CDO constants, you can set a reference to the CDO type library in the global.asa file, or you can reference the available constants from an include file you build yourself, as long as you know what the constants are.

The Send method of the NewMail object actually sends your e-mail message, and the AttachFile method attaches files to the message. The Send method can be used by itself once the appropriate properties are set, or these properties can be used as parameters in a single line sending a message, like so:

```
ObjEmail.Send(From, To, Subject, Body, Importance)
```

The AttachFile method has syntax like the following:

```
ObjEmail.AttachFile(pathandfilename, caption, encodingmethod)
```

The caption can be the filename so the user knows what the attachment is, and the encoding method can be changed from the default (UUENCODE) to Base64.

1-Minute Drill

- What does setting the Importance property do for your e-mails?
- What happens if you send an e-mail without setting the From property?

The Session Object and Child Objects

The CDONTS object model also contains a Session object, and related to this object are a number of children objects that work with it to provide a great deal more e-mail functionality to your applications than just being able to generate and send e-mail messages. The children are

- **The Folder object** Allows access to the default folders (Inbox and Outbox) in the Session, and you can view, add, and delete any messages in it, as well as through its Messages collection.
- **The Message object** Can be accessed through the Messages collection (from the Folder object) and enables you to retrieve the message properties of messages in the collection as well as send or delete individual messages (the Delete method of the Messages collection deletes all messages in the folder).
- **The Attachment object** Allows access to an individual attachment on a message (the Attachments collection of the message allows access to all attachments on a message). You can review the attachments properties to see what kind of attachment it is (name, source, type, and so on), and you can also delete, load data to, or save an attachment.
- **The Recipient object** Represents a single recipient among a group of recipients (accessible through the Recipients collection of the Message object) and enables you to view the name, address, and type of recipient (To, CC, BCC).

Now that you've reviewed the primary objects in CDONTS, you can make a simple application for sending e-mails from a web page.

- Possibly nothing, unless all e-mail servers and the receiving client can make use of the value.
- The e-mail will still be sent, but the From area will be blank.

Project 11-2: An E-mail Sending Web Page

You might never want your users to be able to log in to your website and send e-mails directly, but creating a page to do that can illustrate how you can use the NewMail object to easily send e-mails from an ASP application. What you do with it after that is your business but, please note, just because you can easily send mass quantities of e-mail using a database of e-mail addresses doesn't mean you should. Spam is usually unwelcome, and making the extra effort to verify those recipients on the list who actually want to hear from you can pay big dividends down the road.

Step-by-Step

1. Make sure your SMTP server is properly set up to send out e-mails. If you installed SMTP service during the installation of Windows 2000 and IIS, there's little to do other than make sure the Default Virtual SMTP Server is pointing to a valid domain. If you didn't install it, do so using the administrative functions and the setup procedures under IIS.

2. To start the application, build the user a nice e-mail sending screen (shown in Figure 11-3), using an HTML form to collect the appropriate value for each property you're going to send, like this:

```
<html><head><title>Project 11-2</title>
<meta http-equiv="Content-Type"
 content="text/html; charset=iso-8859-1">
</head>
<body bgcolor="#FFFFFF" link="#663333">
<table width="100%" border="1"
 bordercolordark="#CC9966" bordercolorlight="#CC9966">
  <tr><td colspan=2>
      <table width="100%" border="0">
        <tr><td width="100%" valign="top"
 height="247" colspan="2">
            <table width="100%" border="1"
 bordercolor="#FFCC99" bordercolorlight="#CC9966"
 bordercolordark="#CC9966">
            <tr bgcolor="#CC9966">
                <td><b><font face="Arial, Helvetica,
 sans-serif" size="+1" color="#FFFFFF">SEND E-MAIL
</font></b></td>
            </tr></table><form method="POST"
 action="SendE-mail.asp" name="">
```

```
            <table width="100%" border="0"
 bordercolordark="#CC9966"
 bordercolorlight="#CC9966">
             <tr valign="top" bgcolor="#CC9966">
<td> </td>
             </tr><tr valign="top"><td>
                 <table border="0" width="100%">
                   <tr bordercolor="#CC9966"
 bgcolor="#FFCC99">
                     <td align="right" colspan="2">
                       <div align="left"><b>
<font face="Arial, Helvetica, sans-serif"
 color="#FFFFFF"><font color="#663333" size="+1">
Fill In All Fields, Please</font></font></b></div>
                   </td></tr>
                   <tr bordercolor="#CC9966"
 bgcolor="#FFCC99">
                   <td align="right" width="12%">
<div align="center"></div>
                     </td><td align="right"
 width="88%">
                       <div align="left"><b>
<font face="Arial, Helvetica, sans-serif" size="+1"
 color="#FFFFFF"><font color="#663333">
<font size="-1"></font></font></font></b></div>
                     </td></tr><tr><td width="12%"
 align="right">
                       <div align="left"><font
 face="Arial, Helvetica, sans-serif" color="#663333"
 size="-1"><b>From: </b></font></div>
                     </td><td width="88%">
                       <input type="text" name="From"
 size="40" tabindex="1">
                     </td></tr><tr><td width="12%"
 align="right">
                       <div align="left"><font
 face="Arial, Helvetica, sans-serif"
 color="#663333" size="-1"><b>To:
                         </b></font></div>
                     </td><td width="88%">
                       <input type="text"
 name="To" size="40" tabindex="3">
                     </td></tr><tr><td
```

11

```
 width="12%" align="right">
                        <div align="left">
<font face="Arial, Helvetica, sans-serif"
 color="#663333" size="-1"><b>CC:</b></font></div>
                      </td><td width="88%">
                        <input type="text"
 name="CC" size="40">
                      </td></tr><tr><td width="12%"
 align="right">
                        <div align="left"><font
 face="Arial, Helvetica, sans-serif" color="#663333"
 size="-1"><b>BCC:</b></font></div>
                      </td><td width="88%">
                        <input type="text" name="BCC"
 size="40" tabindex="6">
                      </td></tr><tr><td width="12%"
 align="right">
                        <div align="left"><font
 face="Arial, Helvetica, sans-serif" color="#663333"
 size="-1"><b>Importance:</b></font></div>
                      </td><td width="88%">
                        <select name="Importance">
                          <option value=2>High</option>
                          <option value=1 selected>
Normal</option>
                          <option value=0>Low</option>
                        </select>
                      </td></tr><tr><td width="12%"
 align="right">
                        <div align="left"><b><font
 size="-1" face="Arial, Helvetica, sans-serif"
color="#663333">Subject:</font></b></div>
            </td><td width="88%"><input type="text"
 name="Subject" size="40">
               </td></tr><tr><td align="right"
 bgcolor="#FFCC99" colspan="2">
                        <div align="left"><font
 face="Arial, Helvetica, sans-serif"
 color="#663333" size="-1"><b><font
 face="Arial, Helvetica, sans-serif"
 size="+1" color="#FFFFFF"><font
 color="#663333">BODY</font></font>
                      </b></font></div></td></tr><tr>
```

```
                    <td width="12%" align="right">
<font face="Arial, Helvetica, sans-serif"
 color="#663333" size="-1"></font></td>
    <td width="88%"><textarea name="Body" cols="100"
 rows="10"></textarea>
                    </td></tr><tr
 bordercolor="#CC9966" bgcolor="#FFCC99">
                    <td width="12%" align="right">
<font face="Arial, Helvetica, sans-serif"
 color="#663333" size="-1">
                      <input type="submit"
 value="Send E-mail" name="B1">
                      </font></td>
                    <td width="88%">  </td>
                  </tr></table></form></table></td>
        </tr></table></td></tr></table></body></html>
```

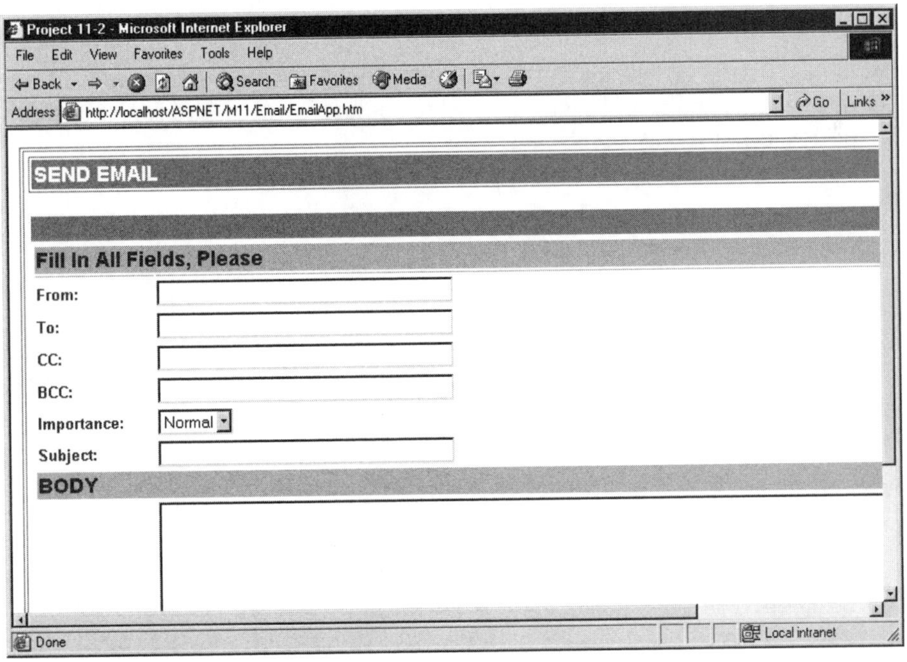

Figure 11-3 The e-mail sending form

3. Now that you have a beautiful form, you can set up the backend processing like this:

```
<% Option Explicit
Dim objEmail
Set objEmail = CreateObject("CDONTS.NewMail")
objEmail.From = request.Form("From")
objEmail.To = request.Form("To")
objEmail.Cc = request.Form("CC")
objEmail.Bcc = request.Form("BCC")
objEmail.Importance = request.Form("Importance")
objEmail.Subject = request.Form("Subject")
objEmail.Body = request.Form("Body")
objEmail.Send
Set objEmail = Nothing
Response.Write "<HTML><HEAD><TITLE>Project 11-1
</TITLE><BODY><CENTER><B>Message
 Sent</B></CENTER></BODY></HTML>"
%>
```

4. Notice that after you set all the properties for the e-mail, you send it using the Send method, and then respond to the user with a "Message Sent" notice formatted as a web page.

Ask the Expert

Question: I understand how it would be useful to send e-mails to myself when someone submits a form, but how else would I use this capability? Why not just keep the contents in a database?

Answer: One big advantage of using e-mails (and you can use them in addition to putting the contents in a database) is you get instant notification. As soon as a user clicks, the e-mail is sent. If you happen to be online with your e-mail client open and checking for mail on a regular basis, you could almost receive notification in real time.

In addition, plenty of e-mail-to-fax applications are available, and these work well for businesses that either don't have e-mail (still a significant number, believe it or not) or don't want to go online to check e-mail all the time. Sometimes the person collecting the information or taking the order is just an employee working behind a counter and having the fax machine spit out online orders is convenient.

> Other uses for e-mail capability run more toward server and application management. For instance, suppose you want the server to notify you when a certain value in the database reaches a threshold, or when a particular customer is shopping, or when a particular error is generated. Triggering an e-mail through ASP lets you do these things easily.

Optimizing ASP.NET Applications

There are many ways to code any given programmatic function (or web page, for that matter). Depending upon the circumstances, some ways may work better than others in meeting your objectives. Optimization is the process of refining and changing your code and the structure of your application to better meet your objectives.

Not every optimization listed in this section is appropriate in every case because not every project has the same objectives. For example, for a very small, low volume, non-mission-critical application, it may not be necessary to perform extensive optimization, both because the gains will never be evident and because it can add unnecessary expense.

ASP.NET Optimization Measures

The following table includes common measures you can use to optimize your ASP.NET applications:

Disable session state when not in use.	To disable session state for a page, set the EnableSessionState attribute in the @ Page directive to false, like this: <%@ Page EnableSessionState="false" %>. To disable session state for an application, set the Mode attribute to off in the sessionstate configuration section of the application's web.config file, like this: <sessionstate mode="off" />.
Choose the appropriate session state provider.	There are three ways to store session data: in-process session state, out-of-process session state as a Windows Service, and out-of-process session state in a SQL Server database. In-process session state is by far the fastest solution.
Avoid round trips to the server if possible.	Round trips to the server can make it much easier to perform certain operations effectively, but always remember that this can add unacceptable latency to your application.

Disable server control view state if possible.	If you are performing operations that don't require new or stateful data, disabling view state will save processing time. Change the MaintainState attribute to false for the control (or for the whole page, if you like) to disable view state.
Use System.Text. StringBuilder for String concatenation.	The StringBuilder class allows much higher performance than ordinary string operators for concatenating strings.
Use SQL Server stored procedures.	Stored procedures run much faster inside the database than if they are set in code in your application.
Disable debug mode before deploying.	Disable debug mode before deploying an application or performing tests. When debug mode is enabled, application performance noticeably suffers.

Security Overview

High-profile attacks on e-commerce websites are becoming more and more common, and fraudulent transactions are also a growing problem. While these have recently been getting lots of press and attention, security, privacy, and reliability issues have been around practically since data processing began. If you look into the history of commerce and communications in general, you'll find innovative methods employed to verify identity, keep information private, and ensure accurate delivery under adverse conditions since people first started communicating.

The point is that security, in its broadest terms, goes far beyond simply using SSL on your web server or making users provide a username and password. When you think about security, think about all the potential threats to your system, your data, and the services you are attempting to provide users. Start at the highest level and work down to build in security, and you'll have a much more secure and reliable application.

Security Defined

In its broadest terms, building a secure system means protecting the data and services your system works with from all threats that would gain unauthorized access to, misuse, destroy, or render inoperable that data and or those services. This means any potential threat to the system, regardless of whether it is natural or manmade, malicious or just careless, must be factored into the equation. Let's discuss the subtopics implied by this definition:

- **Reliability** An unreliable system is just as bad as a hacked system, especially if you are running mission-critical applications.

- **Privacy** A privacy policy that enables you to sell user's personal data without notifying them (still perfectly legal at this time, by the way) could be damaging to you and your user base in the long run—almost as bad as having a hacker steal the data.
- **Secure transactions and storage** Employing SSL to collect sensitive data but leaving your database files hackable is like closing the barn door after the horses are already gone.

So where do you start building a properly secured system, keeping in mind that no system can be guaranteed completely secure under all circumstances? Good security policy goes hand-in-hand with good security architecture.

Security Policy

Depending on the circumstance under which you are working, you might assist the systems administrator and other members of the IT department (along with other upper-level managers in the organization) in preparing a comprehensive security policy for the organization, or you might be in the position of developing the entire policy yourself, with a little input from your client. From one end of the spectrum to the other, you still need to have a formal, written security policy in hand, even if it's not elaborate. It's like having a business plan or any other kind of plan; if you don't have one, it's much harder to figure out where you're going, much less actually get there.

A good security policy covers specific computer and Internet-related issues such as SSL, encryption, and so forth, but it also covers password generation, permissions for employees or users, training, and other issues having more to do with the way people work with your system. Start your security policy by defining the objectives of the policy—in measurable terms, so you can measure whether it's working. For example, if the system is mission-critical, perhaps you must have it up and accessible 100 percent of the time. Then, if it ever goes down for any reason, you will be missing your objective (not by much, we hope), but at least it's measurable and will give you a means to quantify the effectiveness of the measures built into your security policy.

Next, define the roles and responsibilities of each player or group expected to have access to the system, and make sure to include a discussion of those folks who are uninvited. This means to include not only what users, managers, and administrators are supposed to do, but also hackers, ex-employees, and Internet users in general. Remember, if enough users try to access your site, even by accidentally entering the wrong URL in their browser, they can bring down your application. It's important to define what you expect of authorized users, but it's also important to outline what you think unauthorized users might do and to plan for it.

Finally, your security policy should include regular assessments, updates, revisions, and effectiveness measurements. Security, like so many other areas of interest on the Internet, changes pretty rapidly, and you need to put in place some system of regular accounting for and coping with rapid change.

Software, Applications, and Networking Security

Assuming you have a reasonable security policy in place and it covers non-computer-related issues well, then it's time to look at security concerns about your software, applications, and how your networks are configured. This includes your operating systems, programs, and applications, as well as the physical and logical arrangement of your networks.

Operating System Security

Operating system security is a good starting point because you can do many things at the operating system level to make it more difficult for unauthorized users to gain access to restricted areas or services. For example, you can create partitions on your hard drive with a variety of formats. Making a separate partition for the web server and web applications is a smart move, especially when you format the partition as NTFS, as was done in an earlier module. NTFS enables you to set permissions much more finely than the typical FAT format. And NTFS enables you to set *Access Control Lists* (ACLs), set disk quotas, and encrypt files.

Another area deserving attention is the removal of capabilities not needed to run the application or manage the server. For example, you can remove the capability of the operating system to generate DOS-style filenames and extensions, to allow anonymous network access, and to allow access to common administrator tools. Your system administrators should be familiar with how to disable these functions, but it's a good idea to check with them and see what they've done or plan to do.

The system administrator should also remove access to unneeded network services, such as WINS, NetBIOS, and LMHOSTS lookup, and should set TCP/IP filtering so unnecessary ports are unavailable. The responsibility of the system administrator is also to install and configure the firewall and any proxy servers properly.

Web Server Security

Following a review of operating system security (this is as much or more the job of the system administrator) comes a review of the configuration of your web server software, in your case, IIS 5.0. By default, when IIS is installed, some capabilities that aren't required for all web applications will be installed. For example, FrontPage Server Extensions is only required if the web pages call for them, and this should only happen if you are using the advanced features of FrontPage when you create your pages. If you don't use the advanced features in FrontPage (such as the Search function or the Form Handler), you don't need FrontPage Server Extensions installed. This can be construed as a general rule: namely, that you shouldn't install or should uninstall any services or features not specifically required by your applications.

If you maintain the web server, another area deserving close attention is the release of patches for the server. For example, at the Microsoft site in a search for IIS 5.0, there were many security bulletins about IIS 5.0 vulnerabilities, such as the following:

- **MS00-031** Patch Available for "Undelimited .HTR Request" and "File Fragment Reading via .HTR" Vulnerabilities.
- **MS00-030** Patch Available for "Malformed Extension Data in URL" Vulnerability.
- **MS00-023** Patch Available for "Myriad Escaped Characters" Vulnerability.

Examining the available patches to see if they apply to your IIS configuration or your web application is crucial to the continuing security of your website.

Like most servers, IIS 5.0 can maintain log files and, using the components discussed in previous modules, you can create custom log files to use for whatever you want. For some applications, you may find this capability makes tracking who is doing what within your application easier. This has implications not only for telling what happened after an attack, but also for alerting you during an attack or an attempt to gain unauthorized entry.

Authentication and Certificates

You can set your application to require one of three levels of authentication when users enter your website: Anonymous, Basic, and IWA. Anonymous authentication requires no user name and password; essentially, by requesting a page, a user gets access to it. Basic authentication means users will be requested to supply a username and password when connecting, and they are then transmitted in clear text format. *Integrated Windows Authentication* (*IWA*) makes use of either the Kerberos Network Authentication Protocol, or the old Windows NT Challenge/Response Protocol, depending on the client being used.

The point of authentication is to verify the user is who she says she is. Each of the three methods mentioned has appropriate uses under various circumstances and can work with other security measures to provide secure communications to the appropriate party.

Certificates, which can be bought from a number of sources, provide a layer of encryption to your communications, both personal and server-based. The use of certificates is part of the answer to the problem of making sure the person you are dealing with is actually the person you think he is. Without going into too much detail, the overall problem of security and encryption has been fairly well solved from the standpoint of generating hard-to-break encryption codes, but it hasn't been addressed as well when it comes to verifying identity unambiguously. Certificates from a trusted source help solve that portion of the problem.

You can buy personal certificates and server certificates from companies such as Verisign and then install them on your browser and your web server, respectively. These certificates help prove who you are and make it much easier to communicate securely with e-commerce websites and with your own customers. Once you have a certificate in place, it's a fairly simple matter to set up SSL on IIS 5.0, and you can even become your own certificate authority (rather than buying it from Verisign) if you want.

1-Minute Drill

- What should you have in place before you start setting up security measures for your website?
- Who is responsible for website application security?

- A well-thought-out security policy
- Everyone developing or using the application

Mastery Check

1. What encryption method is unbreakable above a certain bit size?

   A. PGP

   B. RSA

   C. Dual-key

   D. None of the above

2. What kind of security does authentication provide?

   A. Authentication tells you the person or system you are communicating with is actually the person or system they have told you they are.

   B. Authentication verifies the message you are reading hasn't been tampered with.

   C. Authentication hides the contents of a message from unauthorized viewers.

   D. None of the above.

3. What VBScript method could you use to determine whether a password is long enough to be a valid password?

   A. CStr, which counts the length of a string

   B. Fix, which fixes the length of a string

   C. Len, which measures the length of a string

   D. Lbound, which rejects any strings below the lower bound in size

4. What four properties are the mark of a valid transaction?

   A. Atomicity, Synchronicity, Isolation, and Durability

   B. Atomicity, Consistency, Immolation, and Durability

   C. Atomicity, Consistency, Information, and Durability

   D. Atomicity, Consistency, Isolation, and Durability

Mastery Check

5. In the context of a transaction, what does Isolation mean and why is it important?

   A. Each part of an individual transaction is isolated from the other parts, so the failure of one part does not stop the other parts from being completed.

   B. Each transaction is isolated from other transactions, so each transaction operates as if it alone had total control over the resources it is updating.

   C. If one update within a transaction fails, the entire transaction will be rolled back.

   D. None of the above.

6. If you program a script with ASP as a transaction and the transaction fails, how does Component Services tell your script about this, and what measures must you take to support transactions in your script?

   A. Component Services has two events, OnTransactionCommit and OnTransactionAbort, that tell ASP about the success or failure of a transaction, and, upon failure, rolls back all changes made within the transaction.

   B. Your ASP script can detect the events triggered in Component Services signaling the success or failure of a transaction, but you must manually roll back all changes made because Component Services cannot perform the rollback when a transaction is performed within an ASP script.

   C. Although your ASP script can detect the success or failure of a transaction, you must manually roll back the parts of the transaction that aren't supported under Component Services, such as Application and Session variables and file system changes.

   D. None of the above.

7. What is the SQL statement to build a table in SQL Server, and how is an auto-numbering primary key established?

   A. Build Table surname is the statement, and Primary Key is the attribute that sets an autonumbering primary key in SQL Server when a field or column is being named.

Mastery Check

B. CREATE TABLE tablename is the statement, and setting a data type of INTEGER IDENTITY creates an autonumbering field in SQL Server.

C. CREATE TABLE tablename is the statement, and you can use the AUTO attribute to create an autonumbering field in SQL Server.

D. None of the above.

8. What should the connection string to a SQL Server database include?

A. It should include the name of the DSN, the username, the password, and the name of the database.

B. It should include the DSN only.

C. It should include the username, password, and name of the database only.

D. None of the above.

9. What is the difference between CDO and CDONTS?

A. CDO means Comma Delimited Object, while CDONTS means Collaboration Data Objects for Windows NT Server.

B. CDO contains the capability to perform collaborative functions for all platforms, while CDONTS can perform collaboration functions only on Windows NT Server.

C. CDO has more collaborative functions than CDONTS.

D. None of the above.

10. What property would you set to send an e-mail to someone without others knowing the e-mail was sent to that person?

A. To

B. From

C. CC

D. BCC

E. None of the above

Mastery Check

11. Three steps in building security into online applications for an organization are conducting a security ________, identifying and closing security ________, and implementing a security ____________.

12. Describe how (in ASP.NET) to disable session state for a page and for an application, and why you might want to do this.

____

____

13. While developing an application, you should have _______ mode enabled to help you find problems within your application, but once you are ready to deploy the application, you should turn off ______ mode, so your application's performance improves.

14. Describe some features you can incorporate into your applications that help make them more secure.

____

____

15. In regards to the Isolation property of a transaction, what does this property mean, and how might it affect the ability of your application to scale up?

____

____

Appendix A

Answers to Mastery Checks

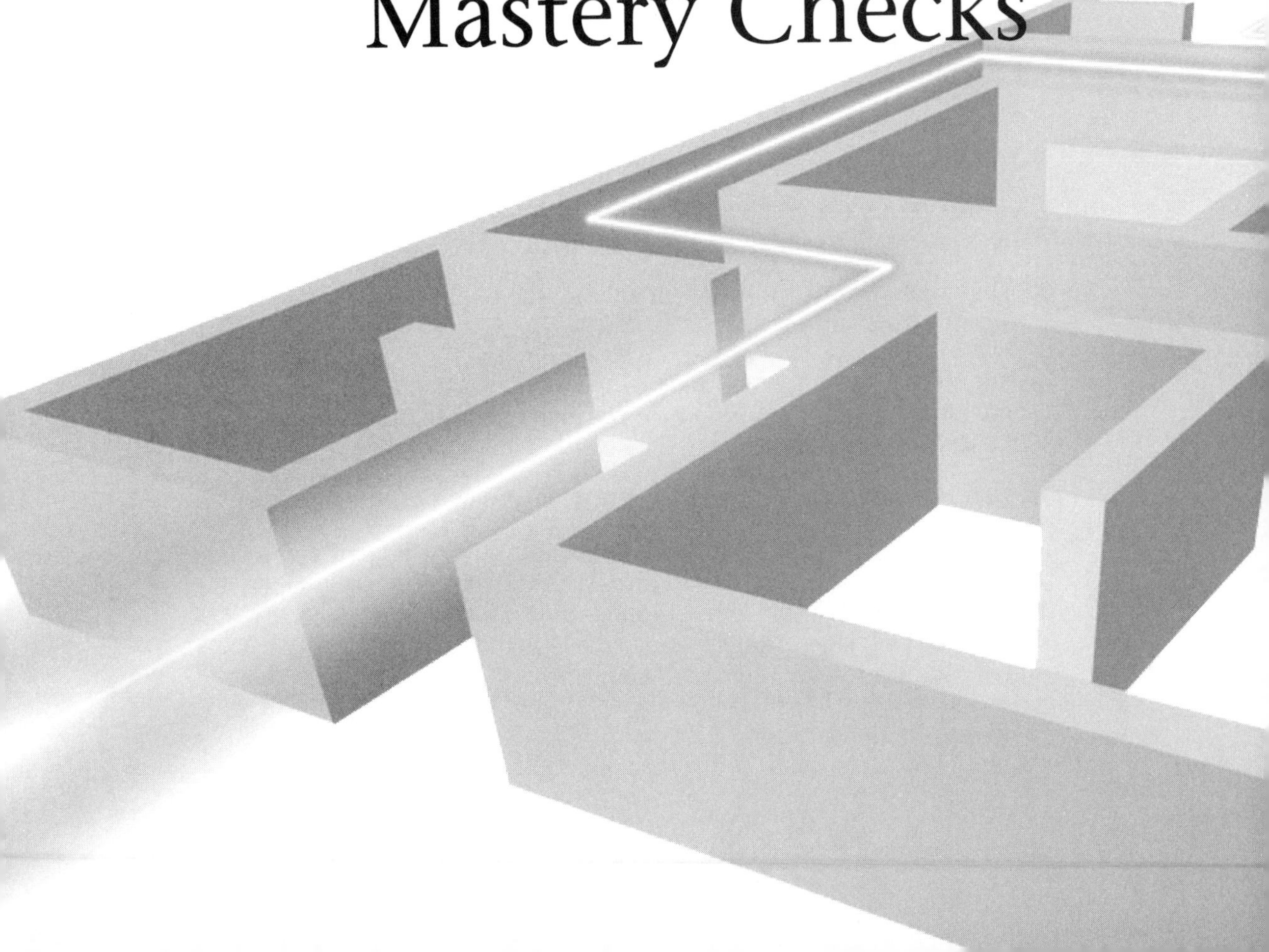

Module 1: ASP.NET: Getting Set Up

1. On what platform does ASP.NET run, and how much does ASP.NET cost?

D. B and C

2. What is the primary functionality ASP.NET brings to a website, and why is it so important?

ASP.NET provides the capability to create dynamic, distributed applications for websites, enabling websites to function much like ordinary desktop applications. It is important because, with its connection to all the other data and resources available on the Internet and its ability to communicate to both humans and machines, ASP.NET applications are much more powerful than ordinary applications.

3. What is a partition, and why does it matter how it is formatted when installing IIS?

A partition is a separate area on a hard drive, and the format of a partition is important because it affects the capabilities IIS has regarding permissions allowed to be set for the partition.

4. What process is advisable to use when designing a web-based application?

C. Ask plenty of questions up front, and then evaluate the client's needs and make recommendations based on those needs.

5. What is bandwidth and why is it an important consideration in the design of a modern website?

Bandwidth is the amount of data that can be transmitted within a given time, and it is important because it constrains website performance (speed of access).

6. What is the difference between interpreted and compiled languages?

B. Compiled languages are for developing programs that are turned into processor instructions specific to the CPUs they run on, while interpreted languages remain in the form of source code until they are accessed. Compiled languages produce executable files that run much faster than code made with interpreted languages.

7. What is XML?

E. B and C above

8. What programming languages are supported in ASP.NET?

C. Any programming language for which a compiler capable of producing IL code is available

9. What ADO objects are used for accessing databases?

B. The Connection, Command, and Recordset objects

10. What ADO.NET objects are used for accessing databases?

A. The DataSet and DataReader objects

11. What kinds of bandwidth are there, and how is usage calculated?

B. There is available bandwidth and used bandwidth. Available bandwidth is calculated as the total amount of data that can be transmitted in a given time frame, while used bandwidth is the amount of data actually transmitted in a given time frame.

12. What is a distributed application, and how is it different from normal applications?

A distributed application works as a set of programmatic functions that may be physically located anywhere on the Internet or any network, while the functions in a normal application are contained within a single program on a single machine.

13. How can you find out what version of the operating system is running on your computer?

D. Any of the above.

14. What is the advantage of using a set of tools such as Visual Studio to develop ASP.NET applications?

D. All of the above.

15. What kinds of features are found in a web page made with ASP.NET?

Web Forms and Web Services.

Module 2: ASP.NET Programming Basics

1. What languages are commonly used to construct web pages and online applications?

   E. All of the above

2. HyperText Transport Protocol defines communications between web servers and web browsers. What kinds of messages are included in these communications?

   F. All of the above

3. Delimiters are characters used to define commands in programming languages. The delimiters for HTML are < and >. The delimiters for ASP code within HTML are ______ and ______.

   <%, %>

4. Describe three common coding practices that make your code more readable, more debuggable, and less error-prone.

   Commenting your code, using standard naming conventions, and using the Option Explicit statement (VBScript) or Option Strict (VB.NET).

5. Who decides what the layout and look and feel of a website should be? Who should have input?

   E. All of the above

6. What languages are used to program ASP.NET pages?

   E. All of the above

7. What does the term *data type* mean? What kinds of data types are there?

   B. Data type refers to the type of data in question, such as strings, numbers, and so forth. Depending upon the data type, certain types of processing are possible. For instance, a string of data may not be added to another string, but if the data types are changed to some numerical type, the two items of data may be added.

8. Hard-coding values into a page or into program code is a bad idea and should be avoided wherever practical because if the value is present in several places, pages, or programs, much more ________ is required to change the value.

effort

9. Describe three ways in which coding XHTML is different from coding HTML.

In XHTML, all elements must be properly terminated, elements and attributes must be written lowercase, and elements must be properly nested.

10. What built-in ASP objects are available? Are these same objects also available in VB.NET?

A. The Request and Response, Application and Session, and Server objects , and they can be used in VB.NET as well.

11. What program structure would be useful for looping through a set of statements until a particular value is reached?

D. The Do...Until loop

12. What does *polymorphism* mean?

Polymorphism means that methods and properties of classes can have the same name and be used in the same way, even though what is happening inside the objects made from those classes may be completely different.

13. An ASP file should have the file extension _____, while an ASP.NET file should have the file extension _____.

.asp, .aspx

14. Describe three things you might see when an error is generated in your code upon compiling it for the first time.

What the problem is, what line it was found on, and detailed output from the compiler.

15. How is your code compiled in the CLR, and when does this happen?

A. All the files in your application, including HTML files, are compiled. They are compiled the first time the application is accessed, and thereafter only the compiled resource is used. If you make a change to a file, that file will be recompiled the next time it is accessed.

Module 3: Programming ASP.NET with Visual Basic.NET

1. What are variables?

B. Variables are placeholders for data that can vary as an application executes.

2. What are VB.NET data types, and how are they related to variables?

A. The term *data type* refers to the kind of data represented within a variable, such as string, date, number, and so forth. VB.NET data types have names assigned to them that may not be the same as the names assigned to data types in other languages.

3. Operators are programming language symbols that perform operations on variable values (or hard-coded values). The arithmetical operators include the __________ to perform addition and the __________ to perform subtraction. The + operator can also be used to concatenate strings as well as perform addition.

plus sign (+), minus sign (–)

4. Describe how the logical operator *And* works.

The And operator works by checking whether or not two expressions are true. If they are, the result is True, but if either or both are false the operator returns False.

5. Suppose you have an And operation in which the first expression is True and the second expression is False. What answer would be produced, and what would the data type of the answer be?

D. The answer would be False, and the data type would be Boolean.

6. When you write **Request.Form("fieldname")**, what does the word *Form* represent?

C. A collection of the Request object

7. What object collection could you retrieve to get a cookie from the user with ASP?

C. Both of the above

8. HTML/XHTML forms are often used to collect values from the user. The ________ attribute in the ________ element contains the information necessary to tell the browser where to send the form contents.

   action, form

9. Describe the relationship between the Request object and the Response object and how they are used with forms to create interactivity.

   Requests made by the user (input) are captured in the Request object, such as name and value pairs in a form submission ending up in the Request object's form collection, and following processing results or output are often transmitted back to the user with the Response object via the write method.

10. What are properties and methods?

    C. Properties and methods are things that objects have. Properties are values assigned to objects, while methods are functions that can be performed with or on an object's data.

11. What program structure would be useful for looping through a set of items in a collection?

    A. The For...Each...Next loop

12. What does a cookie do?

    Cookies store strings of data on the user's computer. They are often used to identify a particular user and session between various requests.

13. A server-side include file makes it easy to include the same code in multiple pages. An include file would be written with the ________ directive.

    include

14. Describe how you could write code so that if processing is taking too long you could keep the processing going until it was done and then return control to the user.

    The script timeout property could be changed to a lower number from the default 90 seconds.

15. What does the CreateObject method of the Server object do?

    A. Objects are made from classes in VB.NET, or are already built into ASP. When the CreateObject method is run, an instance of the object is created, and that instance can be filled with data or otherwise used in any way its programming calls for.

Module 4: Web Forms and ASP.NET

1. What does a Web Form consist of, essentially?

C. An HTML web page with an HTML form and a backend page with programming for processing on the server

2. What does the term *stateless* mean for websites?

B. An ordinary website does not track variables, values, or conditions of controls every time a request/response is performed.

3. Web Forms and their back-end processing pages are __________ into a class based on the ASP.NET ________ class. Because it is __________ it runs much faster than traditional scripting and HTML pages.

compiled, Page, compiled

4. Describe how an easy method of making ASP pages with HTML can hinder code reuse and readability when inappropriately applied to larger, more complex pages.

Mixing ASP and HTML results in programming logic and display properties being intertwined. Called *spaghetti code,* it is difficult to separate later, when changes to the logical flow are required.

5. What are round trips, and why should they be reduced whenever practical?

B. A round trip is one request/response cycle, and it can take too long to go back to the server.

6. What does the term *viewstate* mean?

A. Viewstate means the current condition of controls on the browser.

7. What files are created automatically when you create a new project using the Web Application template in VS.NET?

E. A and C above

8. You can view your files in ______________ in VS.NET, and view the properties of each control in the ____________ pane.

   Solution Explorer, Properties

9. Describe how you would change from GridLayout view to FlowLayout view in your Web Forms page.

   Right-click on the page and choose Properties, and in the dialog box change from GridLayout to FlowLayout.

10. What property of a Web Forms control would you set to specify its name?

    B. The id property

11. What type of control would you add to your Web Form to ensure that a particular field is filled in?

    C. A FieldRequiredValidator control

12. What does the Text property do for Web Forms validation controls?

    If you enter an asterisk in this property, the asterisk will show up when the Web form is displayed in Design mode. Then, you can enter text in the ErrorMessage property, and at run-time this text will be displayed where the asterisk is displayed at design-time.

13. You can add rows or columns to a table on a Web Form by choosing ____________________ from the menu.

    Insert Row or Insert Column

14. Describe three properties of the CompareValidator control that affect the data type, value, and error message displayed when the control operates.

    The Type property affects the data type the CompareValidator uses, the ValueToCompare property contains the value the control compares to user input, and the ErrorMessage property specifies the error message that will be displayed if the value entered by the user is inappropriate.

15. What would you do to test validation on your form after you've built it?

    D. A and B above

Module 5: ASP.NET Configuration, Scope, and State

1. What is the difference between an ordinary ASP or ASP.NET application and a virtual one?

   C. A virtual application is a separate application running in a subfolder off the root folder of the default website.

2. What does scope mean, in the context of ASP?

   C. Defines which variables can be seen by which scripts

3. What is the difference between application and session scope?

   C. Application scope maintains variables that can be seen by any script running within the application, while session scope maintains variables that can be seen only by scripts running within the session of that individual user.

4. By what mechanism does the global.asa file permit you to run code when your applications and session start or finish?

   D. Events

5. How does your ASP application identify an individual user and establish a session?

   C. Using a session cookie

6. The code to add a variable to the Application object is ________________.

   Application("myvariable")

7. The code to abandon a session is ________________.

   Session.Abandon

8. The code to remove all variables from a session is ________________.

   Session.RemoveAll

9. What is the scope of variable values contained in the default application and in virtual applications?

   A. Virtual applications can see variables in the default application unless they happen to have the same names, but the default application cannot see variables in virtual applications.

10. Configuration in ASP.NET is managed using ___________ files. Your computer, individual applications, and even individual pages may each have their own configuration defined in these files.

   Web.config

11. How are ASP.NET configuration files created, and what format are they written in?

   ASP.NET configuration files are automatically created when you create a new project in Visual Studio.NET and are written as XML files.

12. What configuration section handler of an ASP.NET configuration file controls the applications browser capabilities, and what section controls Web Services?

   B. The browserCaps and webServices sections, respectively

13. What methods can ASP.NET use to manage state?

   D. Only A and B above

14. What happens when you make changes to an ASP.NET global.asax file while your application is running?

   C. The changes will be detected and the entire application shut down and restarted, destroying any current state information.

15. What are the practical differences in the way ASP and ASP.NET make use of the Application and Session objects and their event handlers in the global.asa and global.asax files?

   B. There is virtually no practical difference.

Module 6: ASP.NET Objects and Components

1. What is an object model?

   C. A description or illustration of the relationships of objects to each other.

2. What does the Dictionary object contain, and how can it be changed?

   B. Name/value pairs, and they can be changed by using Dictionary object properties

3. In the File object, what attributes can be set when using the CreateTextFile method?

   A. Filepath, overwrite, unicode

4. Which Scripting Library objects can be used to create text files?

   C. Only the FileSystemObject, Folder object, and File object

5. Working with files sometimes requires navigating within them to find and edit particular sections of text. To move from one line to the next within a file, you would use the ____________ method of the ____________ object. To write a blank line into a file you would use the ____________ method of the ____________ object. To determine what column you are in within a text file, you would use the ____________ property of the ____________ object.

   SkipLine(),TextStream, WriteBlankLine(numberoflines), TextStream, Column, TextStream

6. What capabilities does the Ad Rotator component offer?

   C. It provides a means of accessing banner ads for random rotation according to a set percentage for display.

7. Why is the Browser Capabilities component so important, and where is the content it uses kept?

   A. It detects browser types, providing a means to display customized web content based on browser type and version. The content it uses to accomplish this is kept in a text file named browscap.ini.

8. How does the Content Linking component perform its job?

   B. It refers to a content linking text file for information about path, name, and description of the files in your website and uses methods and properties to assist the user in navigating the site.

9. What is one of the primary advantages of using the Content Rotator component?

   B. You can rotate text and hyperlinks across your pages according to the percentage paid for by advertisers.

10. When an object is created with the Server.CreateObject method, the object is instantiated ____________, and when an object is created using <OBJECT> tags, the object is instantiated __________________________.

    immediately, only when first called in your script

11. What method of the FileSystemObject object would be used to find out the extension of a file?

    C. GetExtensionName(filepath)

12. In ASP.NET, there is an AdRotator ______________ in the ____________. You can set the images it displays and the number of impressions each should receive with an _________ file.

    server control, Toolbox, XML

13. What does the ParentFolder property of the Folder object do?

    A. Returns a Folder object representing the parent folder of the current Folder object

14. What capability of a given browser might be critical to know if you are trying to decide how to manage state in your web application?

    B. Whether it supports cookies

15. What function in VBScript can be used to determine whether an object exists?

    A. IsObject(objectname)

Module 7: Web Services and ASP.NET

1. What fundamental difference between Web Services and web applications made with Web Forms affects users?

   A. Web Services have no user interface.

2. eXtensible Markup Language (XML) is not a markup language per se, but instead a specification for writing markup languages. What XML-based languages are used in communications to and from Web Services?

   B. WSDL, SOAP

3. XML documents should be ___________, otherwise an XML processor will generate an error when trying to read them. If an XML document conforms to a DTD, then the document is said to be __________ as well.

   well-formed, valid

4. Describe the purpose of a DTD or an XML Schema and the primary structures they allow developers to build for XML languages.

   The purpose of a DTD or XML Schema is to allow developers to define the structures that are permissible for a given XML language, as well as some of the characteristics of those structures. For example, a DTD allows developers to define the names of elements, names of attributes, and the frequency and content model of the elements and permissible values for the attributes.

5. What is a namespace, and what purpose does a namespace serve?

   C. A namespace represents a particular address containing definitions of elements, attributes, and other named structures and serves to differentiate between structures with identical names.

6. What is the purpose of Web Services Discovery Language (WSDL)?

   E. All of the above

7. What is the difference between WSDL and Universal Description, Discovery, and Integration (UDDI)?

   B. WSDL provides a language for describing Web Services, and UDDI provides a consistent set of statements that can be used to form the WSDL description so that the description will be complete.

8. Web Services created in ASP.NET have ________ for a file extension. They can be stand-alone services or part of a larger ________________.

.asmx, web application

9. Describe three ways in which you can use Web Services in your web applications.

You can create a Web Service that runs on its own (a standalone service), you can create an application that makes use of Web Services you create within the application, and you can create an application that uses Web Services provided by other websites.

10. What data type is the output of a Web Service?

C. None of the above

11. In what file do you enter your Web Service processing code when making a Web Service with VS.NET and the Web Services template?

A. The code-behind file of the service

12. When developing a Web Forms project in VS.NET, how are Web Services accessed?

To access a Web Service from within a Web Forms application when developing in VS.NET, you must add a web reference from the Project menu. A browser-like interface will open and allow you to browse any Web Services available from the location you enter.

13. To use a Web Service from within a Web Form, one way to access that service is by using a button with an ____________ region. Inside that region you call the function and from the results you may perform any additional ____________ required by your application.

event-handling, processing

14. Describe an advantage Web Services have over similar programmed services that have no Internet connection.

When a programmed service is connected to the Internet, it is capable of including within its processing real-time information from other websites. This means the services it provides can be based on the latest information, rather than canned values.

15. In what file is the WSDL description and discovery information kept when making a Web Service with VS.NET and the Web Services template?

C. The .vsdisco file

Module 8: ASP.NET and SQL

1. What is the process of determining the end result and working backward to determine requirements called?

C. Reverse-engineering

2. What is the SQL command for specifying criteria in a SELECT statement?

B. WHERE

3. What are the SQL text field delimiters?

A. Single-quote marks

4. What takes the place of traditional DBMS navigational forms on a website?

E. C and D above

5. Why are databases commonly part of web applications?

E. B, C, and D above

6. To build a table in SQL Server, what steps should you take?

E. All of the above

7. Primary key fields are important because they uniquely identify each record of data entered into the table. Therefore, a given table can be linked to another table in a ______________, such as one-to-one, one-to-many, or many-to-many.

relationship

8. Describe three types of query commonly found in databases.

The SELECT query, which selects certain records from a table (or tables) based on criteria matching data in specified fields. The UPDATE query, which updates value for certain fields for selected records (again using criteria). The DELETE query, which deletes certain records, again based on criteria.

9. What SQL query will retrieve all records from a table named "pets" in which the pet name is "Clyde" with the records including only the pet name field (pet_name) and the pet id field (pet_id)?

D. SELECT pet_name, pet_id FROM pets WHERE pet_name='Clyde'

10. What is the difference between a null value and a zero-length string?

A. A null value means there is nothing in the field (it is unknown whether a value for this field exists), while a zero-length string means the value is known and it is "nothing" (it is known that there is no value for this field).

11. How are values inserted into SQL statements when the SQL query is part of your programming and the value to be inserted isn't known until the program is running and the user enters the value?

C. Using string concatenation operators appropriate for the language you are writing your program in.

12. If a table named "owners" has a one-to-many relationship with a table named "pets", this means that the table named "owners" is the ________ of the table named "pets", and that for every record in the "owners" table there may be ________ child records in the table named "pets".

parent, many

13. Describe the functions of the Connection, Command, and Recordset objects in ADO, and how the Recordset object compares to the DataSet object in ADO.NET.

The Connection object is used to run connection strings and establish a connection to a data store. The Command object is used to run commands against a data store, such as a SQL statement. The Recordset object represents a set of records retrieved from a data store, formatted in a table-like structure that can be navigated and modified.

14. What table joins are available in SQL? What is the purpose of each?

C. Equi-join, outer-join, and left and right joins. The equi-join connects tables and allows all records from both tables to appear where the values in the joined fields are equal, the outer-join connects tables and allows all records to appear with null values for fields in records where the joining fields don't match, and the left and right joins connect tables but allow all records from one side while disallowing unmatched records from the other table.

15. What SQL aggregate function would you use if you wanted to add all values in a particular field, and what SQL aggregate function would you use if you wanted to figure out how many records were in a set of records?

    B. SUM and COUNT

Module 9: The ADO.NET Connection-Related Objects

1. What can you do to optimize your database interactions?

    C. Close connections, use stored procedures, and use only required data

2. What is the SQL command for specifying a parameter in Access?

    A. PARAMETERS [parametername] data type

3. What does the Direction attribute mean for Parameter objects?

    C. Whether data is going to or coming from the stored procedure

4. What lock type is the default?

    B. Optimistic

5. You can establish a connection to a database provided you have the right information, such as a driver, database name, and so forth. This information can be used directly in your program as a ______________, or it can be stored in a ________ or in a ______ file.

    connection string, DSN, UDL

6. Describe stored procedures and why they are often better to use than the same procedures written into your application.

    Stored procedures are procedures that run within a database, such as particular types of queries. When written and run inside the database, they often run much faster than the same procedure written as code in your application.

7. What property of the Connection object may contain information such as UserID and Password?

    A. The ConnectionString property

8. What properties of the Connection object open and close the connection, and what property tells you whether the connection is open or closed?

   C. Open, Close, and State

9. What is a cursor, and what difference does it make what type of cursor you get with a recordset?

   B. A cursor is a mechanism for navigating through records in a recordset. Some cursors are more flexible than others, allowing more operations but requiring more processing power and memory to perform their functions.

10. When setting up a Command object, the records retrieved depend on what is entered in the ______________ property, which may be the name of a ____________, or a ________ statement.

    CommandText, table, SQL

11. Describe how parameters work, in what object they may be set and found, and why they are useful.

    Parameters contain values to be passed or retrieved to or from an operation on a database. They may be set in the Command object as part of the Parameters collection. They provide a method for capturing values to send to a stored procedure and for retrieving values resulting from the stored procedure.

12. What is the relationship between the Errors collection and the Error object? When errors are generated, where do they go?

    C. The Errors collection is a collection of Error objects that is attached to the Command object. Errors become individual Error objects in the Errors collection.

13. When using ADO, why would you include the adovbs.inc file in your program?

    A. This file contains settings that equate ADO constant names with particular ADO values. Using the constant names is easier to correctly remember (and to debug) than using the actual constant values themselves.

14. What features does a Dynamic cursor have?

    A Dynamic cursor allows both forward and backward movement through a recordset and also displays changes made by other users as those changes are added to the database.

15. In a stored procedure in SQL Server, the _______ symbol is used to signify the beginning of a parameter name.

@

Module 10: The ADO/ADO.NET Recordset and DataSet Objects

1. What is the difference between the Requery and Resync methods of the Recordset object?

   B. Requery reperforms the original query, while Resync just refreshes the existing data in the recordset.

2. What property would you set to limit the number of records returned in a recordset?

   C. MaxRecords

3. What mechanism could you use to gather user data for record updates?

   D. All of the above

4. What property of a Stream object is similar to the Recordset object's BOF and EOF properties?

   C. EOS

5. What information does the State property convey, for many ADO objects?

   C. Whether the object is open or closed

6. ADO makes use of the ____________, ____________, and ____________ objects to retrieve and manipulate records and data in databases, while ADO.NET uses the ____________, ____________, and ____________ objects for a similar purpose. The ____________ object represents an entire data store, and when changes are made to records or data the changes are propagated back to the data store with the ____________ object.

   Connection, Command, Recordset, Connection, Command, DataSet, DataSet, DataAdapter

7. Describe how (in ASP) you would address a field named Quantity from a table named Products in a recordset named rcdst.

   The Recordset is an object, and each field in a recordset is part of the Fields collection. Therefore you can use the name of the recordset, then a dot, then the name of the collection (Fields), and then the name of the particular field in parentheses, like so: rcdst.Fields("Quantity"). The name of the table is not required.

8. To navigate among records in a recordset, there are several methods available. Name the methods allowing movement forward, backward, and to a specific record.

C. MoveFirst, MovePrevious, MoveNext, MoveLast, and Move

9. What properties allow you to determine if you have moved past the first or last records in a recordset?

C. BOF, EOF

10. What methods allow you to update or delete records in a recordset?

A. The Update method will update a particular record, and the Delete method will delete a particular record.

11. To open a recordset you must use at least a ____________ object, and to retrieve records you must set a ____________ or ____________ statement. You can create your own name for the recordset, and you can also set the ____________ type, and ____________ type.

Connection, data source, SQL, cursor, lock

12. Describe a workable strategy (based on primary key values) for updating records in a database when the user edits the data in one of a series of records written into a web page and then submits that edited data as a posted HTML form.

In order for your script of program to identify records individually when receiving data from a web page, a common strategy is to attach the primary key value for a given record to the name of each form field representing a field within the table of records from the database. As the field data in the recordset is written into the HTML form fields, the primary key value for the current record is concatenated onto the standard field names. When the updated data is read back after the form is posted, the primary key value may be extracted, and a new recordset created containing only the record that bears the same primary key value. Then the updates are applied only to that record.

13. Why might it be useful to have the Record and Stream objects available in ADO?

A. Not all data sources are formatted as databases, and the Record and Stream objects assist with collecting and manipulating data in nondatabase formats.

14. The DataReader object is best used when:

B. Speed is an issue, and you don't need much flexibility or functionality for manipulating data.

15. What methods are used when a DataReader object is required on a Web Form?

A Connection object must be placed on the form, and the Open() method is used to open it. A DataReader object must be dimensioned, and the ExecuteReader() method must be used to retrieve records. The DataBind() method must be used to bind the data in the DataReader object to whatever control is being used to display the data (we used a DataGrid object in Project 10-1).

Module 11: ASP Transactions and Mail

1. What encryption method is unbreakable above a certain bit size?

D. Dual-key

2. What kind of security does authentication provide?

A. Authentication tells you the person or system you are communicating with is actually the person or system they have told you they are.

3. What VBScript method could you use to determine whether a password was long enough to be a valid password?

C. Len, which measures the length of a string

4. What four properties are the mark of a valid transaction?

D. Atomicity, Consistency, Isolation, and Durability

5. In the context of a transaction, what does Isolation mean and why is it important?

B. Each transaction is isolated from other transactions, so each transaction operates as if it alone had total control over the resources it is updating.

6. If you program a script with ASP as a transaction and the transaction fails, how does Component Services tell your script about this, and what measures must you take to support transactions in your script?

C. Although your ASP script can detect the success or failure of a transaction, you must manually roll back the parts of the transaction that aren't supported under Component Services, such as Application and Session variables and file system changes.

7. What is the SQL statement to build a table in SQL Server, and how is an auto-numbering Primary Key established?

B. CREATE TABLE tablename is the statement, and setting a data type of INTEGER IDENTITY creates an autonumbering field in SQL Server.

8. What should the connection string to a SQL Server database include?

A. The name of the DSN, the username, the password, and the name of the database

9. What is the difference between CDO and CDONTS?

C. CDO has more collaborative functions than CDONTS.

10. What property would you set to send an e-mail to someone without others knowing the e-mail was sent to that person?

D. BCC

11. Three steps in building security into online applications for an organization are conducting a security ____________, identifying and closing security ___________, and implementing a security ___________.

assessment, holes, policy

12. Describe how (in ASP.NET) to disable session state for a page and for an application, and why you might want to do this.

For a page, set the EnableSessionState attribute in the @ Page directive to False. For an application, set the Mode attribute to off in the sessionstate configuration section of the application's Web.config file. Disabling session state makes your application run faster.

13. While developing an application, you should have ___________ mode enabled to help you find problems within your application, but once you are ready to deploy the application you should turn off ___________ mode, so your application's performance improves.

debug, debug

14. Describe some features you can incorporate into your applications that help make them more secure.

One of the most common ways to break into an internal network is to exploit the capacity of the web server to accept data posted from a form. Because web pages can be saved with source code and then modified before the results are returned to the web server, validation routines that run on the client are trivial to defeat. Therefore, you should also build in validation routines that run on the server.

15. In regard to the Isolation property of a transaction, what does this property mean, and how might it affect the ability of your application to scale up?

The Isolation property is part of the Atomic, Consistent, Isolation, and Durability (ACID) properties of a good transaction system, and this property means that all components of the transaction are isolated from all others, so no other user can interfere with any of the records or data being affected by the transaction. While locking the records in this fashion makes the transaction safe, it also means that if numerous records are affected, other users will have to wait to complete their own transactions, thereby slowing the application's performance. Like just about everything, using transactions is a compromise of one feature over another.

Appendix B

Visual Basic/ JScript Reference

Although we've mainly used VB.NET in this book, both VB.NET and JScript (as well as C#) can be used with Microsoft's .NET Framework. The following sections contain tables summarizing key elements of VB.NET and JScript for quick reference.

Visual Basic.NET Keywords, Functions, and Operators

Element	Action
Arrays	
IsArray	Verifies an array exists
Dim, Private, Public, ReDim	Declares and initializes arrays. The Private and Public elements affect scope, and the ReDim element redimensions an array as necessary.
Ubound	Finds the upper bound (limit) of an array
Erase, ReDim	Reinitializes an array by erasing it or redimensioning it
Collection Objects	
Collection	Creates a collection object
Add, Remove	Adds or removes an item to or from a collection
Item	References an item in a collection
Compiler Directives	
#Const	Creates and defines a compiler constant
#If...Then...#Else	Conditionally compiles selected blocks of code
Control Flow Statements	
GoTo, On Error	Branch
End, Exit, Stop	Exits or pauses the program
Do...Loop, For...Next, For Each...Next, While...End While, With	Loop
Choose, If...Then...Else, Select Case, Switch	Makes decisions
Call, Function, Property, Sub	Uses procedures
Conversions	
Chr	Convert ANSI value to string
Format, LCase, UCase,	Convert string to lowercase or uppercase
DateSerial, DateValue	Convert date to serial number
Hex, Oct	Convert decimal number to other bases

Element	Action
Format, Str	Convert number to string
Cbool, Cbyte, Cdate, CDbl, Cdec, Cint, CLng, CSng, Cshort, CStr, Fix, Int	Convert one data type to another
Day, Month, Weekday, Year	Convert date to day, month, weekday, or year
Hour, Minute, Second	Convert time to hour, minute, or second
Asc	Convert string to ASCII value
Val	Convert string to number
TimeSerial, TimeValue	Convert time to serial number
Data Types	
Cbool, Cbyte, Cdate, CDbl, Cdec, Cint, CLng, Cshort, CSng, CStr, Fix, Int	Convert between data types
Boolean, Byte, Date, Decimal, Double, Integer, Long, Object(default), Short, Single, String	Set intrinsic data types. Object is the default data type if no data type is set
IsArray, IsDate, IsDbNull, IsNumeric	Verify data types
Date and Time	
Today, Now, TimeOfDay	Get the current date or time
DateAdd, DateDiff, DatePart	Perform date calculations
DateSerial, DateValue	Return a date
TimeSerial, TimeValue	Return a time
Today, TimeOfDay	Set the date or time
Timer	Time a process
Declarations and Constants	
Property	Assign value
Const, Dim, Private, Public, New	Declare variables or constants
IsArray, IsDate, IsDbNull, IsNumeric, TypeName	Get information about an object
Me	Refer to current object
Option Explicit, Option Strict	Require explicit variable declarations
Directories and Files	
ChDir	Change directory or folder
ChDrive	Change the drive
FileCopy	Copy a file
MkDir	Make directory or folder

Element	Action
RmDir	Remove directory or folder
Rename	Rename a file, directory, or folder
CurDir	Return current path
FileDateTime	Return file date/time stamp
GetAttr	Return file, directory, label attributes
FileLen	Return file length
Dir	Return file name or volume label
SetAttr	Set attribute information for a file
Errors	
Clear, Error, Raise	Generate runtime errors
GetException, SetException	Get and set exceptions
Err	Provide error information
On Error, Resume, Try...Catch...Finally	Trap errors during runtime
Financial	
DDB, SLN, SYD	Calculate depreciation
FV	Calculate future value
Rate	Calculate interest rate
IRR, MIRR	Calculate internal rate of return
NPer	Calculate number of periods
Ipmt, Pmt, PPmt	Calculate payments
NPV, PV	Calculate present value
Input and Output	
FileOpen	Access or create a file
FileClose, Reset	Close files
Format, Print, Spc, Tab, FileWidth	Control output appearance
FileCopy	Copy a file
EOF, FileAttr, FileDateTime, FileLen, FreeFile, GetAttr, Loc, LOF, Seek	Get information about a file
Dir, Kill, Lock, Unlock	Manage files
FileGet, Input, Input Statement, LineInput	Read from a file
FileLen	Return length of a file
FileAttr, GetAttr, SetAttr	Set or get file attributes
Seek	Set read-write position in a file
Print, FilePut, Write	Write to a file

Element	Action
Information and Interaction	
AppActivate, Shell	Run other programs
CallByName,	Call method or property
Beep	Sound a beep from computer
Command	Provide a command-line string
CreateObject, GetObject	Manipulating Objects
QBColor, RGB	Sets color spaces
MsgBox, InputBox	Displays Dialog boxes
Registry	
DeleteSetting	Delete program settings
GetSetting, GetAllSettings	Read program settings
SaveSetting	Save program settings
String Manipulation	
StrComp	Compare two strings
StrConv	Convert strings
Format, LCase, UCase	Convert to lowercase or uppercase
Space	Create string of repeating characters
Len	Find the length of a string
Format	Format a string
InStr, Left, LTrim, Mid, Right, RTrim, Trim	Manipulate strings
Option Compare	Set string comparison rules
Asc, Chr	Work with ASCII and ANSI values
Replace	Replace a specified substring with another substring
Filter	Return a string array based on a specified filter criteria
Split	Return a specified number of substrings

JScript Reference

Functions	Description
GetObject	Returns a reference to an Automation object from a file
ScriptEngine	Indicates scripting language in use
ScriptEngineBuildVersion	Builds version of scripting engine
ScriptEngineMajorVersion	Gives Major version of scripting engine.
ScriptEngineMinorVersion	Gives Minor version of scripting engine.

B

Methods	Description
abs	Absolute value
acos	Arccosine
anchor	Places an HTML anchor with a NAME attribute around specified text in the object
apply	Applies a method of an object, substituting another object for the current object
asin	Arcsine
atan	Arctangent
atan2	Returns the angle in radians from the X axis to a point (y,x)
atEnd	Indicates if enumerator is at the end
big	Places HTML <BIG> tags around text in a String object
blink	Places HTML <BLINK> tags around text in a String object
bold	Places HTML <B> tags around text in a String object
call	Calls a method of an object, substituting another object for the current object
ceil	Gives smallest integer greater than or equal to a given number.
charAt	Returns the character at the specified index
charCodeAt	Returns the Unicode encoding of the specified character
compile	Compiles a regular expression into an internal format
concat (Array)	Concatenates two arrays
concat (String)	Concatenates two strings
cos	cosine
decodeURI	Decodes URI
decodeURIComponent	Decodes URI component
dimensions	Returns number of dimensions in a VBArray
encodeURI	Encodes URI
encodeURIComponent	Encodes URI component
escape	Encodes strings for reading on different computers
eval	Evaluates JScript
exec	Starts a search for a pattern
exp	e raised to a power
fixed	Places HTML <TT> tags around text in a String object
floor	Returns highest integer less than or equal to a number

Methods	Description
fontcolor	Places an HTML <FONT> tag with the COLOR attribute around the text in a String object
fontsize	Places an HTML <FONT> tag with the SIZE attribute around the text in a String object.
fromCharCode	Returns a string from a Unicode value
getDate	Returns day of the month
getDay	Returns day of the week
getFullYear	Returns the year
getHours	Returns the hours
getItem	Returns item at a location
getMilliseconds	Returns milliseconds
getMinutes	Returns minutes
getMonth	Returns month
getSeconds	Returns seconds
getTime	Returns time
getTimezoneOffset	Difference in minutes between UTC and host computer
getUTCDate	Date in UTC
getUTCDay	Day of the week in UTC
getUTCFullYear	Year in UTC
getUTCHours	Hours in UTC
getUTCMilliseconds	Milliseconds in UTC
getUTCMinutes	Minutes in UTC
getUTCMonth	Month in UTC
getUTCSeconds	Seconds in UTC
getVarDate	Returns the VT_DATE value in a Date object
getYear	Year
indexOf	Character position of first substring match
isFinite	Indicates whether object is finite
isNaN	Indicates whether the object is not a number
isPrototypeOf	Returns a Boolean value indicating whether an object exists in another object's prototype chain
italics	Places HTML <I> tags around text in a String object
item	Returns the current item in the collection
join	Concatenates an array to a string
lastIndexOf	Last occurrence of substring within a String object
lbound	Lowest index value in a VBArray dimension

Methods	Description
link	Places an HTML anchor with an HREF attribute around the text in a String object
localeCompare	Indicates whether two strings are equivalent in the current locale
log	Natural logarithm
match	Returns the results of a regular expression search
max	Returns the greater of two numbers
min	Returns the lesser of two numbers
moveFirst	Sets current item in collection to the first item
moveNext	Sets current item in collection to next item.
parse	Returns milliseconds since the date represented by a string and midnight, Jan 1, 1970
parseFloat	Converts a string to a floating point number
parseInt	Converts a string to an integer
pop	Removes last element of an array and returns it
pow	Raises an expression to a power
push	Appends elements to the end of an array and returns the new length
random	Pseudorandom number between 0 and 1
replace	Returns result of regular expression replacement
reverse	Returns array with elements reversed
round	Rounds numeric expression to the nearest integer and returns result
search	Returns position of first match in a regular expression search
setDate	Sets the numeric date of the Date object using local time
setFullYear	Sets the year value in the Date object using local time
setHours	Sets the hour value in the Date object using local time
setMilliseconds	Sets the milliseconds value in the Date object using local time
setMinutes	Sets the minutes value in the Date object using local time
setMonth	Sets the month value in the Date object using local time
setSeconds	Sets the seconds value in the Date object using local time
setTime	Sets the date and time value in the Date object

Methods	Description
setUTCDate	Sets the numeric date in the Date object using Universal Coordinated Time (UTC)
setUTCFullYear	Sets the year value in the Date object using Universal Coordinated Time (UTC)
setUTCHours	Sets the hours value in the Date object using Universal Coordinated Time (UTC)
setUTCMilliseconds	Sets the milliseconds value in the Date object using Universal Coordinated Time (UTC)
setUTCMinutes	Sets the minutes value in the Date object using Universal Coordinated Time (UTC)
setUTCMonth	Sets the month value in the Date object using Universal Coordinated Time (UTC)
setUTCSeconds	Sets the seconds value in the Date object using Universal Coordinated Time (UTC)
setYear	Sets the year value in the Date object
shift	Removes the first element from an array and returns it
sin	Sine
slice (Array)	Returns a portion of an array
slice (String)	Returns a portion of a string
small	Places HTML <SMALL> tags around text in a String object
sort	Returns sorted array
splice	Removes or replaces elements in an array and returns result
split	Returns the array of strings that results when a string is separated into substrings
sqrt	Square root
strike	Places HTML <STRIKE> tags around text in a String object
sub	Places HTML <SUB> tags around text in a String object
substr	Returns a substring beginning at a specified location and having a specified length
substring	Returns the substring at a specified location within a String object
sup	Places HTML <SUP> tags around text in a String object
tan	Tangent
test	Indicates presence of a substring within a String object
toArray	Converts JScript array to VBArray
toDateString	Returns data as string

Methods	**Description**
toExponential	Returns a string representing a number in exponential notation
toFixed	Returns a string containing a number in fixed-point notation
toGMTString	Returns a date converted to a string using Greenwich Mean Time
toLocaleDateString	Returns date as string for host's locale
toLocaleLowercase	Converts string to lowercase, acknowledging host's locale
toLocaleString	Converts date to string using current locale
toLocaleTimeString	Returns time as string for host's locale
toLocaleUppercase	Converts string to upper case, acknowledging current locale
toLowerCase	Converts string to lowercase
toString	Returns object as a string representation
toPrecision	String representing number with specified number of digits
toTimeString	Time as a string
toUpperCase	Converts to uppercase
toUTCString	Date to string using UTC
ubound	Highest index value of VBArray
unescape	Decodes strings encoded with escape
unshift	Inserts elements at the beginning of an array
UTC	Returns number of milliseconds after the epoch in UTC
valueOf	Returns value of object

Objects	**Description**
ActiveX	Enables and returns a reference to an Automation object
Array	Creates an array of any data type
Boolean	New Boolean object
Date	Enables date manipulation
Dictionary	Stores key/value pairs
Enumerator	Enables enumeration of items in a collection
Error	Information about runtime errors
FileSystem	File system access
Global	An intrinsic object whose purpose is to collect global methods into one object

Objects	Description
Math	Provides basic mathematics functions and constants
Number	Object representation of the number type or a placeholder for a number constant
Common Functions	Functionality common to all JScript objects
RegExp	Information about Regular Expression pattern searches
Regular Expression	Contains a regular expression pattern
String	Allows manipulation of character strings including location of substrings
VBArray	Access to visual basic safe arrays

Operators	Action
!	logical negation
!=	expression inequality
!==	expression inequality or value or value inequality
%	modulo division
%=	modulo division assignment
&	bitwise AND
&=	bitwise AND assignment
&&	logical AND
*	multiply
*=	multiply assignment
+	adds two expressions or concatenates two strings
++	increment
+=	addition assignment
,	sequential execution
-	subtract two expressions or negate a numerical expression
--	decrement
-=	subtraction assignment
/	division
/=	division assignment
<	less than
<<	left SHIFT
<<=	left SHIFT assignment
<=	less than or equal to
=	assignment
==	equality

Operators	Action
===	equality and type equality
>	greater than
>=	greater than or equal to
>>	right SHIFT
>>=	right SHIFT assignment
>>>	right SHIFT without maintaining sign
>>>=	right SHIFT without maintaining sign assignment
?:	conditional execution
~	bitwise NOT
|	bitwise OR
|=	bitwise OR assignment
||	logical OR
^	bitwise exclusive OR
^=	bitwise exclusive OR assignment
Addition (+)	adds two expressions or concatenates two strings
Assignment (=)	assignment
Bitwise AND (&)	bitwise AND
Bitwise Left Shift (<<)	left SHIFT
Bitwise NOT (~)	bitwise NOT
Bitwise OR (|)	bitwise OR
Bitwise Right Shift (>>)	right SHIFT
Bitwise XOR (^)	bitwise exclusive OR
Comma (,)	sequential execution
Conditional (ternary) (?:)	conditional execution
Decrement (—)	decrements
delete	deletes an object property or an array element
Division (/)	division
Equality (==)	equality
Greater than (>)	greater than
Greater than or equal to (>=)	greater than or equal to
Identity (===)	equal and same type
Increment (++)	increment
Inequality (!=)	inequality
instanceof	indicates whether the object is an instance of a specific class
Less than (<)	less than

Operators	Action
Less than or equal to (<=)	less than or equal to
Logical AND (&&)	logical conjunction
Logical NOT (!)	logical negation
Logical OR (||)	logical disjunction
Modulus (%)	modulo division
Multiplication (*)	multiplication
new	create a new object
Nonidentity (!==)	not equal or not the same data type
Precedence	information about the precedence of operators
Subtraction (-)	subtraction
typeof	return data type
Unary Negation (-)	unary negation
Unsigned Right Shift (>>>)	right SHIFT without maintaining sign
void	prevent statement from returning

Properties	Action or Value
0...n	Returns value of argument from argument object
$1...$9	The 9 previous regular expression matches found
arguments	Arguments passed to function
callee	Returns function being executed
caller	References function that called current function
constructor	Function that creates an object
description	Returns or sets the numeric value associated with a specific error
E	Returns Euler's constant
global	State of global flag (g)
hasOwn	Indicates whether the object has a property with the given name
ignoreCase	State of ignoreCase flag (i)
index	Character position of first successful match
Infinity	Returns an initial value of Number POSITIVE_INFINITY
input	Returns string that was searched
lastIndex	Character position of last match
lastMatch ($)	Last matched characters of a regular expression search
lastParen ($+)	The last parenthesized submatch from any regular expression search
leftContext ($`)	Number of arguments passed to a function

B

Properties	Action or Value
length (Arguments)	Number of arguments passed to a function
length (Array)	Length of array
length ()	Number of arguments for a function
length (String)	Length of string object
LN2	Natural logarithm of 2
LN10	Natural logarithm of 10
LOG2E	Base-2 logarithm of e, Euler's constant
LOG10E	Base-10 logarithm of e, Euler's constant
MAX_VALUE	Returns the greatest numerical value that can be represented in JScript
message	
MIN_VALUE	Returns the number closest to zero that can be represented in JScript
multiline	State of multiline flag (m)
name	Name of an error
NaN (Global)	Not a number
NaN (Number)	Not a number
NEGATIVE_INFINITY	A value more negative than the largest negative number that can be represented by JScript
number	Returns or sets the numeric value associated with a specific error
PI	Returns mathematical constant PI
POSITIVE_INFINITY	Returns a value larger than the largest value that can be represented by JScript
IsEnumerable	Indicates whether the specified property is enumerable
prototype	Returns reference to prototype of a class of objects
rightContext ($')	Returns characters after last match to the end of the searched string
source	Returns a string containing
SQRT1_2	Returns the square root of one half
SQRT2	Returns the square root of 2
undefined	Returns an undefined value

Statements	Description
/*..*/ (Multiline Comment)	Multiline comment
// (Single-line Comment)	Single-line comment

Statements	Description
@cc_on	Activates conditional compilation support
@if	Conditional execution
@set	Creates variables used with conditional compilation statements
break	Terminates current loop to resume execution at next statement
catch	Statements executed upon error in try block
continue	Terminates current loop iteration and starts next iteration
do...while	Loops while a condition is true; always executes the first iteration
for	Executes a statement for as long as the condition is true
for...in	Executes a statement for each element in an array
	Declares new function
if...else	Conditional execution
Labeled	Identifies a statement
return	Exits current function and returns a value
switch	Executes statements based on several sets of conditions
this	Reference to current object
throw	Activates an error to be handled by a catch statement
try	Error handling
var	Declares variable
while	Loops while a condition is true
with	Assigns the default object for a statement

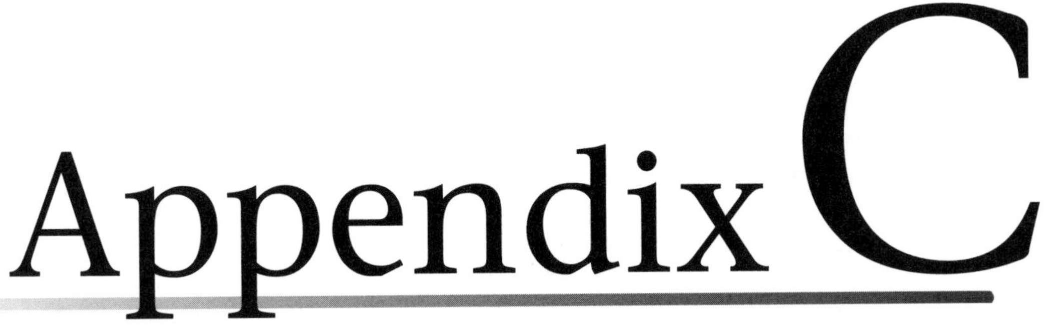

Appendix C

ASP.NET Server and HTML Controls

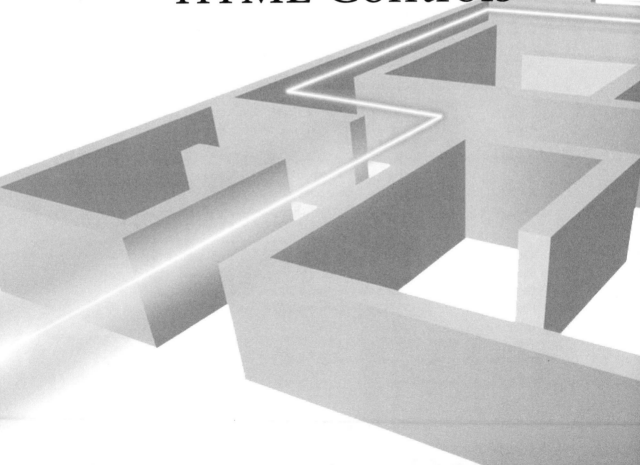

When developing a web application with Visual Studio.NET (VS.NET), there is often a requirement to fill your Web Forms with controls designed specifically for common interactive application functions, such as obtaining user feedback. ASP.NET includes server controls that run on the server but present the user with an HTML-like control, HTML-related controls, and special validation controls as well. This appendix is a quick reference to the names and functions of these controls.

ASP.NET Server Controls

There are a variety of built-in ASP.NET server controls that are available in the toolbox inside VS.NET. The following table lists the available controls and their functions:

Control Name	Description
Label	Displays uneditable text.
TextBox	Captures data entered by a user (displays a blank text box on the screen) and can be preset to a desired value in your programming.
DropDownList	Displays a drop-down list of choices for the user to select, and the user may also enter text as if in a TextBox.
ListBox	Displays a list of choices from which the user can select a single or, optionally, multiple selections.
Image	Displays an image.
AdRotator	Displays a predefined or random sequence of images.
CheckBox	Displays a check box that returns a Boolean value if selected or not.
CheckBoxList	Sets several check boxes into a group and can be used to create check boxes attached to data through the data binding property.
RadioButton	Displays a radio button that can be clicked on or off.
RadioButtonList	Forms a group of radio buttons that can be selected in a mutually exclusive manner (only one of the group can be selected at any given time).
Calendar	Exhibits a calendar from which users can pick a date.
Button	Initiates a function, such as posting the form.
LinkButton	Works like a button but looks like a hyperlink.
ImageButton	Works like a button but looks like an image.
HyperLink	Creates a link.
Table	Creates a table.
TableCell	Creates a table cell.

Control Name	Description
TableRow	Creates a table row.
Panel	Creates a section on a form that is a container for other controls.
Repeater	Repetitively displays data from a dataset inside HTML elements specified by the developer.
DataList	Repetitively displays data from a dataset but with a table-like structure.

HTML Server Controls

There is a variety of HTML controls available in the toolbox inside VS.NET. These controls are equivalent to their HTML counterparts, and any HTML can be treated as a control with a standard set of properties and methods. The following table lists the available controls and their functions:

Control Name	Description
HtmlForm	Creates an HTML form whose control values are posted to the server when the form is submitted. The location to which the form is posted can be set by the developer.
HtmlInputText	Captures user input and can display predefined values set by the developer. Can be set for normal text or to capture data as asterisks when used as a password textbox.
HtmlTextArea	Captures multiple lines and columns of text data.
HtmlAnchor	Creates a link.
HtmlButton	Initiates a function, such as form submission.
HtmlInputButton	Initiates a function, such as form submission, and is broadly compatible.
HtmlInputImage	Works like a button, but displays an image.
HtmlSelect	Displays a list of text and images as icons.
HtmlImage	Displays an image.
HtmlInputHidden	Stores state information for a form.
HtmlInputCheckbox	Creates a check box that can be clicked on and off.
HtmlInputRadioButton	Displays a button that can be clicked on or off.
HtmlTable	Creates a table.
HtmlTableRow	Creates a table row.
HtmlTableCell	Creates a table cell.
HtmlInputFile	Allows users to specify files for upload to the server (if the server allows uploads).
HtmlGenericControl	Creates an object model (properties, methods, and events) for any unlisted HTML element made into a control.

Validation Controls

There is a variety of validation controls available in the toolbox inside VS.NET. These controls do not display directly to the user on the finished Web Form, but instead are activated when the form is submitted. They can check values of other controls and respond in various ways depending upon the values they find (or don't find). The following table lists the available controls and their functions:

Control Name	Description
RequiredFieldValidator	Checks to make sure required fields have a value entered by the user submitting the form.
CompareValidator	Checks to make sure an entry falls within comparison guidelines by using operators and constant or property values.
RangeValidator	Checks to make sure an entered value falls within a range set by the developer, including numbers, dates, and alphabetic values.
RegularExpressionValidator	Checks to make sure that an entered value is a valid match for a pattern specified by a regular expression (such as making sure that an e-mail address has characters followed by the @ sign, followed by more characters, a period, and more characters).
CustomValidator	Allows the developer to create customer validation logic using values that may only occur when the form is actually in use.

Appendix D

XHTML 1.0 Reference

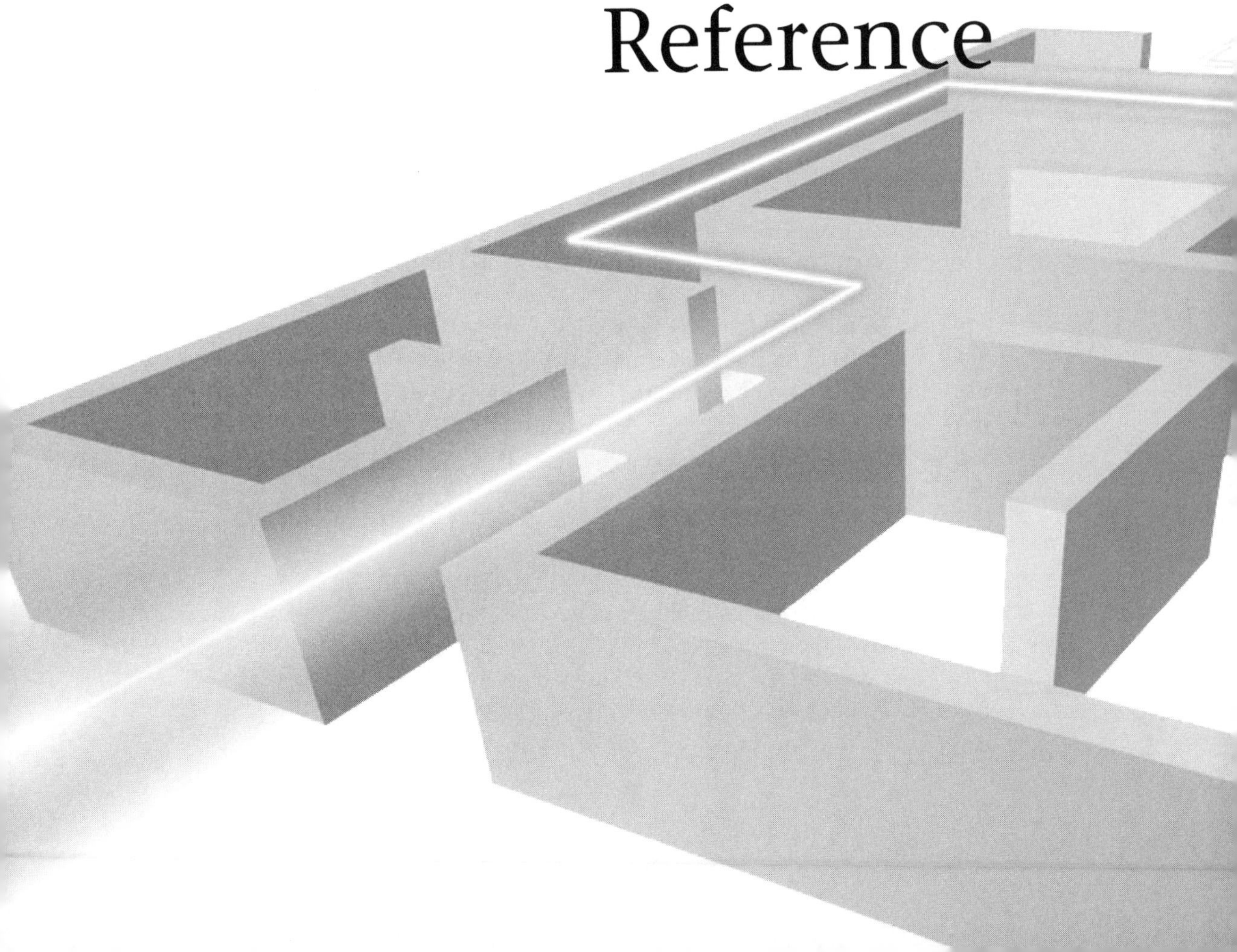

XHTML 1.0 is the successor to HTML 4.01. It contains all the same elements, attributes, and features of HTML 4.01 but is compliant with the XML 1.0 standard. In practice, this means that you may code your documents in a manner very similar to ordinary HTML, but you must follow certain rules to ensure the finished document is compliant. This reference first outlines the rules and how to properly follow them, and then sets out the HTML 4.01 elements in a table for quick reference. More information about HTML, XHTML, and XML may be found on the World Wide Web Consortium's website at **www.w3.org**.

Differences Between HTML and XHTML

Converting HTML to XHTML or writing XHTML manually is not very difficult if you already know HTML, and many HTML editors write code that, with a few minor changes, conforms to the XHTML standard. The primary differences are listed here:

- **All documents must have a DOCTYPE declaration.** In XHTML, all documents are required to have a DOCTYPE declaration that must occur before the root element in the document, such as (for the Frameset DTD):

```
<!DOCTYPE html PUBLIC "-//W3C//DTD XHTML 1.0 Frameset//EN"
"http://www.w3.org/TR/xhtml1/DTD/frameset.dtd">
```

- **The root element of the document must be <HTML>.** Except for the DOCTYPE declaration, no other elements may come before the starting <html> tag, and no other elements may come after the ending </html> tag. Therefore, XHTML documents must begin with a DOCTYPE declaration immediately followed by the starting tag for the HTML element (comments may appear before the <HTML> element, but no other elements). The starting tag must also contain a reference to the XML namespace the document uses. Here is an example of the coding for the HTML element in XHTML:

```
<html xmlns="http://www.w3.org/1999/xhtml">
```

- **Elements and attributes must be lowercase.** Unlike HTML, *XML is case-sensitive*, and by convention all XHTML elements and attributes are written lowercase. Note that attribute values are excluded from the case rule. This makes sense, because things like file names in URLs may be upper- or lowercase and so cannot be restricted to lowercase.

- **Attribute values must be encased in quotes and not minimized.** All attribute values must be in quotes, and minimized attributes are not allowed. In XHTML all attribute values are indicated by quotation marks. This is a good coding practice anyway. Minimized attribute values are those where simply entering the name of the attribute causes its function to occur, such as the "selected" attribute value in the Option element, and this practice is not allowed in XHTML.
- **Leading and trailing spaces in attribute values will be stripped.** Leading or trailing white spaces in an attribute value will be stripped out. If there are white spaces within an attribute value, they will be mapped to a single space between words. For western scripts, this is an ASCII space character.
- **Only the *id* attribute can be used to identify an element uniquely.** In HTML, many elements rely on the name attribute to identify them within the hierarchy of elements, but in XHTML only the id attribute may be used for this purpose, and it must provide a unique identifier, differentiating the element from all others in the page.
- **Nonempty elements must be terminated or have an ending tag.** Any elements that have both a starting and ending tag must use both in XHTML. For example, whereas in HTML a paragraph could be delimited by only the starting <P> tag (placed at the end of every paragraph, if desired), in XHTML both the starting and ending tags must be in place.

  For empty elements, an ending symbol with a space and a slash must be used, as shown here for the line break tag (<BR>):

  ```
  <br />
  ```

  The exception is when a nonempty element is used but has no content (so that it appears empty). In this case, the author must not use the previous syntax but must instead rely on the syntax using both the starting and ending tags, like this (for a paragraph with no content in it):

  ```
  <p></p>
  ```

- **Elements must be nested, not overlapping.** In HTML elements may overlap each other, meaning that the ending tag of a child element can be outside the ending tag of its parent element. In XHTML, all child element tags must occur inside the element tags of the parent element.

- **SCRIPT and STYLE elements must be marked as CDATA areas.** In XHTML, the method for excluding script and style sheet code is to mark the code in these elements as a CDATA section. In the following example, the CDATA section delimiters take the place of HTML comment markers and are boldfaced so they stand out:

```
<script language="Javascript">
<![CDATA[
function clickme() {
alert("Hello")
}
 ]]>
</script>
```

HTML 4.01 Reference

A	The anchor tag. Used for creating hyperlinks. Most commonly used with the HREF attribute to open another web page.
ABBR	Indicates a sequence of characters that compose an acronym.
ACRONYM	Indicates a sequence of characters that compose an acronym.
ADDRESS	Indicates a portion of text that constitutes contact information, like an address, phone number, or URL.
APPLET	Executes Java or other executable code.
AREA	Used for inline image-mapping. Defines a "clickable space" in the client-side image map.
B	The Bold tag. Encapsulated text will be bold. *Do not overuse this tag.*
BASE	Specifies the URL from which all relative links are referenced.
BASEFONT	The default font for the web page.
BDO	Turns off the bidirectional rendering algorithm for selected fragments of text.
BIG	Makes text larger.
BLOCKQUOTE	Denotes a long quotation. Separates the quote from the body text.
BODY	Begins and ends the main section of the web page. Defines many key properties of the web page such as bgcolor (background color) and background (background image).
BR	Line break.

BUTTON	Renders an HTML button. The enclosed text is used as the button's name.
CAPTION	Specifies a caption to be placed next to a table.
CENTER	Centers the enclosed information. Frequently one tag will enclose *lots* of stuff.
CITE	Renders text in italics.
CODE	Renders text as a code sample in fixed-width font.
COL	Used to specify column-based defaults for a table.
COLGROUP	Used as a container for a group of columns.
DD	Definition of an item in a definition list. Usually indented from other text.
DEL	Indicates a section of the document that has been deleted since a previous version.
DFN	The defining instance of a term.
DIR	Renders text so that it appears like a directory-style file listing.
DIV	Defines a container section within the page and can hold other elements.
DL	Definition list.
DT	Definition term.
ME	Renders text as emphasized, usually in italics.
FIELDSET	Draws a box around contained elements to indicate related items.
FONT	Specifies font attributes for contained text such as size and typeface.
FORM	Contains form elements and describes what is to be done with the gathered data.
FRAME	Used to create a frame within a frameset. Can include several attributes to control borders, spacing, and so on.
FRAMESET	Defines a group of frames and their collective properties such as the number of columns and rows.
H1–H6	Heading tags, H1 being the largest; H6 the smallest.
HEAD	Denotes the header portion of the document.
HR	A horizontal rule. Used for separating sections of a web page.
HTML	Contains the entire web page.
I	Italicizes enclosed text. *Do not overuse.*
IFRAME	Creates a floating frame within the page.
IMG	Embeds an image. The attribute src defines the location of the desired image.
INPUT	An input field to be used with a form.
INS	Indicates a portion of text that has been inserted since the previous version.
ISINDEX	Part of a searchable index.
KBD	Renders text in a fixed width format.
LABEL	Creates a label which may be linked to directly, even if it's in the middle of the page.

LEGEND	Defines the title text to be used by the "box" created by the fieldset tag.
LI	List item. Used with UL or OL.
LINK	Defines a hyperlink. Used most commonly with the HREF attribute.
MAP	Defines an inline image map.
MENU	Renders the following block of text as individual items.
META	Provides instructions and information to the browser. This information is not seen in the rendered view of the page.
NOFRAMES	Encloses text that will be seen only on a browser that does not support frames.
NOSCRIPT	Encloses text that will be seen only on a browser that does not support scripting.
OBJECT	Inserts an object or other non-HTML item or control into the web page.
OL	An ordered list. Used with LI.
OPTGROUP	Creates a collapsible and hierarchical list of options. Not widely supported.
OPTION	An item in a selection field.
P	Starts a new paragraph. End tag optional.
PARAM	Used in an OBJECT or APPLET tag to set the object's parameters.
PRE	Renders text in fixed-width type.
Q	A short quotation such as the URL of the source document or a message.
S	Renders text in strike-through type.
SAMP	Renders text in code sample listing, usually in a smaller font.
SCRIPT	Specifies a script for the page.
SELECT	Creates a list box or drop-down list.
SMALL	Renders text with a smaller font than the current font.
SPAN	Used to define nonstandard attributes for text on the page. Used only with style sheets.
STRIKE	Renders text in strike-through type.
STRONG	Renders text in bold-faced type.
STYLE	Specifies the style properties used from a style sheet.
SUB	Renders text in subscript.
SUP	Renders text in superscript.
TABLE	Creates a table. Used with TR and TD and contains control attributes for borders, cell spacing, and so on.
TBODY	Denotes the body of the table. Not required.
TD	Contains the data for one cell in the table.
TEXTAREA	A large text-entry field used with forms.
TFOOT	A set of rows to be used as the table footer.
TH	Defines a header row in the table.

THEAD	Denotes a set of rows to be used as the header for the table.
TITLE	Defines the title for the web page.
TR	Defines a table row. Includes one or more TD tags.
TT	Renders text in fixed-width type.
U	Renders text with an underline.
UL	Unordered list. Used with the LI tag.
VAR	Renders text as a small fixed-width font.

Index

A

D

E

F

G

H

I

N

O

P

Q

R

T

U

V

W

X

INTERNATIONAL CONTACT INFORMATION

AUSTRALIA
McGraw-Hill Book Company Australia Pty. Ltd.
TEL +61-2-9417-9899
FAX +61-2-9417-5687
http://www.mcgraw-hill.com.au
books-it_sydney@mcgraw-hill.com

CANADA
McGraw-Hill Ryerson Ltd.
TEL +905-430-5000
FAX +905-430-5020
http://www.mcgrawhill.ca

GREECE, MIDDLE EAST, NORTHERN AFRICA
McGraw-Hill Hellas
TEL +30-1-656-0990-3-4
FAX +30-1-654-5525

MEXICO (Also serving Latin America)
McGraw-Hill Interamericana Editores S.A. de C.V.
TEL +525-117-1583
FAX +525-117-1589
http://www.mcgraw-hill.com.mx
fernando_castellanos@mcgraw-hill.com

SINGAPORE (Serving Asia)
McGraw-Hill Book Company
TEL +65-863-1580
FAX +65-862-3354
http://www.mcgraw-hill.com.sg
mghasia@mcgraw-hill.com

SOUTH AFRICA
McGraw-Hill South Africa
TEL +27-11-622-7512
FAX +27-11-622-9045
robyn_swanepoel@mcgraw-hill.com

UNITED KINGDOM & EUROPE (Excluding Southern Europe)
McGraw-Hill Education Europe
TEL +44-1-628-502500
FAX +44-1-628-770224
http://www.mcgraw-hill.co.uk
computing_neurope@mcgraw-hill.com

ALL OTHER INQUIRIES Contact:
Osborne/McGraw-Hill
TEL +1-510-549-6600
FAX +1-510-883-7600
http://www.osborne.com
omg_international@mcgraw-hill.com